Contents

The Story of Love   Pages 17-36
In which we follow the
turbulent history of love from the
ancient Greeks to the present day.
Together with certain amorous anecdotes: of
Daphnis and Chloe, of Sir William Roper and his
private view of a choice of brides, and of the
preparation of a meticulous map of Love's
terrain. And arguing that after the
adventures of Aphrodite and the
cunning of Cupid, we may once
more persuade the gates of
Eden to creak open.

Falling in Love   Pages 37-56
In which the reader is invited
to consider, or perhaps remember,
first love—the sudden surprising
realization that of a hundred thousand
people, it is *one* who matters. With a glance
at the lovers provided by astrology, the computer
or the newspaper column, and at the interesting
customs of other ages; and tales of first
meetings from the pages of history and fiction.
In fact, showing how and in
how many places, unexpectedly
or foresightedly, love may
be born.

Courting   Pages 57-96
In which the reader is invited
to view the world of the chase,
where men and women, suitably
dressed and perfumed, pursue each other
through ballroom or wood, past maypole or
skyscraper. We recall the old traditional dreams
of love, look over the shoulder of a lover as he pens a
Valentine or a love letter, or in a Victorian garden
catches the scented message of a bunch of
carefully-chosen flowers. Keepsakes and
customs, food and drink, and the very
breath of love, invite us to the
courtship and its
culmination.

Falling in Love: An Anthology   Pages 97-112
In which, in pieces of poetry and prose,
from Shakespeare's sonnets to Tolstoy's *Anna
Karenina,* all the many contradictory
faces of love are captured and
reflected.

The Compleat Lover

The Compleat Lover

Derek and Julia Parker

McGraw-Hill Book Company
New York   St. Louis   San Francisco   Toronto

Library of Congress
Catalog Card Number: 77-39063
First Edition
SBN 07-048500-3

Printed in Holland

Making Love   Pages 113-160
In which, in photographs, in
paintings and in words we explore
the physical world of love and the
infinite capacity of the human body for
expressing love and tenderness. We show too
the newness which the experience of love can bring
with it—the rebirth of our appreciation of sight,
sound and touch, in which poetry and life
meet; a rebirth which gives us a new
vocabulary, the language of love,
with which we can explore a
whole and unsuspected
new world.

Making Love: An Anthology   Pages 161-176
In which all the intensity and tenderness of physical
love is expressed in poetry and pieces
of prose.

Great Love Stories   Pages 177-192
In which, from the annals of
the history of love, we pluck seven
stories to illustrate the varied course
of true love: from the tragedy of Romeo
and Juliet and Tristan and Iseult to the
rebirth of life which love brought to the Brownings;
and from the mythical magic of Beauty and the Beast
to the fact-become-fiction of Marguerite
Gautier, the Lady of the Camelias; and
ending with the greatest public love
story of this century—of the young
king who gave up his throne
for the woman he loved.

Introduction

The prospect of writing any kind of book about
'love' (perhaps the most indeterminate and
indefinable word in the English language!) is a
daunting one. Indeed, to attempt in the 1970s
a book on love is to court criticism and even abuse
of a varied kind. Never in human history have the
nature of love and the practice of love-making
been so controversially and violently debated as
they are now.

One of our main reasons for writing *The
Compleat Lover* is that we believe that in the midst
of all this confusion the individual capacity to
love is still the most intimate, the most powerful,
the most gentle gift bestowed upon all of us at birth.
We believe too that love is the only means whereby
we can each establish and explore our identity and
self-fulfilment as individuals in relation to others.
Through love, we can, in part, transcend the basic
state of loneliness in which we are all born.
Perhaps immodestly, we wanted, therefore, to set
out our feelings about love for anyone who cared to
read them; and like most writers we wanted at
the same time to clarify our feelings on the subject –
to remember, expand and develop some of the
emotions we felt during two years of courtship
and fifteen years of marriage, and to share them with
other people.

It might be argued that love is too difficult a
subject to be tackled by any but the greatest poets,
that they are the only ones who can write about love
without stooping to triteness or excessive sentimentality. Other lesser mortals, writing of love from the
humble 'molehill of personal experience', can so
easily run the risk of making bores or fools of
themselves. So we have in fact taken out a sort of
insurance against this point by reprinting some of

the finest love poems ever written, and by reproducing paintings and drawings in which some of the world's greatest artists have set out with tenderness, compassion or gusto their feelings on the subject of love. While the poems and paintings we have chosen form a personal anthology of our own favourite pieces, they are certainly more than 'just' literature or art; they come as near as any human utterances can come to expressing 'the life force', the extraordinary, delightful and infinitely complex phenomenon of love.

In the end, however, once one stops writing about history and starts talking about 'love' in the abstract, one has to rely very much on one's own experience: on the view from the 'molehill'. So, in addition to presenting others' opinions and attitudes, we have underlined throughout the book the qualities *we* think are essential (not just helpful, but *essential*) to a happy partnership: lack of selfishness, and selfconsciousness; lack of shyness and inhibition, understanding, kindness, a sense of humour and fun. Even in the games section at the end of the book, which is obviously mainly for amusement, a reader may perhaps recognize his own faults or his partner's virtues, or some aspect of a love affair which he has so far missed.

If we are asked what made us think *we* were qualified to talk about love, the only answer is that our experience of love and life together has been extraordinarily happy. This kind of statement can only sound smug, if not dull – it is only unhappiness, like bad news, that hits the headlines. We shall no doubt be accused of being romantics, of showing an idealized picture of love. Well, this is a happy, an 'upbeat' book; we all know that love can tear a being apart, as well as hold two beings together.

But if we have to speak of our own experience, we can only repeat with what may seem boring self-satisfaction that we *are* extremely happy, and attempt to say why.

If we face facts, we have undoubtedly been extremely lucky: in the first place, lucky that we happened to meet – something that no-one can really 'arrange'. But apart from that, we are inclined to think that one of the main ingredients in our partnership has been a shared sense of fun. So many people seem to take love, and life, over-seriously. We hope our own insistence on the *fun* of love comes across throughout the book, and particularly in some of the illustrations and livelier poems. Like pomposity in human beings, no problem within a partnership can survive being laughed at: it simply deflates and vanishes.

We have tried to reflect most of the faces of love in *The Compleat Lover*, and in that we are of course lucky to be writing in the 1970s. Some of the pictures here, and some of the poems too, would doubtless have shocked our Victorian grandparents. Yet how safe and unshocking they seem today, compared with the 'full frontal' approach to love that is now so prevalent in books and periodicals, on stage and screen. In the past two hundred years, the pendulum of taste has swung violently from one extreme to another – from almost total repression to almost total licence. There are obviously some dangers in each position: it seems to us that there is a civilized middle course, and we have tried neither to suppress anything we felt needed saying, nor to say anything with unnecessary or shocking crudity. We know *The Compleat Lover* is manifestly incomplete in the sense that we boast no ambition to include an encyclopedic catalogue of all types of

overleaf: 'In a somer seson whan soft was the sonne . . .'

13

loving and love-making. But we never intended our book to be a charter for budding Don Juans!

True, we incorporate a gentle guide to the discipline and understanding of the body: but what this book tries to do is *much* more than any love-making manual! There are plenty of sentimental anthologies and plenty of sex manuals on the bookshelves already: we wanted *The Compleat Lover* to be something different, growing out of the experiences of lovers over two thousand years, but yet completely of our own time.

We hope that everyone, whether they are about to scribble a first heart-and-arrow on the wall of a schoolyard, or are planning a golden wedding celebration, will find something in this book with which they can identify: a picture, or a poem, or a passage of prose, which will underline the fun, the romance, the excitement, and perhaps even the heartache, of their own experience.

And whether it sounds smug or not, the best we can hope for every reader is that they find, or have found, someone with whom their life will be as happy and as much fun as ours is with each other.

Derek and Julia Parker

Foxton, Cambridgeshire,
England. 1972

The Story of Love

The turbulent history of love
from the ancient Greeks
to the present day

The Forbidden Fruit

Adam and *Eve* by Albrecht Dürer. For Western civilization the history of love conventionally begins with Adam and Eve in the Garden. Without shame, without guilt, they were at one with everything in the created world.

Then they ate of the forbidden Tree – the Tree of the knowledge of Good and Evil – and became aware of themselves as free agents, and the brightness fell away. Self-awareness brought doubt, shame, division of purpose. Paradise, oneness with life, was lost, as we lose it with the end of childhood; only by

becoming as children again could we ever regain our primeval innocence. This is how most modern thinkers would interpret the myth of Adam and Eve today. But for the early Christian Church the apple of the Tree of Knowledge was the apple of Carnal Love. Tasting the apple of sensuality Adam and Eve lost for ever, according to the teachings of the Church, the capacity for true, lasting love.

For most of us however, most of the time, the words Adam and Eve conjure up neither version of the great biblical story – they are merely Adam and Eve, the first lovers of all.

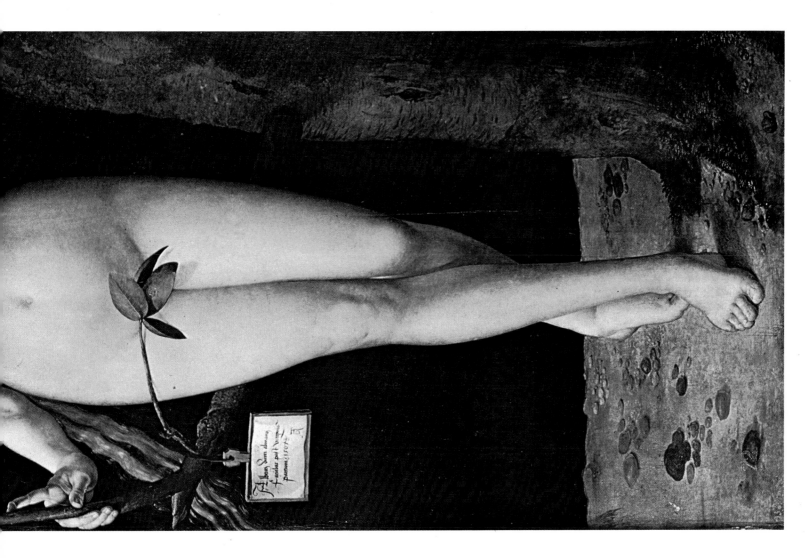

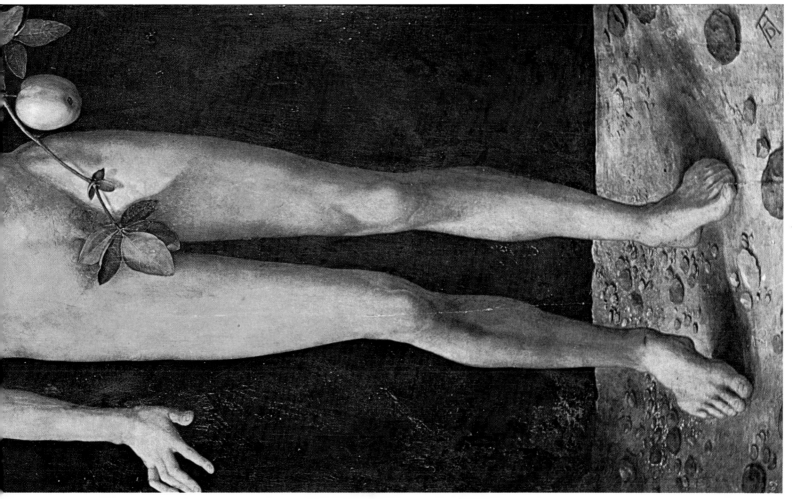

Love in Antiquity

Love is such an elemental feeling. It may arrive without warning as though carried by the wind, taking root without heed of the conventions that men and women usually prefer to live by. Love has been likened so many times to a tornado, a summer storm, a whirlpool or some other event of irresistible power that in the language of romance men and women have come to seem frail victims in its path, unable to withstand its engulfing presence.

Perhaps we enjoy the idea of being overthrown, the threat to what we fondly call our innocence. Even the most assertive of people are prone to relish seeing themselves in the role of the innocent, flung this way and that in a trance-like agony of pleasure and uncertainty. It is all, of course, part of a game, if at times a deadly serious one. Lovers without their blissful deceptions would scarcely qualify as lovers at all.

For the Ancient Greeks, love was very much a game. And their pantheon of lusty gods faithfully mirrored the outlook of the society that created them. If Zeus, the God of Heaven, could spend so much of his time arranging the mechanics of his affairs with beautiful mortals – ravishing Danaë in a shower of gold, or carrying off Europa in the shape of a white bull – then why should mortals be denied similar pleasures? The young Greek looking for such love found it in the arms of a succession of courtesans. Aphrodite, the goddess of physical love, was worshipped throughout Greece as the mistress of all things, vegetable, animal and human. Meanwhile, according to legend, her son Eros, the god of romance, had been romping about heaven and earth since the beginning of the earth itself. His wings took him swiftly from lover to lover; arrows flicked from his ready bow to wound the most unlikely of mortals with the sting of love. 'He whom thou touchest straightway runs mad', wrote Sophocles (*c.* 496–406 BC); and Eros was even ready to edge his mother, Aphrodite herself, into the most ill-considered of entanglements.

But if, in Greece, love was the most enjoyable of parlour games, it was not a game to be played with a possible future wife. Marriage was, in fact, a kind of business transaction in which the interests of the woman's parents and those of her prospective husband were of paramount importance. As one of Xenophon's characters remarks to his new wife:

> We could easily have found someone else to share my bed. I'm sure you recognize that. But after thinking it over, I in my interests and your parents in yours, and reviewing all the possible candidates for our household management and the care of our children, I selected you and your parents myself.

Indeed the role of women, aside from those courtesans who were at the top of their profession, was wholly lacking in promise. Deprived of any worthwhile education or of independence of action, women were reduced to the drudgery of organizing their husband's domestic comforts.

Because their wives made such indifferent companions, men turned to each other for love relationships. Much of the romance, the fervour of love which men could not express otherwise was poured out to boys, and is enshrined in poetry, in carvings, and in historical texts.

In due course, as the centre of Western society moved to Rome, women became more accepted in society. But it was a slow and gradual process before man's respect for women had risen to a point where love as we would understand it today could take its place in marriage.

Was there, then, no classical golden age of love, no ideal vision through which the love of man for woman was celebrated? A great many ideals, it is probably true to say, were realized in myth alone, and not in reality. And yet there are so many delightful fairy-tales in the literature of antiquity, so many romances and happy endings that it does seem as though, beneath the hard everyday veneer of arranged marriages and kept women, the Ancients had a sense at least of the joys which their unequal society denied them.

Perhaps this short extract from the story of *Daphnis and Chloë* may serve to represent the purest essence of romantic love as it was conceived in the age of the Greeks. 'Love, sweet Chloë, is a god, a young youth, and very fair, and winged to fly. And therefore he delights in youth, follows beauty, and gives our phantasy her wings. His power's so vast; that of Jove is not so great. He governs in the elements, rules in the stars, and domineers even o'er the gods that are his peers . . . There is no medicine for love, neither meat, nor drink, nor any charm, but only kissing and embracing, and lying naked together.'

A Greek dish showing Persephone banqueting with Hades, the god of the Underworld. Persephone was the daughter of Demeter, the goddess of fruit, crops and vegetation. While picking flowers with her friends one day, she found herself alone in a field of blue flowers. Tugging hard at one particularly beautiful one, she pulled up its root, and a yawning gap opened in the earth. Hades saw Persephone as he drove past in his chariot, and, falling in love with her, carried her off to live with him. The distracted Demeter searched the earth in vain for her daughter. Finally, at the intercession of the other gods, Persephone was allowed to return to her mother provided she had eaten nothing while imprisoned in the land of the dead. But she had eaten six pomegranate seeds, so she was allowed to return to earth for only six months in the year.

above: A chivalrous knight comes to the rescue of a damsel in distress in *St George and the Dragon* by Paolo Uccello.

opposite: 'Outside the courts, love was decidedly more natural . . . the woods and fields throbbed with the cries of large-eyed country girls and the triumphant laughter of their young men.' (Detail from *Fête de la Libération* by Bauchant.)

Pleasures and Prudery

Cupid, blindfold, firing one of his arrows at a young man.

Despite their improved station by Imperial Roman times, women in their battle for recognition still had a great deal to do. Indeed, from our more enlightened viewpoint today their position appears to have been little short of desperate. The Church, in particular, was one body that needed more than gentle persuasion. (Men were another, but more of them anon.) Love in official Christian circles was considered to be, ideally, of the spirit; occasionally, in order that the earth might be peopled, as God expressly commanded, fleshly love had (alas!) to be permitted. It was, in all, a melancholy situation, rather gloomily summed up by St Paul, who asserted that it was 'better to marry than burn', but he would go no further than that.

The gloom persisted for many centuries; not surprisingly, though, people's natural inclinations could not be entirely repressed. In the twelfth century, for example, the extraordinary conventions of 'courtly love' were devised. Suddenly (perhaps because a good number of lords rattled off to the Crusades leaving their ladies, tight-bodiced and chastity-belted, alone in the high but nonetheless accessible towers of moated castles) women seemed at once infinitely desirable and strangely unobtainable.

In numerous legends, tales and ballads sung by the troubadours in the galleries and courtyards of medieval Europe, the highest prize was a woman's love. To obtain it, men challenged and slew all manner of hirsute, one-eyed monsters, dragons that could be seen in the dark, and witches of incalculable ugliness who shrank and poisoned the unfortunate hero before right prevailed in the closing stanzas. All the while, as these incomparable warrior-lovers rode into the fight, they dreamed of their beloved. Then, not unnaturally, when the goal was reached and the dragon was slain, real life had a habit of taking over from the ballad, and ladies were no longer quite so unobtainable. Not all the troubadours' performances were given in public; others took place in gardens, beneath windows, in the dark of a secret passageway. And many such efforts were amply welcomed by the ladies; there was, incidentally, a popular tradition that it was simply not done to be in love with one's husband: as Marie, Countess of Champagne, put it: 'Love cannot exert its powers between two people who are married to each other.'

Innocence was skin-deep only: the courtly games, in which 'courtesy, generosity and fair speech' were the rule, soon gave way to something rougher and ruder, in which a courtly verse was replaced by the vow:

> *God grant I die not by any man's stroke*
> *Till I have my hand 'neath her cloak.*

Outside the courts, love was decidedly more natural than it was civilized, and was at least in part a seasonal activity. It waxed irresistibly in the spring and early summer – when the woods and fields throbbed with the cries of large-eyed country girls and the triumphant laughter of their young men. Physical strength still counted for a great deal. And while the ladies of the courts of love leant from their windows to hear the latest air, down in the village the blacksmith's wife bore her eleventh child.

With the Renaissance came a new version of the ideal of Platonic love; a love seeking divine love through human love. The ideal was carried over into Elizabethan England but common practice fell far short; in the battle between reason and passion, the passionate element in human life finally triumphed and gained acceptance so that it was no longer considered sinful to enjoy life and love. Yet, even in the sixteenth century, marriages were still arranged in a fashion more suited to the cattle market than to the 'lists of love'. Take the story of Sir William Roper, who one day came to call on Sir Thomas More, with a view to marrying one of his daughters. Perhaps he had read Sir Thomas's latest book, *Utopia*, in which it was advised that 'the woman . . . is shown naked to the suitor by a worthy and suitable matron, and similarly the suitor is presented naked before the maiden by a discreet man.' Showing no sign of doffing his own hose, Sir William accompanied Sir Thomas to the girl's room, and tweaked the bedclothes off them. There they lay, 'on their backs, and their smocks up as high as their armpits'. Waking in surprise, they instinctively turned over. 'Now,' Sir William said, 'I have seen both sides.' He tapped one girl on the buttocks, and said 'Thou art mine.' History does not record how Sir Thomas reacted, but the marriage was apparently a success.

Public behaviour was as rough and ready as ever. At the theatre, for instance, as one puritanical observer, Philip Stubbes, put it, you could see 'such itching and shouldering, such heaving and shoving, to sit by women; such giving them pippins to pass the time . . . such tickling and toying, such smiling, such winking and such manning them home . . . Every sawcy boy of ten, fourteen, sixteen or twenty years must have his pretty pussie to huggle withal'.

Stubbes, in his outcry against the licentious ways of his contemporaries, was a true spokesman for the Calvinists in Europe and the Puritans in England and America. According to their creed, human love, in almost any form, was wickedness – the Devil's work. Only a seemly love within marriage was to rated, and that barely. Physical love was expressly for the purpose of procreation, in accordance with the Lord's commandment; gratification of the senses was out of the question. As for woman, her very charms, once extolled by troubadour and Elizabethan suitor alike, were now considered evil. In no way should she, with a single careless look or gesture, risk tempting man from the strict path of righteousness and virtue. Her hair was to be knotted severely from her face; she was to dress in the drabbest greys and browns, and in the coarsest of stuffs, and to keep her glance downcast and modest.

It was certainly a pleasure-negating, life-denying creed; but as usual the pendulum of reaction was soon to swing in a very different direction.

overleaf, left: A Tantric temple carving, one of many hundreds illustrating the mystical Hindu view of physical love.

right: A nineteenth-century Indian miniature, *Lady and Prince Wrapped Together in a Quilt*. '. . . the wedded ones court each other slowly, by pleasing, and by giving and taking happiness. Each seems only to look upon the lovely things in the other.'

Sir John de la Pole and his wife hand-in-hand in formal repose in this brass from Chrishall Church, Essex.

Love in the East

The Spirit of Eden, if it dwelt anywhere, did so in the Far East. In ancient China life was simple and full of gaiety. Chinese poems, for instance, tell of girls and boys encouraged to meet, to dance on the banks of the river and freely to pledge their love. In India, the *Kama Sutra* of Vatsyayana encouraged young men to conduct their courtships with tenderness and grace, gathering flowers with their girls, writing them glowing love-letters, and finally making a *gandharva* marriage in which both partners had a full say in their commitment to each other.

But later things began to change. Confucius (the St Paul of the East) made known his feelings on the subject of woman, whose duty, as he saw it, consisted simply in 'obedience'. In childhood she obeyed her father; in marriage, her husband; in widowhood, her son. Then she died, as unobtrusively as possible. A little further west, in India, the Hindu laws of Manu pointed out that 'a woman whose mind, speech and body are kept in subjection, acquires high renown in the world, and in the next, the same abode with her husband'.

In many schools of Buddhism as in Christianity, woman as a sexual creature was connected intimately with the sense of sin, and any sensuality in her was to be properly rebuked. And the idea of sensuality as a means of demonstrating the love of woman for man, or of man for woman, in or out of marriage, simply did not exist.

Just as, in Greece, men had courtesans to resort to, so in the East there were respected classes of prostitutes: the temple prostitutes of India, and in Japan the Geisha, who lived in luxury and were accomplished not only in sensuality, but in singing and dancing and conversation.

A principal difficulty in discussing 'love' in the East is that since antiquity, the tables have nearly always been turned: the functional aspect of sex, procreation, was of paramount importance. Love, if one was fortunate, followed a marriage; it was certainly not considered before the ceremony. A Japanese legend tells how a god and goddess, after centuries of innocent celibacy, suddenly discovered how to make love – and then gave birth to the whole world: man, woman, fish, fowl, sea, plain and mountain. By comparison with that performance, which resulted from the discovery of *sex*, what did love matter? What mattered more was the fusion of the principles of *yin* and *yang*, the male and the female: with what emotions that fusion was accompanied, seemed immaterial. This principle naturally led to the Confucian idea that, if the purpose of sex was to produce children, and if it had no place of any real importance in life other than this, then one could theoretically decline to have anything to do with it unless for the purpose of procreation. Making love thus became not only inessential, but was declared positively dangerous, leading to a loss of health and a weakening of intellect.

Hinduism, on the other hand, embraced a wide-ranging variety of beliefs and practices. Some branches of the religion took the line that it should be possible to achieve a life in which asceticism and sensuality were perfectly balanced: men vowed to continence lived in temples alive with the carvings of erotic artists; boys were expected to remain completely celibate until at least after they had finished their studies; sex was permitted inside marriage. Manu was not quite as strict on the subject of sex as Confucius: 'Let not a man, from a selfish appetite, be strongly addicted to any sensual gratification. . . In caressing women there is no turpitude; for to such enjoyments men are naturally prone; but a virtuous abstinence from them produces signal compensation.'

Other branches of Hinduism, especially those influenced by Tantric thought, attached special importance to woman and to sex. Physical love was regarded as an art and a ritual, a joyful religious act in which the human act of creation mirrored the divine creation. Woman was seen as the receptive creature embodying the divine principle of 'insight-wisdom'; man embodied the creative, dynamic principle, and the sexual union of the two represented the ultimate unity, celebrated in erotic temple carvings all over India.

Yet, for the most part, love as we would recognize it has been absent from the East for the past two thousand years. This may be partly as a result of the lowly status of women, but it is perhaps mainly because of the importance attached to the procreation of male children. This was too important a matter to be left to lovers, their eyes muddied by romance. It was seen to be safer for elder relatives, helped by astrologers and advisers, to arrange a marriage, and for the bride and groom not to meet until the ceremony – a practice which still prevails today: Indian newspapers carry regular advertisements, inserted by parents, for possible partners for their sons or daughters.

There was, and still is, however, a saving grace; the chance of love *after* marriage. Thus, in the months after marriage, a husband might court his wife as ardently as a boy experiencing his first love. Savitri Devi Nanda described how 'the wedded ones court each other slowly, by pleasing, and by giving and taking happiness. Each seems only to look upon the lovely things in the other, forgetting or not seeing the unlovely things. Thus in time they mould each other to the one common way, which is their way of life. Once given, the love of a Hindu girl can never be taken back.'

This still seems a strange idea to Westerners, but one that they might profitably listen to. How many marriages, after all, tend to grow stale when a young couple's relationship moves from the violence and lushness of spring to the stillness of summer, faltering as familiarity dulls the senses? It will take a few centuries for East and West to be reconciled on this theme. But we notice – from our experience of Eastern films and literature, and from what we see around us in the West – that as the world grows smaller, the face of love is beginning to wear the same expression all over the world; and it is an expression on the whole of tenderness. The pendulum, having swung violently between two extremes of sensuality and celibacy for three thousand years, is perhaps slowing down to a regular middle beat.

overleaf, left: A detail from *La Perspective* by the eighteenth-century French painter Jean Antoine Watteau, showing a group of decorous lovers playing music among the trees.

right: Love played according to the rules, within the safety and conventions of the middle-class family. (*Le Déjeuner dans un Jardin à Villeneuve-sur-Yonne* by Edouard Vuillard.)

Onward to Eden?

From the repressiveness of the Puritan era in the West, the pendulum swung with great gusto in a very different direction. With the founding of Versailles in 1661, Europe witnessed the birth of 'polite society', an innovation which greatly strengthened the position of women, as well as prescribing new standards of behaviour for the people at large.

Some of the results of the cult of refinement were not without their comic side – in Paris, in the late seventeenth century, in London in the eighteenth, the aristocracy even walked in a stylized balletic fashion. And there were other excesses of preciosity such as a map drawn up in total seriousness by Mme de Scudéry (1607–1701) and published in her novel *Clélie*. The map is called the *Carte du Tendre* (Map of Tenderness) and it charts the progress of a slender river from a town labelled New Love past another called Tenderness; the river then debouches into the Sea of Danger, strewn with jagged rocks. On either side of the river stand small hillocks named after emotions and stages of love: there is Billet doux, Billet galant, Generosity, Respect, Probity, Obedience, etc etc. To one side of the map yawns the Lake of Indifference, on the other stands a boiling Sea of Enmity.

Despite such excesses of preciosity, civilization was undoubtedly set on a fresh course. Gentility was revered in men, and a new morality was formulated in which philosophers and poets came most to respect the *honnête homme*, the decent man, moderate and tolerant in his views. After the excesses of arduous wars and the Inquisition this was a major step forward. It was also in many ways a concept ideally suited to the rising middle classes. However, this was not altogether good for love. What every woman of spirit most enjoyed was not an *honnête homme* but someone much more exciting, a dark-eyed rebel in the Casanova mould who would sweep aside the conventions and avidly transport her to wherever in her imagination she most wanted to be – to Rome, the Far East, a couch behind locked doors, or even a nearby forest. And so, behind the ideal flourished a rather different practice.

These were the first ages of the 'beautiful people', and of the beautiful hostess to whose salon and masked balls the entire capital feverishly sought to be invited. Once there, desirable partners were to be met, looks exchanged and secret notes pressed into gloved hands. The nature of the chase was irrevocably changed. It had become an urbanized and highly polished procedure, and it gave women an altogether firmer say in who should have his way with them – and who should be cast aside to declaim his agony on some lonely shore.

There were, of course, strict conventions to be observed: all forms of relationship were condoned providing they remained invisible from public view. Breaking the rules might involve the trespasser in severe penalties – a duel, imprisonment, a ponderous and costly lawsuit. But successful lovers would seldom begrudge their loved one a three-hour wait in a darkened coach beneath the trees – if their passion were then to be fulfilled. Giacomo Casanova (1725–98) flourished in a secret underworld of his own making, lying hidden for hours in cupboards and behind curtains, and, on one occasion, waiting in vain all night on a rat-ridden back staircase. Refusing to admit failure, he returned the following night, waited several more hours – and was granted his triumph! The idea, incidentally, that women did not enjoy sex was not much in evidence before the nineteenth century. It was then widely put about in order to maintain appearances among the bourgeoisie, and to discourage young girls from trying too much too quickly and so bringing possible disgrace on their families. Up till then, however, it can safely be said that sex was the agreeable lubricant of every civilized society.

The nineteenth century saw a widespread tightening up of morals; the church spoke out strongly against the sins of the flesh. Suddenly ashamed of themselves, the men and women of the nineteenth century began to see indecency everywhere. Statues were draped, even the legs of tables and piano stools had to be covered. Any physical contact that there might be in marriage was widely regarded as an unpleasant duty for the woman and as an insensitive need for the man, to be controlled as far as possible.

But the hypocrisy was transparent. Victorian women, baring their upper breasts, whitening their skins, drawing in their waists, did everything in their power to make themselves as seductive to their menfolk as

'Today there is an ever-increasing recognition of woman's right to live, work and love as an equal.' Mistress of her own destiny, the elegant owner of the glamorous open car and the pedigree dog is free to decide whether or not she needs the man. (*Photograph by John Hedgecoe.*)

possible. The men, paying lip-service to the conventions, kept mistresses, haunted the stage doors of the music halls. And families were larger than any before or since . . .

And so we come to the infinitely more relaxed attitudes of the present day; the veil of hypocrisy has been cast aside; physical love is recognized as an integral and fulfilling part of a relationship. And, perhaps more importantly still, there is an ever-increasing recognition of woman's right to live, work and love as an equal. If the gates of the Garden of Eden have remained shut for so long that the lock seems to have rusted, then in a sense man only has himself to blame for his persistent denial of these rights. For there can be no real partnership where there is no equality. Courtly life set the pattern in former times but was almost exclusively a game for the rich. Women of the upper classes habitually enjoyed power of which lowlier women could only dream.

Quite suddenly, since the end of the nineteenth century, man has begun to recognize this. A woman no longer has to accept that her place is 'in the home' – unless that is how she wants it. A woman no longer has to wait for the man to make the first move, in any situation. Slowly (and revolutions take time if their results are to be enduring) she is moving away from a position of complete submission to a position in which she will be truly free. When she has settled into that position, the gates of Eden may even creak open. And this time we can all enjoy the apple, the serpent will have vanished, the sunshine will be real.

Falling in Love

The sudden surprising realization
that of a hundred thousand
people, it is one
who matters

Young Love

Many people say that 'first love' is different from any other. But it is not. A boy of sixteen can be in love with all the passionate purity of a Dante, with a girl to whom he has never spoken. At the same time, he can be discovering the first pleasures of physical love with quite another girl. Or, reaching out automatically for any girl to take out, he can be surprised to find a new sensation stirring within him – a feeling which seems to have nothing to do with kissing and touching, but a longing simply to be in the same room as her, to exist in her presence.

No-one who remembers their teenage years will easily forget the idealized image of their first 'true love'. Young love is the dream of eternal love, of a love softly wandering through sunny fields of growing corn; the dream of hands and eyes that will hold us in them until a final kiss; the dream of a shared affection that gradually strengthens with the years; the dream of a lifetime fulfilled, of deeds achieved, memories treasured, lives created, and shared. Young love is all these things; but love, young, is rare.

Even in wiser years love rarely proclaims itself. Often we imagine ourselves immersed in a love so strong that its end is impossible to see. And just as often such love fades like a morning mist. So how in our youth can we possibly know the heights and depths of love? Yet Romeo died for his Juliet, and she for him. The tenderness of a young boy for his girl and her care for him can be remarkable, and hold lessons for adults. But the stirrings of the body are often very confusing. Many girls are physically mature at thirteen years, young men are often most sexually potent before they are twenty. Yet some adults still tend to discourage emotional relationships between teenagers; even at co-educational schools the fourteen-year-old boy and girl are expected to be unaware of each other except as class-mates. This has two results: the shyness in admitting love, which parents may have remarked is silly at their age; and a secret discovery of the facts of sex, a discovery which is often tinged with guilt and even shame.

As time goes on, and we know more about the working of men's minds and bodies, it is evident that the basic procreative instinct is combined with a mass of other factors – natural intelligence, particularly, or the home conditions and social situation of the partners. The conventions of the group in which the individuals find themselves more often than not strongly condition their attitude to love, especially to a declaration of it. Many misunderstandings, and much sorrow, have arisen because one or other partner is too shy, too worried, or sometimes too selfish to commit himself. Warm friendships have foundered when a boy says, 'I love you' and a girl makes no reply, or a girl's devotion goes unrecognized and unreciprocated in however small a way. To open oneself in a gesture of friendship or love and to be received in apparent coldness, through fear or diffidence on the part of the other person, can induce a sense of foolishness and impotence which it will take a long time to dispel.

The physical signals the body gives out when a boy sees an attractive girl, or *vice versa*, are no doubt in part the signals it was trained to make when man was still an ape, and the urge to procreate was above all vital to the survival of the species. As man becomes more sophisticated and complicated, the basic procreative instinct becomes mingled with a mass of other factors, and inevitably confusion results, both among young people awakening to physical love and in the minds of adults, the 'older generation'. One of the main reasons for this confusion is that scarcely any civilized country has yet worked out a proper system of sex education – much to our shame. Whereas Margaret Mead, in her famous book *Sex and Temperament in Three Primitive Societies* outlines methods of sex education among people we might misguidedly call 'savages', which are natural and right.

Ideally children should learn about sex as early as possible, and at home. But a recent survey in England revealed that a quarter of all boys and a third of all girls felt they should have been taught more about sex by their parents; most boys and girls felt they should have learned more about it at school; and almost all of them agreed that adults seemed to think they should be able to find out about sex for themselves – while discouraging them from the means of doing so. By the time one is capable of making love, one obviously ought to know the facts of life. There is no evidence at all that sex education leads to promiscuity: indeed there is evidence to suggest that ignorance or a scant knowledge of the workings of sex leads to greater sexual activity as girls and boys follow their own strong instincts, their desire to experiment, without having learned of the social consequences.

It is foolish to suppose that love and sex can be completely divorced; recognition of one implies the presence of the other, and if love is sometimes absent from sex, the opposite is practically never true. The relationship between them is so mysterious that adults, let alone adolescents, can scarcely comprehend it. It would certainly appear, however, that the child who grows up afraid of sex, or shy of expressing the spiritual side of love, is unlikely to be happy in his adult relationships. But love is so entirely personal an affair that it is presumptuous to lay down rules. Even as adults we can say little that is definitive about love. It affects some people one way, others completely differently. Some may search desperately and rarely find it; others may find that they seem to 'fall in love' constantly. And each experience can be as truly love as the other.

'Young love' may well be a traumatic experience, whenever it comes. But if we seem to make heavy weather of an experience poets praise as idyllic and crystalline, it is because it is too important to lie about. Young love deserves our respect, our concern, our sympathy, and the best chance we can give our children of finding true love – lasting, permanent and satisfying love – is by transferring to them our own sense of pleasure and delight in it.

Dreams of Love

When we are young, it can seem all too impossible to find someone who can be loved at anything but a chill distance. Even among the teenagers of the 1970s, one suspects that a very great number live in a desperately isolated cocoon. Shyness is by no means dead; the happy promiscuity of the pop festival is not nearly as promiscuous as adults may believe (or, reflecting, hope). And on our own in a crowd, our feeling of loneliness may reach its most intense level, our chances of finding a girlfriend or boyfriend can seem as remote as ever. So we turn to dreams – often, for the moment, all we have.

Often when we are young, we create for ourselves ludicrously perfect partners – beautiful, witty, considerate, lively, sensuous, self-sufficient yet utterly dependent upon ourselves for fulfilment. Accompanied by the echoes of our dreams, it is not surprising that we see the real people around us with a slight squint, finding the nearest approach to our ideal in the highly polished, plastic, inhuman shadows of the cinema or television screen, or the advertisement hoardings. And later, however happy we may be in a partnership, there can be few men or women who are not conscious every day that they are surrounded by other men and women with whom they might, had situations been otherwise, have fallen in love, and perhaps have been as completely happy. It is a thought which we probably suppress – happily in love, we hesitate to believe that it might have been with anyone else: it seems, irrationally, a kind of betrayal. But of course it is not. It would be ludicrous to suppose that in a world of 3,600 million people there could be only one person with whom we could be happy!

So we wonder, from time to time, how it would have been if the cards had not fallen out *so* – perhaps because we are conscious that like everything else in life, we and our partners are imperfect; and still we instinctively search for the ideal, for the dream lover who has haunted man and woman throughout history. We see him, or her, mainly through art: the perfection of form of the Venus de Milo, or Michelangelo's David; the spirit of Tess of the D'Urbervilles, or the vigour of D'Artagnan, tell us a great deal about the dream visions of their creators in their generation. The artists show us their dreams of perfect lovers, and reflect our own.

Sometimes, we think we glimpse our ideal in the street, or at a party, and may even think of making a gesture of recognition: but more often we simply look, as Samuel Pepys, who was married to a pretty, vivacious Frenchwoman, one morning at church 'stood privately at the great doors, to gaze upon a pretty lady; and from church dogged her home, whither she went to a house near Tower-hill; and I think her to be one of the prettiest women I ever saw'.

At home, of course, she may have been a termagant; but the dream is pleasant, and harmless. Some Victorian doctors, however, believed that dreams of any kind, whether horrific nightmares or pleasant dreams of love, were unhealthy – dreamless sleep was the sign of a contented

man (or woman). Now, we would argue that everyone dreams, just as everyone at some time dreams of love. In one sense, dreams may be safety valves in which we can indulge the inevitable, half-wistful 'if only'; in another sense, they are projections of ourselves in love, and to that extent we shall possibly see them come true. It is just as likely, however, that our ideal love, made flesh, would drive us mad with boredom inside a week. The reality of a personal relationship with another thinking human being, of one individual personality meeting with another, is an essential part of a fulfilling love affair. There may be friction between the partners, frustration and misunderstandings. There will more than likely be arguments which to outsiders would seem to rend the union so far apart that reconciliation is impossible. But such dissension can hide a deep concern for each other, and can turn in a moment to warmest affection.

However ideal the dream, the reality is undoubtedly better, more honest – and, anyway, real! If we are lucky, dream and reality may become as one. As Stephen Spender expresses it, in a beautiful poem,

> *'My dream becomes my dream,' she said, 'come true.*
> *I waken from you to my dream of you.'*

An idealized nineteenth-century painting of voluptuous women. (*The Garden of the Hesperides* by Lord Leighton of Stratton.)

overleaf: 'Often, when we are young, we create for ourselves ludicrously perfect partners . . .' (*Photograph by John Hedgecoe.*)

The Search for Love

The ways of conducting the search for love are as innumerable as the forms of love itself.

The lazy way (or perhaps the way of mild desperation) is through an agent: and the newspapers and magazines have always been a help. Today, most periodicals, hippy or stately, glossy or pulp, carry advertisements phrased in more or less polite terms, announcing that a Miss A seeks Mr B, for any one or more of several motives; as in the advertisement which appeared in an English provincial newspaper in 1972: 'Lady with long grass wishes to meet gentleman with power mower; view also friendship'.

An advertisement, a marriage bureau, an astrologer (much used in India, where a notice might say: 'Alliance sought by rich young businessman worth six figures, with beautiful vegetarian Brahmin girls; reply with horoscope'), or a computer dating system, all provide opportunities for the vital first meeting – hopefully with someone compatible. Sometimes, indeed, *too* compatible. Fed with details of hair colour, height, religion, personal tastes, a dating system in London went into full swing, and after much cogitation came up with a date for one man. Having waited at the meeting place for two hours, he telephoned the agency, to discover that he had been paired with himself. Another man found himself at a meeting with a six-foot, slim, intelligent blonde – of his own sex. A beautiful friendship resulted, but was not precisely what either had in mind.

Where one may meet a prospective lover depends on a number of factors – not least, the social climate. Parents who worry about their children dating at pop festivals or meeting on some protest march, might bear in mind that in another age they could well have met for the first time in bed. In the Middle Ages in France, for instance, it was a custom in many villages that on a certain evening in each week the single girls left their bedroom doors or windows open, and any eligible young man might come in, 'to lie all night talking and playing' – though any extensive love-making was frowned upon. Bedrooms in those days were not lit, so the face you found on your pillow in the morning might be a nice surprise, or otherwise.

The custom was not strange to England, even as late as the 1840s, when the Rev. William Jones, Vicar of Nevin, in Wales, complained that he could not keep servants unless he agreed to them entertaining their particular friends in their beds.

But most people in the villages and small towns of Europe met their lovers out-of-doors:

> *Among the acres of the rye*
> *The pretty countryfolk do lie*

and 'many a squire's daughter has clambered over hedge and stile to give a rampant jump into the arms of a jolly young haymaker or ploughman', wrote one historian in the 1880s.

Flirtation by John Seymour Lucas.

In town, when houses had few private rooms, or were full of prying servants, the mazes, arbours and bowers of large private (or public) gardens provided secluded corners for assignations. In Restoration days, Greenwich, Vauxhall and Ranelagh Parks were extremely fashionable and popular: it was at Ranelagh that the elderly Lord Carteret was introduced to his young bride, and was seen 'all fondness, stopping every five steps to kiss her'.

The theatre, and even the church, was considered a very proper place in which to keep one's eye open for 'the beautiful fair'; Ben Jonson pointed out in one of his plays that if one wanted to meet beautiful young women, one should go where they were likely to be – 'to courts, to tiltings, public shows and feasts, church, and sometimes plays. In these places a man shall find out whom to love, whom to play with, whom to touch once, whom to hold ever'.

And it is still true that only a tiny minority of people need the excuse provided by the computer or the advertisement: chance is enough for most of us; when we see a girl or a man who is particularly attractive, in a train, or a park, or a street, or at a party, it is usually possible to arrange an exchange of a few words – to place the tip of one's toe in the water, so to speak, and take the temperature. Often the water is merely tepid, sometimes icy cold. But occasionally it scalds, and life will never be the same again.

overleaf: 'Among the acres of the rye . . .' First meetings as we may imagine them are seldom as romantic as this. (*Photograph by John Hedgecoe.*)

The First Meeting

How many thousands of ways there are for a fateful first meeting to occur! By chance or plot, by formal introduction or by being thrown together, there is scarcely a circumstance or situation which could not provide the setting for a meeting to which two lovers look back with nostalgia, amazement, amusement, or simple affection. Many times, too, we don't even know it has happened until days or weeks after the event. Sometimes the first glance can tell all, and seal a union as firmly as any ceremony ever performed.

One royal meeting was as happy as anyone could wish: introduced to Prince Albert as a possible suitor, Queen Victoria was in little doubt. She found him 'so charming, and so excessively handsome, and such beautiful blue eyes and exquisite nose, and such a pretty mouth with delicate moustachios . . . a beautiful figure, broad in the shoulders and a fine waist'.

But her predecessor, the Prince Regent, had not been so fortunate: although he loved Maria Fitzherbert from the moment he saw her on the arm of a friend outside the opera house, the facts remained that she was a Roman Catholic, and he was the heir to the throne and to the leadership of the Church of England. Their marriage was never officially recognized, but he loved her until he died. And while Nelson and Emma Hamilton were attracted to each other at their first meeting, she was after all both the wife of a distinguished British Ambassador and a lady of no extraordinary virtue – on neither ground a proper match for a hero (who himself was married). They let nothing stand in their way, however, and their affair was one of the most famous in history.

Sometimes a first meeting passes without incident, the occasion going by without a hint of a love match remotely approaching the heads or hearts of either person concerned: as when Tolstoy, dining at Pokrovskoye-Streshnevo with his old friend Lyubov Behrs, was served at table by her eleven-year-old daughter Sonya, little thinking that six years later that little girl would become his wife.

And while love may grow from nothing, or announce itself with a violent clash of cymbals, some lovers, meeting for the first time, react very coolly indeed. When John Keats met Fanny Brawne, for instance, he found her beautiful 'but silly, fashionable and strange . . . ignorant, monstrous in her behaviour, flying out in all directions, calling people such names that I was forced lately to make use of the term Minx'. Yet within weeks, he was writing her some of the most impassioned love letters in the English language.

And in one of the most celebrated first meetings in fiction, in Jane Austen's *Pride and Prejudice*, Mr Darcy appeared to the heroine Elizabeth Bennet 'the proudest, most disagreeable man in the world'; while he found her 'tolerable, but not handsome enough to tempt *me*'. Jane Austen knew human nature: very often the first reaction is one of distaste – sometimes for the very qualities which later seem admirable; sometimes for traits of personality which have to be tactfully curbed!

Of course, a meeting can take place before lovers are introduced, or introduce themselves: an intuitive awareness of each other is the most effective of all introductions – the exchange of glances across a room which is not just a device of the romantic novelists, nor just wishful thinking, but can be an intense instant of contact which can compel an immediate reaction or stun us into delighted amazement.

If that glance is the very opposite of magnetic – a purely dismissive one such as Mr Darcy gave Elizabeth at the ball – it may be months or even years before the awareness of love grows, through a slow attraction: 'I cannot fix the hour, or the spot, or the look, or the words which laid the foundation', Mr Darcy was to say later, when Elizabeth asked him when he came to love her: 'I was in the middle before I knew that I had begun'. But the first meeting will always be remembered, for this one thing is certainly true of lovers' first meetings – that neither of them will ever forget it.

And as for the occasions: they too can scarcely be catalogued, they are so varied. They can be completely accidental: Byron, whose capacity for loving was generous to the point of indiscrimination, met his last and greatest love, the beautiful young Countess Guiccioli, at a party to which they had both gone with the utmost reluctance, and only out of politeness to their hostess.

Then of course there are the calculators, the handkerchief and glove droppers, the men and women who engineered first meetings with great care: like Isabella Harvey, who was leaning from her window in Kensington one afternoon in the early 1660s, and saw the Earl of Sussex passing in brilliant procession below, his handsome young son Sir Humphrey among the company. She dropped her glove at the feet of Sir Humphrey's horse; the knight speared it with his lance and lifted it high to her window; soon afterwards they were married.

And sometimes true love begins under unpromisingly businesslike circumstances. A newspaper of 1754 printed an advertisement from a suitor which somehow has a genuine tone:

'If the beauteous Fair One who was in the front boxes at the play *Romeo and Juliet* last Wednesday night dressed in a pink satin gown with a work'd handkerchief on, and a black feather in her hair with bugles; also a black ribbon round her neck with a solitaire; has a soul capable of returning a most sincere and ardent love to one who thinks he had the honour of being taken notice of by her as he sat in the side box; let her with all the frankness of a Juliet appoint in the paper or any other where, how and when she will give her Romeo a meeting.'

The modern equivalent would be a meeting arranged by computer; love might result, or a disappointment – but without a meeting, there can be nothing, and the first meeting can be the doorway to a lifetime of happiness.

overleaf: 'The first meeting can be the doorway to a lifetime of happiness.' (*Photograph by John Hedgecoe*.)

The first kiss. (*Photograph by John Hedgecoe*.)

Courting

*The traditions and techniques
of the world of the chase*

The Sprightly World of the Chase

above: The ardent red rose, symbol of passionate love, paying court to the white rose in Walter Crane's illustrated book *A Masque of Flowers.*

right: The Swing by Jean Honoré Fragonard. The kicked slipper, the flying petticoat, the flaunting frills – all weapons in the armoury of the flirt.

In the annals of love two forces – man's desire to conquer the woman to whom he feels himself drawn, and the woman's enjoyment of her status as his ideal of beauty and love – have provoked a whole enchanted World of the Chase. As for the intrigues we indulge in, well, men have laid traps for women ever since Adam was a gardener – even though it was Eve who proffered the first, climactic apple.

For those of us who lack Casanova's overbearing sense of purpose, or Don Juan's wit, authors have always been ready with advice. Ovid, the witty Latin poet (43BC–*c.* AD17), wrote a delightfully lighthearted guide to the chase, the *Ars Amatoria.* Although in his private poems Ovid agonized over his own love, in the *Ars Amatoria* he directed other lovers to be more calculating. Gifts, food, drink, perfumes, dress . . . all of these, Ovid wrote, could carry the power to provoke love – and not necessarily frivolous or temporary love, but, equally, the kind that endured for ever.

Artichokes and Lizard's Leg: Foods to Inflame your Desire

Some blandishments are more subtle than others. There is, for instance, the matter of inflammatory foods. Almost every kind of food has from time to time been thought to stimulate an erotic desire in man or woman, from cocoa to the powdered horn of the mythical unicorn. But there is, and always has been, a great difference between the aphrodisiac which simply prepares the way for love, and the preparation which specifically provokes lust.

The idea of the aphrodisiac dates back to the time when the important thing about life, love and marriage was the production of children; and in very ancient times it was often considered that fertility was not a matter for man alone but an affair in which the supernatural assistance of the gods could, without disgrace, be sought. Anxious for children, man relied on aphrodisiacs not only to provoke his initial desire, but also to spur himself to great erotic heights, in the belief that the greater his lust, the better the chances of conception. The true seducer naturally was quick to turn the whole idea to his own advantage, but even so there were those who felt that an infallible aphrodisiac somewhat destroyed the fun of the game. To them, it was rather like beginning a chess tournament with one contestant being at once deprived of her Queen, both Bishops, and all recollection of the rules! But, in more moderate, less racy circles such aids were not altogether spurned. Then, as now, a good dinner and good wine were seen as a totally pleasant and enjoyable preamble to making love.

A closer look at the history of 'serious' aphrodisiacs – food or drinks specially prepared to increase potency, or to promote irresistible desire – reveals that the more unpleasant the mixture, the more efficient it was supposed to be. The most unspeakable drinks were solemnly prescribed, carefully prepared, and more or less enthusiastically consumed – drinks beside which the witches' brew in *Macbeth* ('Eye of newt, and toe of frog, Wool of bat, and tongue of dog, Adder's fork, and blindworm's sting, Lizard's leg and howlet's wing') seems a pleasant evening postum. These drinks were often taken from cups cast in the form of human parts, and there was for some centuries a belief that any food remotely erotic in outline must be an efficacious aphrodisiac.

There has always been danger in 'real' aphrodisiacs: the notorious 'Spanish Fly' (the insect Cantharides, dried and powdered) for instance, which works by acutely inflaming the gastro-intestinal system; and while its results delighted the Marquis de Sade by driving the guests at a certain ball to the utmost reaches of debauchery, it can cause serious damage. And in Africa there is yohimbine, a substance derived from the bark of the central African yohimbé tree which has been used for centuries to increase sexual powers. Yet modern scientific research has shown that it can cripple and that stimulative effects are in fact obtained only with toxic doses.

The more innocent aphrodisiacs such as the sweet potato, enjoyable for their own sake, were very rarely truly aphrodisiac: or if so, like alcohol (as Shakespeare pointed out) they 'provoke the desire, but take away the performance'. Almost every vegetable or herb at some time or another has been held to have aphrodisiac properties, especially if it was unfamiliar. The Elizabethan garden was a hot-bed of potential lust (one wonders how ladies could bring themselves to walk in them!) The famous *Herbal* of Nicholas Culpeper (1616–54) readily suggested herbs to assist the limping lover, and the powers of onions and all kinds of bulbs, chestnuts, eringo and asparagus were universally recognized; carrots, too, were held to be 'a great furtherer of Venus her pleasure, and of love's delights'. And by the nineteenth century advertisers by the score were ready to announce that the definitive aphrodisiac had at last been found: in the 1880s, a 'Balsamic Corroborant, or Restorer of Nature' was declared to have 'received flattering encomium from a certain Royal and several Noble personages'.

More simply, though, is not the mere presence of woman (or man) enough to excite us? Even the air we breathe can assume fresh and intoxicating powers. Take, for example, the experience of an eighteenth-century gentleman, a certain Captain Philip Thicknesse, who, 'in general, though I have lived in various climates, and suffered severely both in body and mind, yet having always partaken of the breath of young women, wherever they lay in my way, I feel none of the infirmities which so often strike the eyes and ears in this great city of sickness by men many years younger than myself.' Not that he was the first; other men than Captain Thicknesse have found it extraordinarily enlivening to partake of the breath of beautiful young women lying in their way! But by his gentle and imaginative approach, his willingness to draw strength from the passing breeze, to be thrilled by the mere proximity of a desirable woman, it is clear that Captain Thicknesse had all the makings of a Compleat Lover!

overleaf: '. . . a good dinner and good wine were seen as a totally pleasant and enjoyable preamble to making love.' (*Photograph by John Hedgecoe.*)

Cockney lovers in a *tête-à-tête* by Robert Seymour, the nineteenth-century English caricaturist.

Clothes to Kindle a Wantonness

Men have always taken pride in decking out their mistresses, looking on them as companions not only to covet, but to decorate as well; the most popular courtesans in Europe have always tended to appear in public, on fashionable occasions, looking rather like Christmas trees. Joseph Addison wrote, in 1711 in *The Tatler*, 'I consider woman as a beautiful romantic animal, that may be adorned with furs and feathers, pearls and diamonds, ores and silks. The lynx shall cast its skin at her feet to make her a tippet; the peacock, parrot and swan shall pay contribution to her muff; the sea shall be searched for shells, and the rocks for gems; and every part of nature furnish out its share towards the embellishment of a creature that is the most consummate work of it'.

Addison was being no more than gallant by the standards of his age; and although his ideal of a beautiful woman, or a beautifully dressed one, may seem far removed from the casual fashions of the present day, there is something undeniably modern in his assessment of woman as a '*romantic* animal'.

The 'romantic' image is, of course, very much cultivated by the advertising media of today, and we are all to some extent influenced by the advertisers' message in our search for an image for ourselves. From the time we can read, or even earlier, we are deluged by a rival flood of films and printed matter, the outpourings of the image-making industry, all of which hints broadly that sexual and romantic love are of very great importance. And so they are. However, commercial interests are apt to drive their message hard. In posterland, all the girls are incredibly beautiful, incredibly passionate; dressed in flowing silk, their newly-washed hair streaming golden in the wind, they travel by fast car or steady jet to sunny sparkling beaches, where incredibly handsome, incredibly healthy, incredibly rich young men lie waiting for them.

With most young people the message is quickly taken, and they begin to formulate an appearance that is at once fashionable within their age-group and distinctive to them as individuals and – most important of all – alluring to the opposite gender. But how can clothes and hairstyles and all the rest of the pre-packaged so-called 'romantic' paraphernalia be emotionally arousing? Men and women are born naked, and it would be ironic if it were true that the main reason for wearing clothes was as a kind of ceremonious preamble to removing them for amorous purposes. Perhaps, nevertheless, it is so.

The English costume historian James Laver set out some years ago his theory of 'the shifting erogenous zone'. By this he sought to show that the design of women's clothes varied simply in order to satisfy men's eyes. At any particular time, women emphasized one area of the body – constricting the waist to display slenderness, placing bustles to draw the eye to the buttocks, deepening the neck of a dress to display the breasts, and so on. Then, when men began to show signs of boredom, they shifted the emphasis to another part of the body. Men's eyes invariably followed.

It does in fact seem that clothes can have aphrodisiac qualities, controlled by the wearer, who decides just which area to reveal and how much of it. It is the selection that matters, and society in the end lays down the rules. With, possibly, a glance back at the erotic, bare-breasted Egyptian women of three thousand years ago, designers in the last decade tried to bring in the topless dress, but failed. Perhaps it was too explicit a move. The Victorian woman, on the other hand, showed considerable areas of breast – though her ankle was taboo. Now, after the miniskirt era, the eye is moving again, perhaps once more to the breasts.

The man is in a more equivocal position; it is doubtful whether women are on the whole particularly susceptible to what men are wearing, or even to their wearing nothing at all; women's magazines which have tried to introduce the concept of male nudes managed only to raise a storm of yawns from their indifferent readers. No, it seems that if a woman finds a man's clothes attractive, it will be for the sake of the clothes themselves as much as for the man inside them; while the man who enjoys what a woman is wearing, is very probably thinking of what is beneath them:

Nineteenth-century 'posterland': the handsome, attentive soldier in full regalia; the accomplished girl, fashionably bustled, at her piano.

> *Young men's love then lies*
> *Not truly in their hearts, but in their eyes.*

WILLIAM SHAKESPEARE, Romeo and Juliet

Of course, in our own time man has been handicapped: we are now (it is to be hoped) at the tail-end of the only period in history during which man has been reduced to being, fashion-wise, a cipher. Sometime after the middle of the nineteenth century, Euro-American man began to sober up in terms of dress to the extent that by the middle of the twentieth century any attempt to show individuality in dress was suspect. Sociologists have seriously suggested that women preferred their men in sober suits during the first half of this century, because, at a time of unemployment and general uncertainty, this indicated a faithful and sober husband and a good worker.

Over the past fifteen years – and it is no coincidence that affluence has reached new peaks in this period – the peacock principle has returned to male dress. Men suddenly began to 'display' once more, as the male animal has always done; and Mr. Laver's erogenous zone theory could now be seen to apply to men's fashions – at one stage tight trousers emphasizing the buttocks and thighs, at another the tee-shirt drawing attention to a muscular torso, or the cut of a coat exaggerated to show off the width of the shoulders.

But, however that may be, we are inclined to think that man (as distinct from woman) has little to gain in the courts of love, either by dressing or undressing! The recent focus on men's fashion may simply depend on boredom with the old, dull clothes that men were forced to wear for so long. Only in time, perhaps, will all be revealed.

overleaf: 'The cosmetic arts are as old as time . . .' (*Photograph by John Hedgecoe.*)

Venus Provoked: the Heady Power of Perfumes

Fashionable eighteenth-century lady receiving an overdose of hair powder.

The cosmetic arts are as old as time. The women of Egypt were using *kohl* to darken their eyelids centuries before Cleopatra was born, and the drug belladonna (*digitalis*), distilled from foxgloves and still prescribed today for the treatment of heart disease, got its name from the use to which Italian ladies first put it: to dilate the pupils of their eyes so that only a faint rim of iris remained. To all appearances intoxicated with emotion, her eyes dark with love, the *bella donna* would swoon towards the lover who was just a vague blur before her unfocusing pupils. In close-up the effect was slightly bizarre, however, and it was through such excesses that the heavily made-up woman became a universal target for rumour – just like the woman whose *décolletage* was too deep, or who wore her hair loose when everyone else's was severely pinned. Indeed it is doubtful whether cosmetics as such were ever such a practical aid to Venus as their sister – perfume.

Perfume, in some form or other, has probably been used by man for some 25,000 years. Its uses have not of course been strictly confined to the would-be seductress – or seducer! Derived from the Latin 'per fumum' ('through smoke') perfume was originally associated with ancient religious ceremonies. In an attempt to propitiate the gods, the Indo-Europeans offered up 'pleasant odours'; little did they realize that some 25,000 years later, their modern counterparts would be offering these aromatic powders, if in a somewhat different form, to a mere mortal – woman. Yet even if the recipient has changed, the propitiatory element may still obtain!

Diogenes, the Greek cynic (412–323 BC), used to buy aromatic ointments to anoint his feet! 'When you anoint your head with perfume', he declared, 'it flies away into the air and only the birds benefit; whilst if I rub it on my lower limbs, it envelops my whole body and gratefully ascends to my nose'. A few centuries later in ancient Rome the practice of using perfume on clothing and on the skin became quite commonplace. The wealthier citizens even used to perfume their villas; and the emperor Nero is alleged to have had fragrant gums and scents showered on to his guests through silver tubes in the ceiling of his banqueting halls. Royal households in the middle ages were not, it seems, complete without a resident perfumier. When Catherine de Medici married Henry II of France, she was accompanied to Paris by her cosmetician and perfumier. Perfume was not merely a blandishment, however; before the uses of soap and hot water had been properly explored, it was extremely important as a disguise; and, during those periods of history when a high excise duty was levied on soap, both men and women were obliged to use perfume as a substitute.

But that perfumes were often used in the pursuit of love is inescapable. Plutarch tells how Cleopatra relied partly on perfume for the seduction of Mark Antony. Shakespeare, in *Antony and Cleopatra*, vividly evokes the scene as Cleopatra sailed up the river Cydnus to meet the waiting Antony:

The barge she sat in, like a burnish'd throne,
Burn'd on the water; the poop was beaten gold,
Purple the sails, and so perfumed, that
The winds were love-sick with them . . .

Ever since Cleopatra's conquest, perfumes have at the very least been luxurious gifts which might purchase a lady's smile, and make the ensuing conversation more rewarding. Indeed, in the eighteenth century matters reached such a pass that the British Government was forced to introduce a Bill preventing 'women of whatever rank, profession or degree, whether virgins, maids or widows' from seducing or betraying into matrimony 'any of His Majesty's subjects by the scents, paints, cosmetic washes, artificial teeth, false hair', or other means. Serious penalties were incurred for the perpetration of such heinous offences!

Since then, moderation has been used; but most people still assume (and advertisers positively assert) that colognes, after-shaves, bath rubs, toilet waters and perfumes in general have an aphrodisiac value for both men and women. How much truth is there in this? Are scents 'surer than sounds or sights to make your heartstrings creak', as Kipling claimed for them? Certain scents do indeed bring back the past more evocatively than any photograph or recording. Baudelaire, in one of his erotic poems, commemorates this very attribute:

When, on an autumn evening, with closed eyes,
I breathe the warm dark fragrance of your breast,
Before me blissful shores unfold, caressed
By dazzling fires from blue unchanging skies.
Your perfume wafts me thither like a wind:
I see a harbour thronged with masts and sails
Still weary from the tumult of the gales;
And with the sailors' song that drifts to me
Are mingled odours of the tamarind,
– And all my soul is scent and melody.

A modest glance from a Victorian woman – and a far from modest display of ankle.

But the interesting thing about that poem (just to disappoint the perfumiers) is that Baudelaire was referring not to any artificial scent, but to the warm animal smell of his mistress's unanointed body.

The glands with which all animals attract a mate (sometimes over great distances) give out odours specifically for that purpose. Similar secretions are also naturally present in humans. It has moreover been discovered that the perfumes which seem most to attract men to the women who wear them, are those nearest in tone to our glandular secretions. And recently scientists have issued warnings that by continually using perfumes and deodorants, we may well be destroying much of our appeal to the opposite sex! It is a great irony that, in our efforts to attract, we should end by destroying our power to do so.

above: Silks and satins, elaborate jewellery, carefully dressed hair and a peach–bloom complexion in this design for a mosaic wall by Gustav Klimt.

right: The peacock principle in Elizabethan male dress. (*Youth Leaning against a Tree among Roses* by the miniaturist Nicholas Hilliard.)

The Joys and Heartaches of Dreamland

In the nineteenth century the interpretation of dreams became a highly fashionable pastime. Already, before the advent of Freud and Jung, it was beginning to be suspected that dreams were connected with man's most secret thoughts and wishes, and a number of 'dream books' were published in which dreams were interpreted and also used to indicate future events. Naturally enough, such works were in greatest demand when they offered guidance in matters of the heart. Below is a selection of entries, all of which relate to courtship, taken from the *Dictionary of the Interpretation of Dreams* of 1818, said to have been culled 'from the learned writings of Artemidorus and Others'. The moral tone is stern and unmistakably of its day. Is it all too fantastic to be credible? Perhaps. But there were many who believed its findings at the time. Dreams, after all, occupy a strange corner of our existence; and it is just possible that beneath the sweeping prophecies of Artemidorus and his friends, there lurks an element compounded of truth and common experience. The reader must decide.

Adultery For persons to dream they have committed it, shows that they shall meet great contentions and debates; but to dream they have resisted the temptation to it shows victory over their enemies, and that they shall escape great dangers.

Boots To dream that one is well booted, or hath good boots on, signifies honour and profit by marriage.

Cards To dream one plays at cards or dice signifies deceit and craft in love: your loved one should be less trustful of you! He that playeth at cards in a dream, shall be a great gamester as well with Joan as with my lady.

Coalpits To dream of being at the bottom of a coalpit signifies matching with a widow: for he that marries her must be a continual drudge, and yet shall never sound the depth of her policies.

Confections To dream that one makes confections and sweetmeats signifies great ease in courtship.

Deer To dream of hunting deer signifies a hard and lengthy courtship, but victory in the end (should you capture the prey).

Dragons To dream you see a dragon is a sign that you will marry some great lord or mistress, or a law-maker; it signifies also riches and treasure.

Earthworms To dream of earthworms signifies a secret enemy to the marriage, or a secret lover, who is the mere worm of the earth.

Figs To dream of figs in season is a good dream and signifies joy in love, and pleasure. But out of season, the contrary.

Grapes To dream of eating grapes at any time signifies the celebration of love's rites. To tread grapes signifies the overthrow of a reluctant love; to gather white grapes signifies the gain of a much-sought love.

Harpies To dream one sees harpies, which are infernal creatures, half women and half serpents, or else furies, such as the poets feign them to be, signifies tribulation and pains occasioned by envious men or women, and such as seek our ruin, shame or other misfortune by seduction.

Ladder The ladder is a sign of travelling, to or from a loved one; to ascend a ladder signifies success in love; to descend one betokeneth failure.

Leeks To dream of leeks signifies a discovery of secret domestic matters.

Lentils To dream of lentils signifies corruption, either of the dreamer or the beloved.

Logs To dream that one is cleaving logs is a sign that a stranger shall come to the house, with a danger to virtue.

Marry To dream that you marry signifies often a desire that you shall not be married.

Meat To dream you see the meat you have already eaten signifies that you desire the end of a love match.

Monster To see a monster or monstrous fish in the sea is not good, and signifies your love may wish you harm; but out of the sea every fish and monster is good, because then they can hurt no more, or save themselves. And therefore besides that our dream signifies that though one we love may wish us harm, they have no power.

Nettles To dream of nettles, and that you sting yourself, shows that you will venture hard for the love you desire. And if young folks dream thus, it shows they are in love, and are willing to take a loved one though they be stung thereby.

Nightingale To dream of this pretty warbler is the forerunner of a good-tempered lover. For a married woman to dream of a nightingale shows she will have children who will be great lovers. It signifieth also principally weddings and music, and promiseth a housewifely wife.

Organs To dream that you hear the sound of organs signifies joy.

Oysters To dream of opening and eating oysters shows great hunger in love, which the party dreaming shall suddenly sustain; or else that he shall take great pains in courtship, as they do that open oysters.

Pigeons To dream you see pigeons is a good sign; to wit that you will have content and joys at home. To dream you see a white pigeon flying signifies good success in love, providing your motives are for the good of your beloved. Wild pigeons signify dissolute women, and tame pigeons denote honest women and matrons.

Plough To dream of a plough is good in love, and affairs, but it requireth some time to bring them to perfection.

Rice To dream of eating rice denotes extreme fecundity.

Saddle To dream you are riding a horse without a saddle signifies outrageousness in love, lack of real concern, a disposition to deceive.

School To dream you begin to go to school again and you cannot say your lessons right, shows that you are a novice in love, and must take pains to learn its niceties.

Velvet To dream you trade with a stranger in velvet signifies joy from your lover, who shall bring you richness, and not only in gold.

Wrestling He that dreams that . . . he wrestles with a woman . . . is too forward in love. A woman who dreams she wrestles with her husband, will certainly bring him shame.

'Dances are a great and perennial spur to flirtation.' (*Artist unknown.*)

Ballrooms and Maypoles: the Unbridled Ecstasies of the Dance

'The delightful unison of their unerring feet, the movement, the music, her cool breath saluting his cheek – it was not a waltz, it was an Ecstasy!'

Dances are a great and perennial spur to flirtation – from the splendid balls at which polite behaviour was at least presumed to be the rule, to the kind of rude assembly that the puritan Philip Stubbes (*fl.* 1583–91) had in mind when he wrote of dances as 'an introduction to whoredom, a preparation to wantonness, a provocation to uncleanness, and an introite to all kinds of lewdness . . . I have heard many impudently say that they have chosen their wives and wives their husbands by dancing, which plainly proveth the wickedness of it. Every leap or skip in dance is a leap towards hell'.

More sympathetic was the novelist Charles Reade, who in 1863 painted a telling portrait of two lovers breathless in a first encounter: 'To most young people love comes after a great deal of waltzing. But the pair brought the awakened tenderness and trembling sensibilities of two burning hearts to this their first intoxicating whirl. To them, therefore, everything was a thrill – the first meeting and timid pressure of their hands, the first delicate enfolding of her supple waist by his strong arm but trembling hand, the delightful unison of their unerring feet, the movement, the music, her cool breath saluting his cheek. . . It was not a waltz, it was an Ecstasy'.

In country districts dancing embodied a blend of religious and magical belief as well as a great deal of boisterous physical activity. May dances were and still are held throughout Europe, from Sweden to the South of France, their function being inextricably allied to the ceremonies of increase customarily held at that time of year to promote the crops and fertility in general. In the seventeenth century the poet Robert Herrick noted that boys and girls rose early 'to observe the rite of May.' But to the ever-watchful Stubbes, there was more to it than that. According to him, on the eve of May Day young people 'run gadding over night to the woods, groves, hills and mountains, where they spend all the night in plesant pastimes'. As to the Maypole dances, Stubbes 'heard it credibly reported (and that viva voce) by men of great gravitie and reputation, that of fortie, threescore, or a hundred maides going to the wood to deck the maypole, there have scaresly the third part of them returned home againe undefiled'.

And Stubbes, with his eye gluttonously fixed to the keyhole of his society, was not one to spurn such titillating statistics. But, for all that, the message of the maypole remained clear enough; ornamented with nosegays, garlands, red ribbons, flags, handkerchiefs or gilt egg-shells, depending on the country of origin, it announced that warm summer days had arrived again:

> Come lasses and lads, get leave of your dads,
> And away to the Maypole hie,
> For every he has got him a she,
> And the fiddler's standing by.

ANON. *c. 1670*

76

All Cupid's Heraldry: the Irrepressible Rise of the Valentine

The occasion in the year when the heart of every Compleat Lover beats a little faster is 14 February, St Valentine's Day. The Saint himself is a very shadowy, perhaps totally mythical, figure; his day seems to have been associated with love through the ancient notion that it was on that day that birds began to mate. Robert Herrick, the English lyric poet, wrote rather mournfully,

> Oft have I heard both youths and virgins say
> Birds chuse their mates, and couple too, this day;
> But by their flight I never can divine
> When I shall couple with my Valentine.

Certainly from Elizabethan times the term had been well-known; Margery Brews married 'her well-belovyd Valentyn John Paston, Squyer', in 1477; and in 1535, in a will, a man wrote: 'I gyf and bequeth to my Valentyn Agnes Illyon ten shillings'. Often a Valentine received much more: Samuel Pepys recorded that the Duke of York in 1667 gave Lady Arabella Stewart a Valentine gift of a ring worth £800; and two hundred years later an embarrassed lady in Norwich, England had to cope with the unexpected arrival of a grand piano!

More modestly, the Valentine card became the recognized mark of anonymous affection. The tradition started in the early part of the eighteenth century, when manufacturers began issuing sets of verses which the largely illiterate public could mount on cards of its own devising. The fashion really caught on in the nineteenth century: in 1850, Lord Macaulay commemorated the events of St Valentine's Day:

> On earth the postman toils along
> Bent double by huge bales of song,
> Where, rich with many a gorgeous dye,
> Blazes all Cupid's heraldry –
> Myrtles and roses, doves and sparrows,
> Love-knots and altars, lamps and arrows –
> What nymph without wild hopes and fears
> The double rap this morning hears!
> Unnumbered lasses, young and fair,
> From Bethnal Green to Belgrave Square,
> With cheeks high flush'd, and hearts loud beating
> Await the tender annual greeting.
> The loveliest lass of all is mine!
> Good morrow to my Valentine!

The fashion limped a little during the 1880s, but now seems as popular as ever. Each year token hearts are given and exchanged. Solitary hearts pound in expectation, ache and are broken, flutter wildly and are saved; 'my true love hath my heart and I have his'.

overleaf: Nineteenth-century Valentine cards. (*Photograph by John Hedgecoe.*)

My Uncle Toby and the Widow Wadman by Charles Robert Leslie.

Love-Letters

In his great anthology *Love*, Walter de la Mare pointed out how 'lovers never weary of craving to communicate what no mere words unaided can. Their parcels stubbornly refuse to be unpacked. . . . Sighs elude ink; crosses must stand for kisses; and, though not from any apprehension of wasting time, they have to find haven in such piteous exclamations as "Words cannot express", "I cannot tell you", "If only I could say!", "My heart. . ."'

In a few love letters which have survived, the heart speaks aloud, and so movingly that one feels guilty at invading the lover's privacy. The love-letters of John Keats, for instance, are almost unbearably moving to read. His was an unhappy love; a victim of tuberculosis, which in his time was almost always fatal, and of the social conventions of the early nineteenth century, Keats could celebrate his love only in words. And the illness so built up erotic tension within him that his jealousy and even envy spilt over into anger and pain. These are not heartwarming or comforting love-letters; but they expose the naked nerves of love more clearly than any others we know, and more clearly than more self-conscious works of art.

Again and again in them we hear the note of astonishment that we all know – astonishment that the heart should be capable of such deep feeling:

> 'I am almost astonished that any absent one should have that luxurious power over my senses which I feel. Even when I am not thinking of you I receive your influence and a tenderer nature steals upon me. All my thoughts, my unhappiest days and nights have I find not at all cured me of my love of beauty, but made it so intense that I am miserable that you are not with me: or rather breathe in that dull sort of patience that cannot be called Life. I never knew before, what such a love as you have made me feel, was; I did not believe in it; my Fancy was afraid of it, lest it should burn me up . . .'

In his letters Keats expressed that infinite longing which is the mark of love at its most intense. To read them is to stare into the open abyss which waits for any lover, if circumstances turn against him. No one could wish to receive them; they show the extremes of despair in love, and, by contrast, the extremes of delight. Other surviving, happier letters remind us of a more pedestrian, yet infinitely easier love. There are the charming letters of Dorothy Osborne and Sir William Temple, parted by the English Civil War. He sent her, to keep, a lock of his hair:

> '. . . How fond I am of your lock. Well, in earnest now, and setting aside all compliments, I never saw finer hair, nor of a better colour; but cut no more on't. I am combing, and curling, and kissing this lock all day, and dreaming on't all night. The ring, too, is very well, only a little of the biggest. Send me a tortoise one that is a little less

than I sent for a pattern. I would not have the rule absolutely true without exception that hard hairs be ill-natured, for then I should be so. But I can allow that all soft hairs are good, and so are you, or I am deceived as much as you are if you think I do not love you enough. Tell me, my dearest, am I? You will not be if you think I am,

Yours.'

The tone in this courtly letter from Henry VIII to Anne Boleyn is, by contrast, formal but ardent:

Mine own Sweetheart,
This shall be to advertise you of the great melancholy that I find here since your departing, for I ensure you methinketh the time longer since your departing now last than I was wont to do a whole fortnight. I think your kindness and my fervency of love causeth it; for otherwise I would not have thought it possible that for so little a while it should have grieved me. But now I am coming towards you, methinketh my pains be half removed. Wishing myself (especially of an evening) in my sweetheart's arms whose pretty duckies I trust shortly to kiss. Written by the hand of him that was, is and shall be yours by his own will,

H.R.

Napoleon's letters to Josephine were wild and passionate:

I awake all filled with you. Your image and the intoxicating pleasures of last night, allow my senses no rest. Sweet and matchless Josephine, how strangely you work upon my heart. Are you angry with me? Are you unhappy? Are you upset? My soul is broken with grief and my love for you forbids repose. But how can I rest any more, when I yield to the feeling that masters my inmost self, when I quaff from your lips and from your heart a scorching flame? Yes! One night has taught me how far your portrait falls short of yourself! You start at midday: in three hours I shall see you again. Till then, a thousand kisses, mio dolce amor! but give me none back, for they set my blood on fire.

Dec. 29 1795

To read such letters is disquieting – because of the invasion of privacy – and yet at the same time extremely rewarding. What we hear when we read Henry VIII's love-letters is his very voice. This does not mean, of course, that it cannot be a false voice; men were deceivers ever. But it is not an artificial voice. And that is how to write a good love-letter (how indeed to write a good *letter*): forget about the niceties of syntax, and be oneself; the success of a love-letter has nothing to do with literature or education.

overleaf, left: Escaping to read a love-letter in private. (*Photograph by John Hedgecoe.*)

overleaf, right: The course of true love may not always run smoothly. (*Broken Vows* by Philip Hermogenes Calderon.)

Hearts and Flowers for Ever

A written message was not the only way of conveying amorous sentiments, even from a distance. Long before the invention of printing, and possibly even before the invention of writing, flowers served as a mark of admiration, as a testimony of affection, love or adoration. A thousand years before the birth of Christ, a Greek poet, Meleagros, wrote:

White violets I'll bring
And soft narcissus
And myrtle and laughing lilies
The innocent crocus
Dark hyacinth also
And roses heavy with love.
And these I'll twine for Heliodora
And scatter the bright petals in her hair.

The petals will fall from different flowers in different countries, of course – in England, perhaps daisies and buttercups, roses and cowslips; in America, goldenrod and stargrass, June daisies, Mayapple and asters; in India, hibiscus and dattura and champa flowers; and in Australia wattle, and strange heathflowers; in Mexico, cactus flowers – 'roses of the desert' – or the feet-long clusters of the cream bells of the yucca.

In any country, to compare your mistress to a flower is fairly obvious; to do it with grace has always been the aim of a lover. For years, the simple *gift* of flowers was enough; Napoleon sent Marie Louise flowers every day he was absent from her. But the Victorians, bringing sentimentality to an art, were not content to pay the simple tribute: they *literally* 'said it with flowers', inventing a language for the purpose. Some 'phrases' were ancient: a single red rose had always meant, plainly, 'I love you'; but then enterprising students of love compiled whole dictionaries of flowers, which could only be properly interpreted if the person beloved happened to possess the same dictionary, for there were endless nuances of meaning in even the most common of flowers.

One industrious floral etymologist was G. R. M. Devereux, who in *The Lover's Guide*, published in 1909, pointed out that one could send one's love stephanotis, enquiring 'Will you accompany me to the East?' A spiderwort, returned, would mean: 'I esteem, but do not love you.' 'Jonquil!' you might reply (or, 'I desire a return of affection!') To which the girl might respond with a single dandelion, meaning, simply, 'Go!' Whole sentences could be composed – provided one's garden were big enough! A sequence of garden daisy, Virginia creeper leaf, speedwell and bay leaf, would be translated by the initiated as: 'I share your sentiments, offer a woman's fidelity, and change but in death.' But, even in the presentation of a bouquet or a single flower, care was needed: a moss-rosebud, handed to one's love, was widely interpreted as an honest confession of adoration. If, however, one had the bad luck or absent-mindedness to hand it to her upside down, it signified something quite different.

It was all, of course, a carefully contrived game, fun to play and not to be taken too seriously by the participants. As a novel language it paved the way for many a pretty compliment made later in earnest, and many a daring proposal doubtless followed such introductory ice-breaking moves. And if the various books disagreed amongst themselves as to the meaning of some flowers, confusing the issue and covering one's traces at an instant gave the game added spice. No bones or hearts would be irrevocably broken at that stage. Or so we might be tempted to think today. But the moods of lovers are devious and deep and it is quite likely that a romance at the turn of the century could in fact be wrecked by a casually inverted moss-rosebud. Even today most of us have mental corners where a belief in magic dies hard. The ancient superstitions of love are, moreover, still celebrated in many rituals and customs throughout the world, as we shall shortly see.

Black humour from an artist's brush: *The Persecuted Lovers* by the Australian painter Arthur Boyd.

THE LANGUAGE OF FLOWERS

ROSEMARY
Remembrance

PHLOX
I agree with you

AZALEA
Do not be frivolous or you
may run into trouble

IVY
For ever true

ACACIA
Deep and true love

DAFFODIL
Hope on

SUNFLOWER
Someone loves you
very much indeed

IRIS
A letter is on its way

VIOLET
Love

CYCLAMEN
Do not worry.
You need not be afraid

LILY OF THE VALLEY
You will be
happy again

TULIP
I love you

ORANGE BLOSSOM
A wedding is
on its way

RED CARNATION
Have pity on my poor
long-suffering heart

EVERLASTING FLOWERS
I shall never forget you
as long as I live

ROSE
True love

MIMOSA
Try not to be so
sensitive

ANEMONE
Someone
you love is ill

WILD DAISY
I will think of it

APPLE BLOSSOM
Beware. You will be
tempted to folly

Rhymes and Spells and Amorous Potions

Jealousy and Flirtation by Haynes King.

Love and magic have always been attracted one to the other. The great love stories of antiquity hummed with activity as gods changed into swans or bulls, and Jupiter roamed about disguised as a fly in order to surprise many an unsuspecting mortal. Later, wizards busily stirred bubbling cauldrons of love charms, and mumbled abstruse spells. In ancient Britain, King Uther Pendragon launched the Arthurian saga by commissioning Merlin to change him into the likeness of Gorlais, Duke of Cornwall, so that he could enjoy the latter's wife, Ygerna. And young King Arthur, the result of that union, ruled over a country in which lovers fought unrelentingly against, or with the help of, strange magic.

Other European sagas – the Ring, for instance – are equally alive with love-spells. Tristan and Iseult were thrown into their catastrophic affair as the result of a magic potion, and incantations visited unsuspecting lovers with drama, delirious joy, or sometimes deep tragedy. Gradually, the incantations turned into love-rhymes and spells, and often they were specially designed to comfort young girls who had not yet found a lover or husband. One amateur magician in the early nineteenth century set out this recipe for discovering a future husband:

'The seeds of butter-dock (coltsfoot) must be sowed by a young unmarried woman half an hour before sunrise on a Friday morning, in a lonesome place. She must strew the seeds gradually, on the grass, saying these words –

> I sow, I sow
> Then, my own dear,
> Come here, come here,
> And mow and mow!

The seed being scattered, she will see her future husband mowing with a scythe at a short distance from her. She must not be frightened, for if she says "Have mercy on me!" he will immediately vanish. This method is said to be infallible, but it is looked upon as a bold, desperate and presumptuous undertaking.'

John Aubrey, the inveterate seventeenth-century scholar and gossip, noted down several country spells, among which, 'on St Agnes night, 21 January, take a row of pins, and pull out every one, one after another, saying a paternoster, sticking a pin in your sleeve, and you will dream of him or her you shall marry. You must lie in another county, and knit the left garter about the right-legg'd stocking . . . and as you rehearse the following verses, at every comma knit a knot:

> *This knot I knit,*
> *To know the thing I know not yet,*
> *That I may see*
> *The man that shall my husband be,*
> *How he goes and what he wears,*
> *And what he does all the days.*

Accordingly in your dream you will see him.'

Superstition also had much to do with the little keepsakes of love: the band of hair worn in a ring or locket – no doubt this had connections with the Samson and Delilah legend; the idea was that with a little of the loved one's hair one possessed a little of his or her strength, for ever.

Within living memory, gifts have been given with some faint idea of their magical properites; and girls have used rhymes and charms to bring their loved ones into their dreams, or even their arms. No doubt the spells often seemed to work: if a girl was so determined to win her man as to go through the complex procedures sometimes demanded by these spells, she probably won him in the end!

overleaf: Keepsakes of love. (*Photograph by John Hedgecoe.*)

Keepsakes and Customs

Victorian girl showing her lover's portrait to her admiring friends.

Individuality has always been one of the happiest marks of courtship: the man who could afford to send his love a diamond the size of his fist achieved more if he could think of something more original – which would show his mistress that he loved her with all his heart as well as, hopefully, all his fortune. New ideas were eagerly seized upon by lovers anxious to demonstrate the liveliness of their affection.

In the sixteenth century, for instance, handkerchiefs became a fashionable mark of amorous sentiments, and by the end of the century 'maydes and gentlewomen gave to their favourites, as tokens of their love, little handkerchiefs of about three or four inches square, wrought round with a button at each corner'. By 1800, the craze was for musical-boxes, and a lover might give his mistress a seal with a tiny musical-box in it, or she might give him a watch that played a traditional air.

The history of love is full of movingly *personal* gifts, too: when Keats left Fanny Brawne, for instance, among the gifts she gave him was a large oval white cornelian, used for cooling ladies' hands when they were at needlework – something she had handled every day, and which could communicate to him the very touch of her hand. Such objects were often very private. Perhaps, for one reason or another – shyness, or a family's disapproval – it was necessary to keep love a secret. In other cases love could be proudly displayed, as by the knight who wore his lady's glove in his helm; or today, in America, by the girl who wears her boyfriend's fraternity pin – though that can be more a trophy than a real mark of love! Real love gifts tend to be quietly given and as quietly kept; a charm worn under the shirt, a ring round the neck on a chain, a little note folded small and kept in a pocket . . .

Today, most people in love will have a photograph of their partner, and a likeness has always been a popular love gift: at first, a painted miniature – but this was of course expensive, and it was only with the development of the silhouette that everyman could give everywoman his face to keep in her purse. Then came the photograph, and by the late 1840s many a young woman possessed a small leather folder from which her beloved's face looked stiffly out in daguerreotype, his neck firmly fixed in the photographer's iron clamp. Love gifts *as* love gifts (ignoring Christmas or birthday presents) are probably less popular now than they used to be, particularly among the youngest generation. A favourite disc or tape, a meal, a coffee or a Coke – these have replaced the hand-kerchief or the bottle of perfume; a boy gives his girl, it seems, *himself*; and she seems happy with the gift.

In our time the pledging of boy to girl, girl to boy, may well take place without the kind of formal 'engagement' that was necessary in almost all strata of society until ten or fifteen years ago. In the 1970s, the landmarks of commitment in love seem to be breaking down, after almost two thousand years. Until not long ago a romantic setting, a formal dialogue followed by a semi-official announcement were thought to be essential ingredients in a traditional rite. But here may be the place to reveal that the authors of *The Compleat Lover*, became engaged during a motorscooter ride, about twenty-eight miles east of Plymouth, England, and many engagements certainly take place in even less romantic situations.

The custom of betrothal seems to have originated in medieval times – and for the most practical of reasons. Often in country areas there would be no resident priest, and lusty lovers could hardly be expected to wait until one happened to come along. So they could choose between two forms of engagement: *sponsalia de futuro* (more or less the counterpart of a modern engagement: a promise to marry at some future date), and the more immediate *sponsalia de praesenti*, which they usually preferred because it constituted a true if somewhat irregular marriage which entitled them to live together as man and wife until a priest was available to make the union official.

Engagements took place at a surprisingly early age: a boy between seven and fourteen, or a girl between seven and twelve, could be betrothed (though not married), and nothing could then sever them! One wonders how many accidental betrothals took place, for the kind of ceremony involved seems to have been very simple, usually comprising an exchange of rings, a kiss, and the joining of hands (in France before a priest; elsewhere, simply in the presence of a witness). The clergy were bound to accept the *fait accompli*, despite the fact that they disapproved (particularly, on moral grounds, of *sponsalia de praesenti*). In fact so strong did their disapproval become that the Council of Trent, in the middle of the sixteenth century, abolished the latter method of engagement altogether.

In the twentieth century, the idea of 'trial marriage' has been much discussed. What has been forgotten is that trial marriage has existed in Europe for most of the past two thousand years: it has been called 'engagement'. And except perhaps during the Victorian age in England, it has given a man the right to share his sweetheart's bed (or a corner of the cornfield, at all events). Today, 'engagement' often means simply 'an understanding' – and not always a very clear one. A survey made during the late 1960s revealed that while 100% of all engaged girls were confident that a marriage would take place, only 60% of engaged boys felt they had actually committed themselves, even if they had given the girl a ring.

An exchange of rings has always, it seems, been a part of the betrothal ceremony, however unofficial; and certainly part of the marriage ceremony for most of its history. It is likely that the first engagement rings were given in Imperial Rome, simply as a pledge that a marriage would take place at some future date. At first iron, then gold rings took their place on the fourth finger of the left hand; and by the eleventh century the Church had taken up this secular idea, and the ring had become part of the official betrothal ceremony, and subsequently of the marriage service. And still today, the plain gold band has a sentimental significance that even the most unsentimental girl finds difficult to resist.

overleaf: 'The simple magic of togetherness.' (*Photograph by John Hedgecoe.*)

Eloping lovers – one of the possible hazards of denying lovers to each other.

The Simple Magic of Togetherness

Sometimes the course of true love runs smoothly but such cases have usually been the exception. Yet love is often strengthened by the prospect or the experience of danger: a man who fought a duel for his mistress could show no more fiercely how much he loved her than to risk life and limb; while she could only hope that the right man won. Similarly, there is no surer way of driving lovers together than to deny each to the other, as many worried parents have found. What is perhaps not so clearly understood is that jealousy is an admirable aphrodisiac, too, and can rebound. There is a story told by Inge and Sten Hegeler of a young man who for years had been the lover of a girl who one day began to show an interest in someone else; she began turning down his invitations, obviously became bored with him, and seemed to want to end the whole affair. At first he thought of bursting into her flat; then he wrote her a seven-page letter, filled with sentimental memories and pleas. Then he tore it up, and instead sent her two dozen dark red roses, with a card on which he wrote; 'Dear Else – Thank you for the time we had together. Thanks for – you. Hans.' They have now been happily married for several years.

Not all love stories have happy endings. And the greatest are often tragic: Antony and Cleopatra, Hero and Leander, Petrarch and Laura, Dante and Beatrice, Romeo and Juliet – these real and fictional lovers, loving with all their strength, loved finally in vain. It seems that living 'happily ever after' is really the reward of those who love steadily, truly and passionately but in a more relaxed fashion – a prescription that may prove very difficult to follow, however hard we try.

If there is any truth in the simple ideal of 'love in a cottage' it is that the company of one's lover is enough. Diamonds, perfume and mink stole – all the accoutrements of courtship – are in the end superfluous.

> *Come live with me and be my love,*
> *And we will all the pleasures prove.*
> CHRISTOPHER MARLOWE

Togetherness is what matters.

Falling in Love
An Anthology

Introduction

Words are almost as natural to the expression of love as bodily caresses. And love can turn the least adequate of us into a poet. The first hint of it and we are away, carefully rhyming *love* and *dove, moon* and *June*!

But most of us in our moments of emotion find ourselves turning to the song writers and the poets and novelists to express our love for us. Passionate or light hearted, flip or tender, ironic or ecstatic, all the many contradictory faces of love are caught and reflected in their writings.

from Anna Karenina

Vronsky followed the guard to the carriage, and at the door of the compartment he stopped short to make room for a lady who was getting out.

With the insight of a man of the world, from one glance at this lady's appearance Vronsky classified her as belonging to the best society. He begged pardon, and was getting into the carriage, but felt he must glance at her once more; not that she was very beautiful, not on account of the elegance and modest grace which were apparent in her whole figure, but because in the expression of her charming face, as she passed close by him, there was something peculiarly caressing and soft. As he looked round, she too turned her head. Her shining grey eyes, that looked dark from the thick lashes, rested with friendly attention on his face, as though she were recognizing him, and then promptly turned away to the passing crowd, as though seeking someone. In that brief look Vronsky had time to notice the suppressed eagerness which played over her face, and flitted between the brilliant eyes and the faint smile that curved her red lips. It was as though her nature were so brimming over with something that against her will it showed itself now in the flash of her eyes, and now in her smile.

LEO TOLSTOY, *1828–1910, translated by Constance Garnett*

Not to Sleep

Not to sleep all the night long, for pure joy,
Counting no sheep and careless of chimes,
Welcoming the dawn confabulation
Of birds, her children, who discuss idly
Fanciful details of the promised coming—
Will she be wearing red, or russet, or blue,
Or pure white?—whatever she wears, glorious:
Not to sleep all the night long, for pure joy,
This is given to few but at last to me,
So that when I laugh and stretch and leap from bed
I shall glide downstairs, my feet brushing the carpet
In courtesy to civilized progression,
Though, did I wish, I could soar through the open window
And perch on a branch above, acceptable ally
Of the birds still alert, grumbling gently together.

ROBERT GRAVES, *b.* 1895

Madam,

It is the hardest thing in the world to be in love, and yet attend to business. As for me, all who speak to me find out, and I must lock myself up, or other people will do it for me.

A gentleman asked this morning, 'What news from Lisbon?' and I answered, 'She is exquisitely handsome.' Another desired to know 'when I had last been at Hampton Court?' I replied, 'It will be on Tuesday come se'nnight.' Pr'ythee allow me at least to kiss your hand before that day, that my mind may be in some composure. O Love!

> *A thousand torments dwell about thee,*
> *Yet who could live, to live without thee?*

Methinks I could write a volume to you; but all the language on earth would fail in saying how much, and with what disinterested passion,

I am ever yours,
Rich. Steele.

SIR RICHARD STEELE *to Mrs Scurlock*

The Two

She carried the goblet in her hand
—Her chin and mouth shaped like its rim—
Her walk was light and sure,
Not a drop fell from the cup.

So light and sure was his hand:
He rode a spirited charger
And with one casual gesture
Brought it to a shivering halt.

But when from her gentle hand
He went to take the goblet
Difficulty overtook them:
Both began to tremble,
Their hands never came together
And dark wine stained the ground.

HUGO VON HOFMANNSTHAL,
1874–1929, translated
by Derek Parker

Girl Lithe and Tawny

Girl lithe and tawny, the sun that forms
the fruits, that plumps the grains, that curls seaweeds

filled your body with joy, and your luminous eyes
and your mouth that has the smile of the water.

A black yearning sun is braided into the strands
of your black mane, when you stretch your arms.
You play with the sun as with a little brook
and it leaves two dark pools in your eyes.

Girl lithe and tawny, nothing draws me towards you.
Everything bears me farther away, as though you were noon.

You are the frenzied youth of the bee,
the drunkenness of the wave, the power of the wheat-ear.

My sombre heart searches for you, nevertheless,
and I love your joyful body, your slender and flowing voice.

Dark butterfly, sweet and definitive
like the wheat-field and the sun, the poppy and the water.

PABLO NERUDA, *b. 1904, translated by W. S. Merwin*

from The History of Mr Polly

And Mr Polly fell in love, as though the world had given way beneath
him and he had dropped through into another, into a world of luminous
clouds and of a desolate, hopeless wilderness of desiring and of wild
valleys of unreasonable ecstasy, a world whose infinite miseries were
finer and in some inexplicable way sweeter than the purest gold of the
daily life, whose joys—they were indeed but the merest remote glimpses
of joy—were brighter than a dying martyr's vision of heaven. Her
smiling face looked down upon him out of the sky, her careless pose
was the living body of life. It was senseless, it was utterly foolish, but all
that was best and richest in Mr Polly's nature broke like a wave and
foamed up at the girl's feet, and died, and never touched her. And she
sat on the wall and marvelled at him, and was amused.

H. G. WELLS, 1866–1946

The Dalliance of the Leopards

Very afraid
I saw the dalliance of the leopards.
In the beauty of their coats
They sought each other and embraced.
Had I gone between them then
And pulled them asunder by their manes,
I would have run less risk
Than when I passed in my boat
And saw you standing on a dead tree
Ready to dive and kindle the river.

ANON. *From* the Sanskrit, *5th Cent. A.D.*

Blow, Wind, to Where My Loved One Is

Blow, wind, to where my loved one is,
Touch her, and come and touch me soon:
I'll feel her gentle touch through you,
And meet her beauty in the moon.
These things are much for one who loves—
A man can live by them alone—
That she and I breathe the same air,
And that the earth we tread is one.

Translated from the Sanskrit of the RĀMĀYANA
by John Brough

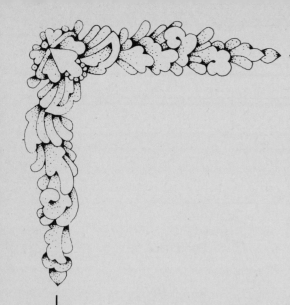

from *Marriage and Morals*

I believe myself that romantic love is the source of the most intense delights that life has to offer. In the relation of a man and a woman who love each other with passion and imagination and tenderness, there is something of inestimable value, to be ignorant of which is a great misfortune to any human being.

BERTRAND RUSSELL, *1872–1971*

Upon Julia's Clothes

Whenas in silks my Julia goes,
Then, then (methinks) how sweetly flows
The liquefaction of her clothes.

Next, when I cast mine eyes and see
That brave vibration each way free,
O how that glittering taketh me!

ROBERT HERRICK, *1591–1674*

Teresa Guiccioli meets Lord Byron

I became acquainted with Lord Byron in the April of 1819; he was introduced to me at Venice by the Countess Benzoni at one of that lady's parties. This introduction, which had so much influence over the lives of us both, took place contrary to our wishes, and had been permitted by us only for courtesy. For myself, more fatigued than usual that evening on account of the late hours they keep at Venice, I went with great repugnance to this party, and purely in obedience to Count Guiccioli. Byron, too, who was averse to forming new acquaintances – alleging that he had entirely renounced all attachments, and was unwilling any more to expose himself to their consequences – on being requested by the Countess Benzoni to allow himself to be presented to me, refused, and, at last, only assented from a desire to oblige her. His noble and exquisitely beautiful countenance, the tone of his voice, his manners, the thousand enchantments that surrounded him, rendered him so different and so superior a being to any whom I had hitherto seen that it was impossible he should not have left the most profound impression upon me. From that evening, during the whole of my subsequent stay in Venice, we met every day.

From a letter from the COUNTESS TERESA GUICCIOLI *to Thomas Moore*

from *To Earthward*

Love at the lips was touch
As sweet as I could bear;
And once that seemed too much;
I lived on air

That crossed me from sweet things,
The flow of – was it musk
From hidden grapevine springs
Down hill at dusk?

I had the swirl and ache
From sprays of honeysuckle
That when they're gathered shake
Dew on the knuckle.

ROBERT FROST, *1875–1963*

A Birthday

My heart is like a singing bird
   Whose nest is in a water'd shoot;
My heart is like an apple-tree
   Whose boughs are bent with
      thickest fruit;
My heart is like a rainbow shell
   That paddles in a halcyon sea;
My heart is gladder than all these,
   Because my love has come to me.

Raise me a daïs of silk and down;
   Hang it with vair and purple dyes;
Carve it in doves, and pomegranates,
   And peacocks with a hundred eyes;
Work it in gold and silver grapes,
   In leaves and silver fleurs-de-lys;
Because the birthday of my life
   Is come, my love is come to me.

CHRISTINA ROSSETTI, *1830–94*

The Sonnets

Between about 1593 and 1600, William Shakespeare wrote a sequence of 154 sonnets, which are among the greatest records of love in world literature. There is still some mystery about the men and women mentioned in the poems, though various scholars claim to have solved the puzzle: but the handsome young man to whom many of the sonnets are addressed, the stolen mistress, the rival poet and the 'dark Lady' immortalized by Shakespeare remain shadowy figures whose clothes we may all wear. . .

18

Shall I compare thee to a summer's day?
Thou art more lovely and more temperate:
Rough winds do shake the darling buds of May,
And summer's lease hath all too short a date:
Sometime too hot the eye of heaven shines,
And often is his gold complexion dimm'd;
And every fair from fair sometime declines,
By chance, or nature's changing course, untrimm'd;
But thy eternal summer shall not fade,
Nor lose possession of that fair thou ow'st;
Nor shall Death brag thou wander'st in his shade,
When in eternal lines to time thou grow'st:
    So long as men can breathe, or eyes can see,
    So long lives this, and this gives life to thee.

29

When, in disgrace with fortune and men's eyes,
I all alone beweep my outcast state,
And trouble deaf heaven with my bootless cries,
And look upon myself, and curse my fate,
Wishing me like to one more rich in hope,
Featured like him, like him with friends possest,
Desiring this man's art, and that man's scope,
With what I most enjoy contented least;
Yet in these thoughts myself almost despising,
Haply I think on thee, – and then my state,
Like to the lark at break of day arising
From sullen earth, sings hymns at heaven's gate;
    For thy sweet love remember'd such wealth brings,
    That then I scorn to change my state with kings.

30

When to the sessions of sweet silent thought
I summon up remembrance of things past,
I sigh the lack of many a thing I sought,
And with old woes new wail my dear time's waste:
Then can I drown an eye, unused to flow,
For precious friends hid in death's dateless night,
And weep afresh love's long since cancell'd woe,
And moan the expense of many a vanish't sight:
Then can I grieve at grievances foregone,
And heavily from woe to woe tell o'er
The sad account of fore-bemoaned moan,
Which I new pay as if not paid before.
  But if the while I think on thee, dear friend,
  All losses are restored, and sorrows end.

116

Let me not to the marriage of true minds
Admit impediments. Love is not love
Which alters when it alteration finds,
Or bends with the remover to remove.
O no! it is an ever-fixèd mark
That looks on tempests, and is never shaken;
It is the star to every wandering bark,
Whose worth's unknown, although his height be taken.
Love's not Time's fool, though rosy lips and cheeks
Within his bending sickle's compass come;
Love alters not with his brief hours and weeks,
But bears it out even to the edge of doom.
  If this be error and upon me proved,
  I never writ, nor no man ever loved.

from *To His Coy Mistress*

Had we but world enough, and time,
This coyness, lady, were no crime . . .
. . . My vegetable love should grow
Vaster than empires, and more slow.
A hundred years should go to praise
Thine eyes, and on thy forehead gaze;
Two hundred to adore each breast,
But thirty thousand to the rest.
An age at least to every part,
And the last age should show your heart.
For lady you deserve this state,
Nor would I love at lesser rate.
But at my back I always hear
Time's winged chariot hurrying near,
And yonder all before us lie
Deserts of vast eternity.

ANDREW MARVELL, *1621–75*

In Praise of Cocoa

*(Lines written upon hearing the startling
news that cocoa is, in fact, a mild
aphrodisiac)*

Half past nine – high time for supper;
'Cocoa, love?' 'Of course, my dear.'
Helen thinks it quite delicious,
John prefers it now to beer.

Knocking back the sepia potion,
Hubby winks, says, 'Who's for bed?'
'Shan't be long,' says Helen softly,
Cheeks a faintly flushing red,

For they've stumbled on the secret
Of a love that never wanes,
Rapt beneath the tumbled bedclothes,
Cocoa coursing through their veins.

STANLEY J. SHARPLESS, *b. 1910*

The Message of the Rose

Go, lovely Rose—
Tell her that wastes her time and me,
   That now she knows
When I resemble her to thee,
How sweet and fair she seems to be.

Tell her that's young,
And shuns to have her graces spied,
   That hadst thou sprung
In deserts where no men abide,
Thou must have uncommended died.

Small is the worth
Of beauty from the light retired:
   Bid her come forth,
Suffer herself to be desired,
And not blush so to be admired.

Then die—that she
The common fate of all things rare
   May read in thee;
How small a part of time they share
That are so wondrous sweet and fair!

EDMUND WALLER, *1606–87*

from Washington Square

He looked straight into Catherine's eyes. She answered nothing; she only listened, and looked at him; and he, as if he expected no particular reply, went on to say many things in a comfortable and natural manner. Catherine, though she felt tongue-tied, was conscious of no embarrassment; it seemed proper that he should talk, and that she should simply look at him. What made it natural was that he was so handsome, or, rather, as she phrased it to herself, so beautiful. The music had been silent for a while, but it suddenly began again; and then he asked her, with a deeper, intenser smile, if she would do him the honor of dancing with him. Even to this inquiry she gave no audible assent; she simply let him put his arm round her waist—as she did so, it occurred to her more vividly than it had ever done before that this was a singular place for a gentleman's arm to be—and in a moment he was guiding her round the room in the harmonious rotation of the polka.

HENRY JAMES, *1843–1916*

viva sweet love

'sweet spring is your
time is my time is our
time for springtime is lovetime
and viva sweet love'

(all the merry little birds are
flying in the floating in the
very spirits singing in
are winging in the blossoming)

lovers go and lovers come
awandering awondering
but any two are perfectly
alone there's nobody else alive

(such a sky and such a sun
i never knew and neither did you
and everybody never breathed
quite so many kinds of yes)

not a tree can count his leaves
each herself by opening
but shining who by thousands mean
only one amazing thing

(secretly adoring shyly
tiny winging darting floating
merry in the blossoming
always joyful selves are singing)

'sweet spring is your
time is my time is our
time for springtime is lovetime
and viva sweet love'

E. E. CUMMINGS, *1894–1962*

from **The Angel in the House**

'I saw you take his kiss!' ''Tis true.'
'O, modesty!' ''Twas strictly kept:
He thought me asleep; at least, I knew
He thought I thought he thought I slept.'
COVENTRY PATMORE, *1823–96*

Recuerdo

We were very tired, we were very merry—
We had gone back and forth all night on the ferry.
It was bare and bright, and smelled like a stable—
But we looked into a fire, we leaned across a table,
We lay on a hill-top underneath the moon;
And the whistles kept blowing, and the dawn came soon.

We were very tired, we were very merry—
We had gone back and forth all night on the ferry;
And you ate an apple, and I ate a pear,
From a dozen of each we had bought somewhere;
And the sky went wan, and the wind came cold,
And the sun rose dripping, a bucketful of gold.

We were very tired, we were very merry,
We had gone back and forth all night on the ferry.
We hailed, 'Good-morrow, mother!' to a
                shawl-covered head,
And bought a morning paper, which neither
                  of us read;
And she wept, 'God bless you!' for the
             apples and the pears,
And we gave her all our money
        but our subway fares.

EDNA ST VINCENT MILLAY,
1892–1950

The Look

Strephon kissed me in the spring,
   Robin in the fall,
But Colin only looked at me
   And never kissed at all.

Strephon's kiss was lost in jest,
   Robin's lost in play,
But the kiss in Colin's eyes
   Haunts me night and day.

SARAH TEASDALE, *1884–1933*

Meeting at Night

The grey sea and the long black land;
And the yellow half-moon large and low;
And the startled little waves that leap
In fiery ringlets from their sleep,
As I gain the cove with pushing prow,
And quench its speed i' the slushy sand.

Then a mile of warm sea-scented beach;
Three fields to cross till a farm appears;
A tap at the pane, the quick sharp scratch
And blue spurt of a lighted match
And a voice less loud, thro' its joys and fears,
Than the two hearts beating, each to each!

ROBERT BROWNING, *1812–89*

My dear Teresa,

I have read this book in your garden; – my love, you were absent, or else I could not have read it. It is a favourite book of yours, and the writer [Madame de Staël] was a friend of mine. You will not understand these English words, and other will not understand them – which is the reason I have not scrawled them in Italian. But you will recognize the handwriting of him who passionately loved you, and you will divine that, over a book which was yours, he could only think of love. In that word, beautiful in all languages, but most so in yours, – *amor mio* – is comprised my existence here and hereafter. I feel I exist here, and I fear that I shall exist hereafter, – to what purpose you will decide; my destiny rests with you, and you are a woman, eighteen years of age, and two out of a convent. I wish that you had stayed there, with all my heart, – or, at least, that I had never met you in your married state.

But all this is too late. I love you, and you love me, – at least you *say* so, and act as if you *did* so, which last is a great consolation at all events. But *I* more than love you, and cannot cease to love you.

Think of me, sometimes, when the Alps and the ocean divide us, – but they never will, unless you *wish* it.

Byron

LORD BYRON *to the Countess Teresa Guiccioli*

Summer Poem

I will bring you flowers
every morning for your breakfast
and you will kiss me
with flowers in your mouth
and you will bring me flowers
every morning when you wake
and look at me with flowers in your eyes

HEATHER HOLDEN, *b. 1946*

from *In the Midnight Hour*

When we meet
In the midnight hour
country girl
I will bring you nightflowers
coloured like your eyes
in the moonlight
in the midnight hour

I remember

Your cold hand
held for a moment among strangers
held for a moment among dripping trees
in the midnight hour

I remember

. . .

walking in city squares in winter rain
kissing in darkened hallways
walking in empty suburban streets
saying goodnight in deserted alleyways

in the midnight hour

ADRIAN HENRI, *b. 1932*

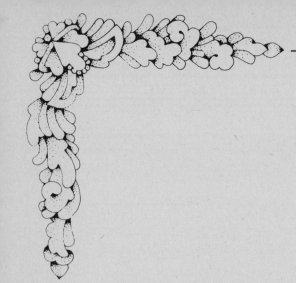

from Cyrano de Bergerac

But all this time your letters—every one was like hearing your voice there in the dark, all around me. At last I came to you. Anyone would. Do you suppose the prim Penelope had stayed at home embroidering if Ulysses wrote like you?

I read them over and over. I grew faint reading them. I belonged to you. Every page of them was like a petal fallen from your soul, like the light and fire of a great love, sweet and strong and true. Forgive me for loving you only because you were beautiful . . . afterwards I loved you for yourself too—knowing you more and loving more of you. It is yourself I love now, your own self.

EDMOND ROSTAND, *1868–1918*

The Passionate Shepherd to his Love

Come live with me and be my Love,
And we will all the pleasures prove
That hills and valleys, dales and fields,
Woods or steepy mountain yields.

And we will sit upon the rocks,
Seeing the shepherds feed their flocks
By shallow rivers, to whose falls
Melodious birds sing madrigals.

And I will make thee beds of roses
And a thousand fragrant posies;
A cap of flowers, and a kirtle
Embroidered all with leaves of myrtle;

A gown made of the finest wool
Which from our pretty lambs we pull;
Fair lined slippers for the cold,
With buckles of the purest gold;

A belt of straw and ivy-buds
With coral clasps and amber studs;
And if these pleasures may thee move,
Come live with me and be my Love. . .

CHRISTOPHER MARLOWE, *1564–93*

Making Love

*An exploration of the physical
world of love*

The Language of the Body

It is only when we are freshly in love that we realize the enormous potential that we have for feeling rather than thinking. Everything is sharper, brighter and richer.

Suddenly we look at the world from a different angle and new vistas open up. We feel more in tune with our surroundings and with ourselves. Half the joy of love is this unchaining from mental constraint.

As children we live primarily in the world of the senses. A baby examines his toes with his eyes, hands and mouth. A child hears the sound of leaves, feels the wind on his cheek and sees branches swaying. This combination of sensations mingles to produce the experience of trees on a windy day. If we say to the child, 'Imagine a tree on a windy day,' his mind-picture will be a positive one, but to an adult it will be an idea not a fact, for as adults we live primarily in a world of abstract thoughts, shut off from the senses by the pressures and speed of everyday living. Many of us suffer from an almost total sense-deprivation, most of us from blunted perceptions.

In the following pages we have tried to capture this world of feeling in pictures that express some of the variety and wonder of the sensations of the body.

The first step towards a full reawakening of the senses is to slow up. Concentrate on the thousands of everyday things you do but take for granted: for example, the most automatic of your life-processes – breathing. Try for a change focusing your attention on the air moving slowly through your nostrils and down into your lungs. Imagine the oxygen flowing through your body, bringing life. Then

concentrate on breathing out. Become conscious of how you feel.

Repeat this process for everything that you do – drinking, eating, yawning, laughing, stretching, growing. Run your hands over your face and body, experience the different textures of hair and skin, feel the cells you are made of, get to know yourself.

An essential part of reawakening to the world of the senses is to become alive to the world outside. To do this you have to isolate a single experience from the crowding world, like picking up a stone and feeling its smoothness lying in your hand, or trickling sand through your fingers. Return to the simplicity of a child's involvement with kicking up dead leaves in the street, or running in the rain.

It is the individuality and uniqueness of your experience that is important. Learn to encourage and treasure it.

As with exploring the world of your own senses, so with caressing your partner; the secret is to take time to notice and appreciate details of texture and feeling. All too often we are totally absorbed in our own sensations, hurrying on from one feeling to another without savouring them to the full. This is the antithesis of love and of the giving that is inherent in it.

The whole of the body is sensitive and needs to be explored. The skin, all of it, is our biggest sexual resource and capable of great variations of feeling. Remember that you can caress with your hands, hair, nose, mouth, eyelashes.

There are no hard and fast rules – everyone is different, everyone is special. Slowly, by gentle exploration you will discover both yourselves and each other. It is this affectionate journey over the most sensitive areas of your bodies that is much of the joy of love.

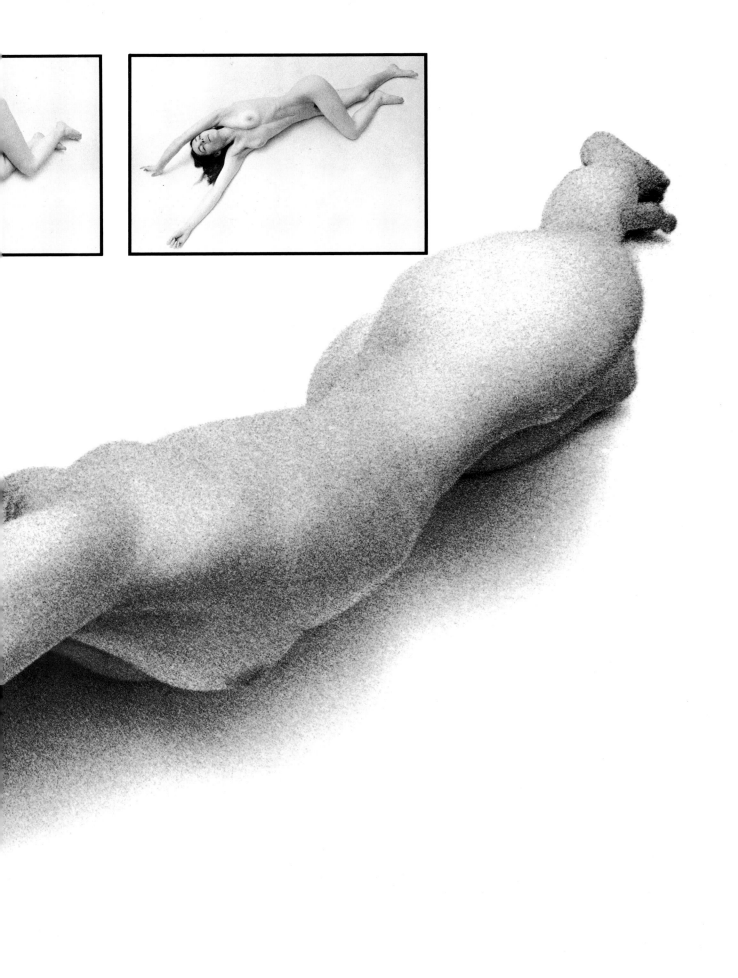

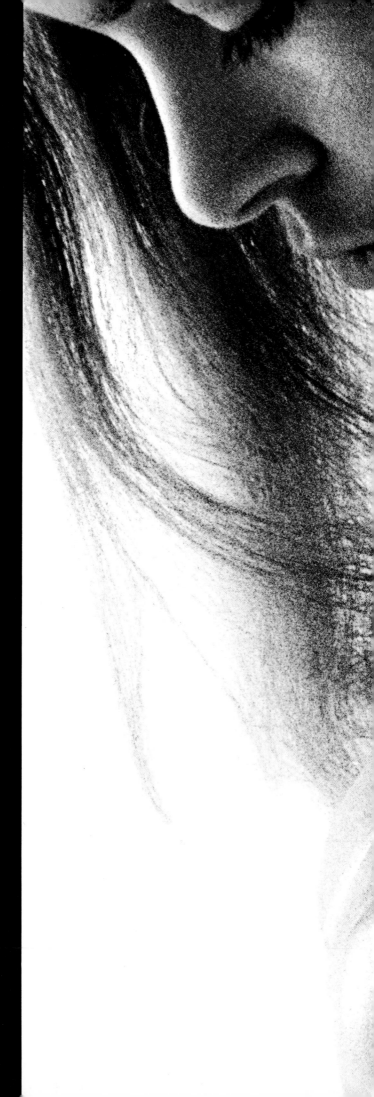

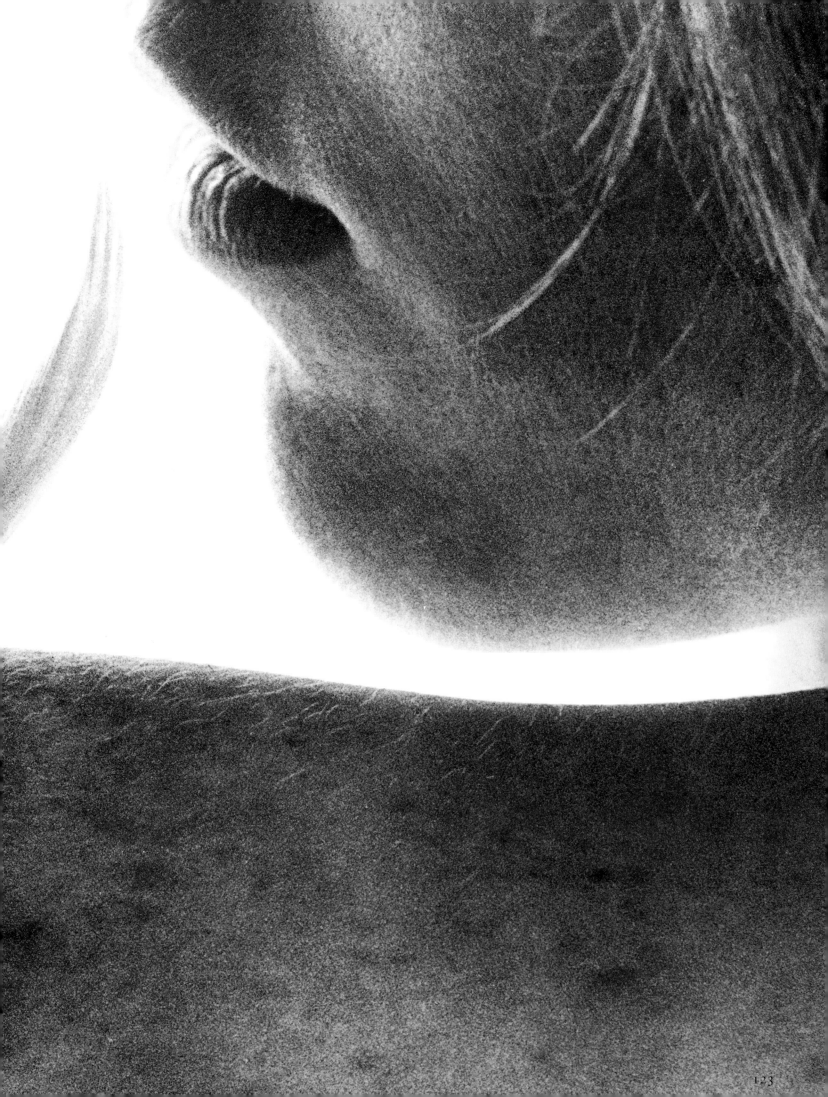

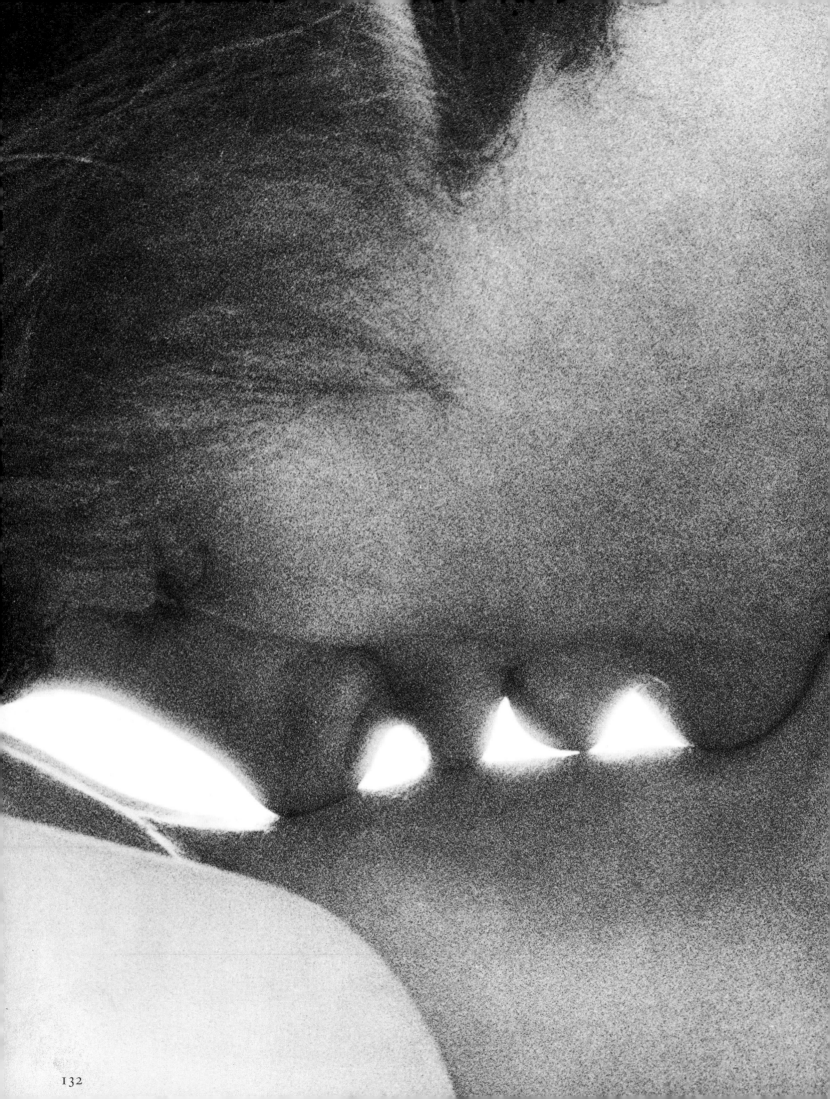

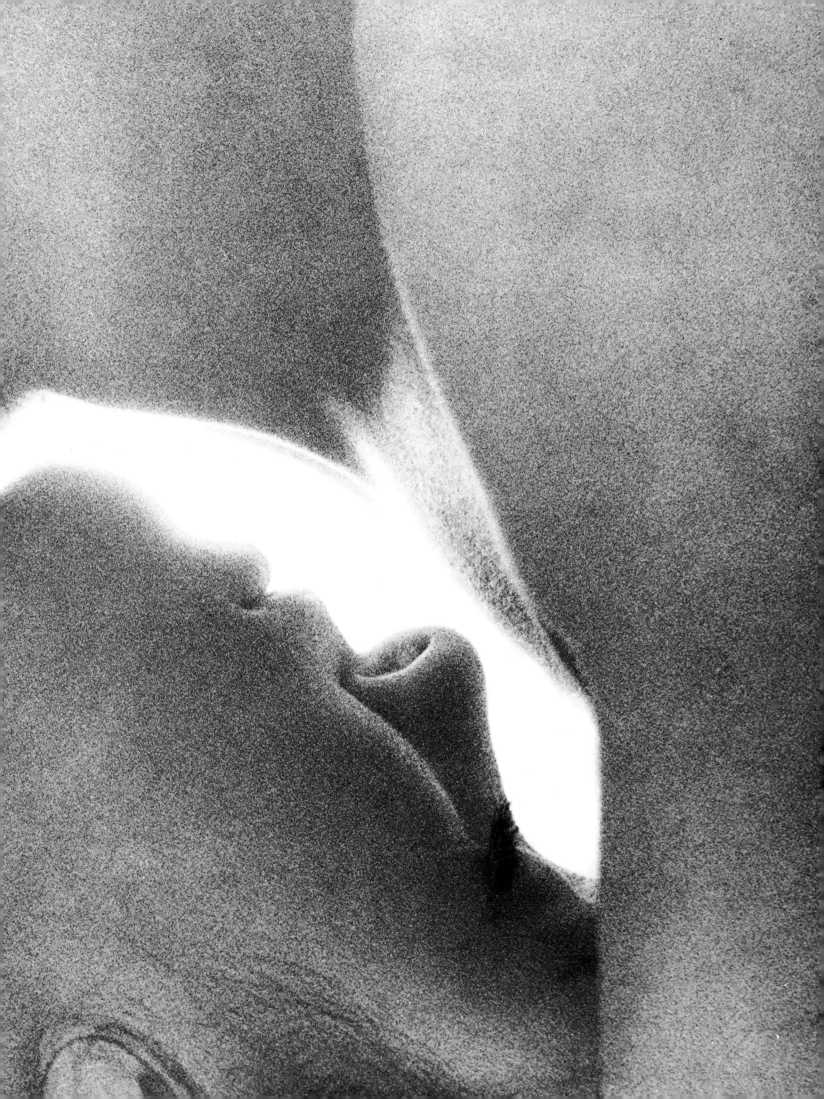

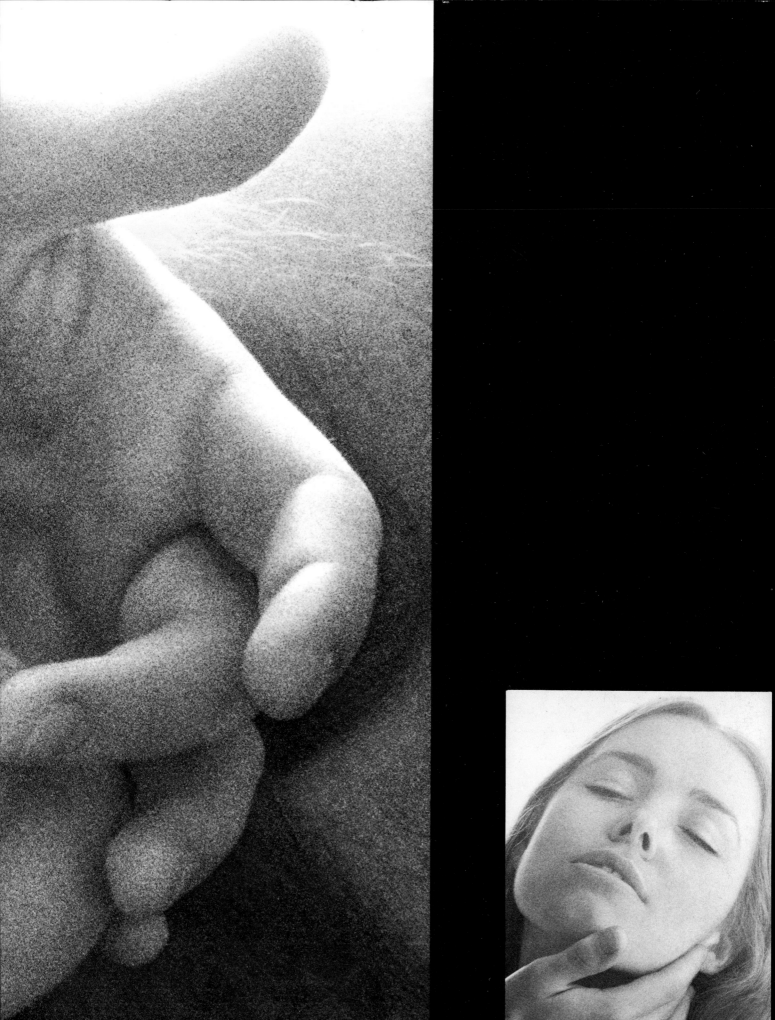

On Making Love

It is only when we have lost ourselves in the totally relaxed, glorious freedom of true love-making that we can begin to glimpse its life-enhancing nature, or the wonderful sense of peace and fulfilment which follows. This is indeed to be born anew, to have every nerve and sinew, every apprehension of life refreshed, for both man and woman. It is as though in making love we re-make our whole world in reflection of our happiness, and with it comes a pleasure – no, more than a pleasure, a joy – which should be at the very centre of life together.

Physical love is so much a part of the whole love relationship that it is silly and even dangerous not to pay it great attention. Who, travelling in a strange country, does not consult a phrase-book and make at least some attempt to understand the general style of an unknown language? It would of course be horrible to force anyone to read one of the explicit pornographic magazines which are now very freely available. But it would be sad, too, if anyone in the 1970s felt that it would be improper or immodest to read one of the many tactfully and often very well written books of sex education that are also available. It should at last, almost for the first time since the destruction of our primal innocence, be possible for every man and woman to relax and free themselves from fear of embarrassment, or the tendency to suspect that anything in love-making can be 'wrong' that the partner accepts and takes pleasure in.

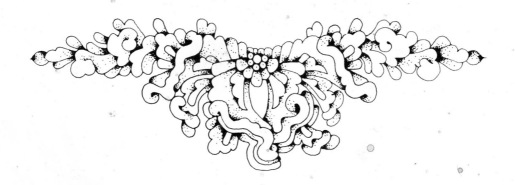

They were alone once more; for them to be
    Thus was another Eden; they were never
Weary, unless when separate: the tree
    Cut from its forest root of years – the river
Damm'd from its fountain – the child from the knee
    And breast maternal wean'd at once forever, –
Would wither less than these two torn apart . . .

They found no fault with Time, save that he fled;
    They saw not in themselves aught to condemn;
Each was the other's mirror, and but read
    Joy sparkling in their dark eyes like a gem,
And knew such brightness was but the reflection
Of their exchanging glances of affection.

The gentle pressure, and the thrilling touch,
    The least glance better understood than words,
Which still said all, and ne'er could say too much;
    A language, too, but like to that of birds,
Known but to them, at least appearing such
    As but to lovers a true sense affords;
Sweet playful phrases, which would seem absurd
    To those who have ceased to hear such, or
            ne'er heard.

LORD BYRON *(1788–1824)*
Don Juan, *Canto IV, X–XIII–XIV.*

above: '... With our clothes we should also shed our inhibitions, any sense of embarrassment, let alone shame.' (*Boisgeloup* by Pablo Picasso.)
right: The tenderness of love. (Detail from *The Month of April* by Francesco del Cossa.)

The language of love is complex and difficult, rewarding and delightful; the greatest fun, yet able to communicate the deepest and most tender truth. We pity the illiterate whose vocabulary is so small that it only allows him to express himself in the simplest, most basic terms; no-one denies that he misses a great deal. And similarly, if we lack the grammar and dictionary of love, if we are not able to express ourselves through our bodies with elegance, charm, force and humour, we are missing out on something essential to happiness. The language of love, of the body, is as individual and personal as our own speech: properly understood and spoken, it never fails. It is the language of life itself.

But only a hundred years ago a main tenet of the Victorian attitude to love-making was expressed in the often stated opinion that 'a lady does not move'. Although there were no doubt many happy couples in the Victorian age, there were also many marriages in which, inhibited from the slightest physical expression of her feelings, the frightened bride remained a frightened wife throughout her married life, the beauty and fulfilment of physical love a closed book to her. Indeed few things are more pitiful to contemplate than the fear and horror with which so many Victorian girls entered marriage, knowing nothing about the physical side of love, told only that there were certain actions on the part of their husbands with which it would be their duty to bear – forced to suffer virtual rape even from the kindest lover, simply because of the conspiracy of silence that surrounded the whole subject. And that conspiracy was virtually complete: in 1887, a doctor was struck off the

A long, long kiss, a kiss of youth, and love,
    And beauty, all concentrating like rays
Into one focus, kindled from above;
    Such kisses as belong to early days,
Where heart, and soul, and sense, in concert move,
    And the blood's lava, and the pulse a blaze,
Each kiss a heart-quake . . .

LORD BYRON (1788–1824)
Don Juan, *Canto II*, *CLXXXVI*.

register in Britain for selling for sixpence *The Wife's Handbook*, a simple, straightforward and tactful book of sex education. Nor should we pity only the wife: many a husband, too, must have been deeply frustrated by the coldness of his wife, loving enough during their courtship, but, married, 'the sort of girl who while being made love to would calmly reflect that tomorrow was the day for cleaning the parlour' (as Arnold Bennett depicted her).

At least the fear bred of ignorance has now largely vanished. But knowledge and a lack of fear are not in themselves sufficient to make love, early or late, a happy experience. If the new freedom of thought and expression in our own time means anything, it should mean that the last barriers of inhibition are broken down between man and woman; that the disappointments and failures which are almost inevitable in the early stages of a relationship, can be talked about, laughed over, surmounted. There must too be a sense of fun, adventure and enjoyment, and – perhaps most important – a deep desire for the happiness of one's partner. Even today, some people find it difficult to relax, to make love not only without nervousness but without embarrassment. In 1972, the copious nightgowns of the 1880s (when man and woman prepared for bed were often almost as fully dressed as for a tea-party, certainly more fully than for bathing) have gone. And with our clothes we should also shed our inhibitions, any sense of embarrassment, let alone shame. We must realise that we cannot, naked, hold on to the pretences which may be (perhaps essentially) a part of our everyday life. Love-making must not be betrayed by the polite social graces with which we fill our daily lives: our partner is more important than that. We must in fact strive once more to enter Eden, where man and woman were 'both naked, and were not ashamed'.

Lack of ignorance and anxiety in love-making is perhaps one of the greatest gifts the twentieth century offers us. Yet ironically, there is today, perhaps mainly among an older generation, an unmistakable feeling that everyone knows, and says, and writes, a great deal too much about 'love'; that there is no mystery left; that almost before they leave school, a boy and girl know too much about 'the facts of life'.

Even if this were true – and it is at least arguable that there is no such thing as too much information on *any* subject – what is forgotten is that all this information is simply academic: that the most explicit illustration of love-making does not begin to convey the real mystery of the act. The danger is that a boy and girl may 'know' precisely what *happens* in the act of love without beginning to realize even faintly the depth of emotion stirred by its very first gesture, or the extent to which one's body can become the instrument of one's very self, so that making love can be 'a gesture of the spirit'.

The danger of 'knowing too much' is that with the vanished mystery, with the final disappearance of the fear which always accompanies the unknown, will vanish also the gentleness, the tenderness which at

Dalliance by Eric Gill.

left: The Kiss by Gustav Klimt.

It was such pleasure to behold him, such
    Enlargement of existence to partake
Nature with him, to thrill beneath his touch,
    To watch him slumbering, and to see him wake;
To live with him for ever were too much;
    But then the thought of parting made her quake:
He was her own, her ocean-treasure, cast
    Like a rich wreck – her first love, and her last.

LORD BYRON (1788–1824)
Don Juan, *Canto II, CLXXIII*

best accompanies it. The most sensitive Victorian man approached his waiting bride with a tenderness which was the more careful, the more considerate, because he knew the depths of her apprehension. That tenderness is essential at all stages in a relationship, whether in the hesitant initial stages or after years of living together. It should show itself in consideration of time, place, atmosphere; in being ready to offer love when it is needed, or to set aside one's own need if necessary. However desperate the young, awakening body may be for love, however joyfully boy or girl may meet to express the height of that joy, there is still need to remember that the body is the most sensitive, the most apprehensive of instruments: that it must, in love, not be *used*, but *given*.

Giving implies receiving – and receiving the greatest gift anyone is ever likely to receive: the gift, entire and whole, of another human being, body and soul – for if anything is held back, the relationship will be incomplete, and ultimately unsatisfactory.

Just as the giving is important, so is the receiving: the rejection of a gift is always painful, and if the rejected gift is oneself – one's whole self – the rejection can mean a death, the death of the soul. Once the gift has been offered and accepted, there should be no quibbling: in love one must accept not only the advantages – physical beauty, or wit, or gentleness – but the disadvantages too.

Physical love, the mutual offering and accepting of the gift of the body, may be seen as a kind of pact, a bond of faith between two people. Indeed, it is of as much importance as any pact in which a man may promise a woman his worldly goods, or a woman promise a man her fidelity. It plays a greater role in some marriages than in others; for some couples complete happiness in love-making is absolutely central to their life together; in other cases it is less important; in yet others there are great difficulties – if physical love is more important to one partner than to the other, for instance. A man or woman to whom physical love is not very important can scarcely guess at the agony of frustration someone more highly-sexed can endure.

Various societies have had various attitudes towards this gift of physical love, and how and when it should be made. Even now, what may seem strange or even wicked to someone living in a small village in central Europe may seem natural to someone in down-town New York; what seems immoral to someone of one religious persuasion will be natural and permissible to someone of another.

Perhaps the one certain fact is that the gift of one's body to the person one loves, being a gift, can under no circumstances be forced, any more than it should be rejected without great sympathy and tenderness. There will come, in every full relationship, a moment when the gift can be offered, and when what has been a deep and even passionate friendship will be expressed in the completed act of love – maybe only hours after meeting, perhaps years later. When that time comes, and only the two people concerned can say when that should be, the total heights of love are within reach.

Daphnis and Chloe by Francesco de' Bianchi Ferrari, a painting illustrating the idyllic love of Daphnis, a Sicilian shepherd, and Chloe, a young shepherdess. Abandoned as children, they grew up together, fell in love and eventually married.

So fared they night and day as queen and king
Crowned of a kingdom wide as day and night.
Nor ever cloudlet swept or swam in sight
Across the darkling depths of their delight
Whose stars no skill might number, nor man's art
Sound the deep stories of its heavenly heart . . .

Deep from the starry depth beyond the stars,
A yearning ardour without scope or name
Fell on them, and the bright night's breath of flame
Shot fire into their kisses; and like fire
The lit dews lightened on the leaves, as higher
Night's heart beat on toward midnight . . .

Only with stress of soft fierce hands she pressed
Between the throbbing blossoms of her breast
His ardent face, and through his hair her breath
Went quivering as when life is hard on death;
And with strong trembling fingers she strained fast
His head into her bosom; till at last,
Satiate with sweetness of that burning bed,
His eyes afire with tears, he raised his head
And laughed into her lips; and all his heart
Filled hers; then face from face fell, and apart
Each hung on each with panting lips, and felt
Sense into sense and spirit in spirit melt.

So sped their night of nights between them: so,
For all fears past and shadows, shine and snow,
That one pure hour all-golden where they lay
Made their life perfect and their darkness day . . .
Nor woke they till the perfect night was past,
And the soft sea thrilled with blind hope of light.
But ere the dusk had well the sun in sight
He turned and kissed her eyes awake and said,
Seeing earth and water neither quick nor dead
And twilight hungering toward the day to be,
'As the dawn loves the sunlight I love thee'.

ALGERNON CHARLES SWINBURNE *(1837–1909)*
from Tristram of Lyonesse

The most tender and moving moments of love-making often follow the most passionate; after the storm comes the still centre of love at which lovers can feel more at one with each other than at any other moment in their lives. To reach this ideal, perfect equilibrium, one needs sympathy, patience, understanding, skill. Yet the skill cannot really be taught, however many books we may read: there are no specific rules: we learn to love by loving – by trial and error, tact, adventure, exploration. There is no more important lesson to learn in life, than the lesson of love.

From Pablo Picasso's *Vollard Suite.*

Making Love
An Anthology

Introduction

Urgent demand or tender wooing, fierce possession or intimate communion, this experience of physical love is so individual and so unlike anything else in life that it may seem impossible to convey it adequately in words. Yet it has been done, both in verse and prose. In this anthology from the writings of the poets and the novelists the door to this private world is set ajar for just a moment. For this brief segment of time we are allowed to share their deepest emotions, and sharing them recognize them as our own.

Bid Adieu to Maidenhood

Bid adieu, adieu, adieu,
　　Bid adieu to girlish days.
Happy Love is come to woo
　　Thee and woo thy girlish ways—
The zone that doth become thee fair,
The snood upon your yellow hair,

When thou hast heard his name upon
　　The bugles of the cherubim
Begin thou softly to unzone
Thy girlish bosom unto him
And softly to undo the snood
That is the sign of maidenhood.

JAMES JOYCE, *1882–1941*

162

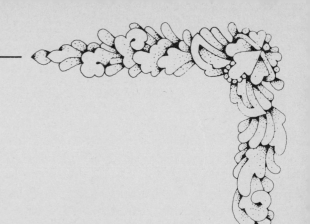

A Red, Red Rose

O my love's like a red, red rose
    That's newly sprung in June;
O my love's like the melody
    That's sweetly play'd in tune!

As fair art thou, my bonnie lass,
    So deep in love am I;
And I will love thee still, my dear,
Till a' the seas gang dry.

Till a' the seas gang dry, my dear,
    And the rocks melt wi' the sun;
I will love thee still, my dear,
    While the sands o' life shall run.

And fare thee well, my only love!
    And fare thee well awhile!
And I will come again, my love,
    Tho' it were ten thousand mile.

ROBERT BURNS, *1759–96*

The Kiss

For Love's sake, kiss me once again!
I long, and should not beg in vain,
    Here's none to spy, or see;
        Why do you doubt, or stay?
    I'll taste as lightly as the bee,
That doth but touch his flower, and flies away.

Once more, and (faith) I will be gone,
Can he that loves ask less than one?
    Nay, you may err in this,
        And all your bounty wrong;
    This could be called but half a kiss.
What we're but once to do, we should do long!

I will but mend the last, and tell
Where, how it would have relished well;
    Join lip to lip, and try:
        Each suck each other's breath.
    And while our tongues perplexèd lie,
Let who will think us dead, or wish our death!

BEN JONSON, *1572–1637*

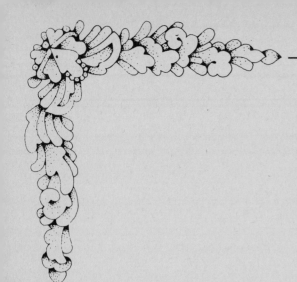

from *The Courtier*

Although the mouth be a parcel of the body, yet is it an issue for the words, that be the interpreters of the soul, and for the inward breath, which is also called the soul. And therefore hath a delight to join his mouth with a woman's beloved with a kiss; not to stir him to any dishonest desire, but because he feeleth that that bond is the opening of an entry to the souls, which, drawn with a coveting the one of the other, pour themselves by turn the one into the other body, and be so mingled together that each of them hath two souls.

BALDASSARE CASTIGLIONE, *1478–1529*,
translated by Sir Thomas Hoby

Warm Are the Still and Lucky Miles

Warm are the still and lucky miles,
White shores of longing stretch away,
A light of recognition fills
    The whole great day, and bright
The tiny world of lovers' arms.

Silence invades the breathing wood
Where drowsy limbs a treasure keep,
Now greenly falls the learned shade
    Across the sleeping brows
And stirs their secret to a smile.

Restored! Returned! The lost are borne
On seas of shipwreck home at last:
See! In a fire of praising burns
    The dry dumb past, and we
Our life-day long shall part no more.

W. H. AUDEN, *b. 1907*

from *Liber Amoris*

In her sight there was Elysium; her smile was heaven; her voice was enchantment; the air of love waved round her, breathing balm into my heart; for a little while I had sat with the gods at their golden tables, I had tasted of all earth's bliss.

WILLIAM HAZLITT, *1778–1830*

The Metaphor

The act of love seemed a dead metaphor
For love itself, until the timeless moment
When fingers trembled, heads clouded,
And love rode everywhere, too numinous
To be expressed or greeted calmly:
O, then it was, deep in our forest,
We dared revivify the metaphor,
Shedding the garments of this epoch
In scorn of time's wilful irrelevancy;
So at last understood true nakedness
And the long debt to silence owed.

ROBERT GRAVES, *b. 1895*

In a Gondola

The Moth's kiss, first!
Kiss me as if you made believe
You were not sure, this eve,
How my face, your flower, had pursed
Its petals up: so, here and there
You brush it, till I grow aware
Who wants me, and wide open burst.

The Bee's kiss, now!
Kiss me as if you entered gay
My heart at some noonday,
A bud that dares not disallow
The claim, so all is rendered up,
And passively its shattered cup
Over your head to sleep I bow.

ROBERT BROWNING, *1812–89*

Sweet, Let Me Go

Sweet, let me go! sweet, let me go!
What do you mean to vex me so?
Cease your pleading force!
Do you think thus to extort remorse?
Now, now! no more! alas, you overbear me,
And I would cry—but some, I fear, would hear me.

WILLIAM CORKINE, *fl.* 17th cent.

165

Jig

That winter love spoke and we raised no objection, at
Easter 'twas daisies all light and affectionate,
June sent us crazy for natural selection—not
Four traction-engines could tear us apart.
Autumn then coloured the map of our land,
Oaks shuddered and apples came ripe to the hand,
In the gap of the hills we played happily, happily,
Even the moon couldn't tell us apart.

Grave winter drew near and said, 'This will not do at all—
If you continue, I fear you will rue it all.'
So at the New Year we vowed to eschew it
Although we both knew it would break our heart.
But spring made hay of our good resolutions—
Lovers, you may be as wise as Confucians,
Yet once love betrays you he plays you and plays you
Like fishes for ever, so take it to heart.

CECIL DAY LEWIS, *1904–72*

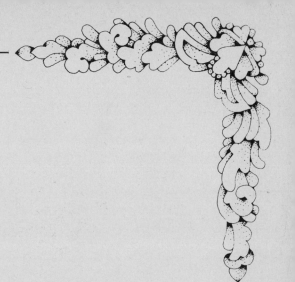

from *Wuthering Heights*

'Do come to me, Heathcliff.'

    In her eagerness she rose and supported herself on the arm of the chair. At that earnest appeal he turned to her, looking absolutely desperate. His eyes wide, and wet at last, flashed fiercely on her; his breast heaved convulsively. An instant they held asunder, and then how they met I hardly saw, but Catherine made a spring, and he caught her, and they were locked in an embrace from which I thought my mistress would never be released alive: in fact, to my eyes, she seemed directly insensible.

EMILY BRONTË, *1818–48*

from *The Morning is Full*

The numberless heart of the wind
beating above our loving silence.

Orchestral and divine, resounding among the trees
like a language full of wars and songs.

Wind that bears off the dead leaves with a quick raid
and deflects the pulsing arrows of the birds.

Wind that topples her in a wave without spray
and substance without weight, and leaning fires.

Her mass of kisses breaks and sinks,
assailed in the door of the summer's wind.

PABLO NERUDA, *b. 1904, translated by W. S. Merwin*

At the East Gate

At the East Gate of the City are young women,
Gracious and light as clouds in Spring time;
But it does not move me that they have the lightness of clouds–
Under her thick veil and the whiteness of her robe, my love gives me
    all joy.

At the West Gate of the City are young women,
Sparkling and beautiful like the flowers of Spring time;
But it does not move me that they have the sparkling beauty
    of flowers–
Under her thick veil and the whiteness of her robe, my love
    gives me all joy.

From the Chinese of SHI KING, *1776 B.C.*

And Your Dress Is White

You have bent your head, are looking at me;
and your dress is white,
and a breast blooms from the loosed
lace on your left shoulder.

The light exceeds me; trembles
and falls on your naked arms.

Again I see you. Your words
were quick, tight–spoken,
giving me heart
in the weight of a life
I knew circus-like.

The road was deep
that the wind went down
certain March nights,
and woke us unknown
like the first time.

SALVATORE QUASIMODO, *1901–71,*
translated by Jack Bevan

from *Day of these Days*

Such a morning it is when love
leans through geranium windows
and calls with a cockerel's tongue.

When red-haired girls scamper like roses
over the rain-green grass,
and the sun drips honey. . . .

When all men smell good,
and the cheeks of girls
are as baked bread to the mouth.

As bread and beanflowers
the touch of their lips,
and their white teeth sweeter than cucumbers.

LAURIE LEE, *b. 1914*

Song of the Pink Bird

Let the pink bird sing; it's at your breast
In a room we're sharing
And your head on my chest confirms
Its glad domination.
Let the world play its games beyond the curtains,
We are certain of only one thing,
Let the pink bird sing.
We have lost interest in wars and political situations,
There are craters in our hearts,
We must not neglect them,
Let the pink bird sing.
Let it sing as long as singing matters,
Look through the curtains
The clouds are blushing,
The moon apologizing –
Let the pink bird bring home to us
One reason for living,
Let the pink bird sing.

BRIAN PATTEN, *b. 1946*

from *Chanson d'Après-Midi*

Your hips are amorous
Of your back and breasts,
And you ravish the cushions
With your langorous poses.

Sometimes, to appease
A mysterious rage
Prodigally, seriously,
You kiss and bite.

You harrow me, dark one,
With mocking laughter,
Then lay on my heart
Your eye, gentle as moonlight.

CHARLES BAUDELAIRE, *1821–67,*
translated by Derek Parker

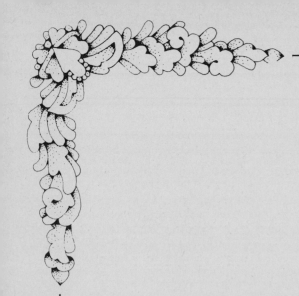

The Goodmorrow

I wonder, by my troth, what thou and I
Did, till we loved? Were we not weaned till then?
But sucked on country pleasures, childishly?
Or snorted we in the Seven Sleepers' den?
'Twas so. But this, all pleasures fancies be.
If ever any beauty I did see
Which I desired and got, 'twas but a dream of thee.

And now good morrow to our waking souls,
Which watch not one another out of fear;
For love all love of other sights controls,
And makes one little room an everywhere.
Let sea-discoverers to new worlds have gone,
Let maps to other, worlds on worlds have shown,
Let us possess one world; each hath one, and is one.

My face in thine eye, thine in mine appears,
And true plain hearts do in the faces rest.
Where can we find two better hemispheres
Without sharp north, without declining west?
Whatever dies, was not mixed equally.
If our two loves be one, or thou and I
Love so alike, that none do slacken, none can die.

JOHN DONNE, *1573–1631*

from 'Sex versus Loveliness'

Why is a woman lovely, if ever, in her twenties? It is the time when sex rises softly to her face, as a rose to the top of a rose bush.

And the appeal is the appeal of beauty. We deny it wherever we can. We try to make beauty as shallow and trashy as possible. But, first and foremost, sex appeal is the appeal of beauty . . .

But the plainest person can look beautiful, can *be* beautiful. It only needs the fire of sex to rise delicately to change an ugly face to a lovely one. That is really sex appeal: the communicating of a sense of beauty. . . .

What sex is, we don't know, but it must be some sort of fire. For it always communicates a sense of warmth, of glow. And when the glow becomes a pure shine, then we feel the sense of beauty.

D. H. LAWRENCE, *1885–1930*

from To His Mistress Going to Bed

Licence my roving hands, and let them go
Before, behind, between, above, below.
O my America! my new-found-land,
My kingdom, safliest when with one man manned,
My mine of precious stones, my emperie,
How blest am I in thus discovering thee!
To enter in these bonds, is to be free;
Then where my hand is set, my seal shall be.
    Full nakedness! All joys are due to thee;
As souls unbodied, bodies unclothed must be,
To taste whole joys. Gems which you women use
Are like Atlanta's balls, cast in men's views,
That when a fool's eye lighteth on a gem,
His earthly soul may covet theirs, not them.
Like pictures, or like books' gay coverings made
For laymen, are all women thus arrayed;
Themselves are mystic books, which only we
(Whom their imputed grace will dignify)
Must see revealed. Then since that I may know,
As liberally, as to a midwife, show
Thyself: cast all, yea this white linen, hence;
There is no penance due to innocence.
    To teach thee, I am naked first; why then
    What needst thou have more covering than a man?

JOHN DONNE, *1573–1631*

Carpe Noctem

There is no future, there is no more past,
No roots nor fruits, but momentary flowers,
Lie still, only lie still and night will last,
Silent and dark, not for a space of hours,
But everlastingly. Let me forget
All but your perfume, every night but this,
The shame, the fruitless weeping, the regret.
Only lie still: this faint and quiet bliss
Shall flower upon the brink of sleep and spread,
Till there is nothing else but you and I
Clasped in a timeless silence.

ALDOUS HUXLEY, *1894–1963*

Lullaby

Lay your sleeping head, my love,
Human on my faithless arm;
Time and fevers burn away
Individual beauty from
Thoughtful children, and the grave
Proves the child ephemeral:
But in my arms till break of day
Let the living creature lie,
Mortal, guilty, but to me
The entirely beautiful.

Soul and body have no bounds:
To lovers as they lie upon
Her tolerant, enchanted slope
In their ordinary swoon,
Grave the vision Venus sends
Of supernatural sympathy,
Universal love and hope;
While an abstract insight wakes
Among the glaciers and the rocks
The hermit's sensual ecstasy.

Certainty, fidelity
On the stroke of midnight pass
Like vibrations of a bell
And fashionable madmen raise
Their pedantic, boring cry:
Every farthing of the cost,
All the dreaded cards foretell
Shall be paid, but from this night
Not a whisper, not a thought,
Not a kiss nor look be lost.

Beauty, midnight, vision dies:
Let the winds of dawn that blow
Softly round your dreaming head
Such a day of sweetness show
Eye and knocking heart may bless,
Find the mortal world enough;
Noons of dryness see you fed
By the involuntary powers,
Nights of insult let you pass
Watched by every human love.

W. H. AUDEN, *b. 1907*

Serenata

Down by the shore of the river
the night embraces itself
and within Lolita's breasts
the branches are dying of love.

The branches are dying of love.

The night, naked, sings
above the bridges of March.
Lolita bathes herself
with salt water and with roses.

The branches are dying of love.

The nights, alcoholic, silver,
Shine over the rooftops.
Silver of streams and mirrors.
Alcohol of your sweet thighs.

The branches are dying of love.

GARCIA LORCA, *1889–1936*,
translated by Derek Parker

from Madame Bovary

The soft night was all about them. Curtains of shadow hung amid the leaves. Emma, her eyes half-closed, breathed in with deep sighs the cool wind that was blowing. They did not speak, caught as they were in the rush of their reverie. Their early tenderness returned to their hearts, full and silent as the river flowing by, soothing-sweet as the perfume the syringas wafted, casting hunger and more melancholy shadows on their memory than those the unmoving willows laid upon the grass . . . now and again a ripe peach could be heard softly dropping from the tree.

'What a lovely night!' said Rodolphe.

'We shall have many!' answered Emma. She went on as though speaking to herself: 'Yes, it will be good to travel. . . . Then why am I sad at heart? Is it dread of the unknown, the wrench of parting? Or is it . . . ? No, it's just that I'm too happy! What a weak creature I am! Forgive me!'

'There is still time!' he cried. 'Think! You may repent!'

'Never!' she declared impetuously. And, moving closer to him – 'What harm could come to me? There is no desert or precipice or ocean where I would not follow you. Our life together will be every day a closer, completer embrace.

GUSTAVE FLAUBERT, *1821–80, translated by Alan Russell*

from *Love and Marriage*

. . . with women love usually proceeds from the soul to the senses and sometimes does not reach so far . . . with man it usually proceeds from the senses to the soul and sometimes never completes the journey.

ELLEN KEY, *1849–1926*

The Mosquito

Fly to her, swiftly fly, Mosquito, bearing my greeting:
Perch on the tip of her ear, and whisper it to her:
Say 'He lies waking, longing for you: and you sleeping,
Sleeping, O shameless girl!, have never a thought for
                                who loves you!'
Buzz!
    Chirr!
                Off to her, sweetest Musician!
Yet speak to her softly, lest
Her bedfellow wake and hurt her because of my love.

. . . or bring me the girl herself, Mosquito, and I
Will crown your head with the lion's mane and give you
Strong Hercules' bludgeon to brandish in your paw.

MELEAGROS, *c. 700 B.C., translated by Dudley Fitts*

from *Glory of Life*

When, as occasionally happens, there is an utter, impassioned, and heroical love between two people, when the thought of each other's bodies causes them day and night to stand as worshippers before the throne of Aphrodite, quivering, shivering with idolatry, fidelity becomes as natural as to breathe . . . When love of this kind visits the earth, as it does visit the earth rarely and by chance, then preserve it, shelter it, sacrifice everything to it! . . . To know that you will be loved, even to the grave's edge, deprives the Icarus-like falling from life to death of half its horror . . . In moments of profane love we should be possessed by an ultimate rapture, our spirits under their foolish bewitchment, awake with gladness, knowing the high fortune of so tender, so savage, so God-like an experience!

LLEWELLYN POWYS, *1884–1939*

Break of Day

Stay, O sweet, and do not rise,
The light that shines comes from thine eyes.
The day breaks not; it is my heart,
Because that thou and I must part.
Stay, or else my joys will die,
And perish in their infancy.

'Tis true, 'tis day; what though it be?
O, wilt thou therefore rise from me?
Why should we rise because 'tis light?
Did we lie down because 'twas night?
Love, which in spite of darkness brought us hither,
Should in despite of light keep us together.

Light hath no tongue, but is all eye.
If it could speak as well as spy,
This were the worst, that it could say:
That being well, I fain would stay,
And that I lov'd my heart and honour so
That I would not from her, that had them, go.

Must business thee from hence remove?
O that's the worst disease of love!
The poor, the foul, the false, love can
Admit, but not the busied man.
He which hath business, and makes love, doth do
Such wrong as when a married man doth woo.

JOHN DONNE, *1573–1631*

Daybreak

At dawn she lay with her profile at that angle
Which, when she sleeps, seems the carved face of an angel.
Her hair a harp, the hand of a breeze follows
And plays, against the white cloud of the pillows.
Then, in a flush of rose, she woke, and her eyes that opened
Swam in blue through her rose flesh that dawned.
From her dew of lips, the drop of one word
Fell like the first of fountains: murmured
'Darling', upon my ears the song of the first bird.
'My dream becomes my dream,' she said, 'come true.
I waken from you to my dream of you.'
Oh, my own wakened dream then dared assume
The audacity of her sleep. Our dreams
Poured into each other's arms, like streams.

STEPHEN SPENDER, *b. 1909*

The Postures of Love

There is a white mare that my love keeps
unridden in a hillside meadow – white
as a white pebble, veined like a stone
a white horse, whiter than a girl.

And now for three nights sleeping I have seen
her body naked as a tree for marriage
pale as a stone that the net of water covers

and her veined breasts like hills – the swallow islands
still on the corn's green water: and I know
her dark hairs gathered round an open rose

her pebbles lying under the dappled sea.
And I will ride her thighs' white horses.

ALEX COMFORT, *b. 1920*

Great Love Stories

Tales from history, myth and fiction showing the varied course of true love

Robert and Elizabeth Browning

A more improbable love story – or for that matter, a happier one – has seldom been told than that of Elizabeth and Robert Browning. Under the selfish and tyrannical rule of her father, Elizabeth Barrett, as she then was, was for years condemned to lead the life of a helpless invalid. She was a gay and cheerful child, and particularly fond of riding. But when she was quite young, she was injured in a fall from a horse, and damaged her spine. Her father, Edward Barrett, took the opportunity of exercising his power and confined Elizabeth to the house, later to her room. She was soon not allowed to stir from the sofa, not even to cross two rooms to her bed. Her room was sombre and silent, with lowered blinds and an air of sickness. Apart from the oppressive presence of her father, which seemed as permanent as the dim light and the medicine bottles, her only interest was literature. Visitors were strictly forbidden, and courtship, to say nothing of marriage, was absolutely unthinkable. So she turned to writing as a solace, achieving some moderate success with the poems that were eventually collected into the volume she published in 1844.

This book of poems attracted the attention of Robert Browning, who was already well established as a poet. Browning read the book, and found there a reference to his own work. A mutual friend, John Kenyon, encouraged him to write to Elizabeth. He did so, and proposed that they should meet. Such a suggestion seemed to her fantastic. Her father's overpowering influence had reduced her, as it had reduced her brothers and sisters, to complete dependence on his will, and his will was that the thought of embarking upon even friendship was not to be entertained.

Into her life of sickly seclusion Browning's letter came, therefore, like a breath of fresh air – of warm, sensuous air. He spoke of an occasion when they had been on the point of meeting, but for some reason or other had not done so. He compared it to the sensation of having found a chapel marvellously illuminated, but with its door barred. Elizabeth answered his letter, and he replied. Thus began a correspondence which culminated after a while in the almost blasphemous suggestion that he should call on her. Terrified at the thought of her father's reaction, Elizabeth made every excuse she could think of, above all, the state of her health and the danger from east winds. 'If my truest heart's wishes avail,' Robert replied, 'you shall laugh at east winds as I do'.

Gradually their letters became more personal and more relaxed, and at last, in the early summer of 1846, they met. Not long afterwards, Robert, deeply in love with her, proposed. It was an electrifying prospect. For the first time in her life, Elizabeth was offered the activity and the pleasures of a normal life. But the thought of her father's outraged reaction horrified her. Later, she wrote to Robert: 'I will tell you what I once said in jest: if a Prince of El Dorado should come with a pedigree of lineal descent from some signory on the moon in one hand, and a ticket of good behaviour from the nearest Independent chapel in the other . . . "Why, even then," said my sister Anabel, "it would not *do*." And she was right; we all agreed that she was right'.

And so she would not hear of marriage: not only because her father had forbidden *all* his children to think of it, but also because she genuinely believed herself to be seriously ill, condemned, as G. K. Chesterton wrote, 'to an elegant death-bed, forbidden to move, forbidden to see proper daylight, forbidden to receive a friend lest the shock should destroy her suddenly'.

Then came a sudden crisis: Elizabeth's doctors declared it was essential that she should be taken to

Italy, where there was a faint possibility that she might recover her health. Mr Barrett refused absolutely to consider the idea. Browning thereupon decided there was only one way in which he could save the woman he loved. He proposed that they should elope. How deeply her affections were by this time engaged may be judged from her reaction to this plan. She ordered a carriage to take her and one of her sisters to Regent's Park. There she got out, and for a little while stood leaning against a tree, looking about her at the trees and the flowers and up at the sky. Then she got back into the carriage, drove home, and sent a message to Robert agreeing to elope. The decision was made: a new life lay ahead.

One morning in September, 1846, Elizabeth walked out of her father's house, became Mrs Robert Browning in a church in Marylebone, and returned home as if nothing had happened. A week later, she surreptitiously left her father's house for ever, taking with her her maid and her spaniel, Flush, who had lived almost all his life lying on his mistress' couch. They were met by Robert and together crossed the channel to France, and then travelled south to Pisa.

Before her marriage, Elizabeth's life had been uneventfully miserable; now it became uneventfully happy. She would never perhaps have been a strong woman, but it soon became clear that her sickness had been to a large extent psychosomatic and encouraged by her odiously selfish father. In the summer of 1846, she had seemed on the point of death; a year or two later, in Italy, she was being dragged uphill in a wine hamper, climbing mountains at four in the morning, riding a donkey for five miles over rugged country.

After three years, she bore Browning a son; then in 1861, she died after a supremely happy marriage that had lasted fifteen years.

The elopement was a *cause célèbre*. The publication of Elizabeth's sonnet-sequence, *Sonnets from the Portuguese*, which tells the story of the love affair, revealed not only the depth of her passion but that love had been for her the means of breaking from the oppressive domination of her father, and discovering the reality of a world that hitherto she had only dreamed of.

How do I love thee? Let me
   count the ways.
I love thee to the depth and
   breadth and height
My soul can reach, when feeling
   out of sight
For the ends of Being and ideal
   Grace . . .
I love thee with a love I seemed
   to lose
With my lost saints

With the publication of their letters after Browning died, their romance seemed more like a story than reality. And, indeed, its storybook qualities have turned the lives of the Brownings into a modern legend. Rudolph Besier's *The Barretts of Wimpole Street* was written first as a stage play, then subsequently adapted for the cinema and television. Finally it was made into a musical, bringing the Brownings' story to thousands more people on both sides of the Atlantic. But a reality it was; Browning did call Elizabeth Barrett to life, and they did live a life of great happiness together, so that, as Chesterton wrote, after Elizabeth's death Browning 'closed a door in himself, and none ever saw Browning upon earth again, but only a splendid surface'.

Romeo and Juliet

A number of versions of the story of Romeo and Juliet existed before Shakespeare adapted the theme and through his art transformed it into one of the world's greatest tragedies of love. What follows is an account of his version, the most famous, and the most moving of all.

There lived in Verona two merchant families, the Montagues and the Capulets, between whom there existed a feud. After a public brawl between the members of both families, the Prince of Verona has threatened execution as the penalty for further strife between them. Romeo, Montague's son, is unconcerned by the Prince's warning, being pre-occupied by an unrequited love for Rosaline, a beautiful young Veronese girl.

Capulet decides to hold a feast for all the notable families of the city, and he sends his servant about the city to invite the guests. But the servant cannot read, and the names upon the list are a mystery to him. He happens to come upon Romeo and his cousin, Benvolio, and asks them to read him the names. Romeo, seeing that Rosaline is among them, agrees with Benvolio to invade the party, taking along a group of their friends.

Capulet has decided it is time his only daughter, Juliet, who is fourteen years old, should be betrothed, and chooses as her suitor Paris, a kinsman of the Prince. Many of her friends are already married, and with children; indeed Juliet's own mother bore her at that age. Juliet is uncertain of her own feelings but consents (to the delight of her old Nurse, a cheerful, richly humoured, bawdy companion) to listen to a proposal from the handsome Paris.

At the feast, Romeo and his friends, mingling uninvited with the other guests, is recognised by Capulet's nephew, Tybalt, a fiery youth, who straightway seeks to have them turned out. But on this evening of the year Capulet is in a good enough humour to tolerate their society.

During the evening, Romeo and Juliet see each other for the first time. They touch hands, exchange words, and with soft, courtly gentleness offer to each other the first of many kisses. Immediately they realize that they have fallen in love, but each is unaware of who the other is. Only as all depart from the feast do they discover, through the offices of the Nurse, the truth of their identities. Romeo begins to feel uneasy. When Juliet finds that Romeo is a Montague, she is in despair:

'My only love, sprung from my only hate.'

After the feast has ended, Romeo evades his friends, climbs the orchard wall of Capulet's estate and makes his way to a spot beneath the balcony of Juliet's chamber. There, in the moonlight, they pledge their love for each other, each prepared to deny name and family in order that they may love freely. Both know only too well what difficulties the dispute between their two families must cause, yet with the innocent ardour of youth they are confident that love will overcome all obstacles. At least, up to a point they are confident. In a tense, breathless dialogue their love and their fears are alternately uppermost

in their minds. As dawn breaks, Juliet's Nurse begins to interrupt from an inner room. Their emotion cannot be contained and in rapid whispers they agree to marry. In haste they arrange to exchange messages before nine the next day. Once more they bid each other farewell, the sun rises, and they must part.

Next morning, Romeo tells his father confessor, Friar Laurence, of his love, and the Friar, believing that he sees in the situation a means of reconciling the two families, promises Romeo his support. So, by Juliet's Nurse, Romeo sends her a message telling her to go to Friar Laurence for confession that afternoon and that there in his cell the Friar will marry them.

Later that same day, Tybalt, meeting Romeo by chance, greets him as usual with an insult. But Romeo, since he has now become secretly a kinsman of Tybalt, returns a soft answer. A friend of his, Mercutio, outraged on Romeo's behalf by Tybalt's insult, draws his sword and fights with Tybalt. Romeo comes between them, trying to stop the fray, but instead only hinders Mercutio from ably defending himself. Mercutio is struck, and falls mortally wounded. After his death Romeo turns on Tybalt and kills him. The whole city is aroused, and the Prince, summoned from his Palace, finds Lady Capulet mourning her nephew. After hearing what has happened from Benvolio, the Prince decides not to condemn Romeo to death, but instead to banish him from Verona, whence he has already fled.

The lovers are in despair. To Romeo, banishment from his bride seems like death itself. Juliet, aware that this must be the penalty for his murder of her cousin, is distraught

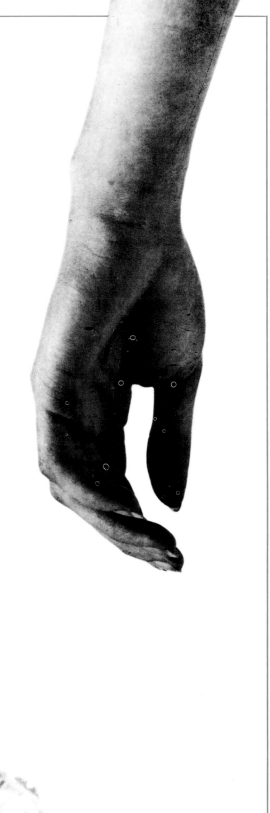

with grief. However, her Nurse contrives the dispatch of a message to Romeo, who, returning secretly to Verona, climbs up to Juliet's balcony and spends the night with her. Once more dawn breaks to part the lovers. Lady Capulet stirs and hurries to Juliet's bedroom to inform her of the betrothal plans. The Nurse warns Romeo and Juliet, they take one final kiss, and Romeo disappears into the garden, to begin his sad flight to Mantua.

Next day, Capulet announces Juliet's betrothal to Paris, whom she is to marry within a few days. Juliet, though unable to explain her reluctance, swears that she will never marry him. Her father becomes furious and declares that if she continues to refuse, he will disown her. Juliet flies to Friar Laurence for comfort, and the Friar suggests a plan. He is skilled as a herbalist and has a potion which, when drunk, induces a temporary appearance of death. He suggests that Juliet shall drink the potion and that then her family, believing her to be dead the night before her wedding, will bury her in the family vault. Meanwhile, the Friar will send a message to Romeo, bidding him to return secretly to Verona, and there to enter the tomb. When Juliet awakes, the two of them will emerge and declare their marriage to their families, who in their relief at Juliet's survival, will become reconciled.

Juliet agrees to the Friar's plan and on returning to her father's house, declares her readiness to marry Paris the next day. That night, in fear and trembling, she drinks the Friar's draught and the next morning is found by her Nurse, apparently dead. With full funeral pomp her body is placed in the family vault, near that of Tybalt.

Meanwhile, plague has broken out in the countryside between Verona and Mantua, and the Friar's messenger has been turned back. But news has nevertheless reached Romeo that his wife is dead. In an extremity of grief, he decides to end his own life, buys some poison from a hermit, and returns post haste to Verona. At night he breaks into the Capulet tomb, after killing Paris, who has come there too to mourn Juliet. He finds her body apparently lifeless lying close to Tybalt's. Without Juliet, Romeo is weary of the world. He mourns by her body, vowing that even in death he will never leave her side. He drinks the hermit's poison and after kissing Juliet farewell, dies.

Friar Laurence, having heard that his message has failed to reach Romeo, hastens to the tomb to explain to Juliet what has happened. As he arrives, Juliet begins to awaken from her drugged state. The Friar tries to bring her away, but she refuses to go with him, and hearing others approaching, he flees. Juliet, seeing Romeo dead, kisses him, hoping some trace of the poison will have remained on his lips; but in vain. Seizing his dagger, she stabs herself and dies.

The Capulets, summoned by Paris's servant, are horrified at what they find. The Prince has also been summoned, and to him Friar Laurence confesses his part in the tragedy. His motive, however, vindicates his actions, for the two fathers mourning their dead children, make peace with each other.

In their deaths Romeo and Juliet transcended the age-old family feud. Their loves were stronger than hate, and eventually brought peace. But peace at what price?

Tristan and Iseult

Fathoms deep beneath the sea, where it runs between the Isles of Scilly and the Land's End, off the westernmost tip of England, lies the drowned land of Lionesse, once a rich and prosperous kingdom ruled by King Meliodas. Meliodas and his beautiful wife Elizabeth conceived a son, but at the time of his birth Meliodas was a prisoner. Elizabeth, seeking her husband, bore the baby unattended and in great distress. She called him Tristan, or 'sorrowful birth', and soon afterwards she died.

King Melodias, rescued from the spell by the magician Merlin, brought up his son Tristan nobly, and sent him into France, where he learned the arts of knighthood, music and hunting. When he returned to his father's court, a handsome young man of eighteen, he was the finest musician and the bravest huntsman ever known, and was greatly honoured.

One day he heard that his uncle Mark, King of Cornwall, was in great difficulty: Agwisance, the Irish king, had sent Sir Marhaus to claim taxes owing to him, and threatened to seize the kingdom. Tristan offered his services to his uncle, who made him a knight, and on his behalf issued a challenge to Sir Marhaus. The challenge was accepted and Sir Tristan and Sir Marhaus fought for many hours, at first on horseback, and then on foot. Sir Marhaus badly wounded Sir Tristan in the side with a poisoned spear; but summoning all his strength, Sir Tristan struck his opponent such a blow that the sword went clean through the knight's helmet and into his skull, and when he withdrew it, a sliver of steel remained in the wound.

For some months it seemed that Tristan might die, and King Mark was told that only in Ireland could the poison in his wound be healed. So under a false name, Tristan travelled dangerously to the court of King Agwisance, where his musicianship and his gentle and noble bearing made him popular. The King was so struck by his nobility that he put him in the charge of his own daughter, Iseult, 'the fairest maid and lady of the world'. Her nursing soon cleansed the wound of poison, and Sir Tristan grew strong again.

But one day Iseult's mother, the Queen, saw Tristan's sword, and matched with the chip in it the sliver of steel which had been recovered from the wound in Sir Marhaus' skull. Sir Tristan, discovered, was banished from the court, and Iseult wept bitterly.

King Mark grew violently jealous of the handsome young knight, and believing that he would be killed if ever he entered Ireland again, commanded him to go to King Agwisance and seek on Mark's behalf the hand of Iseult (of whose great beauty Tristan had spoken) as Queen of Cornwall. As a member of the Irish court, Tristan fought boldly for Agwisance, and the King was once more impressed by his courage and strength. So he granted Tristan permission to take Iseult to Cornwall to be King Mark's bride. And Iseult's mother, wanting to cement an alliance with Mark, gave Iseult's servingwoman, Brangwaine, a love potion to be placed in the drinks on their wedding night, which would ensure immortal love.

But on the journey to Cornwall, by a simple mistake, Tristan and Iseult drank the potion at dinner one evening, and fell immediately into an eternal love.

When they came to Cornwall, King Mark received them with great honour, and led them to his castle on a hill – the Castle d'Or – where the King took Iseult for his Queen. For a while the lovers met secretly, whenever they could; but Tristan at last could no longer bear the sight of his mistress on the King's arm, and left the court for Brittany, where he became a knight of his kinsman King Howel, and fought many battles on his behalf. His adventures became famous: he fought always on behalf of the weak or the oppressed, rescued many beautiful women, and in the Forest Perilous saved the life of King Arthur himself.

All this time, Queen Iseult was faithful to King Mark at his Cornish court. But one day a jealous knight persuaded his mistress to tell Iseult, falsely, that Sir Tristan was dead; and she took a sword, and prepared to kill herself, kneeling down and praying aloud, 'Sweet Lord Jesu, have mercy upon me, for I may not live after the death of Sir Tristan, for he was my first love and he shall be my last'. But King Mark overheard her, took her in his arms, and carried her to her room, where she lay sick for many weeks.

Meanwhile, Sir Tristan had fought the giant Taeleas in a distant part of Mark's kingdom, and was found resting naked in a wood. Mark's knights, not knowing who he was, took him to the King's castle at Tintagel, and entertained him. There, Queen Iseult set eyes on him, but weakened by her illness, did not at first notice him – until a little dog which he had given her when she first came to Cornwall leaped towards him, wild with delight. Then suddenly she recog-

nized her lover, and fainted. The King summoned his Council, and asked them to condemn Sir Tristan to death; but instead they advised that he should be banished from the kingdom for ten years.

So Sir Tristan once more began his travels, and had many more adventures. In much danger, Brangwaine brought him letters from Iseult; but they could not meet.

Then, in Brittany, Tristan was wounded by a poisoned arrow, and fell desperately ill. A Breton noblewoman, deeply in love with Tristan, and also called Iseult, nursed him devotedly; but in his delirium he called again and again for her namesake in Cornwall, and at last

sent by his servant a message beseeching her to come to him before he died; if the returning ship was carrying his love, it was to have white sails; if the sails were black, she would not have come.

Looking one day from the window of Tristan's room, high above the sea, his nurse saw the ship approaching, its white sails glittering in the sun. But unable to bear to see him overjoyed at his love's coming, she told him that the sails were black as pitch. Despairing, he turned his face to the wall, and died. Minutes later, trumpets sounded as Iseult of Cornwall set foot on the Breton coast. She hurried at once to her lover; but too late to be reunited

with him in life, she lay down at his side, and embracing him, she died.

Reunited in death, Tristan and Iseult became legendary. Their story was set down by Thomas of Erceldoune in the thirteenth century, and later by Malory. For hundreds of years it was thought to be purely fictional: but in the last century an inscription on a Cornish cross standing at Castle Dore, near Fowey, in Cornwall, was deciphered, and proved to be the tombstone memorial of Tristan himself. The story has been retold by many poets and musicians, including Swinburne and Richard Wagner, whose *Tristan und Isolde* is perhaps the fullest expression of passionate love in opera.

Antony and Cleopatra

Mark Antony was at the height of his career when he first met Cleopatra. He was one of the foremost generals of Imperial Rome, a brave commander who had fought in Gaul with Julius Caesar. During the civil wars he supported Caesar, and after his murder took arms against the conspirators and defeated them, becoming thereafter one of the triumvirate – Octavius Caesar, Lepidus and himself – that ruled the empire.

Antony was by nature a sensualist and a lover of pleasures, facts that endeared him to the men under his command. But he also drank heavily and gambled, and in his time he had had many love affairs. Indeed, as the result of one of them he had divorced his wife.

In 41 BC, he set forth confidently to conquer Egypt. Paradoxically, it was he himself who was conquered – though not by Egypt. It was to her great queen, Cleopatra, that he fell a victim. She was then twenty-eight years old, he was forty-two. Cleopatra, the daughter of King Ptolemy XIII, had become queen when she was seventeen. Having later been driven from her kingdom by her ambitious brother Ptolemy XIV, she had appealed to Caesar, had become his mistress, and then persuaded him to go to war on her behalf and make her queen once more. She had accompanied Caesar to Rome and was there at the time of his murder; but then had returned hastily to Egypt and declared Caesarion, her son by Caesar, to be her successor.

It was while Antony was voyaging to Greece that he first set eyes on Cleopatra. At Cilicia, where he had made preparations to receive her, she sailed in state up the river Cydnus. The historian Plutarch, writing not much more than a hundred years after the event, recorded her triumphal progress: '. . . in a barge with gilded stern and outspread sails of purple, while oars of silver beat time to the music of flutes and fifes and harps. She herself lay all along under a canopy of cloth of gold, dressed as Venus in a picture, and beautiful young boys, like painted Cupids, stood on each side to fan her.'

So wondrous was the spectacle that the people of Cilicia, leaving Antony alone in the market place where he had gone to greet her, ran to watch the royal progress of this fabled queen.

Cleopatra had no difficulty in capturing the affections of so susceptible a character as Antony. According to Plutarch's description, she must have been one of the most fabulously attractive women in history. 'For her actual beauty, it is said, was not in itself so remarkable that none could be compared with her, or that no one could see her without being struck by it, but the contact of her presence, if you lived with her, was irresistible; the attraction of her person, joining with the charm of her conversation, and the character that attended all she said or did, was something bewitching. It was a pleasure merely to hear the sound of her voice, with which, like an instrument of many strings, she could pass from one language to another . . .!'

She flattered and amused Antony, matching his every mood; and at last captured him entirely. Ignoring the wars which had now broken out in Rome, and forgetting his wife,

Fulvia, who was much involved in them, he went with Cleopatra to Alexandria, where they lived throughout the winter like two young people in love for the first time.

In due course, events forced Antony to leave his mistress and return to Rome. His wife having died, Antony, for reasons of diplomacy, consented to marry Octavia, a cold, passionless woman, but Caesar's sister.

For some years politics and war conspired to separate Antony from Cleopatra; but when once more he set sail for Asia Minor, his passion for her was rekindled, and when they met he presented her with vast tracts of land, the conquests of the empire – Cyprus, Phoenicia, Cilicia, and parts of Judaea and Arabia. He also acknowledged publicly that she had borne him two children, on whom he bestowed the titles of 'Sun' and 'Moon'. This, allied with his treatment of his wife Octavia, proved his undoing. He was deprived of all his titles by the Roman Senate, and war was declared on Cleopatra.

Antony immediately flew to her defence. So tenacious was her renewed hold upon him that when she insisted on commanding her forces personally, he not only consented, but accepted her advice before that of his own commanders. Though his land forces were superior to those opposing him, he agreed to her wish that the first battle should be fought at sea.

While this battle was in the balance, Cleopatra's ships were seen to be in retreat. At once Antony deserted his forces to follow her. Even so, some of those forces remained loyal to him for a time. Then came the final battle, in which they and Cleopatra's faithful Egyptians were defeated.

Such were his feelings of shame

and chagrin that for the time being he could not bear to face Cleopatra. Instead, according to Plutarch, 'without seeing her or letting himself be seen by her, he went forward by himself and sat alone without a word in the ship's prow, covering his face with his hands'.

In his bitterness, he declared at first that Cleopatra had betrayed him. Eventually, he petitioned the Roman senate, asking that his children by Cleopatra should be allowed to become the rulers of Egypt and that he himself should be allowed to live there. The only response to this appeal was a message sent to Cleopatra – that she would be pardoned for her offence against Rome if she would agree to have Antony put to death. This she refused, but fearing that he might attack her, she shut herself in a magnificent tomb that she had built and sent forth a message from it that she was dead. On hearing this, Antony fell upon his sword and was mortally wounded.

When news that he was dying reached Cleopatra, she sent for him to be brought to her, but fearing to unfasten the door of the tomb, had a platform let down on which Antony was raised up and taken into the tomb. 'Those that were present', says Plutarch, 'say that nothing was ever more sad than this spectacle, to see Antony, covered all over with blood and just expiring, thus drawn up, still holding up his hands to her, and lifting up his body with the little force he had left'.

Cleopatra was allowed by the Romans to give her lover a magnificent funeral. Soon afterwards, she entered the tomb where his body was lying, carrying with her a basket of figs in which was hidden a poisonous asp. She provoked the creature into biting her and died with Antony's name on her lips.

Beauty and the Beast

Once upon a time there lived in France a rich merchant whose huge fleets sailed the seven seas, bringing home treasures of gold and jewels, piles of tapestries and barrels of spices.

He had six children – three tall, handsome sons, and three beautiful daughters, the youngest of whom was so fair, so kind and so graceful, that she was known far and wide as 'Little Beauty'. Suitors came from all over Europe to pay court to the merchant's three daughters: but the two elder girls rejected everyone, for they valued themselves so highly that they were determined to wait for a Duke each, at the least. And Beauty, though she was sad to turn away so many handsome young men, declined to marry because she wanted to stay for a few more years with her father whom she dearly loved.

Then, one awful year, disaster struck the merchant's fleets. One by one his ships were seized by pirates, sunk in dreadful storms, or cheated by unscrupulous traders; and within a twelvemonth he was penniless. His great house and most of his fine furniture were sold to pay his creditors, and he was forced to retire to a small farm. He and his sons rose early each morning to work in the fields, and Beauty spent her day cleaning the house, cooking the meals, and feeding the chickens.

Soon the freshness of this new life began to appeal to her, though the work was hard; and she was not unhappy. For her sisters, though, it was another matter: bored to distraction, they remained in bed for most of the day, grumbling at the emptiness of their lives – for no suitors now came to call, not even the sons of gentlefolk.

One day, news reached the merchant that one of his ships, crippled but safe, had come to harbour in a distant port. He set off to welcome its captain, in high hopes of restoring his fortune, and asked his daughters what he should bring them from the town. The elder sisters asked for jewels and trinkets; but Beauty, thinking that her father would need all the money he could raise, asked only for a single rose.

The merchant found the ship alongside the quay; but on board were his creditors, demanding money that he still owed them. He left as penniless as he had been before. To add to his misery, when he was halfway home, he was overtaken by pouring rain which soon soaked him to the skin. At last he noticed some tall gates and went through them to seek shelter. At the end of the drive was a great mansion, every window ablaze with light. As he raised the knocker, the door swung open, and revealed a warm cheerful hall in which a glowing fire was burning. No-one answered his call, and when at length he dared to explore the mansion, he found it empty – though a table was laid with a feast of food and wine. Exhausted, the merchant ate some food, drank a cup of wine, and finding a bedroom, fell upon the bed and slept.

In the morning he was startled to find laid out at the bedside a handsome new suit of clothes, which fitted him perfectly. He dressed and made his way downstairs, where a good breakfast waited for him. Having eaten, he left the mansion, and on his way through the garden he passed a bush of rich red roses. Remembering his promise to Beauty, he picked one and immediately from a nearby maze appeared a terrifying monster, whose face was so grotesque that the merchant cowered from him in terror.

'Not content with my hospitality', the Beast growled, 'you now have the audacity to steal my roses! I

should kill you on the spot – but if within three months you bring me your youngest daughter, I may have mercy upon you. Go! – and take this to sustain you on the journey.' And he threw the merchant a leather bag. Catching it, the man ran, and only paused when he was far from the Beast's estate. To his amazement he found the bag was full of gold pieces. By the time he reached home, the merchant had made up his mind: the gold would sustain his sons and daughters, and he would return to the Beast and give himself up.

After hearing his story, the two elder daughters could barely disguise their joy at the sight of the gold. But Beauty cared nothing for it; she only insisted that she should go to the Beast in place of her father. Battered by the insistence of the other two girls, the merchant reluctantly consented, and escorted Beauty to the Beast's mansion. There, she found a magnificent apartment; with her name on its door; and dressing in one of the wonderful gowns which hung in a vast wardrobe, she made her way downstairs to dinner. The Beast appeared before her, terrifying her to speechlessness by his hideousness. But he was extremely gentle, sitting to watch her eat, and talking with

her in a voice which was harsh and rough, but at the same time seemed soft and almost human. As she rose to leave the table he said: 'Beauty, I have a question to ask you. Will you be my wife?'

Beauty was no longer quite so frightened, but could never bring herself to think of the revolting monster as a husband, and firmly refused him. He looked at her for a moment, and then left. Each evening, he sat to watch her eat, talked politely and kindly with her, and then asked the same question – and received the same answer. Living in the Beast's mansion, Beauty had almost everything she could wish for. Her day was filled by examining the fine books and pictures, and walking in the beautiful gardens. As the time went on she almost forgot the Beast's ugliness, so kindly was she treated. But she still could not think of him as a husband.

Soon, she begged permission to visit her father, and with great reluctance, the Beast allowed her to go to him for a week. Her sisters were intensely jealous when they saw her beautiful clothes, and the fine presents she brought from the Beast. At the end of the week the whole family persuaded her to stay just two more days. But on the second night, Beauty had a dream: in his fine garden, beneath a handsome rosetree, the Beast lay dying.

Next morning she returned in haste and searched the mansion from roof to cellar, but there was no sign of the Beast. Then, in the garden, just as in her dream, she found him. He had starved himself to the point of death for love of her, believing that she had deserted him. 'O, Beauty', he said, 'it is better so; when I am dead you shall live here for ever, untroubled by my hideous presence'.

'Dear Beast', replied Beauty, 'do not die! I know that you have a soul of the greatest purity and simplicity, and I want nothing more than that you shall live to be my husband'.

And immediately she saw before her not the Beast, but a handsome young man of noble bearing. Taking her hand, he told her he was a Prince, changed into a Beast by a witch who promised that he should remain so until he found a beautiful young girl who would marry him. And so, of course, they were married: the Prince and the Beauty lived happily; the merchant became the Prince's Chamberlain, in charge of all his vast domains; and at the entrance to their palace stood her two sisters, turned to stone until their souls should become as pure and loving as that of Beauty. For all we know they stand there still.

Beauty and the Beast was one of the *Contes* retold from ancient sources by Mme de Villeneuve in 1744.

Alexandre Dumas the younger wrote, in 1848, a semi-autobiographical novel which became one of the best-known love stories of modern times, *La Dame aux Camélias*. It was an immediate success and four years later Dumas dramatized it. Later, Verdi used the plot for his opera, *La Traviata*; but perhaps the most popular evocation was in Greta Garbo's film, *Camille*, in which Garbo played Marguerite Gautier, the most beautiful courtesan in France. The character of Marguerite is based solidly on life, on a contemporary of Dumas' who was a farmer's daughter, called Marie Plessis, and whose career very closely resembled that of Marguerite.

Like her real-life counterpart, Marguerite is weary of her so-called 'life of pleasure', and longs to lead a more tranquil life, to escape from the noise and bustle of Paris and live peacefully with someone for whom she can really care—and who really cares for her. Yet the endless social whirl continues; night after night her house is a scene of gaiety. One evening, however, a friend introduces her to Armand, a fashionable and handsome young man, who immediately falls in love with her. She, despite herself, for she knows that she is ill, falls in love with him.

She and Armand go to live in the country together and for a while they are idyllically happy. Away from Paris, the courtesan disappears and is replaced by a beautiful young woman who loves him and is loved in return. She is no longer the friendless love object that she had become, she feels a person again with him, and he in his turn is ardent and happy. But his wealth is not great and soon Marguerite is forced secretly to sell some of her possessions to pay their way. When Armand discovers this, he is deeply embarrassed, though consoled by her explanation that she felt the need to make all possible sacrifices so that *their* love would not be debased by money. He returns to Paris to try to raise some money himself.

While he is away, Marguerite is visited unexpectedly by Armand's father and it is this encounter which is to cause the dying Marguerite to reject her beloved for ever. Armand's sister is to marry, but her fiancé's family are fearful of the scandal provoked by Armand's liaison with Marguerite and have threatened to break off the engagement. Armand's father appeals to Marguerite to reject her beloved and thus avert the ruination of this innocent young girl's life.

Marguerite is moved by his plea and makes the ultimate sacrifice. She summons her maid and writes him a note, saying that she has left him, and she goes back to Paris, longing only for death. Dire poverty forces her to resume her old life style.

Armand is heartbroken and wild with pain. He immediately misjudges her and sets out to persecute her in public by flirting with her companion, the beautiful and heartless courtesan, Olympe. The hapless Marguerite makes a final attempt to see him and to beg for his pity and forgiveness, for she is by this time very weak with tuberculosis. They spend a night together and by morning, she is feverish. Armand sends her the final insult, three thousand francs as payment for their night together. Having failed in her final attempt to explain her conduct to him, Marguerite departs heartbroken from Paris for England. Armand in his turn goes off to the East on a Grand Tour.

It becomes known that Marguerite's illness is incurable and gradually her lovers and admirers, even Count N. . . in London who has kept her in the past, disappear from the scene. Soon, she can no longer afford her elegant and famed house parties. Accompanied only by her faithful maid, she prepares to spend the brief remains of her life in quiet poverty.

Then one day, a letter from Armand's father reaches him in Alexandria and summons him to return, but by the time he reaches Paris, she has been dead for three weeks. All that is left of her are some letters which she wrote to him on her death bed. She fully explains to him everything that happened and why she left him. Armand is overcome by remorse and shocked that he could have treated her so callously. Only his father had been aware of the truth and, in order that Marguerite might not be totally destitute, had given her money while she was living out her final days alone.

This is the story of a social outcast – a woman, who in Dumas' own words, had such a big heart that it killed her. This may be an exaggeration, but there are few women who are able to make the ultimate sacrifice in the way that Marguerite did. In spite of being a so-called woman of easy virtue, she proved to be a woman of dignity and selflessness: a woman of lowly origins who became the envy of Paris, but who wanted more than anything merely to be loved. She gave herself fully and was finally, tragically betrayed by the one man whom she had loved and who in turn had loved her.

In other interpretations of the story, Marguerite has different names: in the film, she becomes Camille, and in Verdi's opera, Violetta. Marie Plessis, upon whom the story is based, was not known to have been particularly fond of camellias, but Dumas created the notion that in her dying state, his heroine could not bear the scent of flowers and therefore selected those, equally sumptuous and scentless, to form her sole adornment.

In the process of time, a tomb was raised to Marie in the cemetery of Montmartre, where Marguerite was said to be buried. A garland of camellias, carved out of white marble, formed an essential part of the decoration. The myth had become reality.

The Duke and Duchess of Windsor

Edward, eldest son of King George V, was brought up strictly by his parents in the knowledge that one day he would be King of England. His childhood was not happy. For much of the time he was severely tutored, and he lived in some fear of his father, who was a stern and punctilious man. But Edward's character was strongly individual, and he maintained his independence of thought and action after he took on the title and duties of Prince of Wales. Early on, his opinions of the life the monarchy should lead were unconventional: after an official visit to Germany he wrote in his diary, 'What rot and a waste of time, money and energy all these state visits are!'

He had great personal charm, and, more important, in the years of unemployment and unrest in the decades after the First World War he had a very pronounced sympathy for families in distress, speaking out against poverty and unemployment in such strong terms that some British politicians began to feel very uneasy.

In 1930 he met for the first time a beautiful American woman, Mrs Simpson. She was born in Maryland, and in 1915 married a young lieutenant in the American Navy. In 1927, she divorced him, and became the wife of Mr Ernest Simpson, a member of a shipping firm, and they lived in London.

The Prince met Mrs Simpson at a house party, found her pleasant company, and began to entertain both her and her husband often at Fort Belvedere, his private home. In 1934, she and an aunt were his guests on a yachting cruise along the French Riviera. Pirated photographs of them together appeared in the American press; but no-one in England outside the Prince's own circle realized what was by now very obvious – that he was deeply in love with her.

Of course there had been attempts to arrange a marriage for him: in 1914 the Queen had tried to persuade him to marry a charming and 'suitable' Princess. But he said he would never marry anyone whom he did not love. Now, he had met that woman. But even if Mrs Simpson left her second husband, for the Prince of Wales to marry a divorced woman would be to many people absolutely unthinkable. As early as 1935 he began to realise that he might have to give up the throne – the only British King ever to do so.

In January 1936 George V died and Edward was proclaimed King Edward VIII. Flying to London, he went to St James's palace, and from a window, hidden from the public view, he heard himself proclaimed King. Newsreels showed a glimpse of him as he stood at that window: but few people who saw the film realized the significance of the smiling woman in black who stood at his side.

Immediately he became King, Edward began to upset the conventional British establishment: he saw no point in many of the customs of court life, and began agitating to have them changed – to the disapproval of many people at court and in the government. Then, on a tour of Wales, he was saddened by the plight of the unemployed miners, and remarked to a local mayor that 'Something must be done'. Some sections of the British press compared his attitude favourably with that of the Conservative Government, to the embarrassment of Stanley Baldwin, the Prime Minister.

Meanwhile, for months the American press had been speculating about the King's future. During the summer, the New York *Daily Mirror* disclosed the 'true story' of the first meeting between the King and Mrs Simpson; *Town and Country* reported 'proofs of his affection are many and varied', and that 'he will go nowhere without her: hostesses who don't invite her don't get the King. In her company he never looks at another woman, he watches her all the time, fondly and intently'. *Town and Country* also speculated that the King might become the co-respondent in Mrs Simpson's second divorce; after the divorce had gone through, the *Washington Post* reported that the King had given his approval to the filing of the suit.

At this time, the British newspapers refrained from publicizing the matter; but sooner or later the storm had to break. It came, unexpectedly, when the Bishop of Bradford, in an address to a conference, referred to the King's 'need for God's grace', and added that he wished he was more aware of it. Although the Bishop always denied that this was a reference to the stories in the American press, the English newpapers took it as such, and the British public at last learned of the contemplation of 'a marriage incompatible with the throne'. Baldwin assured the King that 'the marriage was not one that would receive the approbation of the country'. The King replied instantly that he intended to marry Mrs Simpson the moment her divorce had been granted, and that if the Government opposed the marriage, he was 'prepared to go'. It is difficult to avoid the conclusion, now, that Baldwin may have been relieved at the prospect of getting rid of a monarch who had shown too much regard for 'the ordinary man', and too little respect for the Government. Backed by the influential London *Times*, the Prime Minister insisted after Mrs Simpson's divorce that the King's proposal of a morganatic marriage (by which Mrs Simpson would have married the King, but not become Queen) was impractical. On December 11, ten months after ascending the throne, the King signed the Bill of Abdication, and that evening broadcast a message to the country:

'You must believe me,' he said, 'when I tell you I have found it impossible to carry the heavy burden of responsibility and to discharge my duties as King as I would wish to do, without the help and support of the woman I love.'

On December 12, the ex-King – now created Duke of Windsor by his brother George VI – left Ports-

mouth on a British destroyer, and joined Mrs Simpson in France. In May, 1937, the divorce decree was made absolute, and in June the Duke married her according to French law. A little later, a British clergyman courageously performed the marriage ceremony, without his Bishop's permission.

The only King in history to have given up his throne for love lived in complete personal happiness with his wife until the day of his death. Certainly he lived in exile, in France, returning only occasionally to England, and it must have been painful to him not to have been allowed to make a proper contribution to the war effort. But finally there was a reconciliation with Queen Elizabeth II, his niece; and he said firmly to the end that if the decision was his to make again, he would have taken no other course.

A Lifetime of Loving

*The many faces of love from
childhood to old age*

A Baby's Love

Three ages of love are reflected in this nineteenth-century engraving of a dance: the dependent love of the child, sheltered within its family circle; the tender involvement of the young parents; the generous affection of love in old age.

Early childhood, in John Betjeman's words, 'is measured out by sounds and smells and sights'. Wide open to experience, the baby embraces it with infinite enthusiasm and a will of steel. The whole world is an invitation to love.

Infancy, early childhood – these are the much celebrated ages of innocence, of pure, spontaneous love, unsullied by contact with the world. Only very occasionally can we catch again, all too briefly, the complete simple assurance and confidence of the child's reaction to everything about him – from a blade of grass to a new doll.

Perhaps it is the general helplessness of all young creatures which renders them especially endearing. The helpless infant is totally dependent upon his parents; they are the sole focus of his love. It is they who feed him when he is hungry, who comfort him when he cries. In turn, the baby brings a new dimension to the parent's relationship; he marks a consummation of their love for each other, a love shared through and with the newborn child.

Teething problems aside, infancy is probably the easiest, the most unfraught period of our life. The baby enjoys a love and security, a devoted attention to his wants and needs, which is unlikely to be equalled at later stages in life. Life is rarely as simple again. Nor is love.

The First Age of Love

Childhood Love

The love of the months-old infant soon changes as the months become years. New sensations, new experiences are gradually amassed. The child's dependence on, and unquestioning love for, his father and mother, his delight in toys and books, are constant; but his horizon gradually widens as a new element enters into his life – the pleasure of childhood friends and the first hint of what will very soon become romantic love.

At school and at home, in the playground or in the backyard, the child plays the old, traditional games of childhood, so many of which reflect the complex, stately dances of courtship. Dancing in a ring, girls choose their boys, and after school, perhaps, there is the first reflection of what is to come as the five-year-old chooses to hold the hand of a particular friend, or sit next to him on the school bus. The chosen one's attention may be directed more to his latest comic than his female companion and he may seem light-years from the boy who will be kissing her in ten years' time; and yet the playground is a complete microcosm of adult life, with alternating rejection and acceptance, acts of friendship, acts of violence, cruelty and kindness, often gratuitous, often puzzling.

For the first time we begin to realize that we hardly ever know *exactly* what we mean in our dealings with other people; or what they mean either. Confusion begins. A small girl cries because an equally small boy prefers to play with her friend. The small boy completely fails to understand.

But even at this early stage in our life, the seed of true and lasting love can sometimes be sown. Edgar Allen Poe wrote of his childhood sweetheart:

> I was a child and she was a child,
>   In this kingdom by the sea;
> But we loved with a love that was more than love—
>   I and my Annabel Lee.

And yet for most of us, childhood 'loves' are usually very ephemeral. We transfer our affections as readily from friend to friend – and back again – as we would exchange a stamp or a comic. The favourite of the class one week, the boy or girl whom everyone wants to sit next to or to play with after school, may very well be demoted the next. The footballer hero of the chassroom may find that his quota of love-letters, passed surreptitiously under desks by ardent admirers, suffers a dramatic decline if he fails to show his customary prowess in the next football game.

So far, love itself is still a game; it is still rather 'soppy', a peculiar charade enacted by adults. But none the less, love is knocking on the door. The knocking is insistent. The child may laugh as he slowly turns to answer it. But he already senses what is waiting outside. . .

Young Love

Youth's the season made for joys,
Love is then our duty.

JOHN GAY, The Beggar's Opera

For most of us, love is a very desirable 'duty' which we willingly undertake without any complaint or compulsion! For the adolescent, awakening to new physical and emotional needs, first love can be a very strange, if wonderful experience; a mixture of excitement, eagerness and expectation, and, often, at the same time, a hesitancy, an awkward gaucheness, the fear of venturing out along unknown paths. To the English poet John Dryden, first love was a truly wonderful and enjoyable experience:

Ah, how sweet it is to love!
Ah, how gay is young Desire!
And what pleasing pains we prove
When we first approach Love's fire . .

Love, like spring-tides full and high,
Swells in every youthful vein . . .

But if first love can be happy, can be a wonderful experience, how mysterious and infinitely sad it can be also. The lucky ones, for whom their first deep love is their last love, are few. In spite of what our hearts may be telling us at the time, we know all too well inside ourselves that we may have to love many times before finding a love that will endure.

Love inevitably brings the fear, and often the agony, of rejection, an agony no less intense in the adolescent relationship than in the affairs of later years. Scott Fitzgerald depicted the puzzlement and awkwardness of the young lover very tellingly in *This Side of Paradise*: 'If I start to hold somebody's hand they laugh at me and *let* me. As soon as I get hold of a hand they sort of disconnect it from the rest of them.' That puzzlement, that awkwardness has not suddenly vanished in the 1970s. It is as difficult to grow up now as it was in 1920, 1840 or 1770. In fact, it may be even more so. The adolescent is constantly under pressure, the persuasive pressure of advertising, the expectations of parents and friends, to find a girlfriend or boyfriend. The fourteen-year old may well feel a social outcast if he or she cannot produce a partner for the Saturday night party.

Clumsiness and shyness, inexperience and self-consciousness may all conspire against the adolescent. The boy struggles to control the comic, embarrassing tricks of a breaking voice; the girl is slightly worried, if at the same time proud, of her budding breasts; suddenly downy hair appears on the arms or legs, or worse still on the face. And there is nothing anyone can do about it – even the young lovers. But gradually, the adolescent comes to terms with his or her new physical self; the self-consciousness begins to diminish and the adolescent is ready to embark on the next stage of the labyrinthine highway of love.

The Second Age of Love

The Third Age of Love

The Age of Passion and Folly

Now, at last, the awkwardness of adolescence has fallen away and we are ready to be caught up in another maelstrom of emotions and passions. Life is alive with the prospect of love.

This is the age of flirtation, the averted but inviting eye, the tossed head, the not-so-shy glance. This is the age when a woman begins to know and exert her power; when, in the words of T. S. Eliot, 'lovely woman stoops to folly'.

This is the age all poets celebrate, and the age we go on celebrating in our hearts, our memories long after it is over. For most of us though, this is a relatively short-lived, if exciting phase. It is the in-between stage, the bridge between the transience of adolescent entanglements and a more lasting commitment, a deep and satisfying relationship. It is not always such a carefree whirlwind of excitement and romance as we tend to imagine. Behind the coquettish glances and whims, the gaiety and excitement there may often lurk a more serious note: the seemingly casual air, the frothy exuberance may be a kind of protective mask, concealing an ever-increasing need, a deep-rooted desire to love and be loved.

The search is on; and it may often lead us into dissimulation and self-delusion. It is all too easy to delude ourselves and succumb to an intensity of emotion, to be swept away by an intoxicating tide of passion and pleasure, but all too soon we find that the bubble bursts, and love itself, in its deepest sense, will be swept away on the floodtide of emotion.

For every genuine love-at-first-sight happy-ever-after match there are a hundred bright, bubbling romances that twinkle a moment and are gone. Dorothy Parker wrote:

> *By the time you swear you're his,*
> *Shivering and sighing,*
> *And he vows his passion is*
> *Infinite, undying—*
> *Ladies, make a note of this:*
> *One of you is lying.*

But does it really matter if the bubble bursts? We can after all console ourselves with the thought that the 'next time' may be different; we can always enter the chase anew.

What must be caught and kept, from these blazing years, is a lasting fervour, so that

> *Were the bright day no more to visit us,*
> *Oh, then for ever would I hold thee thus,*
> *Naked, enchained, empty of idle fear,*
> *As the first lovers in the garden were.*
> JOHN MILTON

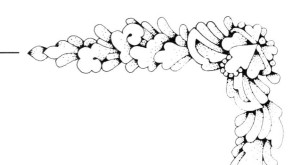

Adult Love

So, the heyday of young love is past; we have found and committed ourselves to the one we love, and it is perhaps in this new phase of life, the middle years, that the real joys of love are within easier reach than at any other age. There is a new sureness, gained only by experience, which deepens emotion and begins to render it eternal. Pleasure comes not only from the sudden recognition of love—not only from its celebration— but from the startling revelation that it can last. Permanence begins to be attainable, a real partnership grows; one delights as much in knowing one's love as in discovering it. Now we begin to build a future through our children; part of our love is built into the course of their lives. Growing together, we grow forward, each year a binding together and an enrichment which touches everything in life:

> *Music I heard with you was more than music,*
> *And bread I broke with you was more than bread.*
>
> CONRAD AIKEN

Lovers on a summer hillside. (*The Bright Cloud* by Samuel Palmer.)

The Fourth Age of Love

The Fifth Age of Love

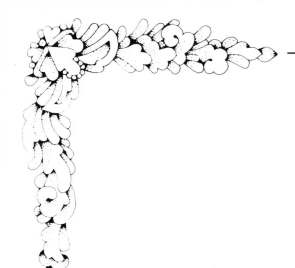

Mature Love

And so *I* has become *we*. Not because, cannibal-like, one has devoured the other, but because by now one has absorbed the other's very essence. Without losing any freedom but the freedom to hurt, one *is* now the other – 'one soul joins two bodies fast for ever'. And this brings unimagined, unimaginable richness. Each enjoys the other's life as well as his or her own.

There is the joy, too, of familiarity and routine; of an intimate knowledge of the other's likes and dislikes, idiosyncracies and habits – good or bad. Each knows how the other will react to a situation, to a word, a gesture, or action, without knowing *precisely* how. The expected phrase may have a new context, a new inflection, yet will still be the expected phrase, will be the person we love. We know the other's taste and will share pleasure in a picture or a play, a book or a hobby, a wine or a flower, even it if does not strictly accord with our own taste or interests. Each leads now a double life, pleasure and pain doubled: *I* has become *we*.

We live vicariously too through our children: now they will be reaching forward into the tensions, the joys, of first love. And, through them, our life is renewed in the repetition of the pattern of nature. Watching them grow, watching the first instinctive love of a baby for his parents, and later watching helplessly as they experience the bitter sweetness of first love, we capture a glimpse of our own past; we relive and renew our response to the drawing together of one individual and another.

Now, love rests on generosity of spirit. Of course there are moments when the expected phrase will be as irritating as one's own clumsiness, or forgetfulness, or lack of sympathy. But the beauty is clearly apparent too: the beauty of knowing someone so well that they are part of oneself, so that the irritation is the more infuriating because it is irritation with oneself. Love is this knowledge, and generous acceptance of it. Love has become safety, dependence on the other as on one's own hand or arm. As Cecil Day Lewis wrote:

> *Live you by love confined,*
> *There is no nearer nearness;*
> *Break not his light bounds,*
> *The stars' and seas' harness:*
> *There is nothing beyond,*
> *We have found the land's end. . .*
>
> *We are where love has come*
> *To live: he is that river*
> *Which flows and is the same;*
> *He is not the famous deceiver*
> *Nor early-flowering dream.*
> *Content you. Be at home*
> *In me.*

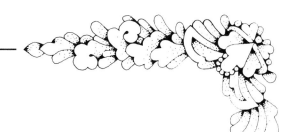

Autumnal Love

Our state cannot be sever'd, we are one,
One flesh; to lose thee were to lose myself.
                                        JOHN MILTON

Neither we nor the person we love are the same at sixty as at twenty, but we will almost inevitably be closer together; we will enjoy a closeness and intimacy that only time can bestow. After a turbulent struggle with the years, Yeats wrote:

Bodily decrepitude is wisdom; young
We loved each other and were ignorant.

And certainly wisdom is one of the great advantages of years of living; wisdom not in any academic sense, but in the sense of experience, the feeling that one 'has been there before'. Very few problems will be new; there may still be passion, there may still be jealousy. Disagreements, differences of opinion may still occur. If, however, we can retain and heighten the balance and assurance of our mature love, if we can reject any uncertainty or imbalance which temporary strains or tensions may impose, then we can enjoy in old age as perfect a union as the world can offer.

The French novelist Honoré de Balzac once heard someone claiming

The Procession of the Dunmow Flitch, 1751, after D. Ogborne.
    He that repents not of his marriage
        in a year and a day either sleeping
        or waking
    May lawfully go to Dunmow and
        fetch him a gammon of bacon,
goes an early anonymous rhyme, commemorating an ancient custom which still exists today. It originated in Little Dunmow, Essex, in about 1246, when Robert Fitzwaller, lord of the manor, awarded flitches or sides of bacon to those couples who could truthfully swear that they had 'had no brawls' and were still as loving after a year and a day of marriage as they had been at the start of their life together. The oath had to be taken in Little Dunmow Priory before the Prior, the monks, and the townsmen The earliest known winner of the flitch was Robert Wright of Badbury, in 1445.

The Sixth Age of Love

The Seventh Age of Love

that in a long life a man needed many women to fulfil his love. 'It is as absurd to say that a man can't love one woman all the time', Balzac replied, 'as it is to say that a violinist needs several violins to play the same piece of music'. Well, every man's, every woman's experience of love will be different – as in each area of life there may be joy, tragedy, success, failure. There are no rules; there are no absolute standards to which everyone must attain; no-one can dictate how love should be. But love is something everyone must practise – and practise – until its music is so much a part of one's life that it scarcely needs rehearsing, until it is as much a part of oneself as one's own past. Indeed it will *be* one's past. So, whether we need one love or many in the course of a lifetime:

Let us always love! Let us love and love again!
Love . . . is the flame that cannot be quenched,
The flower that cannot die.

VICTOR HUGO

An eighteenth-century love knot by the Italian engraver Francesco Bartolozzi.

The Amorous Muse
An Anthology

Introduction

Apart from constantly attempting to define the meaning of love and celebrate its raptures in high poetry, poets have also always versified their minor amatory adventures in rhymes. Sometimes great poets have turned to limericks, sometimes unknown poets have become mildly famous for one amorous squib; and a great horde of completely anonymous poets have turned out ballads and sets of verses which are printed and reprinted in anthologies of poetry, without their author's name ever being known.

In this section, the Muse relates, climbing drainpipes to darkened windows, lifting a petticoat to glimpse a charming leg, or welcoming willing maidens into his arms and beds. Some of these poems are ballads sung three centuries ago, freshly composed for the ale-house by that most rumbustious of all poets, Anon. Others come from such lusty cavaliers as Sir John Suckling, or from the pen of the little clergyman Herrick, stranded in a rough Devonshire parish far from the lights and laughter of fashionable London. If there is sometimes an air of almost desperate gaiety about some of the verses, it is because they are more to do with adventure than with real love; but they are always witty, always fun. And here are some of them. Those printed without authors' names are unattributable and undatable.

Daphnis and Chloe

And at the beginning of the spring the snow melted, the earth reappeared, the grass began to show, and the shepherds went forth again with their flocks to the fields, Chloe and Daphnis leading the way. . . . They sat watching their flocks grazing, kissing the while, and afterwards wandering in search of flowers to weave garlands for the gods. . . . The rams followed the yoes that had not yet lambed, and having caught them, leapt, serving one after the other, and the bucks raced after the she-goats, jumping them in the same fashion and butting fiercely for love of them. Each had his own shes and kept guard lest another should do him wrong. And so by sights and sounds that would have enkindled the fires of Aphrodite in old men, the twain were afflicted, and compelled by their own nature to seek more eagerly than they had yet done that ease and content which kisses and embraces do not afford; but Daphnis the most. For he, being now lusty and well filled out, having spent the whole winter within doors doing nothing, thrilled after the kiss and was big, as the phrase runs, for embraces, more curious in every one, more hardy than he ever was before, pressing Chloe to grant him all he asked for, and to lie with him flesh to flesh longer than was their custom.

opposite: 'Be quiet, Sir! begone, I say:
Lord bless us! how you romp and tear!'

210

Chloe asked what else they could do but kiss and lie together as they were in their clothes, and what he thought he might do if they were to lie together naked. 'That which the rams do to the yoes and the bucks to the she-goats. Thou hast seen that after the jump the yoe runs no longer from the ram; they graze together, assuaged and content, so there is of a certainty a sweetness unknown to us, a sweetness that surpasses the bitterness of love.'

. . .'But hast not seen', said she, 'that our beasties are clothed in wool and hair more closely than I am in these garments?' He believed her, and lay beside her, and for a long time he lay doing nothing, for he was without knowledge how to do that which he desired ardently to do. . . . He sat down beside her and began to weep, for it was sad to find that he knew less about the ways of love than a tup.

From Daphnis and Chloe *by* LONGUS, *c. 2nd cent. A.D.*
translated by George Moore

The Girl Who Caught a Nightingale

Not long ago there lived in Romagna a handsome and comely young man named Ricciardo, who fell deeply in love with Caterina, the beautiful and charming daughter of Messer Lizio de Valbona. He concealed his love with the greatest care. But the girl noticed it, and began to love him too, which naturally delighted Ricciardo. One day he found the opportunity and courage to say:

'Caterina, I beseech you not to let me die of love.'

And the girl promptly answered:

'I hope to God you will not let me die of it.'

This answer gave Ricciardo great pleasure and eagerness; he thought for a while, and then said: 'My sweet Caterina, I can see no way to come to you unless you can sleep on the balcony overlooking your father's garden. If I knew you to be there at night, I would find some means of getting there, however high it might be.'

It was about the end of May, and next day the girl began to complain to her mother that she had not been able to sleep on account of the heat. 'If my father and you are willing, I should like to have my bed on the balcony beside the bedroom overlooking the garden; and there I could sleep, and listen to the nightingale, and be in a cooler place, and be much more comfortable than in your bedroom.'

So that night she had a bed made up on the balcony. And when Ricciardo heard that everything was quiet, he climbed onto a wall with the help of a ladder, and then clinging to the wall, he reached the balcony – with great difficulty, and great danger if he had fallen – and was greeted softly but with the greatest delight by Caterina. After many kisses they lay down together, and took delight and pleasure of each other almost the whole night, making the nightingale sing many times.

Nights are short, and their delight was great, and already the day was at hand, though they did not know it. They were so warm with the weather and their play that they both went to sleep almost at once, Caterina with her right arm round Ricciardo's neck and her left hand holding the thing you are ashamed to mention among men. Thus they slept without waking until dawn came and Messer Lizio got up. Remembering that his daughter was sleeping on the balcony, he softly opened the door, saying to himself: 'Let us see how the nightingale made Caterina sleep last night.'

He crept up and gently lifted the curtain round the bed, and saw Ricciardo and Caterina sleeping naked and uncovered in the embrace I have just described. He called to his wife: 'Get up at once wife, and come and see how your daughter is so fond of the nightingale that she has caught it and still holds it in her hand.'

Then Ricciardo awoke and saw Messer Lizio, and felt as if the heart had been torn from his body. He sat up in bed, and said: 'Sir, I beg you mercy for God's sake.'

'Ricciardo,' said Messer Lizio, 'this is not the reward I should have had for my love of you, whom I have known since boyhood. But take Caterina as your legitimate wife so that, as she has been yours all night, she may be yours so long as she lives.'

So Messer Lizio borrowed one of his wife's rings, and without getting out of bed Ricciardo took Caterina as his wife in their presence. After which Messer Lizio and his wife went away, saying: 'Rest for a while; perhaps you need it more than to get up.'

After which, the two young people embraced each other, and, since they had not travelled more than six miles that night, they went on another two; and a few days later there was an honourable great wedding festival; and afterwards for a long time in peace and quietness Ricciardo hunted birds with his wife day and night as much as he pleased.

Condensed from The Decameron *of* GIOVANNI BOCCACCIO 1313–75, *translated by Richard Aldington*

Approaching Dawn by Eric Gill.

'I'd Have You,' Quoth He

'I'd have you,' quoth he.
'Would you have me?' quoth she,
　'O where, Sir?'

'In my chamber,' quoth he.
'In your chamber?' quoth she,
　'Why there, Sir?'

'To kiss you,' quoth he.
'To kiss me?' quoth she,
　'O why, Sir?'

'Cause I love it,' quoth he.
'Do you love it?' quoth she,
　'So do I, Sir.'

ANON, *17th cent.*

Lucius and Fotis

I found nobody at home but my charming Fotis, who was preparing pork-rissoles for her master and mistress, while the appetizing smell of haggis-stew drifted to my nostrils from an earthenware casserole on the stove. She wore a neat white house-dress, gathered in below the breasts with a red silk band, and as she alternately stirred the casserole and shaped the rissoles with her pretty hands, the twisting and turning made her whole body quiver seductively.

The sight had so powerful an effect on me that for a while I stood rooted in admiration; and so did something else. At last I found my voice. 'Dear Fotis,' I said, 'how daintily, how charmingly you stir that casserole: I love watching you wriggle your hips. And what a wonderful cook you are! The man whom you would allow to poke his finger into your little casserole is the luckiest fellow alive. That sort of stew would tickle the most jaded palate.'

She retorted over her shoulder: 'Go away, you scoundrel; keep clear of my little cooking stove! If you come too near even when the fire is low, a spark may fly out and set you on fire; and when that happens nobody but myself will be capable of putting the flames out. A wonderful cook, am I? Yes, I certainly know how to tickle a man's . . . well, his palate, if you care to call it that, and how to keep things nicely on the boil . . .'

opposite: The Assignation.

From The Golden Ass, *by* LUCIUS APULEIUS *c. 2nd cent.* A.D.,
translated by Robert Graves

Once, Twice, Thrice

Once, twice, thrice, I Julia tried,
The scornful puss as oft denied,
And since I can no better thrive
I'll cringe to ne'er a bitch alive.
So hie away, disdainful sow!
Good claret is my mistress now.

English catch, 17th cent.

Upon the Nipples of Julia's Breast

Have ye beheld (with much delight)
A red rose peeping through a white?
Or else a cherry (double grac'd)
Within a lily? Centre plac'd?
Or ever mark'd the pretty beam
A strawberry shows, half drown'd in cream?
Or seen rich rubies blushing through
A pure smooth pearl, and orient too?
So like to this, nay all the rest,
Is each neat niplet of her breast.

ROBERT HERRICK, *1591–1674*

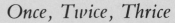

These We Have Loved

Busts and bosoms have I known
    Of various shapes and sizes
From grievous disappointments
    To jubilant surprises.

ANON, *20th cent.*

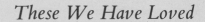

'. . . For though your garter met my eye, my thoughts were far above it.'

Be Quiet, Sir

Be quiet, Sir! begone, I say:
Lord bless us! how you romp and tear!
    There!
    I swear!
Now you've left my bosom bare!
I do not like such boisterous play,
So take that saucy hand away —
Why now you're ruder than before!
Nay, I'll be hanged if I comply —
    Fie!
    I'll cry. . .!
Oh! — I can't bear it! — I shall die!
I vow I'll never see you more!
(But are you sure you've shut the door?)

ANON, *18th cent.*

The Epicure

Let us drink and be merry, dance, joke and rejoice,
With claret and sherry, with lute and with voice,
The changeable world to our joy is unjust.
All treasure uncertain — then down with your dust.
    In frolics dispose your pounds, shillings and pence,
    For we shall be nothing a hundred years hence.

We'll kiss and be free with Nan, Betty and Philly,
Have oysters and lobsters, and maids by the belly;
Fish-dinners will make a lass spring like a flea,
Dame Venus (Love's goddess) was born of the sea!
    With her and with Bacchus we'll tickle the sense,
    For we shall be past it a hundred years hence.

ANON, *18th cent.*

opposite: 'Climbing drainpipes to darkened windows . . .'

Out Upon It, I Have Lov'd

Out upon it, I have lov'd
    Three whole days together;
And am like to love three more,
    If it prove fair weather.

Time shall moult away his wings
    Ere he shall discover
In the whole wide world again
    Such a constant lover.

But the spite on't is, no praise
    Is due at all to me:
Love with me had made no stays
    Had it any been but she.

Had it any been but she
    And that very face,
There had been at least ere this
    A dozen dozen in her place.

SIR JOHN SUCKLING, *1609–1642*

'Busts and bosoms have I known . . .'

opposite: Border for Chaucer's *Troilus and Criseyde* by Eric Gill.

page 220: Border for Chaucer's *Troilus and Criseyde* by Eric Gill.

Young Corydon and Phillis

Young Corydon and Phillis
    Sate in a lovely grove;
Contriving crowns of lilies,
    Repeating tales of love:
And something else, but what I dare not name.

A thousand times he kissed her,
    Laying her on the green;
But as he farther pressed her,
    Her pretty leg was seen:
And something else, but what I dare not name.

Young Corydon grown bolder
    The minute would improve;
'This is the time', he told her,
    'To show you how I love—
And something else, but what I dare not name.'

The nymph seemed almost dying,
    Dissolved in amorous heat;
She kissed and told him sighing,
    'My dear, your love is great:
And something else, but what I dare not name.'

But Phillis did recover
    Much sooner than the swain;
She blushing asked her lover:
    'Shall we not kiss again?—
And something else, but what I dare not name?'

Thus love his revels keeping,
    Till nature at a stand
From talk they fell to sleeping,
    Holding each other's hand,
And something else, but what I dare not name.

SIR CHARLES SEDLEY, *1639–1701*

On Seeing a Lady's Garter

Why blush, dear girl, pray tell me why?
    You need not, I can prove it;
For though your garter met my eye,
    My thoughts were far above it.

ANON, *18th cent.*

Elegy to His Mistress

In summer's heat, and mid-time of the day,
To rest my limbs, upon a bed I lay;
One window shut, the other open stood,
Which gave such light as twinkles in a wood,
Like twilight glimpse at setting of the sun,
Or night being past, and yet not day begun;
Such light to shamefaced maidens must be shown
Where they may sport, and seem to be unknown.
Then came Corinna in her long loose gown,
Her white neck hid with tresses hanging down,
Resembling fair Semiramis going to bed,
Or Lais of a thousand wooers sped.
I snatched her gown – being thin, the harm was small –
Yet strived she to be covered therewithal,
And striving thus as one that would be cast,
Betrayed herself, and yielded at the last.
Stark naked as she stood before mine eye,
Not one wen in her body could I spy.
What arms and shoulders did I touch and see,
How apt her breasts were to be pressed by me,
How smooth a belly under her waist saw I,
How large a leg, and what a lusty thigh.
To leave the rest, all liked me passing well;
I clinged her naked body, down she fell:
Judge you the rest, being tired she bade me kiss;
Jove send me more such afternoons as this!

OVID, *43 B.C.–17 A.D., translated by Ben Jonson*

A Lady Lately

A lady lately, that was fully sped
Of all the pleasures of the marriage-bed
Ask'd a physician, whether were more fit,
For Venus' sports, the morning or the night?
The good old man made answer, as 'twas meet,
The morn more wholesome, but the night more sweet.
Nay then, i' faith, quoth she, since we have leisure,
We'll to't each morn for health, each night for pleasure.

ANON, *18th cent.*

Games

Introduction

The Love Games in this section have been specially designed, with the help of leading psychologists, to help you discover your real attitudes to love. Although they are relaxed and light-hearted and contain a good mixture of straight Fun, they are nonetheless designed to help you to understand yourself and your attitude to others, to help you assess what you want and need from love.

Falling in love is perhaps *the* most unpredictable happening in our lives. And yet many young people today are becoming interested in a more scientific search for a compatible partner, and are turning to the computer-dating system.

The games in this book are a kind of computer questionnaire with a difference – they inject a fun element into the whole process of self-analysis.

What Type of Lover am I?
The success or failure of a relationship may depend on how well you understand yourself and your expectations. Could you be trying to assume a false identity which really runs contrary to your true nature? Start off with Game 1, *What Type of Lover am I?*, and find out which of the twelve categories of lover you belong to or which is the nearest approximation to your own reactions and needs. Are you sensuous, diffident, romantic or what?

The Castle Game
'Love' can be a many faceted word with several rather unromantic under-currents lurking beneath the surface. Could it be that what really attracts you to your latest girl/boyfriend is the promise of financial security or a good sex life? If you feel like taking a cool look at your possible motives, try playing *The Castle Game*.

Consult the Oracle
Game 3 provides strictly light relief from the probings of the first two quizzes. Adapted from a delightful nineteenth-century game, *Consult the Oracle* may provide some surprising answers to questions such as 'Does he/she really love me?' or 'How many times will I fall in love?'

Identilove
Do you often day-dream about your ideal partner and conjure up rather hazy pictures of gloriously handsome young men or glamorous, model-girl women as the case may be? The *Identilove* game will help you design a more concrete picture of your ideal man/woman, and you don't need to be a budding Picasso to do so.

Love Maze
If you don't really like the face you created in Game 4, your girlfriend/ boyfriend difficulties may stem from the fact that you're looking for the

wrong type. You found out what type of lover *you* are in the first game. The *Love Maze* will help you to discover your ideal partner, the kind of person with whom you should be really compatible, and will also help you to sort out your expectations from a relationship. Similar types don't necessarily make a good combination – you may find you need someone to act as a foil to your own personality rather than as a duplicate. Thread your way through the labyrinthine paths of the maze and find out!

Is it Love or Infatuation?

Take a look at your relationship in Game 6 and see if it really is love or just a pleasant, but passing infatuation. Are you trying to delude yourself? Are you so consciously searching for love that you build up every romance into the 'real thing'?

The Steeplechase

No long-term relationship is completely free of problems and upsets and Game 7, *The Steeplechase*, is designed to help you assess how you cope with the ups-and-downs of marriage – or how you are likely to cope if you are not yet married. Will your relationship survive the hurdles of the course? Will you get a soaking at the water jump? Play and find out!

Where's Your Venus? Where's Your Mars?

Lastly come two astrology based games. Both Mars and Venus have a powerful bearing on one's relationships, Venus strongly influencing the capacity for love and affection, and Mars a man or woman's sexual response. All you need to know is your date of birth – or that of your partner – and, with the help of the tables provided, you can work out the influence of the heavens on your love life.

So, 'The game's afoot: follow your spirit' and away you go.

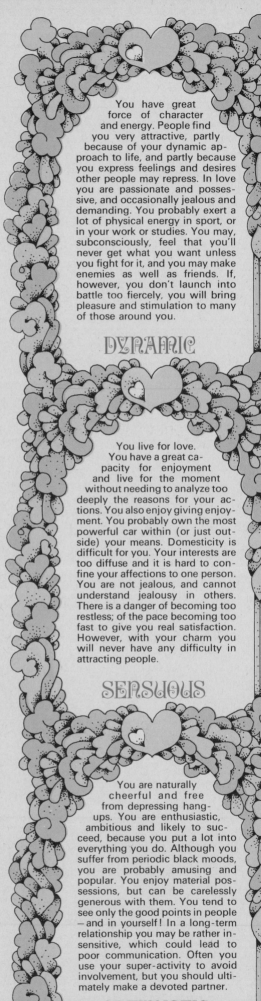

DYNAMIC

You have great force of character and energy. People find you very attractive, partly because of your dynamic approach to life, and partly because you express feelings and desires other people may repress. In love you are passionate and possessive, and occasionally jealous and demanding. You probably exert a lot of physical energy in sport, or in your work or studies. You may, subconsciously, feel that you'll never get what you want unless you fight for it, and you may make enemies as well as friends. If, however, you don't launch into battle too fiercely, you will bring pleasure and stimulation to many of those around you.

REALISTIC

You go for the sensible, the practical, and are hardly ever bothered by irrational fears or self-doubt. You can dress extremely well, and quality is important to you. If you have a car, it will be a reliable make; it may be fast, but you drive carefully. In a relationship you have a lot to give, but are unlikely to choose someone for purely romantic reasons. You cope well with difficult situations and your inbuilt strength enables you to conquer afflictions which would daunt most people, although this same quality sometimes leads to intolerance. However, you have a capacity for great enjoyment and form friendships easily.

SENSUOUS

You live for love. You have a great capacity for enjoyment and live for the moment without needing to analyze too deeply the reasons for your actions. You also enjoy giving enjoyment. You probably own the most powerful car within (or just outside) your means. Domesticity is difficult for you. Your interests are too diffuse and it is hard to confine your affections to one person. You are not jealous, and cannot understand jealousy in others. There is a danger of becoming too restless; of the pace becoming too fast to give you real satisfaction. However, with your charm you will never have any difficulty in attracting people.

INDEPENDENT

Tolerant and understanding, you are able to form mature relationships in which you neither ask for support, nor expect people to lean on you. As a lover you are confident and charming. You have your own brand of loyalty, but, if you feel that too many demands are being made on you, you are likely to slide gently away. Your clothes will have a definite individual touch. You can see other people's points of view, even if you do not agree with them. You tend to feel that you don't need other people, and consequently you may find yourself alone quite often, in spite of your good qualities.

OPTIMISTIC

You are naturally cheerful and free from depressing hang-ups. You are enthusiastic, ambitious and likely to succeed, because you put a lot into everything you do. Although you suffer from periodic black moods, you are probably amusing and popular. You enjoy material possessions, but can be carelessly generous with them. You tend to see only the good points in people — and in yourself! In a long-term relationship you may be rather insensitive, which could lead to poor communication. Often you use your super-activity to avoid involvement, but you should ultimately make a devoted partner.

PROTECTIVE

People are attracted by your inner strength and great sense of justice. You will be admired for the way you cope with life and relationships Love is very real to you, and you have the gift of making people feel loved and secure. You appreciate beauty, and your clothes and possessions are chosen with care. You need to be in control of people, possibly because you feel you can only keep up your own strength by maintaining order around you. Remember that it can be wearing always to be the 'strong' partner; other people can be competent and might like to feel you needed them.

Answer *Yes* or *No*

DO YOU:
1 Tend to quarrel easily?
2 Almost invariably dismiss your dreams as nonsense?
3 Show your affections openly?
4 Take being snubbed in your stride?

Section A
Answer *Yes* or *No*

DO YOU:
1 Remain cheerful, despite missing a train?
2 Like giving and receiving?
3 Choose dependable friends?
4 Cope well with emotional scenes?
5 Remember meals you had years ago?

6 Think modern love stories are unrealistic?
7 Drive a hard bargain?
8 Ever gamble?
9 Sympathize with pacifism?
10 Believe in life insurance

More *Yes's* to the odd numbers — move to left **D.**
More *Yes's* to the even numbers — move to right **F.**

Section C
Answer *Yes* or *No*

DO YOU:
1 Immediately assume your lover is tired of you, if he/she fails to ring?
2 Often feel tired?
3 Find your lover can easily affect your moods?
4 Worry about relationships?
5 Prefer interesting conversation to 'nonsense talk' with your lover?
6 Find emotional arguments irritating?
7 See through people easily?
8 Control your feelings?
9 Let yourself be easily influenced?
10 Feel that your relationships are determined by the other person?
11 Control your temper easily?
12 Usually think compliments from the opposite sex are genuine?

More *Yes's* to questions 1—4 move to **Diffident**
More *Yes's* to questions 5—8 move to **Intellectual**
More *Yes's* to questions 9—12 move to **Tranquil**

Section D
Answer *Yes* or *No*

1 Would you consider camping holiday with yo partner?
2 Do you put ambition b fore enjoyment?
3 Can you have plato relationships?
4 Can you converse easil
5 Do you try to further y reputation as a lover?
6 Is sex important to you
7 Could you tolerate a dr in your standard of living
8 Do you plan your lo life?
9 Do dull-minded peo irritate you?
10 Do you often resort physical violence?
11 Is your seduction tec nique to sweep people their feet rather than a smo approach?
12 Do you find long wa or traffic jams excessiv frustrating?

More *Yes's* to questions 1 move to **Optimistic**
More *Yes's* to question 5 move to **Sensuous**
More *Yes's* to questions 12 move to **Dynamic**

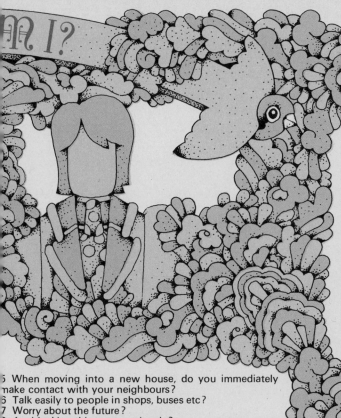

You are kind and gentle, and people like and respect you because of your sincerity and lack of affectation. Although others have a high opinion of you, you do not always have a high opinion of yourself! In your choice of clothes you may be indecisive. When you are feeling happy you know you look marvellous, but, if your mood is low, you tend to be easily discouraged about your appearance. You can be passionate in your love, once you are sure that it is returned. You are an emotional person, and when you get depressed, hang on until you swing the other way, for, in the right situation, with the right people, you have the capacity for great fulfilment in life.

DIFFIDENT

You are capable of deeply satisfying relationships with people. You need love and affection and others recognize this and find you easy to love. Your dependence on others may stem from the fact that you do not feel yourself to be an individual in your own right. Although you seek guidance from your partner you will sometimes find yourself illogically objecting to their interference. This can lead to angry scenes and resentment. However, once you learn to cope with your ambivalent feelings towards your lover, you should be able to derive great pleasure and fulfilment from your relationships.

DEPENDENT

5 When moving into a new house, do you immediately make contact with your neighbours?
6 Talk easily to people in shops, buses etc?
7 Worry about the future?
8 Avoid taking things too seriously?

Mainly *Yes* go to square **A**: mainly *No* go to square **B**.

Section B
Answer *Yes* or *No*

DO YOU:
1 Think love is ephemeral?
2 Become bored without a lover?
3 Avoid seeing friends for fear of intruding?
4 Believe implicitly most things people tell you?
5 Analyze your love-life?
6 Fit in easily with other people's arrangements?
7 Read both heavy and light escapist books on holiday?
8 Often get into difficult situations?
9 Ask people favours?
10 Enjoy calculated risks?

More *Yes's* to the odd numbers—move to left **C**
More *Yes's* to the even numbers—move to right **E**

Logical and thoughtful, you can cope with many aspects of life which bewilder other people. You have a sense of purpose in life and are happiest in a situation you feel that you can understand. You do not attach much importance to material things unless they have a real bearing on your chosen way of life. In a relationship you should prove mentally stimulating, but may perhaps have an excessive faith in your ability to talk things out. Because you fear the irrational, you tend to repress your feelings and emotions. Do not fight against them too much or you may miss out on some important parts of life.

INTELLECTUAL

You tend to idealize and seek perfection, to create fantasies around yourself when life does not come up to your expectations. You can probably get away with unusual or fantastic clothes because you have confidence in your image. In relationships you are not interested in imperfections; in fact you sometimes make yourself believe that there are no faults on either side. You have a tendency to over-dramatize your affairs, and may have a somewhat rosy, idealistic vision of domestic bliss! However, you attract many friends who find your view of life both stimulating and amusing.

ROMANTIC

Section E
Answer *Yes* or *No*

Are you easily hurt?
Do you confide in friends?
Do you listen to advice?
Do you look mainly for warmth and understanding in love?
Are you concerned about impressing people?
Are you sometimes instantly attracted to people?
Do you try to predict what might happen at a party?
Do you try to attract the most glamorous person at a party?
Do you always know when you have hurt someone?
10 Do you know instantly you will fall in love?
11 Do you sometimes instinctively dislike people?
12 Are you sensitive to the atmosphere of a social gathering?

More *Yes's* to questions 1–4 move to **Dependent**
More *Yes's* to questions 5–8 move to **Romantic**
More *Yes's* to questions 9–12 move to **Intuitive**

Section F
Answer *Yes* or *No*

1 Are you intolerant of nonsense in others?
2 Would you stop yourself falling in love with someone who was not free?
3 Do people ask you for advice?
4 Do you find it hard to understand other people's difficulties?
5 Are you open-minded about new ideas?
6 Do you give people the benefit of the doubt?
7 Can you let the other person have the last word?
8 Can you take criticism?
9 Are your standards of integrity particularly high?
10 Are you patient?
11 Do people often cry on your shoulder?
12 Do you think it is only fair to let people get to know you before you launch into an affair with them?

More *Yes's* to questions 1–4 move to **Realistic**
More *Yes's* to questions 5–8 move to **Independent**
More *Yes's* to questions 9–12 move to **Protective**

In a mad world you are a breath of sanity. While others dash round in circles which often prove futile, you are content to wait for the right moment to act, rather than rushing in impetuously. People find you relaxing company because they know that you observe situations calmly. You tend to wait for the other person to come to you rather than making direct efforts at friendships, but once sure of being loved you can be passionate and firm. Underlying your apparent detachment could be the fear of being rejected. However, you attract people easily, so you have no real cause for worry.

TRANQUIL

You act on intuition rather than working out a life-style in advance. You are happiest in situations where you can play it by ear, and have faith in your inner perceptions. As a result you do not feel the need to explain your actions to others. None the less, in love you probably attach a lot of importance to communication, tolerance and understanding. You may dislike relationships involving too much routine. Because you react quickly to new ideas, you may find it hard to finish what you begin. However, intuition will be the ruling factor in your life, so stick to it!

INTUITIVE

Chamber Fifteen

1 Are you hurt if your partner contradicts you in public?
2 Would you mind your partner mixing with people you don't like?
3 Would it ruin your relationship if, in your own interests, your partner shattered your illusions about yourself?
Mostly *Yes*—read Answer 15 on page 228
Mostly *No*—move to Chamber Sixteen

Chamber Thirteen

1 Would you still respect someone you loved if you found they accepted some conventions without question?
2 Could your love survive in a suburban setting?
3 Would you buy clothes which your partner liked but you didn't?
Mostly *No*—read Answer 13 on page 228
Mostly *Yes*—move to Chamber Sixteen

Chamber Nine

1 Would you dissuade your partner from taking a stimulating but badly paid job?
2 Could you forgive your partner if he/she fell out of favour with a rich aunt?
3 Would your honeymoon be ruined if you stayed in a second-rate hotel?
Mostly *Yes*—read Answer 9 on page 228
Mostly *No*—move to Chamber Sixteen

Chamber Twelve

1 Would you make a terrible scene if your partner behaved badly at a dinner party?
2 Would you refuse to go to a discotheque if he/she were wearing a city suit/a tulle party dress?
3 Would you be put off your lover if all your family and friends strongly disapproved of him/her?
Mostly *No*—move to Chamber Sixteen
Mostly *Yes*—read Answer 12 on page 228

Chamber Eight

1 If he/she were the target of criticism, would you find yourself cooling towards him/her?
2 If you discovered major areas of difference between you would this jeopardize the relationship?
3 If you were more successful in the same field than your partner, would your feelings towards him/her be affected?
Mostly *Yes*—read Answer 8 on page 228
Mostly *No*—move to Chamber Sixteen

Chamber Sixteen

Turn to p. 228 and read Answer 16 (*NB*—If you have had to answer questions in more than one Chamber do not read Answer 16 yet. Wait until you have completed your answers in any other Chamber[s] to which you have to go.)

Chamber Seven

1 Would it matter if your friends were scornful of him/her?
2 Would you be put off someone if their income declined?
3 If your partner said the wrong thing when you most wanted to impress, would it mean death to the relationship?
Mostly *No*—move to Chamber Sixteen
Mostly *Yes*—read Answer 7 on page 228

Chamber Three

1 Do you enjoy listening to your partner's confidences?
2 Can you still enjoy an evening when your partner has had a tiring day and wants to curl up with a book?
3 Can you cope with your

Chamber Eleven

1 If your partner objected, would you refuse an attractive job involving travel?
2 Would you try not to talk about your job if your partner wasn't really interested?
3 Would you miss an important business meeting if your partner needed your support over a harrowing emotional problem?
Mostly *Yes*—move to Chamber Sixteen
Mostly *No*—read Answer 11 on page 228

Chamber Six

1 Even though you hate arguments would you determine to fight back if you thought he/she had made a bad decision?
2 Do you think that love always brings some element of suffering?
3 Do you love him/her so much that you would forgive even the most hurtful act or words?
Mostly *Yes*—move to Chamber Sixteen
Mostly *No*—read Answer 6 on page 228

Chamber Two

1 Do you often think it would be awful if your lover left you?
2 Is it proof of your love that you must see or hear from him/her every day?
3 Do you agree that if a couple love each other they

Chamber Fourteen

1 In an argument, would you hate to admit you were wrong?
2 Would you object if your partner tried to convert you to some passionate cause?
3 Would you accept a job abroad if you weren't sure if your partner would be happy?
Mostly *No*—move to Chamber Sixteen
Mostly *Yes*—read Answer 14 on page 228

Chamber Ten

1 Would you still love your partner if you discovered they had invented many of the details of their life?
2 Could you still respect your partner if he/she lost a glamorous job?
3 Could you resist the offer of a rich aristocrat and remain faithful to your partner?
Mostly *Yes*—move to Chamber Sixteen
Mostly *No*—read Answer 10 on page 228

Chamber Five

1 Do you lose interest in someone if the physical side doesn't play a very important part in the relationship?
2 Are you put off when your partner is ill and looks ghastly?
3 Would you be unfaithful if he/she had to go away for a month?
Mostly *No*—move to Chamber Sixteen
Mostly *Yes*—read Answer 5 on page 228

The Castle Game

START

Assemble at the Main Gate to the Castle and answer the following questions:

1 When you are introduced to someone, which goes through your mind—
(a) What do they think of me?
(b) What do I think of them?

2 Which job would you choose—
(a) An emotionally rewarding job working with people on your wavelength?
(b) A job which gives you status and recognizes your talents and abilities?

3 Going unattached to a party, do you aim—
(a) To make a favourable impression on just one person?
(b) To make a favourable impression on everyone?

4 When you see a beautiful stranger, are you more curious to know—
(a) What kind of person are they, how do they think and feel?
(b) What do they do, who are they, where do they come from?

5 When you meet a new group of people, do you—
(a) Tend to let your instincts decide how you feel about them?
(b) Feel you proudly want him/her to meet all your friends and bring him/her into your circle?

6 When you first fall in love with someone, do you—
(a) Only want to see them and tend to forget about your other friends?
(b) Be disappointed, but feel you could not help continuing to love them all the same?

7 If you fell for someone and then realized their opinions and way of life were totally opposed to yours, would you—
(a) Be disappointed, but feel you could not help continuing to love them all the same?
(b) Be put off entirely, deciding that what you thought was love was merely a passing infatuation?

Mainly *Yes* to (a) questions—go to **East Wing of the Castle** and answer Sections 1–8

Mainly *Yes* to (b) questions—go to **West Wing of the Castle** and answer Sections 9–15

WEST WING

If you answer mainly *Yes* to the questions below, move to the appropriate Chamber(s).

Section 1
1 Do you think a relationship should provide security?
2 Do you easily accept other people's judgments?
3 Do you like other people to make decisions for you?
Mainly *Yes*, go to Chamber One

Section 2
1 Would you forego a holiday rather than go alone?
2 Would you enjoy community life?
3 Would you hate to live alone?
Mainly *Yes* go to Chamber Two

Section 3
1 Do you confide in people?
2 Are you a poor listener?
3 Do you often have long telephone conversations?
Mainly *Yes*, go to Chamber Three

Section 4
1 Do you fall in love easily?
2 Do you analyze your love-life?
3 Do you know intuitively if you will fall in love with someone?
Mainly *Yes*, go to Chamber Four

Section 5
1 Do you attach a lot of importance to physical attraction?
2 Before a date, do you plan tactics?
3 Do you make sure *all* your clothes are clean before a date?
Mainly *Yes*, go to Chamber Five

Section 6
1 Can you forgive someone who frequently stands you up?
2 Could you put up with a moody lover?
3 If your lover is less involved than you, do you still plunge in wholeheartedly?
Mainly *Yes*, go to Chamber Six

Section 7
1 Do you admire sophistication?
2 Do your friends' opinions of your date matter?
3 Would you mind if your companion developed a rash in public?
Mainly *Yes*, go to Chamber Seven

Section 8
1 Do you think there is a woman behind every successful man?
2 Would your partner's success give you personal satisfaction?
3 Are you attracted to people similar to yourself?
Mainly *Yes*, go to Chamber Eight

Now try the questions in the Chamber to which your answers have directed you.

(*Important* If your answers have led you to two or more Chambers, answer the questions in each one before moving to Chamber Sixteen or turning to the Answers.)

EAST WING

If you answer mainly *Yes* to the questions below, move to the appropriate Chamber(s).

Section 9
1 Would you go out again with someone who took you to a cheap restaurant?
2 Would you have guilt feelings if you won a fortune?
3 Do you think poverty is a major cause of marital unhappiness?
Mainly *Yes*, go to Chamber Nine

Section 10
1 'The whole world loves a lover'. Do you agree?
2 Would you rather give a separate party for certain friends?
3 Have you thought of having your family tree drawn up?
Mainly *Yes*, go to Chamber Ten

Section 11
1 Would you accept help from your partner's relations, if it put you under an obligation?
2 Would you like to become involved with a colleague more successful than yourself?
3 Does the boss attract you more than the office Adonis?
Mainly *Yes*, go to Chamber Eleven

Section 12
1 Would you be embarrassed to introduce an outlandishly dressed friend to your family?
2 Do you tend to take up your friends' hobbies?
3 Would you be put off by a lover lacking in social graces?
Mainly *Yes*, go to Chamber Twelve

Section 13
1 Do you sometimes say things just to shock people?
2 Do your friends often disapprove of your lovers?
3 Do you avoid 'popular' entertainment on principle?
Mainly *Yes*, go to Chamber Thirteen

Section 14
1 Can you be satisfied with someone who is not your intellectual equal?
2 Do you react badly to criticism?
3 Do you easily tolerate indecision in your partner?
Mainly *Yes*, go to Chamber Fourteen

Section 15
1 Are you put off people if you do not share their views?
2 Do you shun relationships with flamboyant, extrovert people?
3 Do you find opposites attract?
Mainly *Yes*, go to Chamber Fifteen

Now try the questions in the Chamber to which your answers have directed you.

(*Important* If your answers have led you to two or more Chambers, answer the questions in each one before moving to Chamber Sixteen or turning to the Answers.)

why your partner lets you down sometimes?
3 Do you try to give constructive advice if your partner has a problem?
Mostly *Yes*, move to Chamber Sixteen
Mostly *No*, read Answer 1 on page 228

...ber Sixteen

with someone else?
3 If your lover's letters are full of work details, and few endearments, do you find that your feelings cool off a little?
Mostly *Yes*—read Answer 4 on page 228
Mostly *No*—move to Chamber Sixteen

Mostly *No* – read Answer 3 on page 228

The Castle Game: Answers

Answer 1
You need a *parent figure* — what you are really looking for in a relationship, is someone to mother/father you, to give you the degree of tolerance and protection and indulgence that only a child should really expect. . . . .

Answer 2
You want *relief of loneliness* — loneliness is a great problem, and people can be driven to commit themselves very unwisely rather than face any more time alone.

Answer 3
You just want a *listener* — this really has been known to influence the course of true love! To pour your troubles into a sympathetic ear is comforting. You feel you need to be understood and appreciated.

Answer 4
This is a difficult area in which to see clearly, but *emotionalism* seems to be more the question than love. You are 'in love with love'! This can mean either being so fascinated by one's own reactions when in a state of love, that the loved object becomes relatively unimportant, or that all you really want is someone to love *you*.

Answer 5
Sex pure and simple is what you want! Obviously it is fundamental to you, but make sure that 'I love you!' means a little more than 'I want to make love to you!', or that 'I want to live with you for ever!' doesn't only mean 'I want us to make love all day and every day!' A little unrealistic for a long-term policy.

Answer 6
You're confusing love with *martyrdom* — he or she makes you suffer so dreadfully that you must be in love! Because the loved one is either beastly to you all the time, or keeps you at arm's length, your anguish becomes an integral (possibly the most pleasant!) part of the relationship.

Answer 7
Your girlfriend/boyfriend is chosen for *status symbol* value — something to dazzle people with! Friends will burn with jealousy when you sweep off with that dark, handsome man in his super sports car. Conversely, the man with the glamorous blonde in tow must surely impress business colleagues and less fortunate friends!

Answer 8
An *inner foil* is what you want — someone who will enhance or underline the role you see yourself in at the moment, somebody who is an extension, a magnified version of what you aspire to be.

Answer 9
The answer's simple — what you want is *money*! It *is* easier to relax with none of those niggling little quarrels about overspending, or missing the last bus home, but for you the road to happiness is paved with gold — so beware of the Midas touch! Or at least admit it!

Answer 10
Your *social status* is a problem for you — and you may find yourself choosing someone simply because they will open doors to wider, more exciting, social circles. Any combination goes as long as it's advantageous — e.g. from slum to stately home, from conventional moneyed circles to trendy intellectual clique!

Answer 11
As you must have realized by now, your *career*'s the thing! You're climbing up the ladder of success — and he/she will get you there quicker. It is easy to invest such people with a completely illusory glamour without realizing it.

Answer 12
Conformity means more to you than love. You may be choosing the same type of person your friends have chosen; or even someone who will be 'acceptable' in your home environment — worse, getting a boyfriend or girlfriend simply because your friends all have one, or because your parents have pushed you into it.

Answer 13
Non-conformity means more to you than love — at its most exaggerated it means deliberately choosing someone who will cause embarrassment to your family or friends. Motivated by petty revenge, or the desire to prove yourself a superior being — or, of course, just grown-up and independent — it can be worked at all levels.

Answer 14:
Be careful — it's *power* you want! You may be a bit of a tyrant, searching, as you seem to be, for someone weaker than yourself! Try an equal, for a change. You might find it quite a challenge.

Answer 15
You're looking for an *outer foil*, someone who will provide the necessary contrast to allow you to shine in your chosen role! If you want to be the life and soul of the party, you obviously don't want competition!

Answer 16
Love is what you want and give. Like everyone else you may want power, or relief from loneliness, or someone to look after you or set you off interestingly as well; but love for your partner will always come first. Forced to choose between your other motives and love itself, love will always win out. Congratulations! Provided you don't fall victim to any of the above schemes, you should have a very rich and satisfying life.

Consult the Oracle

Play this Victorian game, adapted from Gypsy Rickwood's Fortune Telling Book, and see what the oracle can tell you. All you need is a pack of cards. First shuffle them well and place them face-down on the table in the form of a horseshoe. Then choose one of the six questions below, concentrate hard and draw out one of the cards; the number and suit on the card you have drawn corresponds to the number of the answer to the question which has been asked. You may well be surprised at some of the answers!

(a) Does .... care for me?
(b) Why am I beloved? (Lady)
(c) Why am I beloved? (Gentleman)
(d) How many times shall I fall in love?
(e) Am I blinded by love?
(f) What will first strike me about the person I am to marry?

DOES .... CARE FOR ME?

Diamonds

1 Eternally dreaming of you in absence.
2 No.
3 Not yet.
4 Too selfish to care much.
5 Regards it as a jest.
6 Madly devoted.
7 Less than last year.
8 With silent adoration.
9 Too fickle by nature.
10 Try to forget.
Kn As a friend.
Qn Declare yourself and you will discover.
Kg With increasing warmth.

Hearts

1 With varying intensity of feeling.
2 Sometimes hates the thought of you.
3 Is trying to forget.
4 Yes, do not misunderstand the long silence.
5 Sorrowfully and without any hope.
6 Not one bit.
7 Better in absence.
8 Only when in need of pecuniary assistance.
9 As a safety valve.
10 Against all better judgments.
Kn With great loyalty, seeing how trying you are.
Qn When feeling homesick.
Kg Adores you always.

Clubs

1 Do you expect it? Better not.
2 Is temperamentally shallow, and cannot care.
3 Will care when it is too late.
4 Nothing can alter such affection.
5 Has entirely forgotten you already.
6 Is deliberately unfaithful.
7 Finds distraction elsewhere.
8 Cannot be relied upon for long.
9 You mistake kindness for something warmer.
10 Too unimaginative to care.
Kn Is playing you false.
Qn Never has and never will.
Kg In spite of everything, yes.

Spades

1 Does not feel any too sure.
2 You are one of many.
3 Yes, very dearly.
4 Has departed in a temper.
5 Too jealous and easily upset to care.
6 You are the only pebble on the beach.
7 With increasing intensity.
8 No, it is all pretence.
9 Even though pledged elsewhere.
10 Ever since you first met.
Kn With a passing fancy.
Qn Have not the years proved it so?
Kg Yes, and is very much annoyed that it is so.

WHY AM I BELOVED? (Lady)

Diamonds

1 He does not really mean it.
2 For your material advantages.
3 For your charm.
4 That happy laugh.
5 Your good sense appeals to him.
6 Placidity, verging upon dullness, pleases him.
7 You always agree with him.
8 You are his Aphrodite.
9 Because he wished for somebody just like you.
10 Because you were so good to him.
Kn You cheered his loneliness.
Qn You encouraged his hopes.
Kg For your endless tactfulness.

Hearts

1 He approves of your views on life.

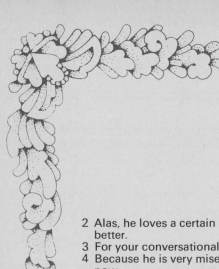

2 Alas, he loves a certain lady even better.
3 For your conversational powers.
4 Because he is very miserable just now.
5 He thinks it adds lustre to his reputation.
6 Vanity on his part.
7 He depends upon you.
8 For purely selfish reasons.
9 For your beauty.
10 He is sentimental by nature.
Kn Because you are an heiress.
Qn He likes clinging ivy.
Kg He thinks you are wonderful.

Clubs

1 Because you are good and trusting.
2 Not for your beauty.
3 He thinks you very practical.
4 He wants a good housekeeper.
5 He is tired of change.
6 He feels you to be his mental equal.
7 Because you are young and kittenish.
8 He wants to take you from another.
9 For the sake of variety.
10 He wants a good comrade.
Kn You have stood by him through so much.
Qn A mad and passing fancy for you only and no more.
Kg Out of contrariness.

Spades

1 From long association.
2 Your spirited repartee pleases him.
3 You are the tragic centre of his life.
4 You remind him of his first wife.
5 Because you caught him on the rebound.
6 No one can explain it at all.
7 You fascinate all, why not him?
8 He likes to be in the fashion.
9 For your fortitude.
10 You bring romance into his life.
Kn The circumstances under which you met account for it.
Qn He sees in you a darner of socks.
Kg Youth calls to youth.

WHY AM I BELOVED?
(Gentleman)

Diamonds

1 Pity's akin to love.
2 You are not beloved, you are respected.
3 Because you are a coming man.
4 It is your hearty manner.
5 She has great faith in your judgments.
6 She prefers quantity to quality.
7 Because everyone else dislikes you.
8 She adores success.

9 Weakness appeals to her.
10 She isn't sure that she does.
Kn Because you always make a point of avoiding her.
Qn There is no one else in her life at the moment.
Kg Long habit accounts for it.

Hearts

1 She likes your grand manner.
2 You are her last chance.
3 She has angled for you for a long time.
4 She hopes to make something of you.
5 She mistakes your stupidity for strong silence.
6 You are such a contrast to your predecessor.
7 Your masterful ways impress her.
8 You have the gift of compliment.
9 She thinks you a celebrity.
10 Her demands are not exacting.
Kn She feels that you rely on her.
Qn For your debonaire manner.
Kg Only by way of variety.

Clubs

1 There are times when she detests you.
2 She is maternally affectionate.
3 Because she is never sure of you.
4 You have many tastes and interests in common.
5 Because her people oppose it.
6 'Because you are you', as no doubt she has said.
7 Your youth appeals to her maturity.
8 Because she can trample upon you.
9 She only wants to take you from a friend.
10 She is a man-eater; beware of her, she loves everyone in turn.
Kn She is a slave to your will and adores you.
Qn You know how to manage her.
Kg She thinks you deeply wronged.

Spades

1 For that high-handed way you have.
2 She admires your sulky charm and moodiness.
3 Because you take her out so much.
4 She only pretends it.
5 She could listen to you for ever without being bored.
6 Because weakness appeals to her.
7 She wishes to have a comfortable home.
8 She is too shallow to have a real reason.
9 She looks upon you as her superior.
10 She worships your heroicness.
Kn Your wisdom — of course.
Qn Because you are so generous.
Kg For your great goodness.

HOW MANY TIMES SHALL I FALL IN LOVE?

Diamonds

1 Once and for ever.
2 Every time you go to a new place.
3 Often. With heartbreaking consequences.
4 Once in early and once in very late life.
5 You begin in the schoolroom.
6 Never at all.
7 Once, when it is too late.
8 Once against your better judgment.
9 You are fickle and cold-hearted and do not love anyone but yourself.
10 Your fidelity is the admiration of all.
Kn A lonely life awaits you.
Qn Often, but in vain.
Kg You have a true and loyal heart.

Hearts

1 You are always finding a new star.
2 The last is always the best.
3 Your Irish blood makes you faithful.
4 You are an anchorite.
5 You flit from flower to flower.
6 You will, once too often.
7 Often, but soon over.
8 When it least suits your plans.
9 You will break all records.
10 When you go East.
Kn You boast and will be punished.
Qn Take care; you number is up.
Kg If you go South.

Clubs

1 You cannot resist dark eyes.
2 Oh! Those endearing young charms.
3 With one after another.
4 You enjoy doing so.
5 In Normandy.
6 Very unwisely.
7 Disastrously.
8 Wait a year or so.
9 You will walk slowly into it.
10 It will come and go like a dream.
Kn You are doing so now.
Qn Alas, you cannot forget the past.
Kg Frequently.

Spades

1 You always love unsuitably.
2 You love an illusion.
3 You have put all that aside for good.
4 No one can keep count.
5 You are too fastidious.
6 For a brief spell.
7 A midsummer madness.
8 Once, and never recover.
9 You did, long ago.
10 You are too shallow.
Kn On summer seas.
Qn Twice with the same person.
Kg You love a memory.

AM I BLINDED BY LOVE?

Diamonds

1 You are. Seek not to see.
2 No, you see everything too clearly.
3 You prefer it so — wisely.
4 No, you are too intelligent.
5 You are perfectly correct in your judgments.
6 Yes, you are behaving foolishly.
7 It is not Love which blinds you.
8 Yes, but it does not matter.
9 No.
10 Fate will loose the bandage.
Kn You close your eyes deliberately.
Qn Nothing can blind you.
Kg It is important for you to forget.

Hearts

1 Better so.
2 Wilfully.
3 You desire not to see.
4 Not you!
5 It makes for peace that you are.
6 No, you always suspect everyone.
7 You close your eyes at times.
8 You might alter your judgments were you not.
9 Blinded by selfishness.
10 Indeed you are not.
Kn Through great consideration.
Qn Ever so little.
Kg You are thinking of someone else.

Clubs

1 You will not remain so.
2 Expect a shock.
3 There is nothing to fear.
4 You are very foolish in this respect.
5 All who love well do not love wisely.
6 Remain contentedly short-sighted.
7 You have eyes like gimlets.
8 There is nothing to see except beauty.
9 Your mind is set upon a different object.

10 No, only dazzled.
Kn Do not exaggerate; you see well enough.
Qn You wear rose-coloured spectacles.
Kg You never will be.

Spades

1 Kindness makes you so.
2 Remain so or your vanity will suffer.
3 Not at all.
4 Open your eyes and face facts.
5 To the blind all things are sudden.
6 Greatly to your own advantage.
7 Leave it at that.
8 All is well.
9 No, you do not appreciate what you have.
10 In a special manner.
Kn Occasionally.
Qn You were, but, alas, you are so no longer.
Kg You know all too well that nothing is hidden, nor need it be.

WHAT WILL FIRST STRIKE ME ABOUT THE PERSON I AM TO MARRY?

Diamonds

1 Heartiness.
2 Mournfulness.
3 A fine patriotism.
4 Love of games.
5 The magic of a smile.
6 Eyes of most unholy blue.
7 Piano fingers.
8 A good profile.
9 A certain defiance.
10 Loud taste in clothes.
Kn A high colour.
Qn Red-gold hair.
Kg A determination to do all the talking.

Hearts

1 Down-cast eyes.

2 A very smart appearance.
3 You will be anything but well impressed.
4 Tremendous self-assurance.
5 An aristocratic calm.
6 Eyes of a different colour.
7 Dimples.
8 Raven hair.
9 A very cold, rather aloof and formal manner.
10 Something bird-like.
Kn That thrilling personality.
Qn A silvery voice.
Kg. A slim and graceful poise.

Clubs

1 Your first impression is hostile.
2 After a time you will grow used to a squint.
3 A gushing manner.
4 You will be frankly bored.
5 Undeniable beauty.
6 Strong silence.
7 Sympathy.
8 Happiness of temperament.
9 Buoyancy.
10 Friendliness.
Kn A steady stare.
Qn A determination to become introduced to you.
Kg A charm of weakness.

Spades

1 That southern charm you know so well.
2 Shyness amounting to gaucherie.
3 Pushfulness.
4 A stormy silence.
5 A sort of worldly wisdom.
6 Eagerness.
7 Out-spokenness.
8 An effect of wealth.
9 Good manners.
10 Something wrong somewhere.
Kn Youth and elegance.
Qn Depression.
Kg That all-conquering smile.

IDENTILOVE

Many of us have fairly definite ideas of what we would like in a girlfriend or boyfriend but when it gets down to what they actually *look* like, the picture goes a bit blurry at the edges! So here's a way to design your own 'perfect partner' – even if you don't consider yourself as a budding Michelangelo.

Answer the questions in Part 1 of the quiz, and write down the key letter you choose for each answer. Then look at Part 2 and find the various characteristics signified by the letters. Draw or trace them on to the basic face shown in Part 3. Finally, read the instructions in Part 4, and you can interpret the motives behind your choice!

PART ONE

1 With a completely new girlfriend/boyfriend, would you prefer that they . . .
A Came up and introduced themselves to you in a natural and friendly way?
B Were obviously interested in you from the word 'go'?
C Were someone you knew already?
D Were introduced to you by a close friend?

2 First conversations can be awkward but to your relief you find that he or she . . .
E Has a lot of interesting things to say.
F Is so fascinating and amusing that you don't need to worry about your own conversation.
G Has a lot of interests in common with you.
H Wants to go to a pop concert, so there's no need to talk much.

3 You tell a friend about your new date, and emphasize that . . .
I He/she is tremendously sophisticated.
J He/she is absolutely mad about you.
K You suit each other ideally.
L He's not HER type at all!/she's not HIS type at all!

4 Imagine that your new boyfriend or girlfriend has borrowed the family car. You have a minor accident, damaging a door. Arriving back, you face his or her father who is FURIOUS. Your date . . .
M Keeps cool and takes all the blame.
N Generally defends you and manages to placate father with charm.
O Tactfully keeps out of the way, letting you sort it out.

5 You enjoy going out with this particular date because . . .
P He arranges everything beautifully and seems to know intuitively just what you want to do/She always knows where she wants to go to, and where the most interesting things are going on.
Q He always gets in touch BETWEEN dates/she is always pleased when you phone her.
R He/she fits in with your suggestions.
S He likes to go out on regular days of the week, so you always know where you are.

You should now have five key letters. Match these with the features below (in the appropriate column), and draw or trace them on to the basic face in Part 3.

PART TWO

PART THREE

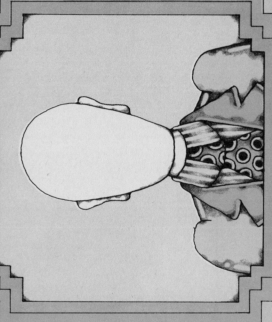

GIRLS

A Well cared-for hair, not too exaggerated in style. B Long, romantic hair. C Soft, fluffy, feminine style. D Casual, slightly fly-away style. E Eyes—dark-looking and steady. Laughter lines. F Eyes—large, long-lashed, and alluring. G Eyes—light-looking, straightforward but far-away look. H Eyes—round, light-coloured, curly lashes. I Eyebrows—well shaped, evenly curved. J Eyebrows—firmly arched. K Eyebrows—fine and almost straight. L Eyebrows—delicate, and higher at inner corners than outer, faintly questioning. M Lips—gently curving and smiling. N Lips—sensuous, full and soft. O Lips—firm, straight, not very full. P Nose—straight, medium-sized, regular. Q Nose—well-shaped, curvy, slightly uptilted. R Nose—small, very uptilted. S Nose—long and a little irregular. **Optional extra**: A liberal sprinkling of freckles.

BOYS

A Young style, hair brushed forward and sideways. B Long, trendy hair. C Slightly casual, untidy style. D Neat, rather traditional hair style. E Eyes—dark with lines around them. F Eyes—heavily lidded, sensuous. G Eyes—ordinary, light and straightforward. H Eyes—with heavy, masculine glasses. I Eyebrows—thick, evenly curved. J Eyebrows—very arched. K Eyebrows—fine and rather straight. L Eyebrows—fine, higher at the inner corners, faintly questioning. M Lips—straight and firm. Not full. N Lips—full and sensuous (above) or wide and smiling (below). O Lips—delicate and somewhat sensitive. P Nose—well shaped and slim. Q Nose—good-sized and masculine. R Nose—uptilted, boyish. S Nose—longish, with indentation on upper lip. **Optional extra**: A well-shaped, thick moustache.

PART FOUR ANSWERS & EXPLANATIONS

INTRODUCTION

There it is—the picture of your ideal girl or boyfriend! Do you feel like keeping it in mind, so that you'll recognize him or her, when you meet? If you don't really like the face, your difficulties may stem from the fact that you're looking for the wrong type! Ask yourself what's wrong with the face, and then see our analysis in the appropriate group. Is it too old or unattractive? (Group 1); lacking in character? (Group 2); weak or immature? (Group 3); or is it basically okay but with one or two bad points? (Group 4).

GROUP ONE

Too Old, Unattractive or Rather Boring

You're not very confident, and consequently you go for the type of person with firm ideas and opinions. After a while you probably find them too over-bearing and this may lead to quarrels which make you feel even less secure! Forget about the "ideal" person for a while. Try to get to know *yourself* a little better, and you'll find it easier to discover the type who definitely would suit you.

GROUP TWO

Nothing Special, Characterless

You just aren't fussy enough! You like almost everybody—especially if they want to go out with you. All you really want is as many dates as possible each week. And, lucky you, you'll probably get them. But you'd better forget your dream of a real 'romance'—that isn't what you really want at present. Don't worry, it will come. For the moment you'd better stick with the less exciting but safer type whose face you have chosen.

GROUP THREE

Too Immature or Weak

You possibly pretend to have a fantastically romantic and exciting life, but underneath you are rather timid. Although you feel you must keep up with your friends, you really find that dating scares you. Try not to be so frightened of the real world. Take up new interests; try to make as many new friends as possible. You'll find most of them are as shy of you as you are of them! As your confidence grows, you'll attract more interesting people, and be able to choose properly!

GROUP FOUR

More or Less Okay

Well, nothing's ever quite perfect, and it's probably asking for disappointment to lay hard and fast rules about what you want in the way of romance! Some of the best relationships are between people who would never have chosen each other in theory!

Don't take this quiz too seriously and above all don't start looking in earnest for the person you've drawn! Remember, though that you shouldn't expect to find complete perfection in one person. Nobody's perfect—not even you!

SENSUOUS

1 Do you like the challenge of opposition?
2 Would you depend on your partner for moral/emotional support?
3 Can you stand criticism?
Mostly *Yes*, answer questions A.
Mostly *No*, answer questions B.

A
1 Do you admire strength of character?
2 Would complete freedom in a relationship drive you too far?

3 Would someone who lives in a dream-world annoy you?
Mostly *Yes*, go to Bay 1. Mostly *No*, bypass B and go on to Bay 6.

B
1 Must your partner have a similar life-style to yours?
2 Would someone without your zest for life bore you?
3 Do you want to be put on a pedestal?
Mostly *Yes*, go to Bay 6. Mostly *No*, go to Bay 1.

PRO-

1 Do you enjoy difficult relatiships?
2 Could you cope with a spethrift?
3 Are a sense of fun and sexprowess of primary importanceyour partner?
Mostly *Yes*, answer questions
Mostly *No*, answer questions

A
1 Would you like an ultra-smissive partner?

ROMANTIC

1 Do you fall for glamorous people?
2 Do you enjoy uncertainty in a relationship?
3 Must life always be a whirl of pleasure?
Mostly *Yes*, answer questions A. Mostly *No*, answer questions B.

A
1 Is strong attraction more important than stability?
2 Do you despise self-pity in others?

3 Are you bored by constancy?
Mostly *Yes*, go to Bay 6. Mostly *No*, bypass B and go on to Bay 4.

B
1 Do you tend to be too unrealistic?
2 Would infidelity upset you terribly?
3 Do you ever think of qualities you'd want in a long-term partner?
Mostly *Yes*, go to Bay 4. Mostly *No*, go to Bay 6.

TRANQUIL

1 Do you need to be pushed into action?
2 Do you like a strong decisive approach?
3 Do you find idealistic people immature?
Mostly *Yes*, answer questions A. Mostly *No*, answer questions B.

A
1 Do you want someone to look up to?
2 Can you cope with arguments?
3 Can you stand physical violence?

Mostly *Yes*, go to Bay 3. Mostly *No*, bypass B and go on to Bay 4.

B
1 Do you want to share your lover's dreams?
2 Would you secretly like a Hollywood-style romance?
3 Are 'sweet nothings' essential to love?
Mostly *Yes*, go to Bay 4. Mostly *No*, go to Bay 3.

THE BO

If you w
meet your
likely
among the o
find you
and answe
questions

DYNAMIC

1 Is being loved an ego-trip?
2 Would you mind if your partner were more successful than you?
3 Is being admired by your partner one of the most important aspects of love?
Mostly *Yes*, answer questions A.
Mostly *No*, answer questions B.

A
1 Are you easily moved to jealousy?
2 Do you see home as a haven?

3 Do you want total devotion?
Mostly *Yes*, go to Bay 3. Mostly *No*, bypass B and go on to Bay 5.

B
1 Should couples be free as individuals?
2 Do you hate the clinging type?
3 Are you bored by people who won't answer back?
Mostly *Yes*, go to Bay 5. Mostly *No*, go to Bay 3.

OPTIMISTIC

1 Are you upset by moodiness or apathy in others?
2 Do you find 'fanciful thinking' boring?
3 Do forceful people attract you?
Mostly *Yes*, answer questions A. Mostly *No*, answer questions B.

A
1 Do you dislike too many demands being made on you?
2 Do you find very deep relationships too restricting?
3 Can you let the person you love

have complete freedom?
Mostly *Yes*, go to Bay 5. Mostly *No*, bypass B and go on to Bay 7.

B
1 Do you think most people are attracted by opposites?
2 Do you find people with different opinions from your own stimulating?
3 Do you often fall in love with quiet people?
Mostly *Yes*, go to Bay 7. Mostly *No*, go to Bay 5.

IF

1 Would you lose respect fo
indecisive person?
2 Could you be happy with s
one less emotional than you
3 Do you want a full social
Mostly *Yes*, answer question
Mostly *No*, answer question

A
1 Do you value independen
2 Is a sense of humour esse
in a partner?
3 Does good-heartedness

o you tolerate weak people?
Would you enjoy playing the
etual protector figure?
tly *Yes*, bypass B and go on to
2. Mostly *No*, move to Bay 1.

Must you always have your
way?
o you like being the boss?
re you a gentle lover?
tly *Yes*, go to Bay 2.
tly *No*, go to Bay 1.

DEPENDENT

1 Are you easily upset by un-flattering remarks?
2 Do you want one steady love?
3 Do you want to be organized by someone?
Mostly *Yes*, answer questions A.
Mostly *No*, answer questions B.

A
1 Is affection ultimately more important than passion?
2 Do you need someone sympathetic to whom you can confide your worries and problems?

3 Would honesty be an essential virtue in someone you loved?
Mostly *Yes*, go to Bay 2. Mostly *No*, bypass B and go on to Bay 8.

B
1 Do you find slightly 'mad' people exciting?
2 Do you believe quarrelling clears the air?
3 Do you want to be understood emotionally?
Mostly *Yes*, go to Bay 8. Mostly *No*, go to Bay 2.

REALISTIC

1 Are you patient with others?
2 Do you like to be responsible for someone's emotional welfare?
3 Would you be upset if you weren't included in your partner's plans?
Mostly *Yes*, answer questions A. Mostly *No*, answer questions B.

A
1 Do you enjoy quiet evenings?
2 Can you always keep cheerful?

3 Do you want to be indispensable to your lover?
Mostly *Yes*, go to Bay 12. Mostly *No*, bypass B and go on to Bay 11.

B
1 Should couples 'live and let live'?
2 Do you find depression catching?
3 Do you want a partner with guts?
Mostly *Yes*, move to Bay 11. Mostly *No*, go to Bay 12.

DIFFIDENT

1 When depressed, do you want to be told to snap out of it?
2 Do unpractical people annoy you?
3 Do you dislike being lectured?
Mostly *Yes*, answer questions A. Mostly *No*, answer questions B.

A
1 Do placid, easy-going people attract you?
2 Do you want to be treated firmly?
3 Do you like strong characters?

Mostly *Yes*, go to Bay 12. Mostly *No*, bypass B and go on to Bay 10.

B
1 Is communication the first requisite for love?
2 Do you like getting very 'involved'?
3 Do you think intellectual ability is all-important?
Mostly *Yes*, go to Bay 10. Mostly *No*, go to Bay 12.

MAZE

r the maze
follow the
till you
h your Bay.
d the direc-
s and all will
evealed!

INDEPENDENT

1 Would you be happy with a 'dreamer'?
2 Do other people's activities interest you?
3 Can you tolerate vagueness in others?
Mostly *Yes*, answer questions A. Mostly *No*, answer questions B.

A
1 Would you be put off by someone whose conversation was boring?
2 Do you dislike the mundane?
3 Does intelligence matter more than looks?

Mostly *Yes*, go to Bay 9. Mostly *No*, bypass B and go on to Bay 11.

B
1 Would you be put off by a forgetful person?
2 Do you value sociability more than intellect?
3 Do you want someone dependable?
Mostly *Yes*, go to Bay 11. Mostly *No*, go to Bay 9.

ate for any faults?
ly *Yes*, go to Bay 7. *Mostly*
ypass B and go on to Bay 8.

st your partner always under-
d you?
o you need a close emotional
n?
o you want to control some-
else's feelings?
ly *Yes*, go to Bay 8. Mostly
o to Bay 7.

INTELLECTUAL

1 Do you prefer independent people?
2 Would you find too many emotional demands irksome?
3 Would an over-sensitive partner annoy you?
Mostly *Yes*, answer questions A.
Mostly *No*, answer questions B.

A
1 Do irrational feelings in others irritate you?
2 Are you embarrassed when adults cry?

3 Would you find a dynamic person fun?
Mostly *Yes*, go to Bay 9. Mostly *No*, bypass B and go on to Bay 10.

B
1 Do you enjoy heart-to-heart talks?
2 Should your partner be a listener rather than a talker?
3 Can you cope with emotional scenes?
Mostly *Yes*, go to Bay 10.
Mostly *No*, go to Bay 9.

The Love Maze: Answers

Bay 1 Protective and Sensuous
Both partners would derive great pleasure from this relationship, giving each other mutual help, and satisfying each other's wishes. If the protective partner realizes and can fulfil the sensuous lover's need for physical stimulation, then it should be a lasting relationship. This concerns not only sex, but also the need for emotional warmth and material comforts. In being made to feel wanted and needed, the protective person can keep doubts about his/her own identity at bay.

The only slight danger in this relationship is that the sensuous partner might find protection too suffocating, and go off pleasure-seeking. The protective person has to make sure that the sensuous partner doesn't entirely lose himself/herself in sensation.
Protective – Turn to Bay 2 for your second-best partner. Then turn to Conclusion 8.
Sensuous – Turn to Bay 6 for your second-best partner. Then turn to Conclusion 7.

Bay 2 Protective and Dependent
It is in the protective person's nature to want to look after someone, and it is in the dependent person's nature to want to be looked after, so in many ways this is an ideal relationship. The dependent person seeks security and a sense of well-being, even the sense of identity, which the protective partner is able to give. The protective partner has a very clear-cut role as a kind of emotional provider, and being one of the strong caring for the weak will gratify his/her emotional needs.

The danger of this relationship is that the dependent person, although wanting support, may sometimes resent dominance and too much interference from the protective partner; and equally the protective partner may tire of protecting. In this case, the less rigidly the roles are played the better.
Protective – Turn to Bay 1 for your second-best partner. Then turn to Conclusion 8.
Dependent – Turn to Bay 8 for your second-best partner. Then turn to Conclusion 1.

Bay 3 Tranquil and Dynamic
This combination of an introverted person (Tranquil) and an extroverted person (Dynamic) is extremely good socially. The couple complement each other, each being attracted by qualities in the other which they lack in themselves. The calmness of the tranquil lover makes a good foil to the adventuring spirit of the dynamic one. The dynamic partner expresses the tranquil partner's feelings, and fights the world for him/her. In return, the tranquil partner brings an atmosphere of peace and serenity and enables the dynamic partner to have a comfortable respite from the competitive pace of his/her life. The tranquil person accepts aggression without hostility and the dynamic person enjoys being the leader.

Possible dangers are that in time the dynamic partner may doubt the value of his/her own aggression as being something which is not displayed in the other person, and that each partner may lose interest in the other because they are so different from each other. However, this is basically a good relationship, and will do both partners good on a short-term basis.

Tranquil – Turn to Bay 4 for your second-best partner. Then turn to Conclusion 2.
Dynamic – Turn to Bay 5 for your second-best partner. Then turn to Conclusion 11.

Bay 4 Tranquil and Romantic
This is a good match and one where both partners should find themselves on the same wavelength. Both are dreamers and tend to find imaginative solutions to their problems. They get on well together, but if the romantic partner is a woman she may find herself wishing that her tranquil lover were more of a hero figure. However, there are compensations for this, for the tranquil partner is easily contented, and will enjoy sharing the fantasy world of the romantic person. In their own minds, they will create a perfect relationship and they are likely to be sentimental and nostalgic and very loving as a couple. It is likely to be a long-lasting relationship which may very successfully lead to marriage.

A possible danger is that their mental image of their relationship as perfect may fade. If it does, both will have a tendency to think that the grass will be greener somewhere else, or with someone else, and if they do split up, this will be the most likely cause.
Tranquil – Turn to Bay 3 for your second-best partner. Then turn to Conclusion 2.
Romantic – Turn to Bay 6 for your second-best partner. Then turn to Conclusion 6.

Bay 5 Dynamic and Optimistic
Each partner here is attracted by the lively qualities the other possesses, and with which he/she can identify. They are both extroverts, and they understand each other, have the same capacity for enjoyment and sociability and the same attitude to the outside world. They will get on well with the same kind of people, and have the same enthusiasms for things. Life for this couple will be fun and vital and very lively, and they can also help each other in many ways: the optimist will cheer the dynamic person when there are setbacks, and will also refuse to take hostility seriously when it occurs: and because the optimistic partner tends to take life at face value, the dynamic partner can help him/her to become more aware of people's motives.

A possible danger is that one or both partners may become dissatisfied with the lack of communication on emotional matters, but on the whole, this should be a good combination of personalities for a long-term relationship.
Dynamic – Turn to Bay 3 for your second-best partner. Then turn to Conclusion 11.
Optimistic – Turn to Bay 7 for your second-best partner. Then turn to Conclusion 10.

Bay 6 Sensuous and Romantic
An excellent combination. Both partners have rich inner worlds, and what goes on in their minds is real to them, so they act out their fantasies together. The sensuous lover is likely to understand the romantic more than the other way round, because the romantic partner is far more involved in his/her own fantasy world, which the sensuous partner may resent. They like love, believe in it, live for it, and radiate it to people around them. In fact, they may satisfy each other so much that they may begin to live entirely in their own world, manipulating the outside world to fit in with their fantasies. Consequently, this combination has a better chance of success as a love affair than a marriage, because the realities of earning a living, paying bills, etc., may interfere too much with the perfect world the two lovers create around themselves.
Sensuous – Turn to Bay 1 for your second-best partner. Then turn to Conclusion 7.
Romantic – Turn to Bay 4 for your second-best partner. Then turn to Conclusion 6.

Bay 7 Intuitive and Optimistic
This is a good combination for a long-term relationship or marriage. Both partners are fairly independent; neither relies on the other too much, yet they have a lot to give each other. Both like taking chances. It's in the intuitive person's nature to take risks, and the optimistic person will take chances and be adventurous without thinking of it as

a risk at all, so they will have an exciting life together. The intuitive partner may be inclined to cut himself/herself off from reality, and the optimistic partner will be a lever on reality. The intuitive partner will help the optimistic one to understand other people's feelings, and give him/her more insight into situations. But the optimistic partner will sometimes find the intuitive person difficult to understand, and the intuitive might sometimes find the optimist lacking in sensitivity.

As a couple they will have to make an effort to understand each other's point of view or they may eventually end up at cross-purposes.

Intuitive – Turn to Bay 8 for your second-best partner. Then turn to Conclusion 5.

Optimistic – Turn to Bay 5 for your second-best partner. Then turn to Conclusion 10.

Bay 8   Intuitive and Dependent
This is a useful combination for a love affair or marriage. The intuitive person has empathy and will be able to sense the needs of the dependent person, though the help given will be emotional rather than practical. It should be a very close relationship if the dependent person is willing to contribute to it. The intuitive person will be able to mediate between the dependent partner and the outside world. Intuitive people are good at adapting to new situations and will carry the dependent person along with them. The intuitive partner, especially in a marriage, will need the dependent person as an anchor and to provide stability for a life-style.

Possible dangers? The intuitive partner might find the dependent person's problems hampering after a while, and the dependent partner may be made to feel insecure by the apparent inconsistency of the intuitive.

Intuitive – Turn to Bay 7 for your second-best partner. Then turn to Conclusion 5.

Dependent – Turn to Bay 2 for your second-best partner. Then turn to Conclusion 1.

Bay 9
Independent and Intellectual
Both partners here mutually agree to 'do their own thing', and there is a lot of freedom in the relationship. The intellectual gives the independent person the stimulation of knowledge and new ideas, while the independent partner helps the intellectual over difficulties in the relationship when the problems are emotional ones. The independent partner, not being over-emotional or over-sensitive, can cope with the intellectual's rational approach to life.

Both partners can pursue their own lives within the relationship, or in marriage. The intellectual has a tendency to bottle up feelings, trying to cope with life by formulating complex theories. To the independent lover the intellectual may sometimes seem intolerant and efforts must be made to understand each other's point of view if this is to be a lasting and satisfying relationship.

Independent – Turn to Bay 11 for your second-best partner. Then turn to Conclusion 9.

Intellectual – Turn to Bay 10 for your second-best partner. Then turn to Conclusion 4.

Bay 10   Intellectual and Diffident
Both the intellectual and the diffident lover find facing life difficult and can be a great help to each other, especially in a short-term relationship. The intellectual can help by rationalizing the diffident lover's view of life, while the diffident lover will give more emotional understanding of life to the intellectual. The more extrovert the intellectual partner is, the greater chance of success for this relationship. It should be a very close relationship, where both partners try to understand each other, and where each feels concerned for the other's welfare. It will also be good for the ego of both partners. In the long term, however, the main danger would be that of lack of communication if one or both partners withdrew into themselves, and it is a socially limiting combination in the long view, as neither partner can be used as a springboard to the outside world.

Intellectual – Turn to Bay 9 for your second-best partner. Then turn to Conclusion 4.

Diffident – Turn to Bay 12 for your second-best partner. Then turn to Conclusion 3.

Bay 11   Realistic and Independent
A very good combination – each should find it easy to live with the other, and the outlook for a long-term relationship is good. Both partners have very separate identities and yet they are not isolated from each other. Both enjoy the present, rather than looking back into the past, and with a realist in the partnership they should be able to plan successfully for the future. They like the same things and have the same aims, and are both intolerant of nostalgia and sentiment. Democratic people, they have an outward direction to their lives and are unlikely to find themselves involved in hair-brained schemes. Each is involved and interested in the other's life, and neither will wish to dominate or take over from the other.

They are both capable of lasting friendships, but the danger might be that as they are both so self-reliant, they may find that they do not need each other much.

Realistic – Turn to Bay 12 for your second-best partner. Then turn to Conclusion 12.

Independent – Turn to Bay 9 for your second-best partner. Then turn to Conclusion 9.

Bay 12   Diffident and Realistic
This is a good combination, with one partner complementing the other. Different in personality and outlook, they yet have a lot to give each other. The realist may be of considerable practical help to the diffident lover, who is inclined to exaggerate problems and dwell on the worst aspect of things. The diffident lover is a help to the realist in their emotional life, bringing understanding and emotional depth to the relationship; he/she is inclined to form very strong affections and this will be both enjoyable and highly flattering to the realist.

In a long-term relationship there is the possibility of lack of communication unless both partners make an effort – impatience on the part of the realist, and feelings of isolation on the part of the diffident lover can put up barriers. If this difficulty can be overcome, long-term prospects should be good.

Diffident – Turn to Bay 10 for your second-best partner. Then turn to Conclusion 3.

Realistic – Turn to Bay 11 for your second-best partner. Then turn to Conclusion 12.

The Love Maze: Conclusions

Conclusion 1 – Dependent

Dependent with *Dependent*: This is not a good combination. Although it might be a close relationship it would become claustrophobic. You are both looking for care and protection, and are unable to fulfil this role for each other. Rather than trying to cling to each other for support, you should find strong partners to suit your needs.

With *Tranquil*. You may be attracted to a tranquil person across a crowded room, but the problem is, who would make the first move? If you leave it to them, you'll still be waiting to start the beautiful relationship when it's time to draw your old-age pension.

With *Diffident.* Not the most cheerful couple in the world, but you should understand each other and have a quiet, cosy relationship. This may easily lead to marriage, but try to resist. You would be happier with someone with a more positive outlook on life.

With *Intellectual*. You would get on well with the intellectual initially, but in the long-term he/she could well cut you out of their way of thinking, and you would have difficulty in understanding their rational approach to life.

With *Romantic*. Madly attracted to each other, and you'll have a beautiful starry trip together. The problem is once the moonshine dies down, you might find him/her a tiny bit too shallow for your depth of feeling.

With *Sensuous*. You'll have a great time with him/her, but then so will everyone else . . . If you want a faithful lover, run away quick!

With *Independent*. Rather a one-sided relationship. Your need for love and companionship is stronger than theirs and this could lead to insecurity on your part in a long-term relationship.

With *Optimistic*. A good match. The optimist is fun and easy to live with. He/she won't always understand your sensitivity, but nonetheless will be a great person to have around, and you could do worse.

With *Dynamic*. He/she will sweep you off your feet all right – but watch out where you land. Dynamic isn't the one to suit your needs, not liking to take responsibility for other people; but it could be a fun relationship if not taken too seriously.

With *Realistic*. Not bad at all. The realist's outlook will be quite good for you, and although your personalities are very different you could try blending. It won't be a very deep relationship, but it will be workable.

Conclusion 2 – Tranquil

Tranquil with Tranquil: Too much tranquility may change to apathy. You would understand each other well and probably be free from conflicts and hostility, but, both wanting to be led, you may be in danger of getting into a rut.

With *Dependent*. Not for you, sorry. There might be an attraction between two people who are similar in many ways and both looking for someone strong, but it would be a bit like the blind leading the blind.

With *Diffident*. You will probably have a mutual understanding with a diffident partner, and a sensitive relationship may develop. However, you would find greater fulfilment with someone who was more out-going and could give you a more action-packed life.

With *Intellectual*. Not ideal. The intellectual would be of no help in your quest for a fun social life, nor would he/she satisfy your emotional needs. Interesting for a while, but not ideal in the long run.

With *Intuitive*. A good combination for friendship or marriage. The intuitive person will lead you into all sorts of interesting situations and get on to your emotional wave-length.

With *Sensuous*. Wonderful for a while, great fun and a great ego-trip for you, but beware of a lasting relationship. The sensuous person needs taming, and you are not really equipped for the task.

With *Protective*. The protective person has your best interests at heart, and you could have an easy, pleasant life, having your problems solved for you. A strong partner like this would give you security – perhaps at the expense of your own personal ambitions!

With *Independent*. A bad deal as far as you are concerned. In marriage you would not be given a sense of belonging, as the independent person can't help going his/her own way, leaving you behind. Even in a short-term relationship you might find a lack of emotional content.

With *Optimistic*. Although the optimistic person isn't emotional, he/she likes to be involved with people, and for this reason you would get on well, and be carried into the swim of whatever was happening around you.

With *Realistic*. Another rewarding relationship between opposites. He/she will take over all practical problems and most of the day-to-day decisions – it will be up to you to make sure that love and understanding are maintained.

Conclusion 3 – Diffident

Diffident with *Diffident*: This would be a close relationship, in which you would sympathize with each other and understand each other's problems. But, although you will communicate well, your moods are so similar that rather than helping each other you may sink each other deeper into gloom.

With *Dependent*. The kind of relationship you might get involved in and live to regret. Both of you tend to stick to what is available rather than breaking new ground, and if this relationship led to marriage it would be very limiting.

With *Tranquil*. A little freer as a relationship, but this one, too, would become heavy after a while. You would be understood by your partner, but a tranquil lover isn't really in a position to do much for you.

With *Intuitive*. Good for a brief love affair or friendship, as the intuitive person can understand you and give sympathy, and you will enjoy the unpredictability of life in the company of an intuitive partner. However, in the long-term you would probably feel irritated by his/her grasshopper mind and lack of stability.

With *Romantic*. Disaster. You would have no time for each other, and probably would never come together in the first place. The romantic's view of life is immature and unreal to you, and you would find yourself without any real point of contact with him/her.

With *Sensuous*. No again. You are miles apart, and would find a sensuous partner superficial, lacking emotional understanding and unsympathetic to your needs.

With *Protective*. A very good combination. A protective person would give you a sense of belonging which would be satisfying and very comforting to you. You could get very involved in this relationship, which could be put successfully on a permanent basis.

With *Independent*. You need a close relationship, and an independent partner wouldn't ever get close enough for a long-term prospect; but it would be interesting and could work quite well as a short-term relationship.

With *Optimistic*. Attraction of opposites maybe, but for anything more than a brief acquaintance this relationship would probably come unstuck, due to the difficulty there would be in seeing each other's point of view, and in understanding each other's needs.

With *Dynamic*. A dynamic person would be good for you, enabling you to

live a more highly-charged life than would otherwise be possible. You would have to forgo a certain amount of communication, but other things would make up for this.

Conclusion 4 – Intellectual
Intellectual with *Intellectual*: You have the same rational approach to life and you stimulate each other mentally, bringing about an interesting and close relationship. However, there is a slight danger of removing yourselves from reality, and emotional problems may be difficult to cope with.

With *Dependent*. The approach to life is too different in this combination, and you would find the dependent's emotional traumas too much to cope with.

With *Tranquil*. Not ideal, but an improvement on the last relationship. The routine would become dreary after a while, with no room for personality expansion.

With *Intuitive*. An interesting combination, although the approach to life is very different. You would each give each other things to think about, although there is a danger of lack of understanding in the long term.

With *Romantic*. Good for a while, a nice break and good for your ego, but if you're thinking in terms of ever-after your outlooks and aims would clash, as Mr/Miss Romantic has never heard of logic or rationality.

With *Sensuous*. Totally opposed. You would find Mr/Miss Sensuous annoying and shallow, and he/she would find you unbearable, too.

With *Protective*. No. Protection is something you can do without and would find mentally restricting. All right if you want a nurse/mother/ benefactor, but not as a soul mate.

With *Optimistic*. Pleasant but not a very rewarding relationship as far as you are concerned. The optimist simplifies life, while you complicate it, and if the differences are exaggerated, lack of communication and misunderstanding will follow.

With *Dynamic*. Very good match – you have all the ideas and theories and your dynamic partner puts them into action. A very useful and stimulating combination.

With *Realistic*. Both being rational people, this would be a good combination. Well worth a try for a short or long-term relationship.

Conclusion 5 – Intuitive
Intuitive with *Intuitive*: A very exciting romance; you are on the same wavelength and can stimulate each other's already vivid imaginations. However, there is a danger of living in a world of your own, and losing sight of all conventional standards.

With *Tranquil*. You could help a passive person become less passive, and their sensitivity, in turn, would give an extra dimension to your life. Good for a long-term relationship if you have enough patience.

With *Diffident*. You would find a diffident person irksome after a while, although in the initial stages you would probably get on well, and understand and sympathize with their feelings and views.

With *Intellectual*. A good relationship, stimulating new ideas in both partners. However, in the long-term you might find that ideas differ too much, a rational approach to life being quite foreign to you.

With *Romantic*. A beautiful relationship for both of you, where you could get carried away into marriage. This would be fine if you could keep a grip on reality, but both being flighty characters you could go off the deep-end together instead.

With *Sensuous*. Very good for a love affair, but not for a deeper relationship. The Sensualist's simple view of life would probably lack interest for you after a while.

With *Protective*. A nice combination for a long-term relationship. The protective person would give you a secure base from which to launch your 'crazy' ways – provided you could have a certain amount of freedom.

With *Independent*. You would get on well with Mr/Miss Independent, who would be a steadying influence on you but wouldn't hamper your movements.

With *Dynamic*. Mr/Miss Dynamic is always on the go, and although you might find him/her exciting company, the pace might become too much after a while.

With *Realistic*. Not for you; total lack of understanding on both sides – and you'd end up wondering whether you and Mr/Miss Realistic belong to the same species.

Conclusion 6 – Romantic
Romantic with *Romantic*: A good relationship at the beginning, making each other's fantasies come true, being able to communicate on a magical level, but problems will come later. Your romantic ideals cannot last for ever, and when they fade you will both find it hard to face the reality of broken dreams.

With *Dependent*. You like to idealize people, and Mr/Miss Dependent wouldn't fit into your ideal. Sorry.

With *Diffident*. As with a dependent person, you would find that Mr/Miss didn't come up to your expectations as a romantic hero/heroine.

With *Intellectual*. The idea of an intellectual might appeal to you, being someone you could put on a pedestal – but in the long term you would realize you had little in common, for your views are totally different.

With *Intuitive*. You would have a beautiful relationship with Mr/Miss Intuitive – it could successfully lead to marriage if you both toned yourselves down a bit and came to grips with reality a bit more.

With *Protective*. You would enjoy this relationship for a while and then become impatient with it, so perhaps it's better not to start it in the first place – Mr/Miss Protective might be inclined to cramp your style.

With *Independent*. He/she just wouldn't live up to your image of an ideal partner and could cause you to lose faith in your fantasies.

With *Optimistic*. Quite a good prospect for marriage. Mr/Miss Optimistic is willing to go for a romantic trip and his/her cheerfulness and practical good sense would be a help to you when times were hard.

With *Dynamic*. Mr/Miss Dynamic probably appeals to you, being someone you can admire. Fine for a while, but thinking further ahead you would find him/her lacking in imagination.

With *Realistic*. Keep well away – you don't want all your illusions shattered, do you?

Conclusion 7 – Sensuous
Sensuous with *Sensuous*: You understand each other's needs and can give each other the love and enjoyment you both want. It sounds an ideal combination, but for a long-term relationship this may not be a stable match. You may find the search for pleasure gets out of hand because neither of you is good at control or order.

With *Dependent*. You would be flattered by the admiration and loving ways of a dependent person, but would probably lose interest after a while. Not for keeps.

With *Tranquil.* A good relaxing relationship if you're thinking of settling down to married bliss – Mr/Miss Tranquil would make a nice, cosy husband/wife for you.

With *Diffident.* You could give Mr/Miss Diffident a very happy time, and you'd enjoy their company for a while, but in the long run the relationship would become heavy-going and you'd look for ways out.

With *Intellectual.* Not right for you. You probably wouldn't strike up an acquaintance with Mr/Miss Intellectual in the first place, but if you did you'd realize your views on life were so different you could be living on separate planets.

With *Intuitive.* Very good for a love affair but not so good for marriage. You'd find their thinking too way-out and quickly tire of someone who lived on another plane.

With *Independent.* If you want someone who will cater for your needs and give you a life of comfort and pleasure you'd best forget Mr/Miss Independent – he/she is too self-reliant and independent for a close relationship of this kind.

With *Optimistic.* A good, easy-going relationship which would work well as a marriage. Mr/Miss Optimistic is fun to be with and would enjoy sharing your beautiful world.

With *Dynamic.* Not for you. You'd find a clash of interests right from the beginning, and Mr/Miss Dynamic is not the person to settle into your life-style – he/she would be off where the action is.

With *Realistic.* No. You'd find Mr/Miss Realist far too spartan for your tastes and he/she wouldn't understand your aims, or sympathize with them.

Conclusions 8 – Protective
Protective with *Protective*: You both feel the need to control and protect a weaker partner, and there is no scope for this in your relationship. You do not cater for each other's emotional needs enough.

With *Tranquil.* A person who would appreciate your protective instincts. His/her gentleness and calm would be an added bonus in your life, too.

With *Diffident.* You would be very good for a diffident person, giving them security – this would be a close relationship on an emotional level, provided you could cope.

With *Intellectual.* Mr/Miss Intellectual would resent your wish to control their

lives, and you would find the relationship unrewarding, because what you offer isn't sought this time.

With *Intuitive.* Not for you. You would find the intuitive person's refusal to see sense annoying, and there would probably be little common ground for communication.

With *Romantic.* You might feel protective towards a romantic person and want to 'save' them. But basically the romantic doesn't want to be saved, so it would be better to concentrate your efforts elsewhere.

With *Independent.* This could be a good alliance between equals. You are both strong people who understand each other's wish for self-assertion, but from the long-term point of view a lack of emotional ties might lead to a sense of isolation on your part.

With *Optimistic.* Although this combination would lead to a trauma-free existence, the optimist is unable to reciprocate in the close relationship you are looking for.

With *Dynamic.* If you enjoy a challenging relationship and are not afraid of fights and some conflicts, this would be a rewarding combination, and Mr/Miss Dynamic would be grateful for the sense of well-being you bring.

With *Realistic.* Another alliance between equals – you would get on together and lead a very constructive life; but because of the lack of emotional need on both sides, this combination is better suited to a business partnership than a marriage.

Conclusion 9 – Independent
Independent with *Independent*: Fine for a modern marriage between two individuals who want to express themselves and achieve their personal life-style. There is a risk that you may both become so independent that after a while you may not need each other any more, and have nothing to give each other.

With *Dependent.* Not for you. You would find Mr/Miss Dependent's emotional demands hampering and irritating and wish you hadn't tied yourself to such a restricting relationship.

With *Tranquil.* No again, for the same reasons but to a lesser degree. You are too self-reliant to understand dependence in any form.

With *Diffident.* Another fruitless relationship – your views on life are so different that understanding and

communication would be doomed from the start.

With *Intuitive.* A good relationship; although you may find Mr/Miss Intuitive difficult to understand sometimes, this would not affect the basic feeling between you.

With *Romantic.* You would not sympathize with the romantic view of life, finding it immature and lacking any kind of sense or interest. Better leave Mr/Miss Romantic to go his/her own way.

With *Sensuous.* You would find the hedonist's view of life easier to understand and to cope with. If you're a pleasure-loving person Mr/Miss Sensuous would appeal to you and make life extremely pleasant for you.

With *Protective.* You would get on well with Mr/Miss Protective and find plenty in common, but you may find difficulties will crop up if this develops into a long-term relationship, for he/she might wish to take control of you.

With *Optimistic.* A very good combination. Mr/Miss Optimist would be easy to live with, not making too many demands on you, and his/her vitality and sense of adventure would add to the relationship.

With *Dynamic.* There would be conflict in this relationship due to the dynamic person's wish to assert their will over you, but if you can compromise and be led sometimes, this will be an exciting and rewarding combination.

Conclusion 10 – Optimistic
Optimistic with *Optimistic*: A good relationship, free from too much tension or hostility. You have the same enthusiasm for life, the same sociability, and you will probably have a lot of fun together and build up a workable life-style. The only slight problem is that the relationship may not be emotionally very deep.

With *Dependent.* You would have a beneficial effect on the dependent person, and your unfailing good spirits would enable you to cope with their emotional difficulties. It may be rewarding for you for a while, but in the end you would probably tire of the responsibility.

With *Tranquil.* A very good combination. Mr/Miss Tranquil would be happy to share their lives with you, and it would be a very enjoyable and problem-free relationship.

With *Diffident.* Not for you. Although you get on well with people in general,

you would quickly tire of someone you felt was always moaning about life. This is a case where opposites don't attract.

With *Intellectual*. Not on the same wavelength, especially if the intellectual is introverted; you would find him/her dull and unco-operative after a time.

With *Romantic*. You will probably be attracted to Mr/Miss Romantic, who is willing to join in the fun and likes an exciting social life. A good combination if you can be tolerant of his/her flighty ways.

With *Sensuous*. A good combination. You will be able to adjust pleasantly to the sensualist's demand for pleasure and ease. Beautiful for a short relationship and could expand into marriage too.

With *Protective*. You would get on with Mr/Miss Protective on a superficial level, but for a deeper relationship you would find his/her concern for your welfare unnecessary and claustrophobic.

With *Realistic*. You get on well with realistic people and although you would both be happy in this relationship, perhaps emotional contact would suffer, both of you having a practical approach to life. You might find a less unemotional partner more rewarding.

Conclusion 11 – Dynamic
Dynamic with *Dynamic*: A fantastic safari or adventure team, but if you're thinking of a domestic life together, take care. Two dynamic people will stimulate each other to achieving great things, but there is a danger that hostilities will arise when you start competing with each other.

With *Dependent*. You would have little patience for a dependent person, and once you felt they had 'clung on to' you you would lose any sympathy you might have had for them.

With *Diffident*. Not for you – you would be unable to understand why you couldn't make Mr/Miss Diffident happy, and the unrewarding

relationship would leave you with a sense of failure.

With *Intellectual*. Although Mr/Miss Intellectual has different aims in life, you find his/her company stimulating, bringing new ideas which you can translate into action. A very good combination if you can be tolerant of the intellectual's seeming lack of 'go'.

With *Intuitive*. Good for a short relationship, as Mr/Miss Intuitive will also bring you new ideas and another approach to life, but in a deeper relationship you might find yourself unable to understand the intuitive's inconsistency and lack of purpose.

With *Romantic*. A good ego-trip – you will be flattered by the romantic's view of you. And then you will probably realize that you and Mr/Miss Romantic have very little common ground, and his/her 'up in the clouds' approach might become very annoying.

With *Sensuous*. A good ego-trip, again, and a good short-term relation-ship – in the long run you may find conflicting interests would prevent a deep relationship.

With *Protective*. Mr/Miss Protective would bring stability into your life, and help you during bad patches – there might be some conflict due to his/her wish to dominate, but if you can agree to be equals this would be a good relationship.

With *Independent*. The same as above, but to a lesser degree – there would be more freedom in this relationship, and a good chance of working out conflicts because of Mr/Miss Independent's tolerance and self-confidence.

With *Realistic*. Another good combina-tion. Mr/Miss Realist can take part in your plans for the future, and be a great practical help, provided interests don't clash. Compromise on both sides would help to make the relationship a success.

Conclusion 12 – Realistic
Realistic with *Realistic*: A fine combina-tion for a secure marriage with common interests, and you will probably be a

successful couple in the eyes of society, planning and achieving the goals you set for yourselves. You may, however, find that practical things take up most of your energy, and as a result emotional contact may be lacking.

With *Dependent*. You enjoy being a strong person with strong opinions, and Mr/Miss Dependent would admire you for this – a good relationship if you are able to cope with the occasional emotional scene.

With *Tranquil*. Mr/Miss Tranquil will fall in easily with your wishes, and you should be able to respond to his/her emotional warmth. Certainly a good combination.

With *Intellectual*. Although you may not regard yourself as an intellectual, you have a lot in common, especially in your rational approach to life, so you have a great deal to offer each other.

With *Intuitive*. This one won't work. Total non-understanding between people whose views are completely opposed. You would find it impossible to sympathize with lack of logic and inconsistency.

With *Romantic*. Even more of a disaster. A total lack of appeal on both sides.

With *Sensuous*. May be fun for a short time, but you would not admire the sensualist's continual demand for pleasure and ease, finding their needs a weakness rather than an attractive quality.

With *Protective*. An alliance between equals, rather like a business partner-ship, but perhaps lacking the emotional content necessary to make the relationship work as a marriage.

With *Optimistic*. A good relationship – Mr/Miss Optimistic could help you build up a good future and would enjoy the present. Emotional understanding may not always occur, but this would be made up for in other ways.

With *Dynamic*. This is a case of two headstrong people together, but if you are both willing to compromise it could be a good relationship.

CAPITAL CITY

1 Do you consider your lover's feelings before making decisions?
2 Does he/she possess qualities you don't often find in others?
3 Would you miss your lover if he/she went away for a couple of weeks?
Mostly *Yes*, read Conclusion Four. Mostly *No*, read Conclusion Five.

CASINO TOWN

1 Are you completely free from jealousy in your personal relationship?
2 Can you love more than one person at a time?
3 Do you need breathing spaces between seeing him/her?
Mostly *Yes*, read Conclusion Five. Mostly *No*, read Conclusion Four.

CASTLE TOWN

1 Could you love anyone as much as your present girl-friend/boyfriend?
2 Can you see any faults in him/her?
3 Can you take partings calmly?
Mostly *Yes*, turn back onto the Highway. Mostly *No*, read Conclusion Three.

HOLIDAY RESORT

1 When you're in love, do you stop flirting with others?
2 Does your ego withstand unflattering remarks from your lover?
3 Would you accept anything less than complete devotion from a lover?
Mostly *Yes*, turn back onto the Highway. Mostly *No*, read Conclusion Two.

COUNTRY VILLAGE

1 Can you imagine a future without your present love?
2 Would you forgive unfaithfulness in your lover?
3 Do you want to be the 'strong' partner in the relationship and dominate your lover all the time?
Mostly *Yes*, turn back to the Highway. Mostly *No*, read Conclusion One.

HIGHWAY TWO
2

HIGHWAY THREE
3

HIGHWAY FOUR
4

IS IT LOVE OR INFATUATION

HIGHWAY FOUR

1 Has your lover made you uninterested in other members of the opposite sex?
2 Does the relationship give you a feeling of constant well-being?
3 Can you forgive his/her faults? *Mostly Yes*, take Lane Four to the Capital City. *Mostly No*, take Lane Five to the Casino Town.

CONCLUSION 5

You are not infatuated and you are not in love either. If you were thinking of a specific person while answering the quiz questions, you don't seem to find the relationship very rewarding. Maybe the affair has taken on the aspect of a duty or a routine you could do without. Or maybe you have a nice pleasant relationship that floats along without much depth of feeling – for you don't appear to be exactly swept off your feet!

Alternatively, perhaps you are experimenting with several different relationships and enjoying the chase for the time being.

When you do meet someone special in your life, try this game again and see if you arrive at a different conclusion!

HIGHWAY THREE

1 Do you think of your lover incessantly?
2 Do you believe fate brought you together?
3 Would you give up anything and do anything for him/her? *Mostly Yes*, turn down Lane Three to Medieval Castle Town. *Mostly No*, carry on along the Highway.

CONCLUSION 4

You seem to have passed through all the stages of infatuation and found the real thing. You have few fantasy illusions about your relationship with your lover, for fantasy is unnecessary if you are satisfied with the real thing. You have confidence in yourself as a lover and you can accept criticism. The responsibility of being in love may sometimes make you feel anxious, but you recognize and accept that anxiety is as much a part of a relationship as loving is, and manage to cope with setbacks without too much upset.

You can enjoy a loving relationship as a natural and integrated part of your life, and you should be very happy with the partner you have chosen.

HIGHWAY ONE

1

Is your present relationship love, or is it infatuation? Follow your route along the Highway to find out.

GO

CONCLUSION 3

This is an infatuation based on sexual fantasy. We all go through such a stage during adolescence, in order to try ourselves out and to prepare ourselves for adult love.

You may find it difficult to cope with strong sexual feelings, and consequently tend to turn them into fantasy rather than acting them out. Some people in this category may have difficulty in separating themselves from their idealized parents, and they may substitute a partner who seems strange and frightening. This subconscious fear causes them to idealize their lover and think of him/her as almost superhuman. It may subside on better acquaintance, and with more experience of relationships with the opposite sex in general.

HIGHWAY TWO

1 Do you find the first meeting the most exciting?
2 Can you say 'I love you' even if you don't mean it?
3 Do you make your lover jealous to test his/her love? *Mostly Yes*, turn down Lane Two to the Holiday Resort. *Mostly No*, carry on along the Highway.

CONCLUSION 2

You are infatuated. Like other forms of infatuation, this form of loving has an illusory quality about it – in your case the illusion is required to support your doubts about yourself. You take to extremes the natural wish to prove yourself desirable to yourself and to other people. You demand extreme love and admiration from your partner to compensate for your lack of ability to form deep emotional relationships. As soon as your lover starts seeing you as an ordinary person with ordinary faults you may well flit away to find someone else, thereby avoiding criticism.

A really deep love will be possible if you stop idealizing yourself, jump off the pedestal and start being human.

HIGHWAY ONE

START HERE
1 Do you find it hard to believe that he/she loves you?
2 Do you always wish you could be alone together?
3 Do you worry constantly about being jilted? *Mostly Yes*, turn down Lane One to Country Village. *Mostly No*, carry on along the Highway.

CONCLUSION 1

Your relationship seems to be an infatuation rather than true love. As a result of an early dependence on your parents, you are seeking security and protection, and because you may lack self-assurance, you feel a need to attach yourself to a strong figure. This need dominates your love. Fear of separation is probably an important factor in the relationship. You want your partner to be both lover and parent, and he/she may soon feel trapped. Try to take into account your partner's needs and see how much you can return his/her love.

Enjoy the infatuation for the time being, but bear in mind that real love should be based on mutual affection and not on a desperate need.

FIVE-BARRED GATE

1 When someone repeats as
their own a clever remark you
made, would you:
(a) smile and let them get
away with it?
(b) point out jokingly that
the remark isn't original?
(c) feel annoyed?

2 A particular business as-
sociate always asks your
partner to dinner without
you. Would you:
(a) make your partner persuade him to invite you?
(b) accept it?
(c) feel furious?

3 You have to consult each
other as to what to do on a
particular evening. Do you:
(a) hope he/she will agree
with your idea?
(b) hope he/she has an interesting idea?
(c) feel you are no longer
independent?

4 Which would be the best
kind of working partnership
for you:
(a) working together on the
same task with equal
recognition?
(b) working together but
with either you or the other
person giving the orders?
(c) working on separate
aspects of the task, with a
clear-cut division of labour?

BALE OF HAY

1 Do you think that the
most important aspect of sex
in marriage is:
(a) the physical attraction
and excitement generated?
(b) the physical satisfaction
of expressing love?
(c) the emotional closeness
and harmony?

2 You want more sex than
your partner. Do you:
(a) dream of other pastures?
(b) argue about it?
(c) try to stimulate him/her
more?

3 If your partner were having
an affair with someone else,
would you:
(a) set about having lots of
affairs yourself?
(b) make a terrible scene
and find it hard to forgive?
(c) be very upset, but forgive
in time?

4 If you found your partner
too sexually demanding,
would you:
(a) think their demands were
abnormal?
(b) give in to their demands
half-heartedly?
(c) think of ways of being
more erotically inclined
towards him/her?

5 If your partner wanted to
draw you in the nude, would
you:
(a) refuse?
(b) agree reluctantly?
(c) agree quite happily?

HIGH BRICK WALL

1 When you are depressed,
do you:
(a) moan away to anyone
and everyone you meet?
(b) avoid people and tend to
be short with anyone you
come across?
(c) seek out a close friend to
talk to?

2 How would you cope with
a partner who liked a newspaper breakfast against your
wishes? Would you:
(a) try to open up a conversation?
(b) stop ordering the newspaper?
(c) share it with him/her?

3 If you bump into an old
girlfriend/boyfriend with
whom you parted on bad
terms, do you:
(a) say a few cool, well-
chosen words and pass on?
(b) cross the road?
(c) make the chance meeting
as friendly as the situation
will allow?

4 You sometimes feel you
don't know what is going on
in your partner's mind. Do
you:
(a) make a few guesses?
(b) get angry?
(c) wait for him/her to open
up?

5 If he/she comes home two
hours late without phoning,
do you:
(a) ask him or her to phone
next time?
(b) sulk for the rest of the
evening?
(c) feel very annoyed at his/
her lack of consideration?

TREB

First Hurdle

1 Invited to dine in rich comp
do you:
(a) make believe you are o
them?
(b) tend not to notice their w
after the initial impact?
(c) simply feel envious?

2 When there's an accide
the street, do you:
(a) walk by quickly?
(b) see if you can help?
(c) stop to look?

Second Hurdle

1 Do you meet your boyfrie
girlfriend's parents for the
time with:
(a) positive dread?
(b) curiosity?
(c) mixed feelings?

2 Your partner finds your rela
difficult. Do you:
(a) agree to keep them as sep
from your partner as you ca

Third Hurdle

1 You have a burglary. Do y
(a) never feel safe in your
house again?
(b) see it as just one of t
unfortunate things?
(c) feel terribly upset about lo
your possessions?

2 When you have a boring
to do, do you:
(a) try not to think about it o
it out of your mind for as lo
you possibly can?
(b) determine to get it over
quickly?

This game will help you
your capacity to cope
the hurdles of marriage

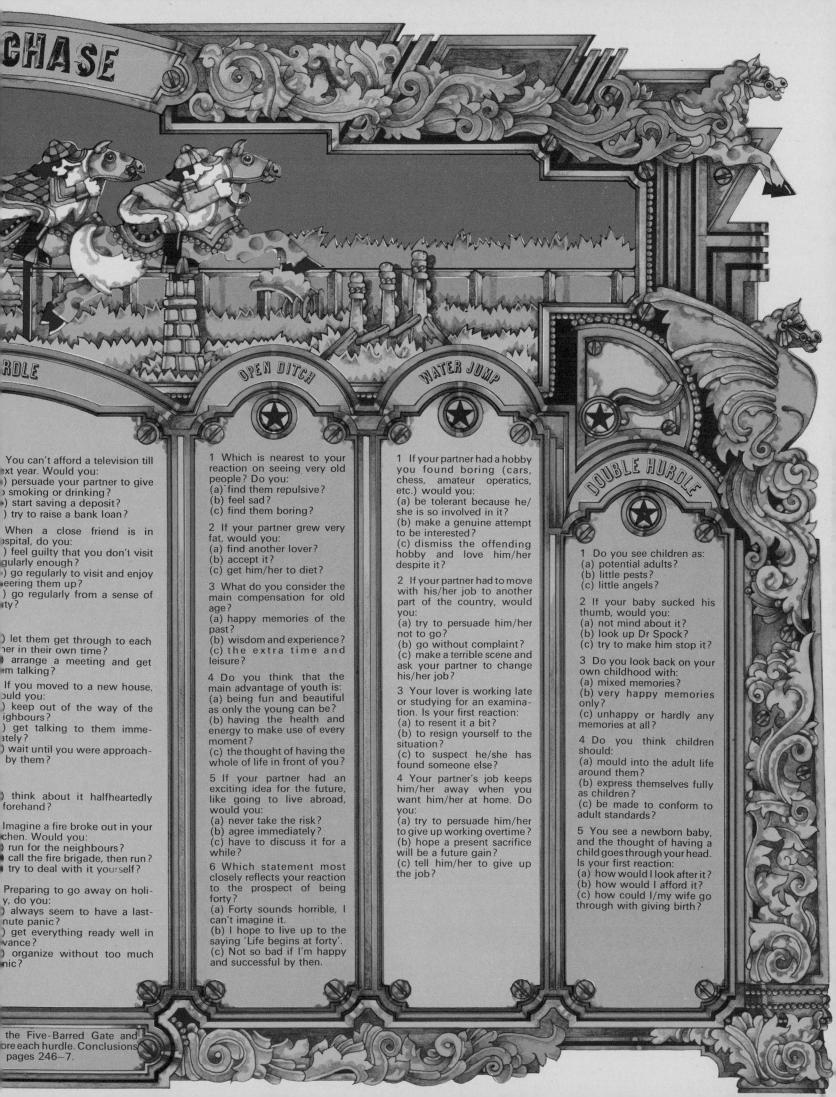

...RDLE

You can't afford a television till
...ext year. Would you:
... persuade your partner to give
... smoking or drinking?
... start saving a deposit?
... try to raise a bank loan?

When a close friend is in
...ospital, do you:
... feel guilty that you don't visit
...gularly enough?
... go regularly to visit and enjoy
...eering them up?
... go regularly from a sense of
...ty?

... let them get through to each
...er in their own time?
... arrange a meeting and get
...em talking?

If you moved to a new house,
...uld you:
... keep out of the way of the
...ighbours?
... get talking to them imme-
...ately?
... wait until you were approach-
... by them?

... think about it halfheartedly
... forehand?

Imagine a fire broke out in your
...chen. Would you:
... run for the neighbours?
... call the fire brigade, then run?
... try to deal with it yourself?

Preparing to go away on holi-
...: do you:
... always seem to have a last-
...nute panic?
... get everything ready well in
...vance?
... organize without too much
...nic?

OPEN DITCH

1 Which is nearest to your
reaction on seeing very old
people? Do you:
(a) find them repulsive?
(b) feel sad?
(c) find them boring?

2 If your partner grew very
fat, would you:
(a) find another lover?
(b) accept it?
(c) get him/her to diet?

3 What do you consider the
main compensation for old
age?
(a) happy memories of the
past?
(b) wisdom and experience?
(c) the extra time and
leisure?

4 Do you think that the
main advantage of youth is:
(a) being fun and beautiful
as only the young can be?
(b) having the health and
energy to make use of every
moment?
(c) the thought of having the
whole of life in front of you?

5 If your partner had an
exciting idea for the future,
like going to live abroad,
would you:
(a) never take the risk?
(b) agree immediately?
(c) have to discuss it for a
while?

6 Which statement most
closely reflects your reaction
to the prospect of being
forty?
(a) Forty sounds horrible, I
can't imagine it.
(b) I hope to live up to the
saying 'Life begins at forty'.
(c) Not so bad if I'm happy
and successful by then.

WATER JUMP

1 If your partner had a hobby
you found boring (cars,
chess, amateur operatics,
etc.) would you:
(a) be tolerant because he/
she is so involved in it?
(b) make a genuine attempt
to be interested?
(c) dismiss the offending
hobby and love him/her
despite it?

2 If your partner had to move
with his/her job to another
part of the country, would
you:
(a) try to persuade him/her
not to go?
(b) go without complaint?
(c) make a terrible scene and
ask your partner to change
his/her job?

3 Your lover is working late
or studying for an examina-
tion. Is your first reaction:
(a) to resent it a bit?
(b) to resign yourself to the
situation?
(c) to suspect he/she has
found someone else?

4 Your partner's job keeps
him/her away when you
want him/her at home. Do
you:
(a) try to persuade him/her
to give up working overtime?
(b) hope a present sacrifice
will be a future gain?
(c) tell him/her to give up
the job?

DOUBLE HURDLE

1 Do you see children as:
(a) potential adults?
(b) little pests?
(c) little angels?

2 If your baby sucked his
thumb, would you:
(a) not mind about it?
(b) look up Dr Spock?
(c) try to make him stop it?

3 Do you look back on your
own childhood with:
(a) mixed memories?
(b) very happy memories
only?
(c) unhappy or hardly any
memories at all?

4 Do you think children
should:
(a) mould into the adult life
around them?
(b) express themselves fully
as children?
(c) be made to conform to
adult standards?

5 You see a newborn baby,
and the thought of having a
child goes through your head.
Is your first reaction:
(a) how would I look after it?
(b) how would I afford it?
(c) how could I/my wife go
through with giving birth?

the Five-Barred Gate and
...ore each hurdle. Conclusions
...pages 246–7.

Steeplechase: Conclusions

You have scored the hurdles separately, now read the Conclusion for each of them. The hurdles you scrape through, or fail altogether, will indicate some areas in your marriage at which you might be able to work a little harder.

Five-Barred Gate: Conclusion
The questions we asked here were to test your ability to adapt yourself to running in double harness! Learning to do so is an important aspect of a successful marriage.

Mostly (a)
You are able to adapt to your partner without feeling threatened, and you will enjoy your image as a couple. Giving and receiving comes naturally to you, and on that basis you should make a very successful partnership in marriage.

Mostly (b)
You have just scraped over this hurdle. Perhaps you have never had to bother with selfish feelings before? It usually takes a long time to settle into a relationship and being wildly in love is a crash course which won't cover every angle. Maybe you can give up some of your independence and let your partner take over occasionally; a partnership can sometimes allow you a good deal more freedom than the solitary state.

Mostly (c)
Sorry, you've failed this hurdle. You seem to be so wrapped up in your own self-image that you find it difficult to share your identity with your partner. You are apt to become resentful if your partner doesn't back up your somewhat romantic view of yourself. A more realistic approach is necessary, so that you can accept criticism sometimes, and realize that everyone has an ugly as well as a beautiful side to their nature. You will have to be prepared to compromise a little more so that you can share your life happily with someone else.

Bale of Hay: Conclusion
This hurdle was to test whether you would be mature enough to cope with the sexual side of marriage. Sex and the expression of love are two of the most important ingredients in a happy marriage.

Mostly (a)
You did not get over this hurdle. You want a perfect sex life with your partner, but you seem to expect this perfection with very little effort on your part. Like all other aspects of marriage, physical happiness comes from mutually understanding each other's wishes and desires. Your present romantic notions about sexual love will probably not be sustained after a few years of marriage. You will then have to take a more realistic look at yourself and your partner.

Mostly (b)
You have just scraped over this hurdle. You may have difficulties at present which could be easily overcome. Affection and the demonstration of it can mean so many things. Who hasn't pulled away from a kiss when feeling angry with the other person? Difficulties often stem from uncertainty about one's emotional and sexual abilities. Look at yourself closely and don't give in to your tendency to underestimate yourself.

Mostly (c)
You have made a clean jump over this hurdle. You have the ability to enjoy sex as an integral part of marriage, and because you see sex and affection as one and the same thing you are likely to adjust well to your partner. As a couple you are close enough to deal with any sexual problems that may arise without losing faith in each other.

High Brick Wall: Conclusion
The Brick Wall tests how easily you can express emotion and communicate with your partner.

Mostly (a)
You have just scraped over this hurdle. Sometimes communication between people breaks down because one feels that what they want to say is unacceptable to their partner. What is *not* being said then becomes the most important factor; which is bound to create tension sooner or later. It would be better if you tried to express your feelings without being afraid of your partner's reaction. But as you did scrape over this hurdle, your communication problems shouldn't be difficult to solve.

Mostly (b)
You didn't get over this hurdle. It is easy to communicate when things are going well, but during difficult times in the relationship you tend to cut yourself off emotionally from your partner. The less you express, the more difficult it is to communicate, and the more easily tension and conflict arise. In a love-situation anger must be expressed too, if you are ever going to come to terms with each other.

Mostly (c)
You are sufficiently aware of your own feelings and those of your partner to be able to communicate adequately. Being well adjusted to each other's personalities you can face discord without loss of communication. You have the ability to express emotion easily, and this isn't an area you need worry too much about.

Treble Hurdle: Conclusion
The questions in the Treble Hurdle were to assess how you would be likely to cope with the domestic and practical problems which can crop up in marriage. Coping with difficult relatives, or poverty, or illness, for instance, can sometimes put a great strain on the marriage.

Mostly (a)
You failed to get over this hurdle. You tend to cut yourself off from unpleasant thoughts, with a feeling of 'it can never happen to me'. This means that in the face of difficulties you may well choose to escape mentally instead of facing up to your problems. You tend to be dependent on other people, and your inability to cope with routine and practical tasks may stem from a dependent wish to be looked after in a parent/child relationship, instead of taking your proper place as a partner in the marriage.

Mostly (b)
You don't have to bother with domestic problems, for you seem to be able to cope. If you were to hit the breadline you could still enjoy life, because you can get satisfaction from your personal relationships, regardless of material factors. You can accept the fact that good and bad things in life come together.

Mostly (c)
You scraped over this hurdle. Strangely enough, it often seems easier for you to accommodate the big dramas in your life than to deal with the minor set-backs, but you seem to be able to cope with *some* of the domestic problems, and probably you find that you can manage until several minor disasters

occur at the same time; then you begin to feel fragmented; and your relationship may suffer in the process. Patience and a little faith in yourself will help. Try to plan your life so that everything doesn't happen at once. This might give you more confidence in your ability to cope.

Open Ditch: Conclusion
The questions at the Open Ditch test how you would be likely to adjust to middle and old age, and how your attitude to age might affect your relationship with your partner.

Mostly (a)
You scraped over this hurdle. You have conflicting feelings about the passage of time. Losing weight if you are too fat, or having a face-lift for your wrinkles is one way of coping with the problem. But really it's best to accept one's age. Middle-aged fauns are a bit of a paradox. There are interesting qualities which help one rise above the aging process and these could be cultivated. Interest and excitement in new ventures and acquaintances, for instance, and flexibility in one's outlook and opinions.

Mostly (b)
You passed well over this hurdle. You have a high enough opinion of yourself as a person not to feel denigrated by becoming old. Because you live life to the full, enjoying the advantages of each age, you are not likely to become a lonely old recluse.

Mostly (c)
You failed this hurdle. Wanting to be young and beautiful for ever seems a nice ideal, but it is an impossible one, and failure to face up to it will make you an unhappy person; and this in turn will make your partner unhappy. You cannot be an eternal adolescent and take on all the responsibilities of a home and children successfully. Life has a beginning, a middle and an end. Each is new and exciting, and each has its own problems and satisfactions.

Water Jump: Conclusion
This was to test how you would cope with your partner's involvement in his/her work and interests. If you failed this hurdle you should be wary of marrying a man who has to take frequent trips away from home/a woman who is very involved in her career.

Mostly (a)
You just scraped over this hurdle. You are probably in two minds about your partner's involvement with his/her work. Perhaps you feel deep down that you shouldn't be reacting in the way you do, and tell yourself that it is silly to be jealous of a mere job. Or perhaps you understand that your partner's job really does mean he/she has to be away from you a lot, and that this is in no way a scheme to avoid you. Remember that a happy but busy partner is often more pleasant to live with than a discontented person with too much time to spare.

Mostly (b)
You passed well over this hurdle. You are able to allow your partner sufficient freedom from the relationship to become involved in work and express his/her individuality. Presumably this means you can trust your partner not to let work ruin your relationship.

Mostly (c)
You failed to get over this hurdle. You tend to be so dependent on your partner that you wish to deny him/her an identity of his or her own. Togetherness is very nice, but not at the expense of your partner's personal ambitions and ideals. You should try to allow your partner more self-expression within the relationship, for your present attitude is bound to lead to conflict.

Double Hurdle: Conclusion
This hurdle was to test the likelihood of your being able to cope well with children, and the resulting problems of adjustment in the relationship with your partner.

Mostly (a)
It sounds as though you have a realistic approach to the strains that children put on a relationship, especially in the areas of responsibility and sharing. Sometimes children expect their parents to take control of their feelings of fear and anger, and it looks as though you will be able to do this.

Mostly (b)
Everyone finds children a problem and the role of parent isn't an easy one, but the art is not to make the problem bigger than it is. As you did in fact scrape over this hurdle there's no reason why you shouldn't be a confident parent. Children often become difficult when their parents are going through a difficult time (uncertainty over a job, resentment in the partnership), but when the cause is removed it becomes easy to enjoy them again.

Mostly (c)
You failed this hurdle. At times the childishness in children becomes intolerable for you. Apart from the real and practical problems here, maybe you have difficulty in accepting your own remnants of childhood, such as the need to be looked after and the enjoyment of being passive in some situations. If you aren't already a parent, you may doubt your ability to deal with children; but nearly everyone else has doubts and once you become a parent you will probably instinctively adjust to parenthood.

Where's your Venus?

Everyone knows whether, in astrology, they are 'Aries', or 'Taurus', or whatever, because on the day they were born the sun was 'in' that particular sign of the Zodiac. What they do not know until it is calculated for them is what signs the other planets were in. For instance, the Moon might have been in Pisces and Jupiter in Leo. When an astrologer casts a birth chart (or 'horoscope', as it was traditionally known) he works from the individual's birth date, the time and place of birth, and from that starting-point calculates (amongst various other things) the exact position of each planet.

Here, we consider Mars and Venus, both of which have a powerful bearing on one's relationships, Venus influencing the capacity for love and affection, Mars a man's or a woman's sexual response. The effects of Venus are strongest when it is in Taurus or Libra, which are the two signs it 'rules'. If your Venus is in the same sign as your Sun, what you read about your love-life under your Zodiac sign ought to be accurate; if Venus falls in a different sign, this gives another dimension to the expression of your love.

In order to find out where your own or your partner's Venus is, turn to the astrological table opposite. First find your year of birth on the top line of the table and then your month of birth at the lefthand side of the chart (1= January, 2=February, etc.). The table shows in which sign of the Zodiac Venus was on the first of each month, and also any date during that month on which it moved to another sign. For instance, if you look at the table, you will see that in January 1947 Venus was in Capricorn on the first of the month, and moved into Aquarius on 26 January.

Venus Through the Signs

Venus in Aries
A warm and affectionate man or woman; probably very emotional, but with fiery, positive emotion. Best summed up as ardent and true—but watch out for selfishness, especially if the Sun sign is Aries when, although there will be kindness, there may also be self-seeking tendencies.

Venus in Taurus
Here is someone who will lavish affection on a partner, and contribute much to the development of a relationship. Possessiveness is bound to be present, and the loved one will almost inevitably be thought of as 'mine', in much the same way as any other treasured possession.

Venus in Gemini
Those who have Venus in this sign will enjoy their relationships, and perhaps take them rather lightly. There is a strong possibility that they will have 'more than one string to their bow', and they can find themselves in love with two people at the same time.

Venus in Cancer
This placing contributes much tenderness, and a strong tendency to look after the loved one. A certain claustrophobic feeling may be in evidence, because the person is so cherishing or sentimental. They may also dwell in the past too much. A high emotional level is very likely.

Venus in Leo
Love, affection and loyalty will be expressed in a grand and probably expensive way, especially if the Sun sign is Leo or Libra. There may be a tendency to dominate or rule the partner, and dramatic scenes are possible!

Venus in Virgo
This tends to contribute over-critical, clinical or chaste tendencies, inhibiting a full, satisfactory expression of love; so conflict can occur, especially if the Sun sign is loving, romantic Libra. The need for a 'perfect' partner may be a root cause of difficulty in relationships.

Venus in Libra
This placing indicates a whole-hearted romantic who is not a fully integrated person until he or she is enjoying a permanent relationship. If the Sun sign is Virgo, this will warm the matter-of-fact, practical Virgoan heart. Powerfully romantic and affectionate feelings are inevitable.

Venus in Scorpio
Considerable intensity, emotion and intuition will be very evident in the expression of affection and feelings. Jealousy and possessiveness may mar the relationship, and a very 'black-and-white' attitude to love is very likely. These tendencies are modified if the Sun sign is Libra or Sagittarius.

Venus in Sagittarius
This is definitely a lively position for Venus, and the overall attitude to love and relationships may not be too serious. More than one relationship is likely, and there is also an idealistic facet, which is very positive. Great warmth, affection and enthusiasm will be fully expressed, however.

Venus in Capricorn
Venus's influence in this sign is chilly; but once the barriers are broken one finds an extremely loyal, faithful, and dependable person. There will be few words of affection, but what is said is meant—especially if the Sun sign is Capricorn, rather than Sagittarius.

Venus in Aquarius
This placing nearly always contributes a sort of filmstar glamour; if the Sun sign is Capricorn it may be a little difficult to come really close to that person—physically or emotionally, but especially emotionally. There is often a marked tendency towards platonic friendships rather than romantic relationships.

Venus in Pisces
A kind, loving, willing slave who cannot do enough for one! Life could become blissfully romantic in an unorganized way. There should be very little difficulty in getting on with a 'Venus in Pisces', though emotions could well run rather high at times.

1913 1914 1915 1916 1917 1918 1919 1920 1921 1922 1923 1924 1925 1926 1927 1928

1929 1930 1931 1932 1933 1934 1935 1936 1937 1938 1939 1940 1941 1942 1943 1944

1945 1946 1947 1948 1949 1950 1951 1952 1953 1954 1955 1956 1957 1958 1959 1960

Where's your Mars?

You may have noticed when looking at the position of Venus that it falls in either the same sign as your Sun, or in the next sign, or in the sign after that. This is because Venus's orbit is inside that of the Earth, and as seen from here it always appears close to the Sun – as a bright morning star or a beautiful evening one.

Your Mars can be 'in' any of the twelve signs of the Zodiac; so while your Sun sign may be Gemini, Mars need not be in that sign – it could be in Libra or any of the other signs. Mars is at its strongest in Aries, the sign it rules, and in Scorpio, the sign whose rulership it shares with Pluto.

Now turn to the table opposite and find out where your Mars (and your partner's!) were on your birthdates. The procedure is exactly the same as it was for finding your Venus, and the table will show you in which sign Mars was on the first day of any month, and the day or days in that month when it moved to another sign.

Mars Through the Signs

♈ Mars in Aries
Mars in Aries will contribute highly-sexed and passionate tendencies. The person will be demanding, but nevertheless straightforward and good company. There will be no lack of enthusiasm, warmth and energy, and a general feeling that life is to be enjoyed to the full.

♉ Mars in Taurus
An extremely passionate and highly-sexed man or woman. Feelings are usually slow to be roused, but once aroused, sexual desire is strong. Jealousy and possessiveness can often creep into relationships. People with Mars in Taurus are extremely sensual and sexually demanding, and will often have expensive tastes.

♊ Mars in Gemini
Here is someone who may not want to become too deeply or emotionally involved with any one partner. A strong sexual desire is unusual, but there is great liking for innovation, variety and change in the style of love-making; many lovers are likely, with relationships kept at a superficial level.

♋ Mars in Cancer
Highly-sexed, but nevertheless roughness and boisterousness will be intensely disliked, so a gentle and sensitive approach is most advisable. Very strong feelings, emotions and intuitions are always present, and there is a tendency to cling to a relationship. In Cancer, Mars often increases fertility.

♌ Mars in Leo
Those with Mars in Leo will appreciate comfort and luxurious, aesthetically pleasing surroundings for their sexual activities, and the result could be a highly sophisticated romp. There should undoubtedly be plenty of lively response to advances, but a slight hint of condescension may make one feel like an ever-grateful subject!

♍ Mars in Virgo
Virgo is purity personified, but Mars is all energy and sex: a contradiction in terms. Desire is certainly present, but the expression of it in a straightforward way may not be at all easy. Psychological difficulties as a result of conflict can cause repression, and deviation is possible.

♎ Mars in Libra
A languid attitude towards sex is very likely, and excuses may be made to put off the over-ardent lover. Once aroused, sensuousness will be evident; but, even so, sex has to be idealistic, colourful and beautiful – 'out of this world' rather than noticeably earthy!

♏ Mars in Scorpio
Mars in Scorpio, more than in any other sign, will make the individual extremely highly sexed. Unfortunately, jealousy and resentfulness can frequently blight relationships. Possibly the best way to combat this is to cultivate demanding interests, so that the excess of energy and emotion is positively and creatively directed.

♐ Mars in Sagittarius
A lively, unserious attitude to sex is likely. The man or woman with Mars in Sagittarius will enjoy relationships, but will make and break them easily, for freedom is highly prized. Those with Mars in Sagittarius will be passionate, but the grass will always seem greener on the other side!

♑ Mars in Capricorn
If those with Mars in Capricorn, caught up in the essential business of getting on in the world, can find the time to indulge in sexual relationships, they will be seething with passion at one moment, and an iceberg the next; but they will admire and identify with faithfulness and constancy.

♒ Mars in Aquarius
Having an affair with someone with Mars in Aquarius will be an interesting experience; but togetherness, in the physical sense, may seem almost a necessary evil to them! They accept the fact that desires must be satisfied, but are somehow 'above it all'. Passion is not really their scene.

♓ Mars in Pisces
Passion must always be combined with a colourful romanticism for those with Mars in Pisces. The emotional level is extremely high, but plain and simple earthy pleasures may not be enough to satisfy some highly individual escapist tendencies. An uncomplicated 'strong' partner will have a beneficial steadying influence.

Acknowledgments

Editorial Director: Christopher Dorling
Art Director: Peter Kindersley
Editors: Michael Leitch, Daphne Wood
Designers: Wendy Bann, Nicholas
Maddren, David Pocknell

Photographers

Michael Busselle: 114–144, 178, 181–192
John Hedgecoe: 2–8, 14–15, 33–36,
46–47, 50–51, 54–56, 62–63, 66–67,
78–79, 82, 86–87, 90–91, 94–95

Artists

Roger Coleman: 146–147, 150–151,
154–155, 158–159
Andrew Farmer: 229
David Roe: Decorative motifs and
games
Justin Todd: 195, 198–199, 202–203,
206–207

Sources of Illustrations

The authors and publishers are
particularly grateful to the following
museums, galleries and photographic
collections for permission to reproduce
the illustrations in this book:

10–11 Uffizi Gallery, Florence/Scala
18–19 Prado, Madrid/Hamlyn Group
Library
21 British Museum, London/C. M.
Dixon
22 Trustees of the National Gallery,
London
23 Musée Nationale d'Art Moderne,
Paris
24 Mary Evans Picture Library
25 Chrishall Church, Essex/Michael
Holford
26 Philip Goldman Collection, London/
Geremy Butler
27 Victoria and Albert Museum,
London
30 Museum of Fine Arts, Boston
31 National Gallery, London
38–39 City Art Galleries, Manchester
42–43 Palazzo Schifanoia, Ferrara/Scala
45 Lady Lever Art Gallery, Port
Sunlight
49 Guildhall Art Gallery, London
58 Mansell Collection
59 Trustees of the Wallace Collection
60, 61 Mary Evans Picture Library
65 Mansell Collection
68, 69 Mary Evans Picture Library
70 Stefan Buzas
71 Victoria and Albert Museum,
London

74–75 Mansell Collection
76 Mary Evans Picture Library
77 Victoria and Albert Museum,
London
78–79 Mary Evans Picture Library
83 Tate Gallery, London
85 National Gallery of South Australia,
Adelaide
88 Victoria and Albert Museum,
London/Geremy Butler
92, 93 Mary Evans Picture Library
96, 98–100 Mansell Collection
101, 103 Editions Graphiques Gallery,
London
105 Mansell Collection
106 Mary Evans Picture Library
107 Mansell Collection
108 Mary Evans Picture Library
109, 111 Mansell Collection
149 Palazzo Schifanoia, Ferrara/Scala
152 Österreichische Galerie, Vienna/
Galerie Welz, Salzburg
153 Mary Evans Picture Library
157 Trustees of the Wallace Collection,
London
162, 163 Mary Evans Picture Library
165 Editions Graphiques Gallery,
London
166 Bibliothèque Nationale, Paris/
Snark International
168 Conway Picture Library
171 Victoria and Albert Museum,
London
172 Private Collection/Hamlyn Group
Library
175 Mary Evans Picture Library
178 *left* Field Talfourd/Radio Times
Hulton Picture Library
178 *right* Field Talfourd/Mary Evans
Picture Library
190–191, 192 *top left, bottom left,
bottom right* Conway Picture Library
192 *top right* Conway Picture Library/
Associated Press
194 Mansell Collection
201 Tate Gallery, London
205 Radio Times Hulton Picture
Library
208, 211, 212 Mary Evans Picture
Library
213 Victoria and Albert Museum,
London
215 Mary Evans Picture Library
216, 217 Mansell Collection
218 Mary Evans Picture Library
219, 220 Victoria and Albert Museum
248, 250 Mary Evans Picture Library

Publishers and Agents

The authors gratefully acknowledge
the kind permission given by the

following publishers and agents to
reproduce copyright material.

From Rex Warner's translation of
Xenophon's *The Persian Expedition*
published by Penguin Books, London.

From *Love* by Walter de la Mare by
permission of the Literary Trustees of
Walter de la Mare and the Society of
Authors as their representatives.

'Flowers for Heliodora' and 'The
Mosquito' by Meleagros translated by
Dudley Fitts from *Poems from the Greek
Anthology*. Copyright 1938, © 1956 by
New Directions Publishing Corpora-
tion. Reprinted by permission of New
Directions Publishing Corporation,
New York and Faber and Faber Ltd.,
London.

From Constance Garnett's translation
of *Anna Karenina* by Leo Tolstoy
published by William Heinemann Ltd.,
London, and Dodd, Mead & Company,
New York.

'Not to Sleep' and 'The Metaphor' by
Robert Graves from *Collected Poems
1965*. Reprinted by permission of
Robert Graves.

'The Two' by Hugo von Hofmannsthal
translated by Derek Parker. Original
German text published by Insel Verlag,
Frankfurt/Main.

'The Morning is Full' and 'Girl Lithe
and Tawny' from *Twenty Love Poems
and a Song of Despair* by Pablo Neruda,
translated by W. S. Merwin. Published
by Grossman Publishers, New York,
and Jonathan Cape Ltd., London.

From *The History of Mr Polly* by
H. G. Wells. Reprinted by permission
of the Estate of H. G. Wells.

'Blow, wind, to where my loved one is'
by Rāmāyana from *Poems from the
Sanscrit* translated by John Brough
published by Penguin Books Ltd.,
London. Copyright © John Brough,
1968.

From *Marriage and Morals* by Bertrand
Russell published by George Allen &
Unwin Ltd., London and Liveright,
Publishers, New York. Copyright ©
R 1957 Bertrand Russell.

From 'To Earthward' from *The Poetry
of Robert Frost* edited by Edward
Connery Lathem. Copyright 1923, ©
1969 by Holt, Rinehart and Winston

Inc. Copyright 1951 by Robert Frost. Reprinted by permission of Holt, Rinehart and Winston, Inc., New York and Jonathan Cape Ltd., London.

'In praise of Cocoa' by Stanley Sharpless published by the New Statesman, London.

'viva sweet love' by e. e. cummings published by permission of McGibbon & Kee Ltd., London, and Alfred Rice, New York.

'Recuerdo' by Edna St. Vincent Millay from *Collected Poems* published by Harper and Row, New York. Copyright 1922, 1950 by Edna St. Vincent Millay.

From 'The Look' from *Collected Poems* by Sara Teasdale, published by the Macmillan Company, New York. Copyright 1915 by the Macmillan Company, renewed 1943 by Mamie T. Wheless.

From 'In the Midnight Hour' from *Tonight at Noon* by Adrian Henri published by Andre Deutsch Ltd., London, and David Mackay Co. Inc., New York. Copyright © 1969 by Adrian Henri.

'Bid adieu' from *Chamber Music* from *Collected Poems* by James Joyce. Copyright 1918 by B. W. Huebsch Inc., renewed 1946 by Nora Joyce. Reprinted by permission of Viking Press Inc., New York and the Executors of the James Joyce Estate.

'Warm are the Still and Lucky Miles' and 'Lullaby' from *Collected Shorter Poems 1927–1957* by W. H. Auden published by Faber and Faber Ltd., London and Random House, Inc., New York.

'Jig' and from 'Live you by Love Confined' by C. Day Lewis from *Collected Poems 1954*. Copyright by C. Day Lewis. Reprinted by permission of Jonathan Cape Ltd. and Hogarth Press, London and the Harold Matson Company Inc., New York.

'And Your Dress is White' translated by Jack Bevan from Salvatore Quasimodo's *Selected Poems* published by Penguin Books Ltd., London, and Henry Regnery, Chicago.

From *Day of These Days* (*The Bloom of Candles*) by Laurie Lee.

'Song of the Pink Bird' from *Little Johnny's Confession* by Brian Patten published by George Allen & Unwin Ltd., London and Hill and Wang, New York. © Brian Patten, 1967.

From 'Sex Versus Loveliness' from *Phoenix II: More Uncollected Writings of D. H. Lawrence* edited by Warren Roberts and Harry T. Moore. All rights reserved. Reprinted by permission of The Viking Press Inc., New York, Laurence Pollinger Ltd., London, and the Estate of the late Mrs Frieda Lawrence.

'Carpe Noctem' from *The Cicadas* by Aldous Huxley published by Chatto and Windus, London and Harper & Row, New York. Copyright, 1929, 1931 by Aldous Huxley. Reprinted by permission of Harper & Row, Publishers, Inc.

'Serenata' from *Selected Poems* by Federico Garcia Lorca translated by Derek Parker. All Rights Reserved. Reprinted by permission of New Directions Publishing Corporation, New York.

From Alan Russell's translation of *Madame Bovary* by Gustave Flaubert, published by Penguin Books, London.

From *Love and Marriage* by Ellen Key published by G. P. Putnam's Sons, New York.

From 'Glory of Life' by Llewellyn Powys Inc., by permission of Malcolm Elwin, Literary Executor to the Llewellyn Powys Estate.

'Daybreak' by Stephen Spender from *Collected Poems 1928–1953* published by Faber and Faber Ltd., London, and Random House, Inc., New York.

From 'The Postures of Love' by Alex Comfort (1946) from *The Signal to Engage* published by Routledge & Kegan Paul Ltd., London.

From *This Side of Paradise* by F. Scott Fitzgerald published by Charles Scribner's Sons, New York, and The Bodley Head, London. From The Bodley Head Scott Fitzgerald Vol. 3.

'Unfortunate Coincidence' from *The Portable Dorothy Parker* by Dorothy Parker. Copyright 1926, 1954 by Dorothy Parker. Published by the Viking Press Inc., New York.

From 'Music I heard with you' from *Collected Poems* by Conrad Aiken (Copyright 1953 by Conrad Aiken) published by Oxford University Press, New York.

From 'After Long Silence' from *Collected Poems* by William Butler Yeats, copyright 1933 by the Macmillan Company, New York, renewed 1961 by Bertha Georgie Yeats. By permission of M. B. Yeats and the Macmillan Companies of Canada and London.

From *The Golden Ass* by Apuleius translated by Robert Graves. Reprinted by permission of Robert Graves.

A condensation of a passage from 'The Girl Who Caught a Nightingale' from Giovanni Boccaccio's *Decameron*, translated by Richard Aldington. © Catherine Guillaume.

Every effort has been made to trace the owners of any copyright material that may exist. Should any material have been included without the permission of the owner of such copyright, acknowledgment will gladly be made in any future edition if attention is called to it.

General Acknowledgments

The following Games were devised by Jane Deverson and Dr Roger Hobdell: What Type of Lover Am I?; The Love Maze; Is It Love or Infatuation?; The Steeplechase. The authors would also particularly like to thank Mr Arwas of Editions Graphiques Gallery, London, Mr and Mrs L. F. Lethbridge, and Dr Charles Rycroft for their help in compiling this book.

General Index

Pages references in *italics* refer to illustrations; the Literary and Art index contains the names of authors quoted in the text, and of artists whose works are reproduced.

A

Advertising, 64, 69
Afternoon, an enjoyable, 220
Albert, H.R.H. Prince, 52
Antony, Mark, 68, 184–5
Aphrodisiacs, 60–1, 65, 96; and *see cocoa*
Aphrodite, 20
Artemidorus, Daldianus, 72–3
Arthur, King, 88
Aubrey, John, 90

B

Balsamic Corroborant, 61
Barrett, Edward Moulton, 178
Beauty and the Beast, 186–7
Belladonna, 68
Besier, Rudolph, 179
Betrothal, 92–3
Boleyn, Anne, 81
Brawne, Fanny, 52, 92
Browning, Elizabeth Barrett, 178–9
Browning, Robert, 172, 178–9
Buddhism, 28
Butterdock, helpful, 90
Byron, Lord, 102, 110

C

Camille, 189
Cantharides, 61
Cards, 229–31
Carteret, Lord, 49
Casanova (de Seingalt), Giacomo, 32
Castle Game, the, 226–8
Catherine de Medici, 68
Champagne, Marie Countess of, 24
Chesterton, G. K., 179
China, ancient, 28
Christianity, and love, 18–19, 24
Church, the, *see Christianity*
Claret, a substitute mistress, 215
Cleopatra, 68, 184–5
Clothes, 66ff
Cocoa, 106
Coltsfoot, *see butterdock*
Computer dating, 48, 222
Confucius, 28
Cosmetics, 68–9
Courtesans, 20, 28
Courtly love, 24
Culpeper, Nicholas, 61

D

Danaë, 20
Dancing, 76
Dante and Beatrice, 96
Demeter, 21
Diogenes, 68
Dreams, 44–5, 72–3
Dumas, Alexandre, 188–9
Dunmow Flitch, 205

E

Eden, a prospect of, 36
Edward VII, *see Windsor, Duke of*
Egypt, 68
Engagement, *see betrothal*
Erogenous zone, shifting, 64–5
Eros, 20

F

Feet, perfumed, 68
Fertility, 76
Fitzherbert, Maria, 52
Flowers, language of, 84–5; love and, 107, 111, 163
Flush, 179
Freud, Sigmund, 72

G

Garbo, Greta, 188
Garter, knitted prophetic, 90; innocent, 219
Gautier, Marguerite, 188
Gods, Greek, 20, 88
Greeks, and love, 20–1

H

Hamilton, Emma Lady, 52
Hand, a saucy, 216
Handkerchiefs, 92
Harvey, Isabella, 53
Henry II, 68
Hero and Leander, 96
Homosexuality, 20–1, 112
Honnête homme, 32
Husband, vanishing, 90

I

Identilove, 232–3
India, *26*
Iseult, 88, 182–3

J

Japan, 28
Jones, Rev. William, 48
Jung, C. G., 72
Jupiter, 88

K

Keats, John, 52, 80, 92
Kenyon, John, 178
Kipling, Rudyard, 69

L

La Traviata, 188
Laver, James, 64–5
Love, parlour game, 20; Christianity and, 24; courtly, 24; outdoor, 24; platonic, 25;

young, 40–1; dreams of, 44; search for, 48–9; and clothes, 64ff; and cosmetics, 68ff; and dreams, 44–5, 72–3; and dancing, 76; and letters, 80–1; and flowers, 84; and magic, 88; and gifts, 92; -making, 145–56; romantic, 102; -games, 222ff

M

Magic, 88
Making love, 113ff
Manu, 29
Marriage, and business, 20; love in, 21; unloving, 24; *gandharva*, 28; arranged, 29; trial, 93; 244ff
Mars, in relationships, 250–1
Maze, a love, 234–41
Mead, Margaret, 40
Meetings, 52, 98, 101, 102, 107
Merlin, 88
More, Sir Thomas, 25
Musical-boxes, 92
Myth, 21

N

Nakedness, *see nudity*
Nelson, Horatio Viscount, 52
Nero, Emperor, 68
Nightingale, an unusual, 213–4
Nudity, pre-marital, 25; preparations for, 64ff; male, 65; as purity, 159; plea for, 171

O

Oracle, the, 229–31
Osborne, Dorothy, 80

P

Paston, John, 79
Pendragon, Uther, 88
Pepys, Samuel, 44, 79
Perfume, 68–9
Persephone, 21
Petrarch and Laura, 96
Photographs, 92
Piano, unexpected grand, 79
Pins, prophetic, 90
Platonic love, 25
Plessis, Marie, 189
Prince Regent, the, 52
Prostitutes, *see courtesans*
Pussies, pretty, 25

R

Renaissance, the, 25
Rickwood, Gypsy, 230
Rings, 93
Romantic image, the, 64ff
Rome, Imperial, 21, 24
Romeo and Juliet, 96, 180–1
Roper, Sir William, 25

S

Sade, Donatien Alphonse, Count ('Marquis') de, 61
St Paul, 24, 28
Sex, for procreation only, 24–5, 28; as sin, 28; as origin of world, 28; as religious act, 29; an unpleasant duty, 36; D. H. Lawrence on, 170; education, 145; proper time for, 220
Sex and Temperament in Three Primitive Societies, 40
Shakespeare, William, sonnets, 104–5
Simpson, Mrs Ernest, see *Windsor, Duke of*
Sleeplessness, 99
Soap, substitute for, 68
Sonnets, Shakespearean, 104–5
Spanish Fly, *see cantharides*
Steeplechase, 244–7
Stewart, Lady Arabella, 79
Stubbes, Philip, 25, 76

T

Temple, Sir William, 80
Thicknesse, Captain Philip, 61
Tolstoy, Count Lev Nikolaye-vich, 52
Tree of knowledge, 18–19
Tristan, 88, 182–3
Troubadours, 24

V

Valentines, 79
Venice, 102
Venus, in relationships, 248–9
Verdi, Giuseppe, 188
Victoria, H.M. Queen, 52
Victorian, attitude to making love, 33, 36, 148, 153
Villeneuve, Mme de, 187

W

Wagner, Richard, 183
Waltz, the, *76*
Wantonness, preparation for, 76
Windsor, H.R.H. Duke of, 190–2
Women, as drudges, 20; accepted, 21; battle for recognition, 24; desirable but unattainable, 24; evil charms of, 25; unquestioning obedience of, 28; equality of, 33, 34–5; breath of, 61; 'romantic animals', 64

Y

Ygerna, 88
Yohimbé, Yohimbine, 61

Z

Zeus, 20

Literary and Art Index

This index lists poems (under both their titles and the first lines of the poem or extract quoted) and their authors; the source and author of prose extracts; and artists and their paintings, drawings or photographs. Figures in italics refer to pictures.

Walking in This World

.

ALSO BY JULIA CAMERON

NONFICTION

The Artist's Way
The Artist's Way Morning Pages Journal
The Artist's Date Book
    (illustrated by Elizabeth Cameron)
The Vein of Gold
The Right to Write
God Is No Laughing Matter
Supplies *(illustrated by Elizabeth Cameron)*
God Is Dog Spelled Backwards
    (illustrated by Elizabeth Cameron)
Heartsteps
Blessings
Transitions
Inspirations: Meditations from *The Artist's Way*
The Writer's Life: Insights from *The Right to Write*
The Artist's Way at Work
    (with Mark Bryan and Catherine Allen)
Money Drunk, Money Sober *(with Mark Bryan)*

FICTION

Popcorn: Hollywood Stories
The Dark Room

POETRY

Prayers for the Little Ones
Prayers for the Nature Spirits
The Quiet Animal
This Earth *(also an album with Tim Wheater)*

PLAYS

Public Lives
The Animal in the Trees
Four Roses
Love in the DMZ
Bloodlines
Avalon *(a musical)*
The Medium at Large *(a musical)*
Tinseltown *(a musical)*
Normal, Nebraska *(a musical)*

FEATURE FILM

(as writer-director) God's Will

Walking in This World
The Practical Art of Creativity

Julia Cameron

JEREMY P. TARCHER/PUTNAM
a member of
Penguin Putnam Inc.

Most Tarcher/Putnam books are available at special quantity discounts for bulk purchase for sales promotions, premiums, fund-raising, and educational needs. Special books or book excerpts also can be created to fit specific needs. For details, write Putnam Special Markets, 375 Hudson Street, New York, NY 10014.

JEREMY P. TARCHER/PUTNAM
a member of
Penguin Putnam Inc.
375 Hudson Street
New York, NY 10014
www.penguinputnam.com

Library of Congress Cataloging-in-Publication Data

Cameron, Julia.   1942 ?
    Walking in this world : the practical art of creativity /
Julia Cameron.
        p.   cm.
    Includes index.
    ISBN 1-58542-183-9
    1. Creative ability.   2. Creation (Literary, artistic, etc.).
I. Title.
BF408.C178   2002   2002020363
153.3'5—dc21

Printed in the United States of America
10   9   8   7   6   5   4   3   2   1

This book is printed on acid-free paper. ∞

Book design by Marysarah Quinn

This book is dedicated to Jeremy P. Tarcher,
editor, publisher, and visionary.
With gratitude for his clarity, wisdom, and wit.
Above all, with gratitude for his friendship.

ACKNOWLEDGMENTS

Sara Carder, for her meticulous care

Carolina Casperson, for her believing eyes

Sonia Choquette, for her visionary optimism

Joel Fotinos, for his faith and vision

Kelly Groves, for his clarity and enthusiasm

Linda Kahn, for her clear-eyed perception

Bill Lavallee, for his optimism and strength

Emma Lively, for her stubborn faith

Larry Lonergan, for his humor and guidance

Julianna McCarthy, for her artful heart

Robert McDonald, for his inspiration and artistry

Bruce Pomahac, for being a believing mirror

Domenica Cameron-Scorsese, for her love and discernment

Jeremy Tarcher, for his friendship and guidance

Edmund Towle, for his good-humored wisdom

Claire Vaccaro, for her sense of beauty

Jerusalem Is Walking in This World

This is a great happiness.
The air is silk.
There is milk in the looks
That come from strangers.
I could not be happier
If I were bread and you could eat me.
Joy is dangerous.
It fills me with secrets.
"Yes" hisses in my veins.
The pains I take to hide myself
Are sheer as glass.
Surely this will pass,
The wind like kisses,
The music in the soup,
The group of trees,
Laughing as I say their names.

It is all hosannah.
It is all prayer.
Jerusalem is walking in the world.
Jerusalem is walking in the world.

CONTENTS

INTRODUCTION

IT IS A DIM DECEMBER DAY. Outside my window, down in Riverside Park, an old woman strolls in the weak sunlight, leaning on the arm of her companion. Slowly and carefully they move along the cobbled path. Every so often they pause to take in the antics of a squirrel scampering along a tree branch or a bold blue jay swooping noisily down in front of them to claim a crumb.

One of my favorite ways to talk with friends is to walk with them. I love being engaged with the larger world and with each other. I love having my thought interrupted by the raven sailing in to land on a stone wall. I love the slow drift of autumn leaves, of snowflakes, of apple blossoms—each in season. Walking and talking humanize my life, draw it to an ancient and comforting scale. We live as we move, a step at a time, and there is something in gentle walking that reminds me of how I must live if I am to savor this life that I have been given.

Savoring this life becomes an automatic and appropriate response the minute I dispense with velocity and pressure. This earth is beautiful and so are we—if I just take the time to notice. At this time I split my life between New Mexico and New York, between walks in Riverside Park and walks on a dirt road through sagebrush, where we need to be alert for rattlers, to whom the road is an inconvenience, an interruption of their fields of rolling sage and fragrant piñon.

It is on these walks that my best ideas come to me. It is while walking that difficult clarity emerges. It is while walking that I experience a sense of well-being and connection, and it is in walking that I live most prayerfully. In New York I am a cave dweller, walking in the late afternoons, dazzled by the gold

I try to catch every sentence, every word you and I say . . .

ANTON CHEKHOV

beribboned sunsets that bedizen the city skyline. When I can, I walk with friends, noting always how companionable our silences become, how effortlessly deep and true our conversations. It is my hope that the careful, slow structure of this book will allow it to approximate such walks for you. By going slowly, we move quickly through our many layers of defense and denial until we touch the living pulse of creativity within us all. The Great Creator made this world to dazzle and move us. When we slow our tempo to match the natural world's, we do find ourselves dazzled and moved.

Ten years ago I wrote a book called *The Artist's Way,* suggesting that our creative unfolding was a spiritual unfolding and that we could work—and walk—hand in hand with the Great Creator. A decade has passed and the teachings of that book still ring true to me. The two pivotal tools, three pages of longhand morning writing called Morning Pages and a weekly solo adventure called an Artist's Date still serve me—and now a million plus readers—very well. In ten years nothing has changed. The drill remains exactly the same. In addition, another powerful tool, the Weekly Walk, has emerged as pivotal.

Nothing brings home the beauty and power of the world that we live in like walking. Moving into our bodies, we embody the truth that as artists we are out to make a "body of work," which means we must encompass more than each day's march. A Weekly Walk helps us to acquire such an overview. It allows us to find both perspective and comfort. As we stretch our legs, we stretch our minds and our souls. St. Augustine, himself a great walker, remarked, "Solvitur ambulando"—"it is solved by walking." The "it" that we solve may be as particular as a bruising romance or as lofty as the conception of a new symphony. Ideas come to us as we walk. We also invite their quieter friend, insight. Walking often moves us past the "what" of our life into the more elusive "why."

Perhaps it would be helpful to give you a sense of what my

Time is not a line, but a series of now-points.

TAISEN DESHIMARU

creative practice is like. It is daily and portable. Its only requirements are paper, pen, and shoes.

I wake up in the morning, reach for a pen and a Morning Pages journal, and I dip my soul into my current life, noting what makes me agitated, what makes me irritable, what finds me excited, what feels like drudgery. I dip my pen to the page with the same methodical devotion that a woman in the high mountains of Tibet scrubs clothes in the stream, scouring them against a rock. It is a ritual, a way to start the day and a way to come clean before myself and God. There's no pretending in Morning Pages. I really am that petty, that fearful, that blind to the miracles all around me. As I write, the light dawns—just as the sun comes up over the mountains—and more is revealed. I see why I am frightened, whom I should call to make amends to, what I need to do in this particular day's march to inch ahead a little. Just as the women washing clothes may pause long enough for that one moment of connection as the sun dazzles the flank of a towering peak, so, too, I get my moments of insight, my glimpses into the why behind the what that I am living. But for the most part, the pages are routine. I do them because I do them. I do them, because they "work." They keep my consciousness scrubbed clean.

Once a week I take some small adventure, an Artist's Date. And I do mean small. I go to the fabric store. I visit the button shop. I sneeze as I enter a dusty secondhand bookstore. I take myself to a pet shop and go to the bird section, where zebra finches, lovebirds, and cockatiels vie for attention under the doleful watching glance of a slow-moving African Gray. If I am lucky, I might visit a rug store and sense a swath of eternity tied down a knot at a time. I might visit a large clock store and hear the rhythmic ticking, steady as a mother's heart.

When I am on an Artist's Date, I stand a little outside the flow of hurried time. I declare an hour off limits from hurried production and I have the chance to marvel at my own "being"

The best thoughts most often come in the morning after waking, while still in bed or while walking.

LEO TOLSTOY

produced. I am just one soul amid so many souls, one life led amid a bouquet of lives. When I step aside from pushing time, from racing the clock, even for just one hour, I feel myself drawn to merciful scale. "We are all in this together," I learn. That and, "It is beautiful."

As driven and stressed as anyone I have ever taught, I had to learn to stop running. Walking did not come naturally to me—and it did not come a moment too soon. I was in my mid-forties before I discovered the power of this essential tool. Now, if I can daily but at least once weekly, I take an extended, soul-refreshing walk.

In our busy lives these walks may be sandwiched in by getting off the subway one stop early, leaving the house a few minutes earlier to walk instead of cab short distances. Lunch hours may become walk times, or a walk may be fit into the very late afternoon. How you walk matters less than *that* you walk. Walking allows the insights of your own inner teacher to enter a dialogue with the teacher you encounter in these pages.

Ideas come from everywhere.
ALFRED HITCHCOCK

Since I wrote *The Artist's Way,* I have heard many stories of the miraculous. Sometimes in a restaurant or on a crowded street someone will stop me and say the sentence, "Your book changed my life." I am glad to have been a conduit, but that is what it is that I have been. I simply wrote down the precepts of divine intervention in our lives the moment we engage our creativity and, through that, engage our Great Creator. What I taught, essentially, is that we are all connected and that as we notice that and surrender to that, we join a long and safe lineage: The Great Creator loves artists and is waiting as a lover waits to respond to our love when we offer it.

What we call God does not matter. That we call on God does. There is an interactive, benevolent, well-wishing something that buoys the sails of our dreams, softens our landings when our parachutes billow closed after a creative flight. This creative something, the Great Creator, takes interest in our creativity, moves naturally and inevitably to support our creativity, recognizing our creative ideas as children of its own making.

Walking in this world, we do not go unpartnered. We do not speak our prayers unheard. There is someone or a something listening with the most tender of hearts. As we open to our inner life, our outer life also shifts. Lives are transformed by a gentle form of listening that is like walking with a cherished friend who listens and then says, "You might want to try X. Oh, look at that great squirrel. . . ."

As artists in tune with the Great Creator, we are coaxed along, cajoled along, coached along. I am not saying that God is Burgess Meredith turning each of us into a Rocky, but that image might not be so far off. God is the Great Artist, and every artist encounters God in the precise form or forms most helpful and necessary to his own creative unfolding. Kindness begins to occur and it occurs as we need it, where we need it, and how we need it. One woman finds a voice teacher. Another finds a source of wonderful yarn. One man gets free editing time on an AVID bank. Another man discovers an art supply store that carries the most beautiful German pencil sharpeners to use on his composing pencils.

Nothing is too small. Nothing is too large. As we practice walking, writing our Morning Pages daily, and venturing into our Artist's Dates weekly, we begin to get a notion of the scope and scale of God—one eye on the sparrow and the other on the vast and starry universe. We are a part of all that, and, by the simple act of reaching out our hand to connect, we become a partnered part of life.

As we go within, we discover that we are not alone there. The loneliness we fear finding in art is actually the loneliness of disconnecting ourselves from our creativity and our creator. As we try our hand literally at the making of something, we do meet our maker. As we try to make more and more, more and more is made of us and through us. "Not I, but the Father doeth the work."

Our aspirations are our possibilities.

SAMUEL JOHNSON

Artists throughout the centuries have talked about inspiration. They have reported the whispers of the divine that came to them when they inclined their ear to listen. Aligning their own creativity with that of their creator, composers exclaimed, "Straight away the ideas flew in on me!" Such ideas can—and do—fly in on all of us. They are the squirrel scampering along the branch. They are the stray pink blossom lighting on a cheekbone. They are the light but definite touch of the unseen world touching our own whenever we are willing to be touched.

Walking in This World is intended as a gentle pilgrimage. We will move issue to issue, walking and talking about the deeper concerns of our souls. I say "souls" because creativity is a spiritual rather than an intellectual endeavor. Creativity is a daily spiritual practice and, like all spiritual paths, it is both mysterious and trackable.

Walking in This World is intended to demystify the obstacles commonly found on the creative path. It addresses issues common not only to creative beginners but to those much further down the creative road. If *The Artist's Way* can safely be said to have launched many travelers on the creative seas, this book is intended to bring to those travelers needed supplies in the form of clarity and encouragement. The creative life is rewarding but difficult. Much of that difficulty is eased by a sense of shared faith and companionship.

Walking in this world a footfall at a time, we walk accompanied by angels, by and large unseen but not unfelt. As we open ourselves to divine guidance—in the form of our own listening creativity—we are brought to the divine in this world and in our all-too-worldly hearts.

It is your work in life that is the ultimate seduction.

PABLO PICASSO

Basic Tools

MANY PEOPLE who have worked with my earlier books *The Artist's Way* and *The Vein of Gold* will have a familiarity with the basic tools of my creative practice. Newcomers will need such a familiarity. Therefore, all readers should take the time to review or learn the three simple tools: Morning Pages, the Artist's Date, and the Weekly Walk. You will be asked to practice them for the duration of this course.

TOOL 1: Morning Pages

Morning Pages are the primary tool of a creative recovery. From my perspective they are the bedrock of a creative life. Three pages stream-of-consciousness writing done before the day "begins," Morning Pages serve to prioritize, clarify, and ground the day's activities. Frequently fragmented, petty, even whining, Morning Pages were once called "brain drain" because they so clearly siphoned off negativity. Anything and everything is fuel for Morning Pages. They hold worries about a lover's tone of voice, the car's peculiar knocking, the source of this month's rent money. They hold reservations about a friendship, speculation about a job possibility, a reminder to buy Kitty Litter. They mention, sometimes repeatedly, overeating, undersleeping, overdrinking, and overthinking, that favorite procrastinator's poison artists are fond of.

I have been writing Morning Pages for twenty years now. They have witnessed my life in Chicago, New Mexico, New York, and Los Angeles. They have guided me through book writing, music writing, the death of my father, a divorce, the

. . . we all need the reassuring and healing messages that treasured rituals provide.

SARAH BAN BREATHNACH

purchase of a house and a horse. They have directed me to piano lessons, to exercise, to an energetic correspondence with a significant man, to pie baking, to rereading and refurbishing old manuscripts. There is no corner of my life or consciousness that the pages have not swept. They are the daily broom that clears my consciousness and readies it for the day's inflow of fresh thought.

I write my Morning Pages in *The Artist's Way Morning Pages Journal* that I designed for just such use. You might write your Morning Pages in a shiny spiral-bound notebook. Some people write their pages by computer, although I strongly recommend writing them by hand. Even the shape of my writing tells me the shape and clarity of my thoughts. Of course, at times Morning Pages are difficult to write. They feel stilted, boring, hackneyed, repetitive, or just plain depressing. I have learned to write through such resistant patches and to believe that Morning Pages are a part of their cure. I know people who are "too busy" to write Morning Pages. I sympathize, but I doubt their lives will ever become less busy without Morning Pages.

It is a paradox of my experience that Morning Pages both take time and give time. It is as though by setting our inner movie onto the page, we are freed up to act in our lives. Suddenly, a day is filled with small choice points, tiny windows of time available for our conscious use. It may be as simple as the fact that we wrote down "I should call Elberta" that cues us into calling Elberta when a moment looms free. As we write Morning Pages, we tend to get things "right." Our days become our own. Other people's agendas and priorities no longer run our lives. We care for others, but we now care for ourselves as well.

I like to think of Morning Pages as a withdrawal process but not in the usual sense, where we withdraw from a substance taken away from us. No, instead, we *do* the withdrawing in Morning Pages. We pull ourselves inward to the core of our true values, perceptions, and agendas. This process takes approximately a half hour—about the same time normally set aside for meditation. I have come to think of Morning Pages as a form of

We must be willing to get rid of the life we've planned, so as to have the life that is waiting for us.

JOSEPH CAMPBELL

meditation, a particularly potent and freeing form for most hyperactive Westerners. Our worries, fantasies, anxieties, hopes, dreams, concerns, and convictions all float freely across the page. The page becomes the screen of our consciousness. Our thoughts are like clouds crossing before the mountain of our observing eye.

When I first began writing Morning Pages, I lived at the foot of Taos Mountain in New Mexico. I was stymied in my life, my art, and my career. One morning I simply got the idea to write Morning Pages, and I have been doing them ever since. A day at a time, a page at a time, my daily three pages have unknotted career, life, and love. They have shown me a path where there was no path, and I follow it now, trusting that if I do, the path will continue. For the duration of work with this book, and, I hope, far longer, I would ask you to write daily Morning Pages. They will lead you to an inner teacher whose profundity will amaze you. Only you can swing open the gate for your teacher to enter. It is my hope you will do so now.

TOOL 2: The Artist's Date

Pivotal to a creative recovery is a second essential tool: the Artist's Date. Grounded in a sense of adventure and autonomy, the Artist's Date is a once-weekly, hour-long solo expedition to explore something festive or interesting to your creative consciousness. If Morning Pages are assigned work, the Artist's Date is assigned play. But do not be misled into skipping it as "less important." The phrase "the play of imagination" has well-earned currency because art *is* made by an imagination at play. The artist who forgets how to play soon enough forgets how to work. The flier into the unknown, the leap of faith onto page, stage, or easel, becomes ever more difficult to take without practice.

At bottom, art is an image-using process. We dip into the well of our consciousness to find images and events for our imagination to employ. Unless we are careful, it is easy to over-

It's a great relief to me to know that I can actually be creative and be happy at the same time.

JAMES W. HALL

fish our inner well, to deplete our reservoir of images. Fishing for something to say, do, or draw, we find new ideas more and more elusive. Nothing "hooks" us.

The conscious use of a weekly Artist's Date, and double that, if we are working flat out, replenishes the inner well and creates a sense of well-being. Synchronicity—that uncanny knack of being in the right place at the right time—picks up markedly as we practice Artist's Dates. Just as cabin fever and a sense of personal restless claustrophobia overtakes an invalid who is sick and too long housebound, so, too, an artist without Artist's Dates suffers a sense of constriction. I know this from personal experience, as I have suffered long periods of ill health. Always, when I return to the practice of Artist's Dates, my sense of well-being increases and my work deepens and enlarges.

For the duration of this course, and longer I would hope, you are asked to take your inner artist on a weekly outing. Expect resistance and self-sabotage—as you plan something adventurous and enjoyable, only to catch yourself sabotaging your date. Our inner artist is a volatile and vulnerable creature, needy as the child of divorce. It wants your undivided time and attention at least once a week so that it can tell you its dreams and difficulties. Painful as these may be, is it any wonder we sometimes avoid such contact? Be alert to resisting your resistance.

A hunch is creativity trying to tell you something.

FRANK CAPRA

TOOL 3: Weekly Walks

Most of us spend life on the run, too busy and too hurried to walk anywhere. Beset by problems and difficulties, we feel walking is a frivolous waste of time—our valuable time. "When will I do it?" becomes one more problem, one more question for our busy mind. The truth is that walking holds our solutions.

It was during a time in which my life felt directionless both personally and creatively that I discovered the solace and direction to be found in walking. At the time I owned a 1965 Chevy pickup named Louise. Every afternoon I would load Louise with a half-dozen dogs and point the truck down a dirt road into the sagebrush. A mile into "nowhere," I would park the truck on the roadside and signal to the dogs that they were free to roam—as long as they stayed within hailing distance. Then I would set off walking. I would walk a forty-five-minute loop, south and east toward the foothills, then north and west directly toward Taos Mountain. As I walked, emotions would wash through me. I was grieving a lost marriage and the death of my father, for many years a close creative companion. I would walk and ask for guidance. Clouds would pass in front of the mountain. I would notice the cloud and then notice that I did have a sense of guidance. I knew what to write, how to write it, and that write it I should. A day at a time, a walk at a time, even a simple step at a time, my sad and tangled life began to sort itself. I say sort itself because all I did was "walk through it." I have been walking ever since.

"Walk on it" is good advice, whether the problem is a persnickety plotline or a persistent personality clash. Native Americans pursue vision quests, Aborigines do walkabout. Both of these cultures know that walking clears the head. Too often in our modern culture we mistake the head for the source of all wisdom rather than the manufacturer of malcontent. For the duration of this course, you are asked to take at least one twenty-minute walk a week. You will find that these walks focus your thinking and instigate your breakthroughs. You will contact the "imagic-nation"—that realm of larger thoughts and ideas well known to shamans and spiritual seekers. It is my hope that the habit of walking and the habit of talking to those you love as you walk will both be awakened by this course.

What we have to learn to do, we learn by doing.

ARISTOTLE

HOW TO Use the Basic Tools

1. **Set your alarm clock to ring one half hour earlier than usual; get up and do three pages of longhand, stream-of-consciousness writing.** Do not reread these pages or allow anyone else to read them. Ideally, stick these pages in a large manila envelope or set them aside and hide them somewhere. Welcome to Morning Pages. They will change you.

2. **Take yourself on an Artist's Date.** You will do this every week for the duration of this course. A sample Artist's Date: Take yourself to your local children's toy store. In the front of the store, near the cash register, you will find "impulse buys" like stick-'em stars, funny pencils and pens, bubbles, and stickers. Let your artist have a treat or two. You may want gold stars for every day you do get your Morning Pages written—that's seven stars for seven days, we hope. The point of your Artist's Date is more mystery than mastery. Do something that enchants and entices your artist.

3. **Take a Weekly Walk.** Outfit yourself in your most comfortable socks and shoes. Set out for a good twenty-minute ramble. You may choose a park, a country road, or an urban route. Where you walk matters less than that you walk. Go far enough and long enough that you feel both your body and your mind "unkink." You may discover that you like walking very much and that you enjoy doing it more than once weekly. Walks definitely help you to metabolize the content of this course.

CREATIVITY CONTRACT

I,_____, commit myself to the regular use of the three basic tools. For the duration of this course, I will write Morning Pages daily and will take an Artist Date's and Weekly Walk once a week. Additionally, I commit myself to excellent self-care, adequate sleep, good food, and gentle companionship.

_____(signature)

_____(date)

Discovering a Sense of Origin

This week initiates your creative pilgrimage.
You are the point of origin. You begin where you
are, with who you are, at this time, at this place. You
may find yourself hopeful, skeptical, excited, resistant,
or all of the above. The readings and tasks in week one
all aim at pinpointing the "you" you have been evading.
When we avoid our creativity, we avoid ourselves.
When we meet our creativity, we meet ourselves,
and that encounter happens in the moment.
The willingness to be ourselves gives us
the origin in originality.

Setting Out

You say you want to make art. You want to begin or you want
to continue. This is good. We need a more artful world, and that
means we need you and the specific contribution that you and
you alone can make. But to make it you must start somewhere,
and that is often the sticking point.

"It's too late."

"I'm not good enough."

"I'll never be able to pull this off."

We all have our fears, and they feel as real as the chair you are
sitting in. Like that chair, they can be slouched into or left behind. Sometimes we need to sit up and ignore the cricks in our

back and shoulders and just begin. That's how it is with art. We just need to begin.

Begin where you are, with *who* you are. In order to go where you want to go creatively, you have to start somewhere. And the best place to start is precisely where you are. This is true whether you are a beginning artist or someone with long miles down the track. In fact, seasoned artists can waste time and energy mulling the dignity of their acquired position in the field when the truth is, they still need to just start again.

Writing doesn't really care about where you do it. It cares *that* you do it. The same is true for drawing. I watched a friend of mine waste a solid year because he "couldn't work without a studio." When he did get a studio and went back to work, what he made were a few largish paintings but a great many beautiful miniature charcoal and pencil drawings that he could have done on a TV table had he been so inclined. No, he didn't work—not because he didn't have a studio but because he didn't work. There is room for art in any life we have—any life, no matter how crowded or overstuffed, no matter how arid or empty. We are the "block" we perceive.

If you are a beginning musician and want to learn piano, sit down at the piano and touch the keys. Great. Tomorrow you can sit down at the piano and touch the keys again. Five minutes a day is better than no minutes a day. Five minutes might lead to ten, just as a tentative embrace leads to something more passionate. Making art is making love with life. We open ourselves to art as to love.

Instead of thinking about conquering an art form, think instead of kissing it hello, wooing it, exploring it in small, enticing steps. How many of us have burned through promising relationships by moving too swiftly? How many of us have burned out in new creative ventures by setting goals too high? Most of us.

Doing any large creative work is like driving coast to coast, New York to Los Angeles. First you must get into the car. You

All serious daring starts from within.

EUDORA WELTY

must begin the trip, or you will never get there. Even a night in New Jersey is a night across the Hudson and on your way. A small beginning is exactly that: a beginning. Rather than focus on large jumps—which may strike us as terrifying and un-jumpable—we do better to focus on the first small step, and then the next small step after that. "Oh, dear," you might be sniffing, "where's the drama in such baby steps?" Think about that for a minute. When a baby takes its first step, it is *very* dramatic.

Today my mail contained a manila envelope from a friend, a born storyteller who spent years wanting to write and not writ-ing. Last June, on a perfectly ordinary day, Larry did an extraor-dinary thing for him: He picked up a pen and started writing. I now have a fat sheaf of stories in my hand. All he needed to do was begin. And then begin again the next day.

Often, when we yearn for a more creative life, we cue up the sound track for high drama. With great dissonant chords crash-ing in our heads, we play out the scenario of leaving those we love and going somewhere lonely and perhaps exotic, where we will be Artists with a capital A. When I hear this plan, I think, *Okay. You do it*. Experience has taught me that my artist per-forms best when the stakes are lower. When I keep the drama on the page, pages accumulate.

I hate to say this, but making art is a little like dieting. One day you just have to start and what you do that day is the begin-ning of success or failure. I cannot write an entire book today, but I can write one page. I cannot become an accomplished pi-anist, but I can put in fifteen minutes of piano time. Today you may not get a one-woman show in SoHo, but you can sketch the battered leather chair with your cocker spaniel sprawled in splendid comfort or you can sketch the curve of your lover's arm. You *can* begin.

Creativity is inspiration coupled with initiative. It is an act of faith and, in that phrase, the word "act" looms as large as the "faith" that it requires.

The realization of the self is only possible if one is productive, if one can give birth to one's own potentialities.

JOHANN WOLFGANG
VON GOETHE

In dreams begins responsibility.
WILLIAM BUTLER YEATS

When we do not act in the direction of our dreams, we are only "dreaming." Dreams have a will-o'-the-wisp quality. Dreams coupled with the firm intention to manifest them take on a steely reality. Our dreams come true when we are true to them. Reality contains the word "real." We begin to "reel" in our dreams when we toss out the baited hook of intention. When we shift our inner statement from "I'd love to" to "I'm going to," we shift out of victim and into adventurer. When we know that we "will," then we couple the power of our will with the power of future events. In this sense, what we "will do" becomes what "will happen." To prove this to ourselves, we need to couple the largeness of our dream with the small, concrete, and do-able "next right thing." As we take the next small step, the bigger steps move a notch closer to us, downsizing as they move. If we keep on taking small enough next steps and therefore keep chipping away and miniaturizing what we like to call "huge" risks, by the time the risk actually gets to our door, it, too, is simply the next right thing, small and do-able and significant but nondramatic. Many of us falter, thinking that in order to begin a creative work we must know precisely how to finish it and, beyond that, to insure its reception in the world. We are, in effect, asking for a guarantee of our success before we have taken the single most important step necessary to insure it. That step is commitment.

When we realize that we want to make something—a book, a play, a sketch, a poem, a painting—we are yearning for the completion of that desire. We hunger to make art the same way we may hunger to make love. It begins as desire, and desire requires that we act upon it if we are to conceive things.

Despite our culture's well-earned reputation for encouraging instant gratification, we are *not* encouraged to act decisively upon our creative desires. We are trained to think about them, doubt them, second-guess them. We are trained, in short, to talk ourselves out of committing art or committing *to* art.

When movie director Martin Ritt told me "Cerebration is

the enemy of art," he was urging that as artists we follow that Nike slogan, "Just do it." He wasn't saying that brains were counter to the creative process, but he was urging us to use our brains to actually make art, not think about making art. Thinking is not the enemy, but overthinking is.

If you *conceptualize* launching a project, you begin to understand the issue of overthinking. Think of your project as "the arrow of desire." Imagine yourself eyeing the bull's-eye, pulling back the bow—and then thinking about it. Worrying about it. Considering whether you are aiming exactly right or whether you should be a smidgen higher or lower. Your arm begins to get tired. Then your aim begins to get shaky. If you manage to finally shoot the arrow, it does not sail with confidence and strength. You have that in your vacillation about exactly *how* you should shoot. In short, you have mistaken beginning something with ending something. You have wanted a finality that is earned over time and not won ahead of time as a guarantee. You have denied the process of making art because you are so focused on the product: Will this be a bull's-eye? We forget that intention is what creates direction. If we aim with the eye of our heart—"*That* I desire to do"—then we aim truly and well. "Desire," that much-maligned word, is actually the best guide for our creative compass. Horseback riders who jump the Grand Prix fences of terrifying heights talk of "throwing their heart" over the fence so their horse jumps after it. We must do the same.

We have attached so much rigamarole to the notion of being an artist that we fail to ask the simplest and most obvious question: Do I want to make this? If the answer is yes, then begin. Fire the arrow.

We take no step unpartnered. We may feel like the fool from the Tarot deck, stepping heedlessly into blank space, but that is not reality. The Great Creator is an artist and he/she/it is an artist in partnership with other artists. The moment we open ourselves to making art, we simultaneously open ourselves to our maker. We are automatically partnered. Joseph Campbell

Action is eloquence.
WILLIAM SHAKESPEARE

speaks of encountering "a thousand unseen helping hands." I think of these hands as an invisible web ungirding any creative endeavor. It is like throwing a switch or toppling the first domino—there is a spiritual chain reaction that occurs the moment we act on faith. Something or somebody acts back.

It is when we fire the arrow of desire, when we actually start a project, that we trigger the support for our dream. *We* are what sets things in motion—people and events resonate toward our fiery resolve. Energy attracts energy. Our arrow is the speeding pickup truck that attracts summer dogs to chase it down the road. We generate the energy and excitement. Then others will give chase. "Build it and they will come."

Nothing great was ever achieved without enthusiasm.

RALPH WALDO EMERSON

Creative energy is energy. When we are worrying *about* creating instead of actually creating, we are wasting our creative energy. When we are vacillating, we are letting air out of our tires. Our pickup is not speeding down the road and may never even get out of the driveway. Our project goes flat.

Does this mean we should race off wildly? No, but it does mean that once we have a heart's desire we should act on it. It is that action, that moving out on faith, that moves mountains—and careers.

The book you are holding now is a book that I am writing on Riverside Drive in Manhattan and in my upstairs bedroom in northern New Mexico—also, in the car and in truck stops as I drive cross-country between the two. None of this behavior matches my drama about being a real writer. In that drama, either I have gone to Australia, where I walk the beaches and beg for inspiration, or else I am freezing in a cabin near Yosemite with nothing to do all winter but shiver and write. When we approach creativity that way, it smacks of the creativity firewalk or the creativity bungee jump—definitely terrifying and not something I'd want to try in the next few minutes or without my will made out. It is one of the ironies of the creative life that while drama is a part of what we make, it has almost no place in how we make it. Even those famous artists who suffered fa-

mously dramatic lives were remarkably undramatic in their actual work habits. Hemingway wrote five hundred words a day,
wife in and wife out. Composer Richard Rodgers wrote a composition every morning, nine to nine-thirty. His colleague, Oscar Hammerstein, rose at six and put in banker's hours on his
farm in Doylestown, Pennsylvania. Unseduced by glamour or
by drama, their output was both steady and prodigious. This argues that we get a lot further creatively by staying put and doing
something small and do-able daily in the life we already have.

So much of the difficulty with beginning lies in our perception that we have "so far to go." We have separated art from
process into product—"So far to go until it's finished"—when
we think like that and we have also separated ourselves from
God. When we are afraid to begin, it is always because we are
afraid we are alone—tiny, like little Davids facing giant Goliaths.
But we are not alone.

God is present everywhere. The act of making art is a direct
path to contact with God, and we do not need to travel any ge-
ographic or psychic distance to experience the grace of creation
in the grace of our own creating.

Goethe told us, "Whatever you think you can do, or believe
you can do, begin it, because action has magic, grace and power
in it." This was no mere bromide. It was a report on spiritual experience—an experience that each of us can have whenever
we surrender to being a beginner, whenever we dismantle our
adult's aloof avoidance and actively seek the Great Creator's
hand by reaching out our own to start anew.

If we stop watching the movies in our head with the scary
sound tracks and start listening to things like "Whistle While
You Work" or "Zippity Doo-Dah," we may begin to make a little headway. We need to get into reality. Art is about making art,
nothing more dramatic than that. Puccini may have written
Madame Butterfly, but he still hummed as he walked on a sunny
street. He still ate pasta and he still spent enough time with his
friends to concoct a plot the village gossip might handily have

*I expect the gift of good and
industrious hours.*

RAINER MARIA RILKE

provided. High art is made by people who have friends and the need to dine on more than inspiration soup.

TASK:

What the Hell, You Might As Well

Often we experience a sense of powerlessness because we do not see any direct action that we can take to concretely alter our sense of being stuck, in a particular way. At times like this we'd do well not to be so linear. Sometimes, we need to exercise just a little elbow grease in any creative direction that we can find. If nothing else, taking a small creative action moves us out of the victim position. Suddenly, we realize that we do have choices and options and that our passivity may boil down to a stubborn laziness, a sort of tantrum that says "If I can't make X better right now, then I am not going to do anything." Instead of a tantrum, try doing this instead:

Take pen in hand and number down from 1 to 20. List 20 small, creative actions you *could* take. For example:

In Heaven an angel is nobody in particular.

GEORGE BERNARD SHAW

1. Paint the kitchen windowsill.
2. Hang lace on my bedroom door.
3. Put the primrose into a good pot.
4. Change the downstairs shower curtain.
5. Buy photo albums and put my dog pictures in one.
6. Send my sister the fudge recipe she asked for.
7. Send my sister fudge.
8. Buy red socks.
9. Wear them to church.
10. Make a computer file of poems I love.
11. Send a great poem to each of my friends.
12. Photograph my current life and send the pictures to my grandmother.

13. Designate something a "God Jar," a special incubator for my dreams and hopes.

14. Designate something else a "what the hell!" basket for my resentment, annoyances, and fears.

15. Throw a slumber party and request that each guest bring a good ghost story to tell.

16. Make a pot of soup.

17. Give away every outfit I even mildly dislike.

18. Get a CD player for my car and stock it.

19. Go to a great perfume store and get one great perfume.

20. Take an elderly friend to a good aquarium.

Commitment

Very often, calling it professionalism, we become too busy to make art for art's sake. We are committed to a certain careerist, professional agenda and we tell ourselves that is all we have energy or time for. This is false. When we make the art we love, it *makes* time and energy available to us for our professional pursuits. Why? Because we feel more vital, and that vitality is assertive energy that makes room for its own desires.

Follow your bliss.
JOSEPH CAMPBELL

When we say "I will articulate my true values, I will express my essence," that word "will" throws a switch. When we "will," then we "will." In this sense we are predicting our future and shaping it simultaneously. Everything is energy. Ideas are simply organized energy, a sort of mold into which more solidified energy can be poured. A book begins as an idea. So does a social movement. So does a building. We cast our dreams and desires ahead of us, and as we move toward them, their content takes on solidity. We cocreate our lives. This is both our responsibility and our privilege. A symphony moves both through and ahead of a composer. As he moves toward it, it moves toward him. In a sense, as artists, we both pitch a ball of creative energy and catch it.

Commit to make something you love and you will find that the needed supplies come to hand. You must "catch" them when they do. A free studio for recording. Use of an editing bank. A windfall of costumes from your aunt's attic. A church space newly renovated and looking for a worthy cause, like your embryonic theater company. Our creative energy triggers a creative response.

Commit to playing the music you love, and the music of life becomes more lovely. Just as making love can quite literally make love, so, too, making art—a form of the verb "to be"—can quite literally make art out of being. The art of creative living, like the actor's art, is a moment-to-moment receptivity, a harmonious leaning into the unfolding melodic structure of existence such as great string ensemble players use in cocreating chamber music. Those who create for love—like the devotees who practice their spiritual tradition with ardor—give off a certain undefinable something that is attractive, and it attracts to them their good.

When we make art for the sake of making art, we tend eventually to make money. Money is energy, and it follows the path we lay down for it. When we commit that we will do something, the finances that allow us to do it follow. Our committed intention attracts supply. This is spiritual law, if not what we are taught to believe. Money is really a codified form of power. Often we think we need X amount of money to attain Y space, but what we really need is the space itself. Intention creates power, often as money, sometimes as access. Art triggers abundance, but it triggers it in diverse forms. Our cash flow may not immediately increase, but our opportunity flow *will* increase. So will many benevolent coincidences or synchronicities that will enrich our lives and our art if we let them. Receptivity is key, and that key unlocks the treasure chest.

Faith moves mountains, and when we see art as an act of faith, then we begin to see that when we commit to our art, mountains may indeed be moved as a path becomes clear. Committed to the "what," we trigger the "how"—needed money may appear in the form of an unexpected bonus, a timely and lucrative freelance job, a surprise inheritance, matching funds, or even a corporate scholarship. When we invest energy in our dreams, others often invest cash. A gifted young pianist receives an unexpected year's financial backing from an older couple from his hometown who are "betting" on him and his talent. A young actor, similarly marooned in a backwater, is given travel funds to audition for the conservatory that chooses him and gives him a scholarship. As we commit to our dreams, something benevolent commits back. Supportive coincidence can be counted upon. Artist to artist, we can safely have faith in the Great Creator's interest in our creative pursuits.

Art is a matter of commitment. Commitment is of interest to the Great Creator. When we display the faith necessary to make our art, the Great Creator displays an interest and an active hand in supporting what it is we are doing. We receive supply in all forms.

A composer who works most often on commission for others recorded for himself a small personal work that he thought of as a musical prayer. It is a simple piece of music and a simple, short recording. So simple and so short that the composer looped it four times and considers the resulting twenty-minute version something a person might meditate to—"just something I made for myself, for my own spiritual use."

Staying a few days as a houseguest at another composer's house, he played the brief recording for his friend. It happened to be running when the doorbell rang and a prominent record company executive came to visit. "What's that?" he immediately wanted to know.

"Just a little personal something I laid down to express myself."

"You mean a prayer?"

"Something like that."

"I've just been made the head of a new division on contemporary spiritual music. Do you think you could build an album around that?"

How often things occur by mere chance which we dare not even hope for.

TERENCE

"Yes, I suppose I could."

Out of the tiny recording, a large and beautiful album was born. Out of the album, a new direction for the composer's career was born. He began to work with larger choral groups and to write more music for voice. This new direction was profoundly satisfying.

"I had always loved chorales, and the idea of a modern oratorio expressing our spiritual values was like an answered prayer for me—a prayer I had barely voiced before it was answered."

It may well be that the "self" in self-expression is not only the voice of our finite, individual self but also the voice of the Self, that larger and higher force of which we are both subject and substance. When we express our creativity, we are a conduit for the Great Creator to explore, express, and expand its divine nature and our own. We are like songbirds. When one of us gives voice to our true nature, it is contagious and others soon give tongue as well. There is an infallibility to the law that as we each seek to express what we are longing to say, there is always someone or something that is longing to hear precisely what we have expressed. We do not live or create in isolation. Each of us is part of a greater whole and, as we agree to express ourselves, we agree to express the larger Self that moves through us all.

To be what we are, and to become what we are capable of becoming, is the only end of life.

ROBERT LOUIS STEVENSON

TASK:
Express Yourself

Take pen in hand and number from 1 to 10. List 10 positive adjectives used to describe you, for example:

1. Inventive
2. Original
3. Zany
4. Hard-driving
5. Humorous

6. Articulate
7. Innovative
8. Generous
9. Enthusiastic
10. Active

Take pen in hand again and write yourself a personal ad using the terms you listed to create a positive and provocative picture of your uniqueness, for example:

Experience the laser insights of an inventive, humorous, and innovative creative guide.

It is worth noting here that the point of this tool is not self-transformation but self-acceptance. If you are intense, so be it. There are those who love intense. If your irreverent humor offends the hyperserious crowd, it *will* be appreciated elsewhere. When we affirm rather than deny the characteristics often singled out, we begin to have a much more accurate idea of by whom, and where, our traits will be appreciated.

Snow

There is a soft and beautiful snow falling outside my window. The ink-black trees in Riverside Park look like a line drawing of trees. The sky is gray and luminous. It's a day for soup and knitting, if we did that anymore. It is certainly a day for knitting up the soul.

We go pell-mell, most of us, and a day like this, when the snow muffles the drumbeat of that insistent sound track that urges us to achieve, achieve, achieve, can come as a relief—the way a bad cold can force us to bed and to getting current with ourselves.

The snowflakes are more than flurries, less than a storm.

The most beautiful thing we can experience is the mysterious.

ALBERT EINSTEIN

They fall each with a particular velocity, feathers from a pillow given a firm celestial shake. Higher realms feel very close in a snowstorm.

As a little girl, my bedroom window overlooked our driveway. The peak of our garage had a floodlight, and when it snowed, I would lie in bed and watch the dancing flakes falling in swirls, sometimes rising in a whirl like a great petticoat. I grew up in Libertyville, Illinois, in a house in the country, yellow wood and fieldstone, a kind of overgrown cottage filled with small rooms and odd corners, places for the imagination to play, to stare out the window at the snow.

We all need a window for the imagination. We need a time and a place to stare out the window at the snow. On a day like today, with a great black crow flapping through the dark limbs, it is easy to see how Poe could write his *Raven,* mere blocks from here, staring at the same snow and some dark bird, a century ago. Artists have stared out of windows and into their souls for a very long time. It is something in the staring-out that enables us to do the looking-in. We forget that.

So often we try to gird ourselves to face a harsh and difficult world when we might instead gentle both ourselves and our world just by slowing down.

We worry rather than ruminate. We fret rather than speculate. Even football teams take time-outs, but it is so hard for us, as artists, to do the same. So often we feel there is so much we yearn to do and so little time to do it in. We could take a cue from music here: "Rest" is a musical term for a pause between flurries of notes. Without that tiny pause, the torrent of notes can be overwhelming. Without a rest in our lives, the torrent of our lives can be the same.

Even God rested. Even waves rest. Even business titans close their office doors and play with the secret toys on their desks. Our language of creativity knows this. We talk about "the play of ideas," but we still overwork and underplay and wonder why we feel so drained.

Genius, in truth, means little more than the faculty of perceiving in an un-habitual way.

WILLIAM JAMES

A friend of mine, a glorious musician, works on two music faculties and tours internationally. Sometimes his great voice, an instrument of beauty as large and soaring as a pipe organ, reaches my ear haggard with fatigue. His great strength becomes his great weakness. He forgets to rest.

As artists living with the drone of commerce, we have forgotten that "rest" is a musical term, and that to hear the music of our lives as something other than a propulsive drumbeat, driving us forward as the war drums drove men into bloody battle, we may *need* to rest.

The ego hates to rest. The ego doesn't want to let God, or sleep, mend up the raveled sleeve of care. The ego would like to handle all that itself, thank you. As artists, we must serve our souls, not our egos. Our souls need rest. This is something my artist-mother knew well.

As artists, it serves us to consciously find windows to the world of wonder—we must locate places that open the trapdoor in our imagination and allow the breath of greater worlds to enter our too-claustrophobic lives. You may find the window for your imagination in the upper cranny of your neighborhood library. There, tucked amid the rafters, amid the high and dusty tomes, you may look out an upper window and sense a world of other writers staring over your shoulder with you. Or you might find your imagination climbing aboard a Persian carpet in an Oriental-rug store, where the leaf-by-leaf turning of intricate patterns, like woven stained-glass windows, might transport you to bygone centuries. A clock store might paradoxically help you step beyond time as you stand amid a small forest of chiming and ticking grandfathers and magical cuckoos.

For Allison, it was always a visit to a grand plant store that gave her imagination room to breathe. Something in the steamy jungle air, the brightly flaming colors, spoke to her of special worlds. Carolina loved antique-clothing stores. She would handle a vintage frock and feel herself transported to a gentler world. For David, the world of vintage model cars lit up the boy

We are the children of our landscape; it dictates behavior and even thought in the measure to which we are responsive to it.

LAWRENCE DURRELL

The most visible joy can only reveal itself to us when we've transformed it, within.

RAINER MARIA RILKE

explorer that is his inner artist. He loves the sleek lacquered shells resembling beautiful oversized bugs. Just whizzing a model along a showcase lid gives him a thrill. For Edward, model trains and great toy stores—more for himself than his "excuses," his young nephews—light up his imagination.

The imagination is not linear. It needs to step beyond ordinary time and space. This is why the world of vintage movie posters gives Michael a thrill. This is why Lorraine loves to visit the large, multifloored fabric stores downtown in Chicago's Loop and the bigger ones over near Greek Town. "I can make anything I want," she often thrills, and although she may choose a dark navy gabardine for a sensible office dress, she has still fingered a rustling taffeta that she would have worn to a turn-of-the-century tea dance.

For each of us, safety and rest come in myriad and very personal forms. My childhood friend Carolina just sent me a long white antique nightgown that makes me feel cherished. Baking pies makes me feel safe—pie making is a tradition among the women in my family. Making vegetable soup, another family tradition, also soothes and calms my hectic citified, careerified soul. My mother, Dorothy, when overwrought, would retreat to the piano and play the Blue Danube waltz until her soul settled back into three-quarter time.

Jean, in the throes of an unexpected and overwhelming divorce, found herself agitated and adrenalized, afraid of "going under" financially. She needed more hours in a day to frantically do all that she felt should be done. A wise older friend familiar with Jean's abandoned hobby, doing needlepoint, and familiar, too, with the fact that such a meditative activity would help Jean to quietly tap her deeply creative sources, suggested that Jean return to needlepoint. When she did, she returned also to a sense of optimism and perspective. A stitch at a time, she began to mend her heart and her life—slowing down, she speeded herself toward recovery and creativity.

I am typing on a manual typewriter, looking at the snow from a window I have curtained in white lace. The white lace reminds me of my mother's love of snow. Maybe because she grew up in a strict wooden farmhouse surrounded by strictly planted fields and level ground, my mother loved a snowy day. Snow brought magic to such landscape, you couldn't see ten miles to the next red barn and silo. You were back to the enchanted land that must have existed before we cleared the great broad-leaf forests of maple and oak. Before you could see too far and not enough. In the winters my mother sat us down at the dining table and taught us to cut snowflakes from folded paper, stiff and white. We would tape them to the windows to have the delight of snow on winter days that were simply dark and short. Reminding me to rest, the snow reminds me of my mother, resting now, in peace.

Sometimes on Sundays in Manhattan, my musical colleague, Emma Lively, and I attend a tiny church where the music consists of nineteenth-century Protestant hymns with uplifting and reassuring literary images. "God is a rock, a harbor, a haven, a sanctuary, a fortress." Above all, God is a place of rest and safety.

The proper use of imagination is to give beauty to the world . . . the gift of imagination is used to cast over the commonplace workaday world a veil of beauty and make it throb with our esthetic enjoyment.

LIN YÜ-T'ANG

TASK:
Do Nothing

This task asks that you do nothing—and that you do it thoroughly for fifteen minutes. Here is how to set your "nothing" up. First of all, cue up a piece of music that is both calming and expansive. Secondly, lie down. Stretch out on your back, fold your arms comfortably, and let your imagination speak to you. Close your eyes and follow your train of thought wherever it leads you—into your past, into your future, into some part of your present that you have not been able, due to busyness, to fully enough inhabit. Listen to the music and to your thoughts gently unspooling and repeat to yourself gently this simple phrase, "I am enough . . . I am enough . . ." Stop striving to be more and appreciate what it is you already are.

CHECK-IN

1. **How many days this week did you do your Morning Pages?** If you skipped a day, why did you skip it? How was the experience of writing them for you? Are you experiencing more clarity? A wider range of emotions? A greater sense of detachment, purpose, and calm? Did anything surprise you? Is there a "repeating" issue asking to be dealt with?

2. **Did you do your Artist's Date this week?** Did you note an improved sense of well-being? What did you do and how did it feel? Remember, Artist's Dates can be difficult and you may need to coax yourself into taking them.

3. **Did you get out on your Weekly Walk?** How did that feel? What emotions or insights surfaced for you? Were you able to walk more than once? What did your walk do for your optimism and sense of perspective?

4. **Were there any other issues this week that felt significant to you in your self-discovery?** Describe them.

Discovering a Sense of Proportion

This week inaugurates an ongoing process of self-definition. As you redraw the boundaries and limits within which you have lived, you draw yourself to a fuller size. Coming into ourselves, we sometimes encounter resistance from those in our immediate environment. The readings and tasks of this week aim at bolstering the sense of a realistic self in the face of difficulty and even discounting.

Identity

All of us are creative. Some of us get the mirroring to know we are creative, but few of us get the mirroring to know *how* creative. What most of us get is the worried advice that if we are thinking about a life in the arts, we'd better plan to have "something to fall back on." Would they tell us that if we expressed an interest in banking?

It could be argued that as people and as artists, we are what we are—however, we also become ourselves, *all* of ourselves, by having our largeness mirrored back to us. I think of a scene from the Disney version of *Cinderella,* when the heroine sees herself in the dress for the first time and realizes she is a beauty. It's like the scene when the young hero first puts on his military uniform and becomes who he is. There is a magical "click" of recognition when the looking glass says back, "Yes, we are what we dream."

Too often we lack such mirrors and such transforming moments. No magic wand taps our life to make us into what we dream.

Like Rumpelstiltskin, the artist most frequently has to name himself. "I am an artist"—a filmmaker, a composer, a painter, a sculptor, an actor, a something—something the outer world has yet to acknowledge. Often braced by scanty support, an artist's identity is tied to a stubborn seed of inner knowing, a persistent "unrealistic" certainty in the face of sometimes daunting and difficult odds, sometimes doubting and difficult friends, sometimes dismaying and even arid creative circumstances. The fledgling composer composes, the fledgling writer writes, the fledgling painter paints from an inner imperative.

As artists, we are often in the ugly-duckling position. We have been born into families that regard us as "odd"—and we come to regard ourselves that way. (Sometimes our families are supportive, but our culture, as a whole, is not.) Our desire to make things and to make something of ourselves in the arts is often reflected back to us as "Who do you think you are?" I call this "growing up in the fun house," where our soul's aspirations are mirrored back to us in a distorted and distorting fashion that makes them appear egotistical and unrealistic: "Don't get too big for your britches," "Who do you think you are?" We often don't really know the answer to that. We know something along the lines of "I think I might be . . ." When we are surrounded by people who either cannot see us or cannot acknowledge what they see, our image blurs. We begin to feel both a certain self-doubt *and* a certain stubborn inner knowing that we may then dismiss as crazy. Part of us knows we're more than they see; part of us fears we're less than we hope. This inner friction is painful.

As artists, when a shoe doesn't fit us, we may try to walk in it anyway. If we are told that it fits, we may start to use our ex-

It is Nature who makes our artists for us, though it may be Art who taught them their right mode of expression.

OSCAR WILDE

cellent creative imaginations to imagine that it fits. We may further tell ourselves that our own discomfort at the pinching and the pain of a wrong shoe—and a wrong personal and creative identity—is just our "ego." And, we might add, just our "grandiosity." For many of us, declaring ourselves an artist is a "coming-out" process. "I think I am, I think I might be, I really identify with . . . oh, dear God, I think I am." Like any coming-out process, this is turbulent.

If we have been raised to be "officially talented" in one arena and not in another, we can be deaf and blind to the guidance that tries to nudge us toward an expanded role. "You are so musical," Julius was frequently told—but he couldn't hear it. In Julius's world, his concert pianist brother was musical and so was his operatic younger sister. "I'm just the appreciator," Julius would say. "Everybody needs an audience." A full two decades' worth of musical compliments fell on Julius's deaf ears. He wrote lyrics to "help out" his songwriter friends. When they said "You've really got an ear," he ignored them—despite the mounting evidence that he had something musical that kept slipping into expression. Oddly, it took a trip to foreign soil—to a locale where no one knew his famous family and his musical limitations—for Julius to begin writing music. A summer's European vacation became a musical odyssey.

"I swear there was music in the air. It was everywhere," Julius reported back. Away from his family role and definition, Julius began jotting down his "tunes," humming them into a tape recorder, putting them down in rudimentary fashion on children's notation paper. He didn't call himself a composer, a songwriter, or even a musician, but he did call himself happy. "Maybe I am a little musical," he finally conceded. He has been writing music and slowly learning to make music ever since. At this writing he's just started piano lessons, and when his teacher says "With your gifts you could go far," he no longer argues or turns a deaf ear. He just says thank-you and continues his exploration of unwrapping his newly acknowledged musical gift.

An ounce of action is worth a ton of theory.

FRIEDRICH ENGELS

I was born at the age of twelve on a Metro-Goldwyn-Mayer lot.

JUDY GARLAND

It could be argued that as artists we are less made than born, and often into circumstances that mask our identity. The realization often comes like something from a fairy tale—a glimpse in a cracked mirror of a creature they did not know they were. It is here the phrase "takes one to know one" comes into play. It is often an older artist who says "This is what you are, or what you might be."

All of us need and require accurate Believing Mirrors. Believing Mirrors reflect us as large and competent creatively. They mirror possibility, *not* improbability. They ignore "the odds" against us. These mirrors are held by people large enough and expansive enough spiritually not to be threatened by the size and grandeur of another artist shaking out his sizable wings. When I was twenty-two and a fledgling artist, veteran literary agent Sterling Lord took me on. The same year, William McPherson, who later won a Pulitzer of his own, hired me to write for him at *The Washington Post*. These men saw something, and all artists tell stories like mine of older artists who "mysteriously" gambled on them.

As artists, we are often grateful and indebted to those who help us know the things we know. An unhappy violist encounters an older composer who suggests a possible affinity for arranging. An arranging career sprouts wings. A singing teacher tells a young pianist, "Don't sing, play!" A photo-shop owner tells a farmer's wife, "You've got quite an eye. I wonder what you could do with a real camera." The answer is "Be a photographer," and that answer, like the film itself, develops over time when exposed to the right encouragement.

Sometimes our encouragement bubbles up unexpectedly in the passing interest of a neighbor, an art-supply clerk, an elderly aunt. Sometimes we come across a magazine article or book, catch a half hour of talk radio in our area of interest, run across a video or an Internet site specializing in our interest. We also experience a phenomenon that I call "inner support." This is an insistent and private inner knowing that tells us we are meant to be, do, or try something—even when there appears to be no outer support.

Richard Rodgers grew up with a doctor father and a brother who also entered medicine. When his own interests ran straight to the Broadway footlights, his family was supportive but unschooled in how to lend that support. Rodgers remembers going to see Saturday matinees of Jerome Kern musicals and knowing he had to grow up to be a composer—but just how to do that was uncharted territory. He tried "regular" high school, and when that failed to compel his interest, he went to the forerunner of Juilliard, where he was the only declared Broadway-bound composer on the premises.

No bird soars too high, if he soars with his own wings.
WILLIAM BLAKE

"Everyone was very kind," he remembers—his classically oriented classmates regarded him with fondness as well as curiosity. They shared his love of music, but after that and beyond that he was on his own, making his way as best he could through friends of his brothers and schoolmates and a certain lucky break involving a family friend. There was no map and, in later years, he would remark that he found his way by "just doing it." That inner itch to "just do it" is the artist's compass.

Although as artists we make maps, we seldom find them. An artistic career does not resemble the linear step-by-step climb of a banker's career trajectory. Art is not linear, and neither is the artist's life. There are no certain routes. You do not become an novelist by moving from A to B to C. Novelists are made from schoolteachers, journalists, and grandmothers. You do not become a composer by attending music school. That might make you a splendid theoretician, an avid structuralist, a discerning critic, but a composer? That is something made by music itself.

Sometimes, in the throes of an identity shift, we say in despair, "Sometimes I don't know who I am," and we are absolutely right. We are correctly sensing that some part or parts of our self are not yet spoken for—or perhaps not yet listened to.

We are far more multiple and rich than most of us assume. We are far larger and more colorful, far more powerful and intricate, far more deep and far more high than we often concede.

This is the way it is with artists. The painter becomes a potter in a fit of pique and boredom, only to discover an unsuspected passion. Like Joshua Logan, the actor becomes a director, the writer steps forward to act. None of it is expected, none of it is predicted, and yet, in cozy retrospect, the tracery of what might be called destiny is often clear. "This is what I am. This is what I am meant to do."

Curiosity is one of the permanent and certain characteristics of a vigorous intellect.

SAMUEL JOHNSON

It is one of the mysterious happinesses of the creative life that when we become willing to listen, the "still, small voice" seems to grow louder. The web of life is interconnected and an artist's prayer in Omaha is as clearly heard as the same prayer uttered in Manhattan. "Help me become what I am," we pray—and we do.

Cole Porter was from Indiana, not a hotbed of composers, not a musical Mecca, although it now features a marvelous music school. In his day it featured only his mother's gentrified encouragement. From birth Porter was a citizen of the world—and a worldly citizen at that. He knew because he listened to what he "knew." Art begins in the heart. By listening to our heart's desires and listening to them closely, we are not only led into making the art we dream of making but also into the dream of that art being realized on a meaningful scale. Like the farmer in *Field of Dreams,* we must trust enough to build it—whatever "it" is—and trust that "they" will come.

For each of us the "they" will be different. For one it will be the loving recognition from a spouse or admiring neighbor. For another the scholarship to study abroad. For another the photo published locally. For yet another the chance to perform the Christmas solo. It is a spiritual law that no art blooms without an artist also blossoming. Like the wild rose, we may be spotted by the wayside in Nebraska or drifting with a gracious tendril on the weathered wallpaper of a country home. All art calls forth art. When we say "I am," those around us speak up. Some will say "I always knew you were." Some will say "I am too."

Mystics hear voices. The question "Do you hear voices?" is used to sort the sane from the insane. And yet, as artists, we do hear voices and most insistently when we seek the guidance for our art. We are led. We are prompted. We are urged. We are *called*.

We do experience synchronicity—the fortuitous intermeshing of an inner need with an unexpected and grace-filled outer circumstance. We are forced—and reinforced—to know our path, and the more willing we are to ask what our true creative identity is, the clearer and more unmistakable our guidance becomes.

As a young, inexperienced writer, I was working at my babysitting job, when my phone rang and a high school colleague inquired whether I would like to take a job at *The Washington Post,* opening letters. I went for the interview. "I hope you don't think you're a writer," the man who hired me dolefully warned. I responded, "Oh, I am a writer. I hope you don't think I'm a journalist." He hired me and in the end we were both right—I became a first-rate journalist, writing for him and covering arts for *The Post.*

This is not to say that we will always believe our guidance or trust it. It is simply to say that the guidance is there. We are made by the Great Creator and we are intended to be creative ourselves. As we seek to cooperate with that intention, the still, small voice that all spiritual paths speak of becomes an ever more present reality. When we "go within," there is someone or something there to meet us and it is *not* mute as to our identity.

"I don't know where I got the strength of character to believe in myself," an artist will say. "It was just blind faith." And yet, faith is not blind. It is farseeing and, even as we claim to stumble in believing darkness, we are led inch by inch and hunch by hunch into what we are becoming—and so is our art.

As artists, we often speak of our creations as our "brainchil-

> *Guided by my heritage of a love of beauty and respect for strength—in search of my mother's garden, I found my own.*
>
> ALICE WALKER

dren," but we forget that our ideas and dreams impregnate us. We are inhabited by a larger life than we know. As we doubt our own identity, that identity is still guiding us, still nudging us to our rightful path. We may doubt our creative viability but, like children who *will* be born, our dreams and desires nudge us forward. Something larger and finer than we know calls us to be larger and finer than we dare. So we act on faith, descend into doubt, and watch in amazement as our dreams carry us forward with a knowing of their own. Sometimes our dreams feel born despite us.

As we dare to make our brainchildren reality, our dreams take on flesh and sinew. Not all dreams will come "true," but there will be truth present in all our dreaming. The Great Creator made us. We are ourselves works of art, and as we work to bring forward the art within us, we express our inner divinity. Perhaps this is why so many artists' stories abound with miraculous co-incidence and "inspired" hunches. Art may be the finest form of prayer. Making art is quite literally a path "to our Maker." In the act of creation, the creator reveals himself or itself to us and we, too, are revealed to ourselves as something of the divine spark from which we ourselves are made. It is this primal fact of connection, artist to artist, Great Creator to us as creator, that the truest sense of our own identity is born. We make art not merely to make our way in the world but also to make something of ourselves, and often the something that we make is a person with an inviolable sense of inner dignity. We have answered yes when our true name was called.

Pure logic is the ruin of the spirit.

ANTOINE DE SAINT-EXUPÉRY

TASK:
Identify Your Identity

Take pen in hand and answer the following questions by filling in the blanks as rapidly as you can:

1. When I was a small child, I dreamed of growing up to be _____.

2. In my childhood, my interest in what art was encouraged? _____.

3. In my childhood, my interest in what art was discouraged? _____.

4. If I had had more encouragement, I would have probably tried _____.

5. The teacher who helped me see my gifts was _____.

6. The childhood friend who helped me see my gifts was _____.

7. If I had another life, the art form I would start exploring early is _____.

8. The reason it is too late for me in this lifetime is _____.

9. One action I can take in the direction of my childhood love is _____.

10. I now commit to this dream by _____.

For many of us, questions such as these bring up sadness. Schedule an hour's undivided time and take your adult self on some small walking adventure. Do not be surprised if many feelings and intuitions and insights bubble to the surface during this Artist's Date. For many of us, our artists have been waiting to speak with us for years.

Becoming Larger

One of the pivotal problems in creative growth is the question of accurate self-assessment. How do we know how large we can be if we don't know how large we are? Frightened of being big-headed and egotistical, we seldom ask "Am I being too limited,

Genius is mainly an affair of energy.

MATTHEW ARNOLD

too small for who I really am?" Expansion can be frightening. Growth can feel foreign, even "wrong."

Most of us know the story of the three blind men who are asked to describe an elephant. One feels the trunk and says, "Ah. It is long and thin and wriggly like a snake."

Another feels the leg and says, "Ah. It is round and sturdy and a great deal like a tree."

The third blind man feels the elephant's side. He says, "Ah. An elephant is very like a wall. . . ."

The joke, of course, is that the elephant was very like all of these things and that its sum is something larger than any of its parts.

It is better to ask some questions than to know all the answers.

JAMES THURBER

As artists, we are often in that elephant's position—a large and complicated creature poorly known to itself and others. Like Alice after she ate the mushroom, we experience shifts in size as hallucinogenic events. One day we will feel very large and competent. The next day we will feel that yesterday's grander size was just grandiosity and that we are really much smaller and more wobbly than we knew. Changing sizes, we go through growing pains, and many of those pains are the pangs of an identity crisis. We may pray about it only to discover prayer is no help: God himself seems to be forging our new identity. The more we pray for it to go away, the stronger it actually becomes.

At age forty-five, after twenty-five years as a writer of words, I suddenly began to hear melody. Music piped through my system like a small chapel flooded with sound by an outsized organ. I found this scary. After all, I "knew" I was a writer, but a musician? This was "too much" to even dream.

When we change sizes creatively, we begin to wonder, *Oh, dear.* Now *what kind of animal am I?* And usually we begin to ask people to help us to know. This is where we often get in trouble. Many times our friends will know only the trunk part of us, or maybe even just the tail. In other words, what is mirrored back to us may be only the part of our artist a friend is comfortable with or can easily see.

In this way, quite inadvertently we often get miniaturized. We often get fragmented. We often feel "shattered" as we go through change because we need people who can help us to hold a larger and clearer picture of the whole creative animal we are. And, yes, that animal just might be an elephant. Oh, dear!

Understandably, friends can tend to reinforce the you that they see. They can want to hold on to a you that doesn't threaten them and that gives them a comfortable sense of their own size and importance. It is not that they are competitive precisely, it is just that they are used to thinking of you in a certain way—as a screenwriter, say, not a director—and used to thinking of themselves in relationship to you in a certain way. When you start to get bigger, it can scare both you and your friends. They worry about being abandoned. You worry about being grandiose. It is very hard to say to yourself and to others "Actually, I think I might be an elephant. I think I might be much bigger and grander than I thought. But don't worry, elephants are loyal." More often, we are disloyal to our newly emerging parts. We can allow ourselves to be talked out of our possible creative flights. Like *Dumbo,* we can be made to feel ashamed of our newly discovered, magnificent ears.

Some of our friends might tend to want to downsize us again to what we were. They have our second, third, and fourth thoughts for us. Other times, we deliberately call those friends who we know will downsize us to who we were before. "You're a perfectly good playwright. *Why* would you want to try writing a movie?" We want to be grounded by their negativity back into our formerly comfortable size and shape. The problem is, we aren't that size, and we aren't that shape. Not any longer.

The tricky part about changing sizes creatively is that we want to keep our old friends but not our old identity. We can keep those who are willing to see more of the elephant. But some of our old friends may need—at least temporarily—to be declared off limits, those who see only the elephant's tail. Their doubts of our new size are a poison for our emerging elephant.

The beginnings of all things are weak and tender. We must therefore be clear-sighted in beginnings.

MICHEL DE MONTAIGNE

An alternative is to find new friends who can see, recognize, and support what it is we are becoming. "Ah, yes, you're an elephant, come over here."

When I suddenly began writing music, I thought I might be crazy, and so did a lot of my friends. I wasn't any longer the Julia any of us knew. Following the muse was one thing—following music, quite another.

"You write *books,*" one friend actually wailed.

"You have such a gift for melody," a new friend, a composer himself, told me—and thank God he did. It can be difficult to hold our belief in the emerging parts of our creative identity. We even more than our friends may fear that we are acting crazily. A new gift can seem too good to be true. We can have a debilitating attack of modesty, asking, "Who do I think I am?" Our behavior may feel crazy, especially if the new talent was unsuspected for many years.

It's part of our cultural tradition to believe and act as if artists are crazy. Is it any wonder we sometimes feel that way ourselves? At our craziest-looking, we are sometimes our most sane. Michelangelo looked pretty strange, flat on his back, near the ceiling. With sweat, plaster, and paint stinging his eyes, not even he may always have enjoyed the comfortable certitude that he was painting a masterpiece. Strapped to a plank, with an arm tired from painting at a contortionist's angle, he, too, may have wondered, *What am I doing?*

What the hell *are* we doing? Who the hell *are* we, really? That is what we are trying to find out, and asking people is one way to do it. Often, older or more experienced artists can say, "Of course you're an actor!" or "Of course you are a writer." They can smell out our identity because it resonates with their own. They've seen baby elephants in the pupa stage before. We may not know what we are, but they do.

My friends now number many musicians who routinely think of me as "just a musician." One, who worked with me on two

If a plant cannot live according to its nature, it dies; and so a man.

HENRY DAVID THOREAU

musicals, knew me two years before he realized I "also" wrote books. So, when a new gift puts in a sudden appearance, remember: If elephants have long memories, they also have long lives. And in a single life you may inhabit many different arts.

Nelson Mandela has remarked that we do no one any favors "hiding our light" and pretending to be "smaller than we are." And yet, calling it modesty, we often try to play small and even stay small. When the creative power moving through us asks us to expand, we would rather contract, calling it more comfortable—it isn't really. We are spiritual beings, and when our spirit grows larger, so must we. There will be no comfortable resting in yesterday's definition of ourselves. It is spiritual law that as the Great Creator is always exploring, experiencing, and expanding through its creations, we must cooperate or feel the pitch of spiritual dis-ease. We can try to play small, but if the universe has big plans for us, we are better off cooperating than resisting. Creativity is God's true nature and our own. As we surrender to becoming as large as we are meant to be, great events can come to pass for us and countless others. In a sense, the size the Great Creator makes of us is none of our business. We work on art and we are the Great Creator's work of art. Perhaps we shouldn't meddle.

All aglow in the work.

VIRGIL

TASK:
Size Shifting

Although many of us have accomplished estimable things, although we may hold demanding jobs and have extensive professional résumés, when it comes time to look at our own dreams, we are suddenly struck by a debilitating modesty. Our dreams seem too big and too good to be true. We doubt our ability to accomplish them. Use the following quiz to miniaturize your doubts instead of yourself.

Take pen in hand and finish these phrases as rapidly as you can:

1. If I let myself admit it, I think I have a secret gift for

   _____ .

2. If I weren't afraid, I'd tell myself to try _____ .

3. As my own best friend, I would really cheer if I saw myself try _____ .

4. The compliment I received that seemed too good to be true was _____ .

5. If I acted on that compliment, I would let myself try

   _____ .

6. The best person to cheer me on in my secret identity is

   _____ .

7. The person I should carefully *not* tell my dream is _____

   _____ .

8. The tiniest realistic step I could take in my dreamed direction is _____ .

9. The hugest step I could take in my dreamed-of direction is _____ .

10. The step I am able to take that feels about right to me is _____ .

Sometimes, we are so overwhelmed by our life events, so swamped by the needs and expectations of others and our own feelings of (over)responsibility, we can feel completely lost, wandering in the dark woods of our own life, as hapless and at risk as Hansel and Gretel. *Where am I?* and *Who am I?* we wonder, anguished and often angry. Creating a wish list helps us remember who we are—and take small, concrete, creative actions to reinforce that identity.

Number a blank sheet of paper from 1 to 20. Writing very quickly, finish the phrase "I wish" twenty times. Your wishes will range from large to small, from simple comforts you yourself can provide to large life desires you can begin to outline for later action. This tool *never fails* to point out some small, do-able steps and, even more important, to locate our position in the compass of our own true desires. A wish list might read:

1. I wish my health were more solid.
2. I wish I had a perfume I actually liked.
3. I wish I could see my daughter.
4. I wish workmen would arrive on time or at least call if they're going to be late.
5. I wish I had a pair of nice slacks for walking.

Very often, each "wish" will suggest some small action. For example:

1. Health more solid—step up walking regime and schedule a doctor's visit. Check results of bone density test.
2. Perfume—get to a good department store and "try" a few.
3. See my daughter—schedule a visit from her formally. Call and "really" invite her. Don't just "miss" her.
4. Workmen—call and say, "Where are you? When are you coming?"
5. Slacks—go looking even if you hate shopping. See if you can find a local seamstress if shops and catalogues yield nothing.

A wish list often reveals that we need to take a concrete action for optimism to return. When we are active on our own behalf, we tend to feel less overwhelmed by the needs and wants of others.

Sometimes to "embody" knowledge we must literally get into our bodies. Take the information you have just gleaned from the above task and one more time walk on it. Allow yourself to walk into a new and larger identity in your imagination. It is often there that we first learn to comfortably inhabit a larger self.

The eyes upturned to Heaven are an act of creation.

VICTOR HUGO

Transformation

But not only medicine, engineering, and painting are arts; living itself is an art.

ERICH FROMM

Art is not linear. Neither is the artist's life, but we forget that. We try to "plan" our life and "plan" our career—as if we could. We also try to plan our growth. This means transformation catches us by surprise. The notion that we can control our path is pushed on us by advertisements and by books and by experts who promise us we can learn to control the uncontrollable. "Empower yourself," magazine headlines trumpet. Seminars and whole expos promise the same illusory goal. And yet, experience teaches that life, and especially life in the arts, is as much about mystery as it is about mastery. To be successful we must learn to follow not the leader but our own inner leadings, the "inspiration" artists have acknowledged through the centuries. "Something" is telling us to make art. We must trust that something.

Because we cannot see where we are really going, because we do not believe that the universe has any plan for us, any worthy plan we might like, our imagination begins to fly frantically around the cage of our circumstances like a cooped-up bird. We want freedom—and we will get it—but we need to get it gently and with grounding.

"I am already successful," we may tell ourselves—and rightly. We may have spent years and considerable energy getting to the top of our profession, only to be struck by a bout of inner restlessness and the unshakable, unpalatable, and unwelcome conviction that our life no longer fits us and we must try to find a new one. Tempted to "ditch everything," we may fantasize running off to the South of France or the north of Africa. We may say to ourselves, "It would be wonderful never to have to do X again," naming something for which we are well paid and well respected. Our professional niche may be so perfect, so carefully chiseled, and so "right," we do not see how we can make any change at all without totally shattering the life we have so carefully built up.

It is a spiritual law that when we are ready to transform, transformation will come to us. We are all conduits for a great creative energy that seeks expression in us and through us. When we yearn to be different, it is not just our restless ego. It is our accurate response to the creative energy within us that is seeking a new venue for expression. We are all creative and we are, in turn, creations. Just as we get restless to make something new, so, too, our creator may be restless to make something new from us. We are not experiencing a bout of hubris, we are actually experiencing a bout of humility. As we let go of our ego's demands to be totally in charge, we slip gently and quietly into a series of changes that we may set in motion through our own hand but experience as the hand of the Great Creator working through us. As we do as inwardly directed, a direction emerges.

Nature never did betray the heart that loved her.

WILLIAM WORDSWORTH

Think of taking yoga and receive a yoga flyer in your mail. Develop an interest in France and spot the ad for a bicycle vacation just after you've said, "Oh, but France would be fattening." Clarify any wish or dream or goal and experience the uncanny feeling that you have somehow magnetized information, people, and opportunities to flow toward you. The spiritual shorthand for this is the phrase "Take one step toward God and discover that God has taken a thousand steps toward you."

Call it "open-mindedness" or "the willingness to be always a beginner," but receptivity and openness characterize the temperament of all great artists, and as we consciously foster these qualities in ourselves, we are given the chance to grow and transform—not perhaps by large and immediate strokes but by small. And each tiny shift can be accompanied by inner quaking. "What's going on? Who am I? What am I doing?" we may inwardly howl as our known identity shifts.

When we begin to see that we can actually change our life, we often panic. Of course we do—prisoners often panic when they realize they can open the door of their cell and walk out "free." "Free" is terrifying after confinement. That's why we panic. "I have no idea who I am!" we gasp.

Often we are surprised to discover that there even *are* new parts to our identity. If we have surrounded ourselves with only one set of mirrors—academics, for example, or corporate types, they may see and reflect back only the parts of ourselves that they can understand. They may not show us anything like our full nature. It's a little like bird-watching. Many specimens look a lot alike until they start to fly, then you see a flash of scarlet and say, "Oh, my, that wasn't a . . . It was a . . ."

When Michael first entered creativity work, he was a lonely and alienated man. Of course he was. A man of quicksilver intelligence and rapier wit, he was ill matched to the tightly laced academic circles he traveled in. His humor was viewed with suspicion; his levity was not welcome. Self-importance was the order of the day, and self-important people liked to make Michael feel like nothing. Once Michael realized he was something, just not the something they were buying, he began to seek colleagues and pastimes where his personal traits were appreciated. Eventually, he navigated out of an academic career and into a creative one. The author now of three books, he is in demand for his lively and good-humored lecture style.

When we are changing sizes, we feel large, clear, and powerful one day, tiny and defenseless the next. We feel euphoric and then we feel enraged. This is good. This is healthy. It just doesn't feel that way. Our identified self seems false. It is not "false," just incomplete. We have the reverse of the phantom-limb syndrome, where an amputated arm or leg still itches or pinches where there is no arm or leg. Our itching and pinching may presage the sudden appearance of a new creative limb—an arm or leg of a creative career we hadn't anticipated. No wonder we panic! What are these weird sensations? Why are we suddenly interested by performance poetry, Puccini, oil paints?

We may try several sets of creative hats and shoes looking for those that fit. This is normal, natural, and to be encouraged. It is also very threatening to those who want an artistic career to progress in neat linear increments like an academic or profes-

It is only by risking from one hour to another that we live at all.

WILLIAM JAMES

sional career. Would that it could. More often we experience awkward growing pains as we grope toward a new identity role.

DO NOT INSIST ON BEING LINEAR.

To avoid panic, it helps to think of change as experimental and to treat ourselves a little like a science project. You will need to try small doses of new identity and see how it wears. Your best gift to yourself in this time will be humor. You do not need to "make yourself over" wholesale. You just need to give the newly discovered and varied parts of yourself some gentle play. And the key word is gentle. Your panic does not mean you *are* crazy, just that you feel it.

DON'T PANIC ABOUT PANIC.

If you are panicked, tell yourself, "Ah! Good sign: I am getting unstuck."

It is spiritual law that we are in the process of becoming what we *already* are—perfect creations of a perfect creator. This means that at our most awkward and ill at ease, we are still in divine order and moving ever closer to God's intention. Faith in this process, a belief that we can change and still experience the unchanging support of the universe, is critical to any sense of comfort as we grow.

The lilies of the field began as buds. We are asked to trust that just as they had a glorious and safe unfolding, so will we. In the natural world, we see butterflies emerge from awkward yet protective cocoons. We must remind ourselves to trust that sometimes we, too, are being protected in our growth. Our erraticism, our ungainliness, our panic—these, too, are natural to the passage of change. The Great Creator experiences all his creation in the throes of shifting identity. The unfolding saga of life on all levels is one of constant transformation, constant changing of form. When we cooperate with our need and desire to grow, we

It takes a long time to bring excellence to maturity.

PUBLILIUS SYRUS

are cooperating with spiritual law. Even before we "ask," our coming needs are clear. The trajectory of our growth is not as lonely as it feels. We are experiencing universal growing pains, and our loneliness, alienation, desperation, and doubt have been felt by many before us, survived by many before us—and answered many times before by the Great Creator who made—and is making—us all.

Art, and artful living, is a constant collaboration between what we are made from and what we wish to make of ourselves. As we open ourselves consciously to inspiration and instruction as to our truest current form, we are led not only to creativity but also to comfort.

The bravest are the tenderest—
The loving are the daring.

BAYARD TAYLOR

TASK:
Shape Shifting

When we are changing sizes and shapes as an artist, we often are afraid of looking foolish. We want to be "finished." We want to be "good at it." We want to read the review that exclaims, "Well worth the creative risk!" Unfortunately, change—and the risks that go with it—invite feelings of vulnerability. Sometimes, simply blurting out our secret dream is a tremendous relief, so that's what we will try to do here on paper. Finish the following phrases as fast as you can:

1. If it weren't so foolish, I'd love to try _____.
2. If it weren't so expensive, I'd love to own a _____ _____.
3. If I were twenty-one again, I would let myself study _____.
4. If I could take the next five years off, all expenses paid, I'd study _____.
5. If it weren't so nuts, I'd love to try _____.

6. If I gave in to my secret dream, I would let myself
_____.

7. If I'd had ideal parents and a perfect childhood, I'd be a
_____.

8. The dream I have never told anyone is _____.

9. The artist I admire and think I am a lot like is _____
_____.

10. The artist I secretly look down on because I have more
talent is _____.

Now, rather than feel foolish over what you have just admitted, take pen in hand again and write a letter from your adult self to your inner artist. Spend at least fifteen minutes writing to your inner artist about the dreams it has revealed. Find a concrete form in which you can take an action on your inner artist's behalf.

CHECK-IN

1. **How many days this week did you do your Morning Pages?** If you skipped a day, why did you skip it? How was the experience of writing them for you? Are you experiencing more clarity? A wider range of emotions? A greater sense of detachment, purpose, and calm? Did anything surprise you? Is there a "repeating" issue asking to be dealt with?

2. **Did you do your Artist's Date this week?** Did you note an improved sense of well-being? What did you do and how did it feel? Remember, Artist's Dates can be difficult and you may need to coax yourself into taking them.

3. **Did you get out on your Weekly Walk?** How did that feel? What emotion or insights surfaced for you? Were you able to walk more than once? What did your walk do for your optimism and sense of perspective?

4. **Were there any other issues this week that felt significant to you in your self-discovery?** Describe them.

It requires a direct dispensation from Heaven to become a walker.

HENRY DAVID THOREAU

Discovering a Sense of Perspective

No man is an island, and our creative unfolding
occurs within a distinct cultural landscape. Cultural
mythology permeates our thinking about art and artists.
The readings and tasks of this week aim at detoxifying
your thinking regarding the arts and your place as an
artist in our society. Art is tonic and medicinal for
us all. As an artist, you are a cultural healer.

Medicine

We are all artists—some of us are declared, accomplished, and
publicly esteemed artists. Others of us are the private kind,
making artful homes and artful lives and shying away from the
public practice or pursuit of our art. Some of us—officially "not
artists" and "without a creative bone in our body"—are artists
nonetheless because creativity is in our blood. In our DNA.

There is one and only one label that seems useful to me in
discussing ourselves. That label is "creative." I have been teaching for twenty-five years. (And making art for longer than that.)
I have never, *ever* encountered a person who was not creative in
some form. Most often, people are creative in many forms. It is
the excess of creative energy, not the lack of it, that is what
makes people feel—and get labeled—"crazy."

Sarah, a book writer now, was known to family and friends
for many years as "high-strung," "nervous," "nutty," even crazy.

She had "too much energy" and it spilled out in making dramas out of daily life. She was always in a pitched battle with something—everything she experienced seemed to be heightened and adversarial. She wasn't precisely depressed, but she did tend to view life in adversarial terms. She moved from therapist to therapist, antidepressant to antidepressant, and "quick-fix" enthusiasm to "quick-fix" enthusiasm. She tried meditation, energy work, and self-help groups. All helped—sort of. Nothing seemed to really make her more comfortable in her skin or in the world we live in. At long last, Sarah began to work with creativity tools. She did Morning Pages, Artist's Dates, and a wide variety of Artist's Way exercises. Her mood lightened. Her energy steadied, and her optimism did not so much return as to make a first appearance on the stage of her adult life.

Creative projects of all stripe began to sprout wings in Sarah's household. She and her children made masks for Halloween, cookies and cut-out snowflakes for Christmas. By New Year's she had a resolution—to try writing the book she had always dreamed of. Carving out a wedge of time for herself during her kids' after-school playtime, Sarah began writing. Her children fielded phone calls: "Mom's writing." And Mom was writing—not only her book, but the distorted dramatics her life had undergone when she had channeled all her creative energy into interpersonal theatrics instead of writing. With plots and dialogue and high stakes on the page, Sarah's tendency toward personal melodrama settled down. Self-expression began to heal her character issues that years of therapy had not touched. At this writing, Sarah has written five books and published four of them. She is not "crazy" anymore, but she is crazy about her work. As she found a way to channel and express her colorful inner selves, her life took on a gentler yet more vibrant shape and her dreams took on Technicolor clarity.

"When I was little, I always wanted to be a writer," she says now. "It's just that for years I didn't think I really could be and

Love is exactly as strong as life.

JOSEPH CAMPBELL

so I abandoned my dream and myself." Finding the courage to dream again, Sarah also found that the parts of herself she had misplaced were alive and well—once they were finally welcome.

I have seen incredible creativity practiced by people in their attempts to avoid their own creativity. A therapist might call those contortions neurosis; I call them "creative knots," as in "I will *not* be creative and so I will be miserable." (In a lot of very creative ways.)

Let's start by getting rid of the nasty labels—"crazy," "grandiose," "flaky," "neurotic." Our true nature is *creative*.

Yes, using our creativity is therapeutic, but that is not because we need to be fixed. What we need is to be expressive. What's inside us is not all nasty and horrid and terrifying, not all shame and secrets and neurosis. Our inner world is a complex, exquisite, and powerful play of colors, lights, and shadows, a cathedral of consciousness as glorious as the natural world itself. This inner wealth is what the artist expresses.

The Great Creator lives within each of us. All of us contain a divine, expressive spark, a creative candle intended to light our path and that of our fellows. We are shiny, not tarnished; large, not small; beautiful, not damaged—although we may be ignorant of our grace, power, and dignity.

The human being, by definition, is a creative being. We are intended to make things and, in the old phrase, to "make something of ourselves." When we lose interest in ourselves and our lives, when we tell ourselves our dreams don't matter or that they are impossible, we are denying our spiritual heritage. When we do this, we become depressed and drained, even physically ill. We become snappish, irritable, high-strung. We call ourselves neurotic—this is not the case. We are not neurotic, we are miserable—miserable because we have stifled our creative selves. Those selves are alive—well—and too large for the cage we have put them in, the cage we call "normal."

In our culture we are trained to hide ourselves and punished

For good and evil, man is a free creative spirit.

JOYCE CARY

when we show ourselves. So we hide ourselves from others and from ourselves. It is the hiding of our true nature that makes us feel or act crazy.

We are trained to pick at ourselves, to rectify ourselves, to label ourselves. Most of our religions emphasize the notion of original sin. Most—not all—of our therapies center on our wounds and not on our gifts. Some, not all, of our 12-Step recovery can center on our character defects and not our assets.

Most of us carry what I call "word wounds"—descriptions of certain qualities that have been conveyed to us as pejorative. I for example have been called both "intense" and "hyperfocused." In our culture we have demonized creativity. We are scared of it and by it. We tell scary stories about artists and how broke, nuts, crazy, drunk, selfish they are. In our culture we are afraid of our creativity. We think it's some nitroglycerin compound that could blow us all up. Nonsense.

Practicing our creativity is healing. Not because we are sick but because we are essentially well. As we express our intrinsic nature, which is beautiful and specific, particular and original, we experience a healing transformation less in ourselves than in our relationship to the world. We are not at fault. We are not powerless. We are very large, and in expressing this truth, healing occurs. What is healed is the rift between our spiritual stature and our mistaken perception of ourselves as flawed.

Creativity is medicine. It is not dangerous or egotistical. It is life-affirming and essential. The more we use it, the more steadily and readily and easily we use it. The more we ground it and regularly access it, the better off we are. The "healthier" we are. Humor and acceptance enter the picture. Far more than self-scrutiny or self-correction, self-expression may be the key to a much more synthesized and effective sense of self.

Yes, we are sometimes unhappy. But this is not because we are neurotic and need to be "adjusted" to the existing norm. This is because we need to express ourselves—which will then change both us *and* the existing norm. Creative change begins in

Out of your vulnerabilities will come your strength.

SIGMUND FREUD

the heart. When we start within ourselves and move outward, expressing what we love and what we value, life gets better, we feel better, and the world gets healthier too.

The tools and process of my book *The Artist's Way* are taught by many therapists. Often, they facilitate Artist's Way groups and report back "miracles of healing." To my eye, the healing is no miracle. The health was always there, waiting to be discovered and expressed as creativity.

I am not interested in debating with people over the reality of mental illness. What I want to focus on is the reality of our considerable mental health. Our society, even our world, might be "sick," but we carry within us the exact medicine to heal it and ourselves.

That medicine is creativity.

Most of us are about as eager to be changed as we were to be born, and go through our changes in a similar state of shock.

JAMES BALDWIN

TASK:
Bless Your Blessings

One of the most medicinal tasks we can undertake is a simple walk. It is difficult to remain mired in negativity and depression when we are "shaking it out" a little.

Walking with an eye to the positive can take a gentle vigilance. As a form of medicine for ourselves, we can consciously turn our thoughts to the ancient practice of practicing gratitude—a footfall at a time. Take yourself out-of-doors and set a goal of a simple twenty-minute walk. Aiming toward the outer world, allow your inner world to fall into a brighter perspective by consciously—and concretely—enumerating your life's blessings. People, events, situations—any of these may be cause for gratitude. As you warm to your task of focusing on the good in your life, both your heart and your step will lighten.

Art Is Therapeutic, Not Therapy

I am still learning.

MICHELANGELO

When we are blocked creatively, we often experience ourselves as miserable—and we then wonder, "How neurotic am I?" Thinking that therapy will supply that answer, or at least alleviate our misery, we often turn to therapy only to find that our misery continues unabated. Of course it does. We are miserable not because we are neurotic but because we are creative and not functioning in our creativity. Therapy may help us to "understand" our blocks. We do better to simply get over them. Art is therapeutic. It is *not* therapy. Therapy aims at transformation through understanding. Art aims at transformation more directly. When we make a piece of art about something we don't understand, we come to understand it, or, at least, our relationship to it through our own experience—which is more full-bodied than merely cerebral. In this sense, art "works" therapeutically whether we understand it or not.

Therapy aims at disarming emotion, placing wounded emotions "in perspective." Art, on the other hand, uses wounded emotions—or any other fuel handy—not to alter our perception of an existing outer reality but to alter that reality through a reality we express. Handel's complex, ecstatic, exultant, and conflicted feelings and perceptions about God created *The Messiah. The Messiah,* in turn, helps others to understand God differently.

Harper Lee wrote one book, *To Kill a Mockingbird,* in 1960. She lives in Manhattan now and still has no plans to write another. And why should she? With one small and "simple" book, she accomplished a great swath of healing. Anyone reading her work comes away from it more whole, more compassionate, more in touch with the interior life of his own vulnerable, childlike self.

Books, poems, plays, symphonies—they aim at healing the soul. They take human emotions and human concerns and, through the alchemy of art, make us somehow feel better about all of it—and us.

Bernice, a Jungian therapist, often sends her patients to music rather than introspection. "Music touches something higher in us," she explains. Music may touch something higher more directly, but all of the arts touch something that is beyond the ordinary machinations of life. It is the overview, this "something higher and more," that makes even the most homespun art somehow therapeutic. Baking a good pie, one feels better for having baked it. The same is true of writing a simple song or even dashing off a quick poem to tell your child she is beloved. When the child calls to say "I got your letter," she is also saying "And it made me feel cherished." Feeling cherished, we feel healed, and, perhaps as much as anything else, the act of making art can be described as the act of cherishing our experience, feelings, and perceptions. This, we are told, is how God regards all of creation. Perhaps it is in this careful attention that we contact the divine spark when we create. Contacting that divine spark is always therapeutic.

Healing is a somewhat automatic by-product of self-expression, not a goal per se. This fact can confuse some people—particularly therapists, who want to "understand" the workings of a process that is both mysterious and spiritual. Intellectually, many doctors and therapists do know that something heals beyond their own skill, but understandably, they want to know what that something is, and control it as part of the healing process that they can administer like a good medicine. Therapy and creative recovery are not mutually exclusive, but they do function differently and come out of two very different sets of assumptions.

We may feel different after making something. We may see something in a different light, but that inner shift of focus comes from expressing what it is we do feel and see rather than striving to feel and see things differently, with more balance and less sting. For an artist—and for the artist in each of us—talking

Music produces a kind of pleasure which human nature cannot do without.

CONFUCIUS

The first and the simplest emotion which we discover in the human mind is curiosity.

EDMUND BURKE

about something may be less useful than painting about it, writing about it, or composing about it. Merely cerebral understanding does not heal. Nor, contrary to many therapeutic models, does the simple expression of emotion, verbally or even physically. Humans are complex, creative beings, and when we create something that expresses our own complexity, we arrive at an inner distillate of clarity through our own *creative* inner process. Many therapists, and many art teachers for that matter, are controlling and intrusive in their premature questioning and direction. They encourage creative clients to cerebrate. This is often the last thing we need. Therapy aims at making us normal. Art aims at expressing our originality. The norm has nothing to do with it.

Enlightened therapies urge us to "accept how we feel." Art teaches us to *express* how we feel and so alchemize it. Art acknowledges that feelings are mutable and that we contain the power to mutate the dross of our wounds into the ore of art. In this sense, art gives us the ability to *always* move out of the victim position. Therapy adjusts us to the world. Art adjusts the world itself.

"Art" is a form of the verb "to be." It is not mere cleverness to point this out. At its core, life is artful and creative, each moment contains choice as much as each brush stroke in a painting, each syllable in a poem, each note in a melodic line. It is because of this, its insistence on choice, choice, choice, that art demolishes the victim position. When bullying life demands of us some injustice: "You want to make something of it?" the artful answer is yes.

When we make something of "it," whatever "it" is, we make something else of it. Art allows us to live freely, even within our restlessness, like Dylan Thomas's green sea singing in its chains. Holocaust victims scratched butterflies on the walls of concentration camps. That assertive creative act spoke plainly: "You cannot kill my spirit." At its core, art is triumphant. At its best, therapy is acquiescent: I accept my influences and accommodate myself to their result. Therapy constructs a self; art presupposes and asserts a self. At bottom, art is rebellious: You cannot name me. I am more than the sum of my parts.

In therapy we seek to examine the impact of those in our life and our resultant wounds and adjustments. We see ourselves in relation to person X or event Y. Our inner workings are understood and understandable in theoretical terms. We deduce why we are what we are. And we often deduce from a flimsy set of stock characters—the nuclear family. Life, even the most impoverished, is far richer than that in its mysterious variables and forces.

Art works in primary colors. We dip our pen, our brush, our hand, directly into the self. "I see it this way," we say. We are the origin of our art. It rises like a river head, asking no one's permission. Art says, "I am." Therapy says, "They were, therefore I am." Therapy may be turbulent, but it is tame compared to art. Therapy may be rewarding, but it makes something of what we *were,* while art makes something of what we *are.* Freud complained, "Whenever I get somewhere, a poet has been there first." Of course. An artist flies direct.

Art is alchemy. It turns the ore of life into gold. Learning to make art rather than drama from a heated imagination is a skill best learned early and practiced fully. If we are to make living art—*and* an art of living—we must be willing to stand knee-deep in the rapids of the human condition, accepting that life, by its nature, is turbulent, powerful, and mysterious. It is the artist's bet that life is better encountered and expressed than diminished and discounted by trying to "fix it" therapeutically. It is the artist's conviction that understanding something intellectually is often far less healing than making something artistically transformative from our shattered selves.

"Keep the drama on the page, the stage, the canvas, the film," an artist learns. It is there that the monsters and beauties, the jewels and junkyard memorabilia of the imagination, can be sorted, shaped, and transformed into art. Dexterity at living

I hate that aesthetic game of the eye and the mind, played by these connoisseurs, these mandarins who "appreciate" beauty. What is beauty, anyway? There's no such thing. I never "appreciate," any more than I "like." I love or I hate.

PABLO PICASSO

with the dramatic shadow play of the creative mind comes with time. A younger artist may mistake intense emotion for a cue to act in his outer life, not his inner one. When turbulent emotions pinch the raw nerves of the creative psyche, there is a choice: Act on this, or act out on this.

With art as our alchemy, the pain of the lost lover becomes the pang of the love song. The misery of a misplaced sense of direction becomes the frantic, seething chords of a dissonant jazz anthem. "Nothing is wrong, nothing is wasted, nothing is neurotic, nothing is disowned, everything is possible in art" must become the artist's credo.

Let the world know you as you are, not as you think you should be, because sooner or later, if you are posing, you will forget the pose, and then where are you?

FANNY BRICE

TASK:
You Want to Make Something of It?

Although therapy may have loftier goals, its most common use is to arrive at a different accommodation of our grudges. "They" did "that" and so we feel bad. The aim of most therapy is that we feel less bad. We come to "understand" why "they" may have done "that" and we make our peace with it. Art is more anarchistic.

Art is more aggressive and more assertive than therapy. It is an action, not a reaction. Dipping directly into ourselves as source, we create something new that would not exist without us as its origin. For this reason art is affirming in a way that therapy is not.

Set aside a stack of magazines with pictures. Buy a piece of poster board and some glue. Locate a scissors, tape if you want it, and give yourself a full hour's time. Scan your consciousness for a situation you would like to understand more fully.

Do you have a mesmerizing personal relationship that seems patently destructive yet you cannot end it? Do you have a tyrant boss to whom you are in feudal bondage? Do you have a bond that is so close to someone that you feel joined at the hip? Are you homesick for the wide open spaces of the West but are living in the vertical canyons of Manhattan? Any of these dilemmas make excellent fuel for the task of collaging.

Holding this theme loosely in mind, spend twenty minutes pulling images that attract you and *may* feel connected to your theme. Spend another twenty minutes arranging your images and gluing them in order. Now spend a final twenty minutes writing about what you've found.

What you discover through this process may surprise and intrigue you. A relationship that seems punitive and one-sided may be revealed to be a source of creative fire. A longing for a "greener" life and environment may be overridden by an actual love of urban images and energy. What you find through making a collage may not even address the specific topic you "worked" on. Instead, a far larger and more holistic sense of healing may emerge.

Anger

When we are angry at being overlooked, it is not arrogance and grandiosity. It is a signal that we have changed sizes and must now act larger.

Very often when we feel small and unheard, it is not because we *are* small and unheard but because we are acting small and unheard. We are not intended to be small. Often we are cornered not into being powerless and puny—as we feel—but into being large.

The problem here is our perspective. When we are angry "out of all proportion," that is a very accurate phrase. We have lost a sense of our true size and power, and the intensity of our feelings makes us feel "hopping mad," another telling phrase, as our mental image of ourselves becomes—or can become—very cartooned. We experience ourselves as puny and tiny and futile. The size of our anger has dwarfed our perspective and our per-

One cool judgment is worth a thousand hasty counsels. The thing to do is supply light and not heat.

WOODROW WILSON

Advice is what we ask for when we already know the answer but wish we didn't.

ERICA JONG

sonality. This is because we do not realize that the power we are perceiving is within us as the power for change. When we are "unspeakably" angry, what we really are is large and unspoken. We are not yet speaking in a way that gives voice and direction to our power. When we feel impotent with rage, we are actually potent with rage—we simply have not yet seen how to effectively use our anger as the fuel that it is.

When we cannot sleep, when we are "eaten alive" by an inequity or slight, the monster that is eating us is our anger over our own displaced power. We are very powerful. That personal power is what we are feeling as a "towering rage," and that artificially externalized wall of rage can make us feel small and puny until we figure out that it is a power within ourselves and not the sheer wall of the "odds" stacked against us. The odds are against us until we are "for" ourselves.

Anger asks us to step up to the plate for ourselves and for others. It points to a path we are trying to avoid. Often we try to act "modest," and that is partially a refusal to be as large, clear, and articulate as we really are. Anger signals us that we are being called to step forward and speak out. We hate this and so we fantasize retreating instead.

Rage at a bully or at a bullying situation is actually a wonderful sign. Once we own it, it is our own rage at allowing ourselves and others to be bullied. If it is our own, we can use it. Yes, this rage feels murderous and distorting, but it is actually a needed corrective. If our rage is that large, so are we.

Our reticence can make us angry. We "know" we should speak up for ourselves but sometimes find we just "cannot."

We do not need to shout, but we do need to act and to speak our truth. A word about that order: Actions do speak louder than words, and so we must take actions that articulate our creative values.

A writer angered by a string of rejections might self-publish—as I did and will always do. A musician frustrated by the "state of the art" in the recording business can more cost-effectively cut a disc, DAT, or a small CD for far less money and energy than indulging in years of therapy to "accept" his feelings of frustration. A proactive creative act is far less expensive than the health problems and life-shortening caused by stewing in feelings of resentment and bitterness—or the even more expensive waste of retreating from the fray entirely.

Luckily for all of us, artists are stubborn. The best-selling author advised by her psychiatrist that she should aim for a secretarial career kept writing (me). The famous filmmaker fired from a documentary project kept making movies (Martin Scorsese). The talented actress cut from Boston University's acting program kept acting (Oscar-winner Geena Davis). The lawyer who "should have" spent his time "on his cases" won the argument that he should write as well (John Grisham). Something inside spoke clearly enough that these artists listened, and a few outer "someones" whispered, or shouted, that they, too, knew who we were. These discerning outer voices affirm our identities and alter our destinies.

Sometimes when we get angry enough at being treated as if we are small, we get brave enough to trust those who think— and say—we might be big. One slight too many and we finally say our true name, but we "swallow" a lot of anger first.

Center stage belongs to those who are willing to move there, some talented and some not. Rather than angrily decrying the behavior and lack of talent of the "arrogant spotlight-grabbers," we need to use our anger to turn our own voltage up a little despite our fears. We need to say our own names as artists. When we do, we feel self-respect. Self-respect comes from the Self. The market will say what it will, but we need to say our own name as artists.

Anger is a call to action. It is challenging and important to let our light shine. It is important to name ourselves rather than wait for someone else to do it, or pretend that we can continue to bear it when we can't. When we complain that others do not take ourselves and our values seriously, we are actually saying

I'm not a teacher: only a fellow-traveler of whom you asked the way. I pointed ahead—ahead of myself as well as you.

George Bernard Shaw

that *we* don't. If our aesthetics matter so much to us, we must act on them in a concrete and specific form.

This is why a failed musical comedy means write another song. This is why a bad review of your novel means write a short story, a poem, anything that signals to your inner world that you still believe in yourself. When we fail to endorse ourselves as artists, others also can undercut us. When we endorse and support ourselves as artists—concretely, in some small form—then others may misread us or mishandle us, but they cannot castrate us or our self-respect.

Anger is a profoundly powerful fuel that we can use to make art and to make more artful lives. When we deny our anger or fritter it away in complaints, we are wasting precious fuel and precious clarity. Anger is a searchlight. It shows us our moral terrain and it shows us the damage we feel done to that terrain by others. It shows us, above all, our choices. If something angers us, we can try to "make do" with stuffing our anger or we can "make something of it" in the literal sense of a piece of art.

Anger causes poems, plays, novels, films. Anger causes symphonies and paintings. When we think of our anger as something that should be excised or denied rather than alchemized, we risk neutering ourselves as artists.

Anger asks us for reservoirs of strength that we often do not know we have. We are galvanized into heroics that we did not feel were a part of our emotional repertoire. We act larger than we feel and end up being larger than we were.

A highly acclaimed classical musician angered by the narrow gauge of highly produced digitalized recordings goes out on a limb to encourage a young and talented musician. *The club is too small, too elite, too canned,* the master musician thinks angrily, and throws the door open a little by lending his prestigious name to a more risky project. Anger has opened his heart and his mind.

Anger is not comfortable. The focused use of it to create art requires emotional maturity we must often reach for to muster—and yet we can. When we do, our world changes by a jot. Anger

No man can know where he is going unless he knows exactly where he has been and exactly how he arrived at his present place.

MAYA ANGELOU

sometimes signals not our immaturity but our maturity, our seasoned judgment, and outraged temper into form for the sake of
healthy change.

TASK:
Use Anger as Fuel

Most of us may feel we "get" angry, but we seldom feel we
"are" angry. The tool you are using now is a startling one in this
regard: You are probably angrier than you think, and that
blocked or unused anger is a powerful source of creative fuel
once you are willing to acknowledge it and tap it more directly.

Take pen in hand. Number from 1 to 50. List 50 angering
grievances from the historical to the hysterical. Be as petty as
possible. You will be astonished at what tiny things "still" anger
you. For example:

1. I'm angry the Catholic Church dropped Latin.
2. I'm angry our church uses bad folk songs.
3. I'm angry the candy shop closed.
4. I'm angry my sister is fighting with my brother.

After you have written for a while, you will notice the question popping up: "What can I do about it?" This question pops
up like toast. We do not like being victims of so much anger,
and so we intuitively look for a positive solution. Jot down the
solutions as they come to you. At exercise's end, you will have
cleared fifty negatives and come up with a list of do-able positives. Do some of them, using your formerly stuck anger as fuel.

In the beginning was the Word. Man acts it out. He is the act, not the actor.

HENRY MILLER

Cartography

The artist is a cartographer; he maps the world. The world
within him, and the world as he sees it. Sometimes that world is

very strange. Sometimes our maps are rejected—seen as unrealistic or distorted or unlikely. Magellan sailed with maps made largely of conjecture—as artists, we are always conjuring and conjecturing on the shape of what we see and "know."

A great work of art focuses the imagination of a vast audience on a previously inchoate problem. *The Grapes of Wrath* showed us the Depression. *One Flew Over the Cuckoo's Nest* showed us our democratic horror at institutions run amuck. All novels are "novel" because they are seeking to tell us something new. Known or unknown, famous or anonymous, all art is an attempt to map the territory of the heart.

Let me say it again: As artists, we are cartographers. We draw from our own experience, and we *draw* our experience, sketching in the territory we have encountered and others will encounter. The perceptions of a novel or a musical composition may predate their consensus map of consciousness of their own times. For this reason, artists must have courage, even heroism, to state what they see and hear.

Early in his career, Beethoven enjoyed personal and professional favor. His work was widely heard and widely revered. He was hailed as a large creative talent. His life was sunny and his creative vistas expansive. As his life wore on, Beethoven's cultural fortunes shifted. His work was considered less accessible, too abstract and demanding. As his personal battle with hearing loss deepened his isolation, he was plunged into a harrowing, nearly suicidal depression. He was caught on the horns of a dilemma: He was called to write music and his talent as a musician was called into question by the music he wrote. He could not be true to himself and go back to earlier forms. There seemed to be no audience for his musical work except himself and God. Contemplating suicide, Beethoven chose life and, in one famous letter to God, vowed to continue to write music no matter how ill received it was. He would write "for the glory of God alone." The resultant music, too modern and advanced for Beethoven's peers, has come to be considered masterworks cen-

Whatever creativity is, it is in part a solution to a problem.

BRIAN ALDISS

turies later. A visionary and a leader of musical thought and form, Beethoven wrote for our times and not his own.

Late Beethoven told us more of our century than of his own. As artists, we draw not only consensus reality but the lineaments of approaching reality. This is why Ezra Pound dubbed us "the antennae of the race." This is why our perceptions are so often discounted as "not in reality," when in fact they are a part of a reality that we are not yet in.

George Orwell told us more of the future than *1984*. George Gershwin told us more of the urban—and urbane—revolution than any demographics.

As artists, we explore the territory of the human heart, braving the dark woods to report to our human tribe that a trail can be found, and we will survive. As artists, we are scouts of consciousness, trailblazers for community and culture.

Of necessity, artists report dangers we might wish to ignore. Like the scout who returns to report an unpassable gorge requiring an unforeseen detour, the artist may report perceptions that feel unbearable to others. From Sam Shepard to Samuel Beckett, the artist may encounter and encapsulate the loneliness of missed connections. The heart of darkness *is,* all too often, the human heart. As artists, we must muster self-respect and compassion for the difficulty of our own calling. The great adventure of the creative life lies not only in the territory seen but in the fact that much of what we see has not been seen before. Human stories are as old as the earth, but human consciousness is always the edge of the known world, like fine telescopes focused on deep space. As artists, we routinely step beyond, straining our eyes and vision to discern and record the shapes heaving into birth from darkness.

We function on nerve, daring, stamina, vision, and persistence. Mountains appear where no mountains are known to be. Lakes shine in the light where there are no lakes. The artist does not see as others see. His imagination yokes together disparate images, some fanciful, some frightening, some enlightening.

Thou didst create the night,
but I made the lamp.
Thou didst create clay,
but I made the cup.
Thou didst create the deserts,
mountains and forests,
I produced the orchards,
gardens and groves.
It is I who made the glass out
of stone,
And it is I who turn a poison
into an antidote.

SIR MUHAMMAD IQBAL

The artist's inner world may resemble a fairy tale—there are ogres, trolls, monsters, witches. Everything is heightened, intensified, dramatized. This pitch of intensity forges art from the raw materials of the imagination. As an artist matures, so does his skill at encompassing such pitched emotion.

Does this mean that we cannibalize our lives? Emphatically, no. It does mean that we own them, shaping and reshaping the acreage of our personal experience into a philosophical habitat that expresses accurately our view of the world.

"Look at it this way," the artist says, and shows the world what his inner world has revealed to him. Franz Kafka was Kafka before we had the term Kafka-esque. George Orwell predated Orwellian. Each of us carries an internal lens through which we view the world. The willingness to reveal what that lens sees is what determines an artist. And an artist must continually open that lens to take in new and wider realities.

A woman in her mid-fifties gets up daily to write a song. She has been musically inclined since childhood, but it took her until her forties to muster the emotional courage to express her songs in more than her inner ear.

"I think I am too old for this," she tells me, yet her year's moneys are budgeted to include the expense of cutting a CD of her work. She could be buying expensive clothes or meals out or gifts for her children, but she has learned that what matters most to her is the process of expressing her heart through art.

"If I don't tell my parents' story, who will?" a writer asks me, explaining a decade's diligence on a long family saga.

"My computer class is very exciting," a woman artist tells me. "I am so much less limited now in the ways that I can see. I was defining myself so narrowly as a fine artist."

For each of these artists, the act of making art is the act of revelation. First to themselves and then to the world: "Listen! Look! It looks like this!" they are saying.

Like Audubon sketching his birds, great art is sometimes

Make visible what, without you, might perhaps never have been seen.

ROBERT BRESSON

made by the simple act of witness rendered to the world: "I saw this beautiful thing." Of course, not all of what we see as artists is beautiful, nor do we render it beautifully, yet just as a crude and handmade map gives us a sense of direction, so, too, the mapmaking of art points the human compass straighter toward home.

Everything vanishes around me, and works are born as if out of the void. Ripe, graphic fruits fall off. My hand has become the obedient instrument of a remote will.

PAUL KLEE

TASK:
Mapping Your Interests

Maps begin as the roughest of sketches, approximately whole continents. We can similarly sketch in our areas of creative interest, working in the loosest terms.

Take pen in hand. Finish the following:

Five topics that interest me are
1.
2.
3.
4.
5.

Five people who interest me are
1.
2.
3.
4.
5.

Five art forms that interest me are
1.
2.
3.

4.

5.

Five projects I could try out are

1.

2.

3.

4.

5.

Come forth into the light of things, Let nature be your teacher.

WILLIAM WORDSWORTH

When we map out our "coulds" instead of our "shoulds," we shift from the realm of probability into the more interesting realm of possibility. When we name and claim an interest, we seem to magnetize that area, drawing to ourselves people, places, and things that speak to our emerging interests.

CHECK-IN

1. **How many days this week did you do your Morning Pages?** If you skipped a day, why did you skip it? How was the experience of writing them for you? Are you experiencing more clarity? A wider range of emotions? A greater sense of detachment, purpose, and calm? Did anything surprise you? Is there a "repeating" issue asking to be dealt with?
2. **Did you do your Artist's Date this week?** Did you note an improved sense of well-being? What did you do and how did you feel? Remember, Artist's Dates can be difficult and you may need to coax yourself into taking them.
3. **Did you get out on your Weekly Walk?** How did that feel? What emotions or insights surfaced for you? Were you able to walk more than once? What did your walk do for your optimism and sense of perspective?
4. **Were there any other issues this week that felt significant to you in your self-discovery?** Describe them.

Discovering a Sense of Adventure

This week you are asked to jettison some of
your personal baggage. The essays and tasks are
aimed at helping you claim a greater sense of freedom.
You will be asked to consciously experiment with open-
mindedness. You will dismantle many unconscious
mechanisms that may have impeded your artistic
expression. You will focus on self-acceptance
as a route to self-expression.

Adventure

Too often, we think we know what we love. It is more accurate
to admit we know only some of what we love, and that the "sum"
of what we love can grow larger. This requires an open mind.

An hour's adventure in a nineteenth-century photography
exhibit may do more to spark your visual artist than six months
in a sensible computer-graphics program. A visit to the zoo may
mean more to your creative animal than a virtuous visit to an art
supply store.

Humans are by nature adventurous. Watch a toddler expand
his territory a wobbly step at a time. Watch a teenager test cur-
few. Watch an eighty-year-old grandmother sign up for an art
tour of Russia. The soul thrives on adventure. Deprived of adventure, our optimism fails us. Adventure is a nutrient, not a fri-
volity. When we ignore our need for adventure, we ignore our

*To die will be an awfully
big adventure.*

JAMES M. BARRIE

very nature. Often we do exactly that, calling it "adulthood" or "discipline." When we are too adult and too disciplined, our impish, childlike innovator yearns to rebel. Too often, that rebellion takes the form of a stubborn, self-involved crankiness rather than an exuberant and expansive risk. Risks, we tell ourselves, are too risky. When we avoid risk, we court depression.

Depression is emotional quicksand. Once we get stuck, it's hard to pull free. Our struggles exhaust us and depress us further. It is easier to avoid depression than overcome it, and, yes, we avoid it by taking risks. If we remember that we need to court, woo, and romance our creative selves, we begin to have a notion of what sort of risk best serves us.

Adele lives in Manhattan. On her good days she loves the vigor of the city. She finds the rich red tones of the buildings on her Upper West Side street adult and invigorating. She loves the window boxes and the glimpses of richly painted rooms beyond. On her bad days Adele feels trapped by the city. She is a westerner at heart and she longs for wide open spaces and wide horizons. The city feels claustrophobic. "Tame." And so, on her worst days, Adele calls the Claremont Riding Academy, reserves a horse, and goes riding.

Claremont is not the wide open spaces, but it does have horses and the stench of horse sweat and it is somehow so daring—three stories of horses wedged into a Manhattan brownstone—that it feels anarchistic and rebellious even to crack open the door and step into the hidden world of horseflesh and leather. And so, when Adele feels too dull and too domesticated, she gets on a horse and feels like she's sitting a lot taller in the saddle, living in a world of risk and adventure.

Caroline, a hothouse flower, needs to have a taste of luxury when her world feels too much like a treadmill. She has taught herself that few things lift her spirits more rapidly than a visit to a really good florist shop, where beauty in all its delicacy and daring can be found intertwined amid wicker baskets and faux vertigris vases. Although she seldom spends much—settling on a truly shocking color of Gerber daisy can give her tiny kitchen a transfusion of color—Caroline always feels her money and time is well spent when she buys herself not merely a bouquet but the optimistic sense that this earth is, or can be, a garden of earthly delights.

Adam, a mild-mannered writer, gets his sense of worthy risk by taking himself to travel stores. He cannot always up and leave his job, but he can take daring mental vacations. He sometimes buys a guidebook, *Most-Used Egyptian Phrases,* and learns a few key words to get him to and from a pyramid. Other times he plans a trip he actually can take, *A Pocket Guide to Day Trips in the Greater Boston Area.* What is pivotal to him is not so much leaving life as he knows it as knowing that he could.

"Most of the time my life is fine, but I need to know that I have psychic permission to get away from it all," Adam explains. A stop in a sports store to look at a new model cross-training shoe, a pamphlet from the bike store about a bicycle vacation in France, these imaginary risks add a needed risk to Adam's Mr. Nice Guy persona. "And I love Indiana Jones movies," he adds.

The creative imagination is a will-o'-the-wisp. Wooed best by enticement and not by aggressive assault, the imagination responds to being coaxed and cajoled. Just as in romance, too serious, too fast, and the fun fizzles out. We need to flirt with an interest, approach it with a sidelong glance. Children's books might be a better first date with a new interest than enrolling in a master's program. If you want to write a novel about an automotive inventor and need to know how an automobile engine works, a good children's book may tell you just what you need to know, while a scholarly tome on the laws of physical dynamics may tell you just enough to squelch your budding interest entirely. More is very nice as something to look forward to and not so nice as part of the phrase "More than I could handle or absorb." Adventures should be manageable, not overwhelming.

It is not so much that the creative imagination is shallow; rather, it is selective. Dumping a huge load of facts into your

It's like driving a car at night. You never see further than your headlights, but you can make the whole trip that way.

E. L. DOCTOROW

imagination can stall its gears rather than start them humming. A biographer sifts the truth from a quarry full of facts. A poet or novelist intuits a quarry full of truth from a single fact. Too many facts, too fast, and the artistic attic gets both stuffy and overstuffed. The imagination feels stifled, not stimulated. Creative heights are best reached when we are not overburdened by an overly intellectual freight of facts.

It is one of the paradoxes of the sustained creative life that the more lightly we take ourselves, the more serious work we will probably be able to do. The more we bear down on ourselves, the more constricted we will feel, and the more vulnerable we will be to creative injury.

Very often, consummate artists are consummate enthusiasts. Director Mike Nichols breeds Arabian horses. Coppola grows great grapes. Novelist John Nichols is an avid bird-watcher. Sculptor Kevin Cannon plays formidable jazz guitar. They have taken a cue from the Great Creator and developed a playful appetite for life itself.

If you play softball once a week, it's a little easier to handle the curve ball of a vicious review. If you let yourself bake an apple pie or two, it's a little harder to think the artist's life, or life in general, is so rotten. If you go salsa dancing once a week, or even once a month, it's a little harder to think that the purpose of your art is to make you rich and famous, and that if it hasn't, it's worthless and so are you.

In light of all this, I am not sure where we got the idea that in order to be "real" artists we had to do things perfectly. The minute we see that word "perfect" (and I think critics are the ones who drag it in the door), spontaneity goes out the window. We get so sure that we can't be a great composer that we never let ourselves write our kids a goofy lullaby or play improvisational noodles at the piano. We're so respectful of "great" art that we always, chronically, sell ourselves short. We're so worried about whether we can play in the "big leagues" that we refuse to let ourselves play at all.

To create, you must empty yourself of every artistic thought.

GILBERT (OF GILBERT AND GEORGE)

Here's what I like about God: Trees are crooked, mountains are lumpy, a lot of his creatures are funny-looking, and he made it all anyway. He didn't let the aardvark convince him he had no business designing creatures. He didn't make a puffer fish and get discouraged. No, the maker made things—and still does.

European film directors often enjoy creative careers, during which their films mature from the manifestos of angry young men to the rueful wisdom of great works by creative masters. Is an afternoon siesta the secret? Is their *vita* just a little more *dolce?* We've taken espresso to our American hearts, but we haven't quite taken to the "break" in our coffee breaks. Worried about playing the fool, we forget how to simply play. We try to make our creativity linear and goal oriented. We want our "work" to lead somewhere. We forget that diversions do more than merely divert us.

How did all this sternness get in here? We let it in. We dragged it in. We even begged it to please come in. And why? Our own natural antic and animal high spirits scare us silly. There are few things more fun than exercising our talents, and since most of us keep them on a pretty tight leash, we are scared that if we let them off, we will need a lion tamer.

As little kids, we might fool around rhapsodically on the piano. We might improvise for hours, pouring out our hearts and our adolescent angst. We play so much and so often that people might say we're good, have a talent, could even have a career—"if we're serious enough about it." Then what happens? We get serious. We begin to "practice," not play. We begin to seek perfection like the Holy Grail. We begin to compete. We go to school, music school, and to master classes, and to intensives and . . . and we may end up with quite a hot career. Meanwhile, some of our ardor cools. Music becomes something we "master." We become musical acrobats capable of flying across the keys with amazing ease, performing astounding stunts—but we have forgotten the sheer thrill of flying.

Anything worth doing is worth doing badly.

An original is a creation motivated by desire.

MAN RAY

How we hate *that* idea. We know it as beginners but forget it as we advance. Trial-and-error becomes beneath our dignity. Of course it does. It pulls the rug out from underneath our seriousness. We don't really have a nice big block to stand behind while we "figure things out." What's to figure out? God was humble enough to just doodle, to just noodle, to fool around—why are we so serious?

When making art becomes about making a career, it has the same deadening impact as when making love becomes about making a baby. Rather than enjoy the process, we become focused on the result, everything else is just foreplay. There's a rush to get it over with and move on to the main thrust of things, our Brilliant Career.

Focused on career goals—prosperity, security, celebrity—we remove ourselves from the sensuality of process. The delight of a first published poem becomes First Published, not "Nice paper. Like how they laid it out." The exciting event becomes "I wonder how it will be received" instead of "What do *I* think of it?"

It becomes about perfection and other people's perception, not the joy of creation, the play of ideas.

When our art boils down to a calculated career move, we ourselves tend to become hard-boiled and calculated. Not bad traits for the hero of a detective novel, but we might need one to detect any fun in our lives.

The creative imagination leaps crag to crag and does not chug up the mountain like an automated chairlift. If we treat the creative self like a young and curious animal, we will get the right idea. A young animal pokes its curious nose here and there. Our creative animal must be allowed the same freedom. Nothing—or something—may come to your sortie into reading about the Norman Conquest, and the "something" that might come may be nothing like the "something" you first envisioned. You *could* start out with an interest in Robin Hood, only to find yourself writing the diary of Maid Marian. The greater your appetite for adventure, the more adventuresome the creative elements at hand when you turn to working on something. It does not take much to spark the imagination, but just what will do it is always the question, and the answers can be very queer indeed. Georgia O'Keeffe wrote home: "I got half-a-dozen paintings from that shattered plate." Someone else may simply have gotten a cleaning job. Do not be too hasty to name your soul's delights.

Sticks and stones, marbles and peacock feathers, a smooth gray river rock—what we take to heart is what speaks to us uniquely. As artists, we are like beachcombers, walking the tide line, pocketing the oddments washed ashore—some small stray thing will tell us a story to tell the world. There is a reason we call art a "calling"—but we do have to answer the call. Intuition speaks to us as impulse. We must learn to explore, not repress, our intuition. Intuition is key to creative unfolding.

There is not a sprig of grass that shoots uninteresting to me.

Thomas Jefferson

"I wanted to learn more about the city," Kenton remembers. "After all, I lived there, but I didn't know much about it. I didn't really know how old things were. I didn't know which parts of town were built first. I didn't know significant historical turning points. I was occupying the great new job in the great new town and I was kind of lonely—but lonely for a sense of roots as well."

On impulse, Kenton began browsing the architecture section of his new neighborhood's swank Barnes and Noble. He found a book on Victorian architecture and realized his neighborhood was filled with vintage homes that were only passing for modern. Detecting here a new cornice, there a portico, Kenton began to feel there was a lot more to his neighborhood than met the eye. He next went to a secondhand bookstore and there found a shelf of "local authors." Amid the texts was a how-to-renovate guide that he picked up for fifty cents. A free Saturday afternoon found him showing up for a lecture at the neighborhood library, "Our Historic District and What We Don't Know About It." At the lecture, Kenton found himself picking up a

All are needed by each one:
Nothing is fair or good alone.

RALPH WALDO EMERSON

flyer for a neighborhood garden tour. On that garden tour, thinking, *What am I doing here?* Kenton met two pieces of destiny. He got an idea for a photojournalism essay he would place with a local underground paper and he met a very interesting young woman—who is now his fiancée.

Opening to our intuition *is* like opening to a new love affair. Our first adventure may be a coffee date that feels a little stiff but has a few memorable possibilities. Our second flyer may be a little more bold—say, a kiss good-bye on the cheek. Our third venture may mark the beginning of a budding passion, an interest that we can't quite shake, that companions us through our days. An intuitive leading is a lead we must follow. "Destiny" arrives as a humble lunch, not a fanfare.

TASK:
Draw Yourself to Scale

An adventure does not need to be large or intense to be adventurous and nutritious for our artist. Arguably, most of us lead lives with too much adventure in it. The nightly news and daily headlines are packed with extremes of all sorts. For this reason, this tool, the "adventuring tool," is a gentle one. We all have adventurous lives, but we must see them to know it.

Go to an office supply or art supply shop. Acquire a small blank notebook suitable for sketching. Carry this notebook with you and carry, too, a sketching pencil or pen so that you can begin to capture the many small adventures of life as you actually live it.

When you enter the adventure of each moment by sketching the office where you are waiting for the doctor, sketching the bus stop where the bus is taking "forever," sketching the coffee mug while your friend is powdering her nose, you begin to gain a sense of yourself as leading a life that is crammed with interesting character and characters the moment you take the time to focus. You do not need to sketch well to enjoy sketching.

The summer I was twenty-one, I carried such a sketchbook with me all over New York. I still have the awkward sketch that I made waiting in what was to become my first literary agent's office. I have a drawing of the gawky plant and hard-to-sit-on chair. One glance at the sketch and I am "back there," alive to the great adventure of launching what was to become my literary career. A few pages later in the same sketchbook, I have a drawing of my friend Nick Cariello. "You make me look too old," he complained as I sketched him—he has since aged into and through the Nick I saw as I drew him.

So much of the adventure of the life we lead rushes past us in a blur. Velocity is the culprit. Velocity and pressure. A sketchbook freezes time. It is an instantaneous form of meditation focusing us on the worth of every passing moment. So often the great adventure of life lies between the lines, in how we felt at a certain time and at a certain place. This tool will help you to remember and savor the passing parade.

To me every hour of the light and dark is a miracle.

WALT WHITMAN

The Verb "To Be"

It is all too easy to think of art as something we aspire to, an ideal by which to measure our efforts and find them falling woefully short. Well, that is one way to think of art, and God knows we have bludgeoned ourselves with it pretty thoroughly. Our concepts of "great art" and "great artists" are often less something we aspire to than something we use to denigrate our own effort. We might want to try thinking about art a little differently.

Catherine was a highly acclaimed young singer. She had a very pure and very "scopey" operatic voice. She responded like a Maserati to direction and could corner on a dime, making her a director's favorite. She had been to the finest conservatory in America, studied with the most rigorous and respected teachers, won competitions and fine notices. She seemed set for a career in the world of opera, except for just one thing: Broadway was what made her heart sing. Like *Madame Butterfly* suffering the pangs of unrequited love, Catherine sang opera but dreamed Broadway—until her health broke down.

The time of the singing of birds is come.

SONG OF SOLOMON

"I just didn't have the heart to sing one more tragic aria. I may have the gift for it, but I wanted to return it unopened. Opera was heavy lifting for me, not vocally but emotionally. I was being groomed for a career I didn't want and I was going along with the agenda. As a result, my heart was broken and so was my health."

Fortunately, Catherine encountered a wise older woman who asked her what she wanted in life, to be admired or to be happy? Catherine saw that her motives for pursuing an operatic career were based in a snobbery she herself did not respect. Screwing up her courage, Catherine admitted her heart's desire. "I deviated from being a diva and became a happy hoofer instead." Turning her ambitions and her talents toward Broadway, Catherine has been working steadily ever since. She laughs, "If the shoe fits, you're supposed to wear it—even if it's tap."

"Art" is less about what we could be and more about what we are than we normally acknowledge. When we are fixated on getting better, we miss what it is we already are—and this is dangerous because we—as we are—are the origin of our art. "We" are what makes our art original. If we are always striving to be something more and something different, we dilute the power of what it is we actually are. Doing that, we dilute our art.

A musician with a profound gift for melody decides that dissonance and minimalism are preferable to his flowing musicality. A sculptor who prefers small-format work feels that without a towering and aggressive masterwork he is diminutive in talent. A filmmaker born to cinema verité admires the drawing-room comedy he will never be able to perfect. An artist whose line drawings make people weep with their stunning simplicity decides that only oil painting is high art.

Arthur Kretchmer, a great editor, once remarked to me, "What is it about writers? If something is easy for them, they don't respect it. Instead, they find their métier and kick it in the teeth."

Sometimes as artists, we practice a self-rejecting aesthetic that is like what adolescents do in terms of their physicality. This is a self-loathing that sets in and says whatever we are, it is not as good or as beautiful as whatever it is the other one has. If we are small, dark, and exotic, we want to be tall and bland and blond. If we are a Nordic goddess, we wish our eyes were brown and not cobalt and that our skin looked like a sultry Gauguin. In other words, whatever we are is not what we wish ourselves to be. Comedians yearn for drama; dramatic actors crave comedy. Born short-story writers lust for the National Book Award for their novels; natural novelists scream for the stage. Not that we can't do more than one thing, but one of the things we should let ourselves do is what comes naturally and easily. So why don't we?

Be ye lamps unto yourselves.
Be your own reliance.
Hold to the truth within
yourselves
As to the only lamp.

BUDDHA

Art is not programmatic. We cannot "improve" ourselves into great artists by doing creative sit-ups. Great artists are actually the greatest amateurs—from the Latin verb *amare,* "to love." They have learned to wriggle out of the seriousness of rigid categorization and allow themselves to pursue the Pied Piper of delight. Picasso is a fine case in point. He found beauty in a tin can, in a rusted coiled spring, in a junkyard. Delighted with his roadside finds, he delighted the world by assembling great art out of his simple love of found objects. What a loss if he had said instead, "Pablo, get a grip! You are the maestro! No tin cans for you. Think Guernica! Think serious!"

No surprise that it was Picasso himself who remarked, "We are all born children. The trick is how to remain one." Mozart, we are told, remained one. Why do we get so damn adult?

If we stop trying to improve ourselves and start trying to delight ourselves, we get further as artists. If we lean into what we love instead of soldiering toward what we "should," our pace quickens, our energy rises, optimism sets in. What we love is nutritious for us. If you are crazy about Schubert, play a little Schubert. Your Liszt will be less listless. If you are wild about yellow right now for no apparent reason, paint something yellow and call that closet the sunroom. Instead of resisting yourself, try finding yourself irresistible. Try out the idea that you might be onto something when you catch sight of an amaryllis in the florist's window and think, *Oh, I'd love to have that.*

Children learn at a prodigious rate. If you watch a child learning, you see that he will move from interest to interest, hungrily grazing among multiple appetites: the blocks, the crayons, the Legos, this way and that, experimenting. When we set to structure a curriculum for our artist, we forget that the artist within is childlike and cantankerous. Enticement works better than entrapment. Curiosity gets us further than curriculum. Serious art requires serious play—and play, by definition, is anarchic, naughty.

To be an artist you must learn to let yourself be. Stop getting better. Start appreciating what you are. Do something that simply delights you for no apparent reason. Give in to a little temptation, poke into a strange doorway, buy the weird scrap of silk in a color you never wear. Make it an altar cloth, set your geranium on it, frame it—try letting yourself be that nasty, derogatory little word, "arty." Drop the rock. A lot of great artists work in their pajamas. Ernest Hemingway and Oscar Hammerstein both worked standing up because they liked that.

Sometimes we get a lot further in our art and in our lives when we let ourselves do a little of what comes easily and naturally. If you like to draw horses, stop drawing chairs. If you would love to take ballet, do it and let modern jazz be someone else's winter sport. If you have a deep love for Broadway, tell Chopin you'll be back.

Painting your kitchen is creative. Putting bells on your kid's school shoes is creative. Restructuring the office is creative. Get-

It is the addition of strangeness to beauty that constitutes the romantic character of art.

WALTER PATER

ting the bad stuff tossed from the closet is creative. None of that's going to blow up Western civilization, and it *is* going to cheer us up, our world up, and, by the tiny overflow joie de vivre, help Western civilization by one tiny jot. It is self-expression, not self-scrutiny and "correction," that brings healing and happiness. Bells on the shoelaces, sonnets in the schools. These are not so far apart. Writing a novel and doing something novel on a Saturday afternoon are *both* creative leaps—one large and one small, but each is grounded in the right to express creative choice.

Very often a little friendly and easy art can send us back up those other slithery slopes with a bit more humor and optimism.

Artists of all stripe tend to equate difficulty with virtue and ease with slumming. We do not lean into our ease and enjoy the ride of our gift. Instead, we make firm resolves to work on our areas of difficulty. We call this improving ourselves—okay, sometimes we do improve a wobbly area, but if we do not practice the joy of using our talents where they fall easily, we rob ourselves of self-expression. The "self" has a few things it "selfishly" enjoys—and it is dangerous, as an artist, to ignore these natural affections and predilections.

This is not to say you have to "give up" high art. Instead, I am saying to try "Hi, Art!" like you are waving to someone friendly out the window of your pickup truck.

Today isn't any other day, you know.

LEWIS CARROLL

TASK:
Allow Yourself to Be

Seriousness is the enemy of spontaneity. What we "should" love and what we do love are often two different things. Allow yourself to admit to some of your more anarchistic forbidden pleasures. (Many French romantic liaisons last longer than marriages. Why? Because they are officially a "forbidden delight.")

Take pen in hand and finish this phrase 10 times:

Secretly, I would love to _____.

You have just cast the net of dreams and scooped from your subconscious some secret and hidden desires. Take pen in hand again and for fifteen minutes allow yourself to fully inhabit one of your secret desires. How does it feel to be doing it? Where are you when you do it? Who cheers you on? What surprises you? Make this mental movie as vivid as possible. Be sure to flesh out your supporting cast and color in your setting. Initiative often begins in the imagination. As Stella Merrill Mann summarizes it, "Ask, believe, receive." Give yourself the initial gift of conceptualizing a fully inhabited secret desire.

Invention vs. Convention

As artists, we are innovators. We experiment and explore. We make things new—at the very least, we make things anew. Every painting edges us forward a hair in skill and experience, even if we are in a workshop class that copies an old master. Every time a pianist tackles Franck or Beethoven, interprets Debussy—there is still some personal nuance that the artist brings to the work. A new staging of an old ballet, the millionth high school production of *Romeo and Juliet*—each expression of art breathes new breath into the work and into the world. Even when we are doing something that "has been done," we bring to bear fresh creative energy. And when we deliberately explore and extend our creative territory, we innovate even further and even more.

Some people are innovators by temperament and trade. Other people are conservers. As artists, we are most often innovators. Those who work with our work—agents, managers, publishers, gallery owners, curators, producers—are most often conservers. As innovators, we must not be *so* innovative that we burn our bridges, but we must not allow our conservers to be so conservative that we spend entire careers shoring up the bridges we have already built. Conservers focus not on the forward-

It is the first part of intelligence to recognize our precarious estate in life, and the first part of courage to be not at all abashed before the fact.

ROBERT LOUIS STEVENSON

moving edge but on the known territory of "how it's done" and "the way it is in the business" and "what will sell." They tell us not how to skin the creative cat a new way but how the cat has already been skinned. They talk about "what works" rather than "what *could* work." They say things like "That's not how the business runs."

Conservers want artists to believe that "how it is done" is how it has to be done. They often talk about the odds against accomplishment of an artistic dream. They often come up with the numbers that "prove" the impossible odds stacked against us. They often forget what we as artists know—the odds are not impossible. They never are and they never will be. They may look impossible. They may sound impossible, but those are largely scare tactics. The phrase "scared out of our wits" is a very precise phrase. As artists, when we allow conservers to terrorize us, we *are* being scared out of our wits—wits being those innovative and inventive smarts that allow us to figure out, always, one more way to skin a cat.

As an artist and an innovator, we must always ask, "How *can* we?" We must always look for, and find, still *another* way to skin the cat, publish the book, shoot the film, stage the play—as artists, we are practitioners not of how it *is* done, but of how it *could* be done. We are charged with finding not the problems but the solutions. As artists, we are concerned with making things, while conservers are often concerned with making do with the world as they find it.

When Jean met and married Gordon, she was a working artist with a lively and varied career. Painting, sculpture, and photography were her favorite pursuits. She moved nimbly among the three, making a brisk and interesting career for herself. "You've got to specialize—you've got to market yourself," Gordon solemnly advised her. "You can't just chase whatever whim catches your fancy. It's not good business."

Impressed and intimidated by her husband's "expertise," Jean shaped her career to his wishes instead of to her own. For the

You never know what is enough unless you know what is more than enough.

WILLIAM BLAKE

decade that their marriage lasted, she largely did as she was told, focusing as her husband told her she should. Instead of flourishing, she felt her career growing "successful"—but stagnant and stale. Depression set in before divorce. When her husband abruptly left her, claiming *he* felt stifled, Jean found herself suddenly free. After a few months of dizzy disorientation, she began exploring a variety of creative interests.

"I'd been defining myself so narrowly, as just a painter. I've got all sorts of creative skills I love using." Long a "closet techie," Jean explored new computer skills, studied layout and newsletters. To her delight, people loved paying her to do exactly that. A lively design business was born.

As artists, we are more like inventors than we are like those who mass-produce the inventions. We may do both, of course, and often do, but we are at heart those who make what others may make more of. We create a painting that may later become a greeting card, a poster, or a calendar piece, but the kernel of invention remains with us. We try to see if an idea "flies." Like the Wright brothers, we make the gadget that then becomes the staple of the industry. As artists, we are interested in what can be done rather than how it can't be done.

Some agents, some managers, some producers and dealers and curators, are themselves innovators and creators. They bring to our work their own inventive daring—most do not. As conservers, they are oriented toward what has sold rather than what could sell. They look more often for the downside than the upside. They may additionally be looking most often for the known sale and the proven return and where they can make the most financial reward in the short term rather than thinking of the long-term creative rewards of making a superior work and trusting the market to respond to that.

As artists, we know very well that something can "not be done," only until someone does it. Some artist, somewhere, decides to shove the fence back a little and extend his or her and all of our range. *Showboat* brought serious concerns to musical

Any profound view of the world is mysticism.

ALBERT SCHWEITZER

theater. *Oklahoma!* and *Carousel* brought "real" stories and char-acters and plays that could stand in their own right as dramatic material. The musical was no longer defined merely as boy-meets-girl—from Rodgers and Hammerstein on out, it tackled real issues and ideas. They had moved the fence, buying everyone more creative acreage.

As examples like these make pointedly clear, as artists, we must listen most carefully to our inner guidance and secondarily to our outer advisers. This isn't just spiritual law—trusting the still, small voice to guide us—it's good business practice as well. The interaction of commerce and creativity is a tricky dance, and we as artists must lead it. Show a new direction in your painting to a dealer who is being asked for more of last year's se-ries and you may hear a worried and dispiriting "Mmmm." Do not be fooled. He cannot see what you as an artist may sense, that your direction is the new direction the market will soon be following. For an artist willing to have a learning curve, all di-rections lead to somewhere worthy.

"Nothing succeeds like success" is a truism for a life in the arts. The problem lies in parsing out what constitutes a suc-cess—and for an artist that may be making something new and challenging rather than repeating a known success. It may be having a body of work that is personally respectable, following not merely the market but our own very changing interests. I have been told "short stories don't sell" and then found yes, they did. I have been told "memory plays don't work" and won prizes for the same play. I have been told "never use first person for a novel" and published the same novel to good reviews, good reception, and personal satisfaction.

The business of art is a machine, but an artist is the live, ani-mating spark that runs it. That spark can be extinguished by too much "realism" and too much "I know you don't want to hear this, but . . ." Well-meaning advisers can advise us straight into a creative slump, straight into a fallow period, straight into a wall of inner resistance. They forget that they cannot sell what we do not

Trifles make perfection—and perfection is no trifle.

MICHELANGELO

make and so often urge us to make what they know they can sell, forgetting that if they deaden our spirits too often and too much, the work will deaden as well and there will be nothing to sell.

As artists, we have a form of inner power the advisers can never extinguish or ultimately thwart. And this is always the key.

It is the question of "odds" that always baffles conservers when they deal with artists. Conservers like to think they know the odds. They like to think they know what sells—and they do know until another artist invents another memorable and unpredictable something and thus creates a market for that. As artists, we are first and foremost the origins of our work. Since each of us is one-of-a-kind, the market, for all its supposed predictability, is actually vulnerable to falling in love with any of us at any time.

I say this and I know this because I believe and know creativity to be a spiritual issue. "Faith moves mountains"—Christ told us that, and he may have meant that literally.

We speak of the Great Creator, we speak of Christ but seldom make the connection that the spiritual laws he taught are actually the spiritual laws related to creativity. "Knock and it shall be opened." "Ask and you shall receive"—these are not mere spiritual bromide, they are spiritual laws as they relate to manifestation.

- Ask
- Believe
- Receive

As artists, we routinely ask for inspiration. We need to learn from Christ's example that we can also ask for the material manifestation of our visions to come to us as money, support, opportunity. Our faith, which is a request coupled with an expectation of its successful fulfillment, is no different from the faith of a navigator setting out to prove the world is round. Creative dreams come to us as visions that we are charged with ful-

I find that I have painted my life—things happening in my life—without knowing.

GEORGIA O'KEEFFE

filling. When we allow the Great Creator to do this to us, through us, then we are aligning ourselves with the spiritual power necessary to negate the "odds."

TASK:
Strike Up a Dialogue

In addition to the outer conservers that we encounter in a creative career, we all also carry an inner conserver, who functions as a gatekeeper on our more expansive impulses. The best creative careers are built by a fruitful inner dialogue between our inner innovator and our inner conserver. It is a practical skill that can be practiced. Take pen in hand and allow your two sides to strike up a dialogue. It might look like this:

What a man thinks of himself . . . determines, or rather indicates, his fate.

HENRY DAVID THOREAU

INNOVATOR

*I'd love to go back to school
full-time. I've been shut up
in my painting studio a decade
and I'm lonely and bored.*

CONSERVER

*You make your living from the
work you do in that studio. You
can't just quit.*

INNOVATOR

Well, I'd like to, that's for sure.

CONSERVER

*What about a once-a-week class?
You'd have time to do that and,
if you pick the right one, it's
a lot of stimulus.*

INNOVATOR
*That's a good idea and less of
a radical free fall. Thank you.*

*We all have angels guiding
us . . . What will bring their
help? Asking. Giving thanks.*

SOPHY BURNHAM

All successful creative careers are built upon dialogues like
the one above. As we both move forward and solidify where
we've been, "solid" careers take shape. They are like gardens
that require patient nurturance, where no one plant runs wild.

CHECK-IN

1. **How many days this week did you do your Morning
   Pages?** If you skipped a day, why did you skip it? How was
   the experience of writing them for you? Are you experiencing more clarity? A wider range of emotions? A greater sense
   of detachment, purpose, and calm? Did anything surprise
   you? Is there a "repeating" issue asking to be dealt with?

2. **Did you do your Artist's Date this week?** Did you note
   an improved sense of well-being? What did you do and how
   did it feel? Remember, Artist's Dates can be difficult and you
   may need to coax yourself into taking them.

3. **Did you get out on your Weekly Walk?** How did that
   feel? What emotions or insights surfaced for you? Were you
   able to walk more than once? What did your walk do for
   your optimism and sense of perspective?

4. **Were there any other issues this week that felt significant to you in your self-discovery?** Describe them.

Discovering a Sense of Personal Territory

Saying yes to our creative selves may
involve saying no to our significant others.
This week focuses on boundaries. The essays
and tasks aim at helping us to define our creative
identities as opposed to our many other roles.
Expect to feel heightened emotions as
energy rebounds into your
own court.

Sexuality vs. Caretaking

As artists, our sexual energy and our creative energy are very closely intertwined. This is why we have love songs. Love sonnets. Torch songs. And the phrase "Carrying a torch," because as unrequited lovers we still carry a bright enough spark to speak of being "shot down in flames."

When someone who ignites our creative imagination crosses our path, that person is a "fuse lighter." Our creative engine kicks over. We suddenly have things to say and long for new ways to say them. We say them in paint, in dance, in poetry, in plasticine sculpture. We suddenly "come alive to the possibility." We are galvanized. People ask, "Are you in love?"

In a sense, we are in love—and we are also in love with our own artist, who is suddenly mirrored back to us as exciting and adventurous, powerful, perhaps even dangerous. We experience more energy. We burn the candle at both ends, staying up late to work on a project. Getting up early to grab an hour at the easel, like a stolen bout of lovemaking on the way to work.

Creative energy and sexual energy are both our personal energy. Our use of them is private, and to pretend otherwise is debilitating and abusive. In point of fact, the two energies are so closely intertwined, they may be experienced as nearly identical. We conceive children and we conceive creative projects. Both energies are sacred. They spring from the same source, our inner core. Our creative energy, like our sexual energy, must not be squandered. And yet, we are often asked to do just that.

As artists, we must be alert to what people ask us for and reward us for being. Our partners and friends do condition us into behaviors quite unconsciously. We must be alert to what they reward us for with their thanks and reciprocity. And to what ways they are withholding and manipulative in their lack of approval and generosity. These things condition us, and they are also the conditions in which our art will or will not be made.

Festivity breeds creativity. Rigidity breeds despair. When our high spirits are straitjacketed in the name of virtue or discipline, the vital and youthful spark in us that enjoys adventure and is game for invention begins to flicker like a flame in a draft.

Creativity responds to nourishment and warmth. If we are forbidden to be childlike—told perhaps that it is "childish" or "selfish"—if we are urged to be too sensible, we react as gifted students do to an authoritarian teacher—we refuse to learn and grow. Our considerable energy is channeled into resistance and over time solidifies into a hard-to-penetrate shell of feigned indifference.

The universe is alive with energy. It is fertile, abundant, even raucous—so are we. Most of us are high spirited, humorous, even pranksterish with the least encouragement. What is lacking for so many of us is precisely the least encouragement. We buy in to the notion that life is dreary and difficult and something to be soldiered through. We tell ourselves, "Oh, well, what did I expect?"

The truth is that as children, many of us expected much

more. We had dreams and desires and inklings of delight and full-blown passions. We practiced ballet in the living room, we sang wildly, we loved the goo of finger painting. We loved, period—and love is a passionate and energizing force. In order for our creativity to flourish, we must reclaim our right both to love and to be loved. We must become a little nuts about ourselves, about our notions, whimsies, and ambitions. Instead of chiding ourselves or allowing ourselves to be chided into an "adult" solemnity, we must regain our right to be goofy, earthy, even silly. In lovemaking we speak of "foreplay," and we must allow ourselves to play at the things we love. This means that if our partner is restrictive, we must get a little clever at daring to be ourselves in private. Instead of yanking on our bootlaces and asking ourselves to get better, we need to loosen up the shoelaces, take off the shoes, and wiggle our feet in the green grass of earth.

Creativity is sensual, and so are we. As we celebrate rather than repress our passion, we are rewarded by more passion, and that is the fuel for art.

If our romantic partner insists on always using us to process with, never taking us out to something simply fun, we will begin to feel snappish and hostile. The same is true of our creative partnerships. We may be caring, we may be acute, we may be an invaluable sounding board, but that's not romance, and that's not creative collaboration either. Nurturing is a part of a partnership—overnurturing is the usurping of your creative energy for someone else's agendas.

When we are asked to overcaretake, to "mother" or "father" our friends or lovers or colleagues, our artist reacts with depression and also with rage. Both as artists and as people, such demands can make us feel curiously desexualized, as if we are truly being neutered, castrated, and used.

A woman writer married to an omnivorously needy partner was astounded to discover that after her divorce, both her creative energy and her sexual energy came springing back to life

Be it life or death, we crave only reality.

HENRY DAVID THOREAU

like a lioness waking up after years of medication and depression from living in a too-small zoo cage. As she sharply realized, creative and sexual energy are connected. Dampen our creative ardor and our sexual selves dampen as well. Dampen our sexual selves by demanding we overnurture and parentalize ourselves, and our creativity suffers.

It is no coincidence that artistic annals are filled with the tales of incendiary romantic intrigues, yielding blazing creative work. Our muses *are* fuse lighters, and the blaze they ignite may be passionate, creative, or both. Does this mean we must sexualize all our relationships or creative collaborations? Emphatically, *no*. But it *does* mean that we must be alert to avoid those bonds and entanglements that neuter our exuberance, hence our sexuality and creativity. If someone refuses to share our humor, we are cast as grim parents to their infantile demands. Artists can marry, but they must marry well. And, I would argue, there must be *merriment* in their marriage for their work to continue to flourish. And if the work is dead, the relationship will soon follow suit. If our energy must always be all-nurturing or stern, our creative keyboard is stuck on middle C.

In artist-to-artist relationships, *both* artists need to be nurtured and seen. Neither partner should be neutered or neutralized by excessive caretaking. Agendas cannot replace adventures.

If a man wants to be mothered, he will not respond with enthusiasm to your sexy new dress—*or* your new song. Similarly, a woman artist might demand an all-caretaking daddy from her spouse, saying her "artist child" needs pampering.

Neither sex is immune to creative castration by relationships that drain creative reservoirs without the tenderness to refill them.

Sexuality can be sublimated in the name of art, but it need not be. Damaging sexual entanglements *do* damage our creativity, but enlivening ones nurture and spark it.

Married to a narcissistic and greedy actress, Daniel felt increasingly drained, and his work life withered. Later, involved with a woman artist who found both him and his work attrac-

I cannot understand; I love.

ALFRED, LORD TENNYSON

tive, Daniel's creative life rebounded robustly with plays, novels, films—all the creative brainchildren of a happy coupling.

Our mythology around artists and sexuality tends to dwell on the negative, on the promiscuity of artists, on their self-destructive sexual binging. Far more pernicious is the subtle leeching of creativity and sexuality through overcaretaking, and far less often mentioned is the happy blossoming artists may experience when settled in a relationship that is alive to their creative and sexual energies.

If there is an art to romance, it can equally be said that there must be romance to art.

The aim, if reached or not, makes great the life; Try to be Shakespeare, leave the rest to fate.

ROBERT BROWNING

TASK:
Putting a Tiger Back in Your Tank

When we are in love, we find our partners fascinating and ourselves with them. When we are in a creative recovery, we find *ourselves* fascinating. We fall in love with our own ideas, insights, inspirations, and impulses. We are interested by what we have to say and think. We feel alive, alert, and vibrant—and, if we don't feel that way, we know it and resent it. Admitting those who leave us cold, we warm to our own interests.

Take pen in hand and finish the following phrases as rapidly as you can:

1. Among my friends, a "fuse lighter" who makes me feel creative and powerful is _____.
2. Among my friends, a "wet blanket" who drains and dampens me is _____.
3. Historically, a relationship that left me depleted from overcaretaking was _____.
4. Realistically, a current relationship that leaves me feeling neutered is _____.
5. My most reciprocal, mutually nurturing creative friendship is with _____.

Once you have sorted through your acquaintances and intimates for those who allow you to be fiery, ask yourself the same question: "Do I allow myself to have passion?" Take pen in hand and write yourself a love letter. Be as specific and as affectionate as you can imagine.

Stop Being "Nice," Be Honest

When you are content to be simply yourself and don't compare or compete, everybody will respect you.

LAO-TZU

"Charity begins at home" is not a bromide. It is a direction. It means start with being nice to yourself, your authentic self, then try being nice to everyone else. When we place ourselves too low in the pecking order, we feel henpecked and, yes, we feel peckish. We neglect our work or do it distractedly. Soon our work may develop a querulous tone, sour and dyspeptic, like ourselves. When we undervalue ourselves, we literally bury ourselves in lives not our own. Meeting the expectations of others, we may misplace our own values.

Value systems are as individual as fingerprints. Each of us has a set of priorities that may be baffling to others but absolutely necessary to ourselves. Violating our true selves, we soon feel worthless and undeserving. This in turn prevents our acting on our own behalf, and so we suffer further.

When I was a young single mother, I felt guilty because I craved time away from my daughter. I wanted silence. I needed to hear my own thoughts. I also needed to take my own soul by the hand occasionally and not have to worry about keeping my daughter's tiny hand clutched. Whatever dreams I harbored had better take the back burner, I lectured myself—although I never stopped writing—and so I tried putting my dreams on the back burner, where they proceeded to boil—and so did my temper. Domenica was a delightful child. I began to find her not so delightful. I was snappish, irritable, and guilty. Yearning for more writing time, a luxury of my premotherhood years, I felt cornered and trapped. Wasn't my child more important than my brainchildren? I lectured myself. I could see no way out.

"Take a night off," an older woman friend, an actress, advised me. "Take care of your artist. That will make you a much better mother. You need to get in reality here. Society tells you motherhood comes first, but—with you—it doesn't. If you're honest about that and put your artist first, you might be quite a good mother. Lie to yourself about it—and did you know most child abuse comes from too much togetherness?"

We get our lives wrong because we get our questions wrong. We get our questions wrong because we have been raised in a culture that is punishing to the forms of freedom necessary for artists to flourish. These freedoms are the ones that allow us to be a little less nice so that we can be a little more genuine. Richard Rodgers needed piano time and took it every morning—*then* he was a devoted father—only then.

I had not known that too much "nice" caused child abuse, but I could believe it. Taking my friend's radical advice, I began getting up an hour earlier to write Morning Pages while my daughter slept. I also began a practice of taking Artist's Dates, getting me and my creative consciousness a few of the sort of festive adventures that I had been devising—and resenting—for my daughter. I was rewarded with this self-care by a movie idea—I wrote a script and sold it to Paramount.

What was even more "paramount" was this: I found that my mother had been quite right to post over her kitchen sink a small poem I had always dismissed as doggerel. It read:

*That which we understand
we can't blame.*

JOHANN WOLFGANG
VON GOETHE

> *If your nose is held to the grindstone rough
> and you hold it down there long enough
> soon you'll say there's no such thing
> as brooks that babble and birds that sing.
> Three things will all your world compose—
> just you, the grindstone, and your darned old nose.*

Jump.

JOSEPH CAMPBELL

I've taught for twenty-five years. I've had a great many students worry that they were selfish. It is my considered opinion that most creative people are actually too selfless. Instead of asking "Julia, am I selfish?" they should ask, "Julia, am I selfish enough?" "Selfish enough" gives us the self for self-expression.

As artists, when we are too nice for too long, we stop being nice at all. "I just need to get to the goddamn piano," we say correctly, or "I haven't written in days and it's driving me crazy," correctly, or "If I don't get to the easel, these kids are gonna walk the plank." Our slowly stoked fires of resentment—caused by too many yesses where a timely no would have been more honest and given us time and space to work—begin to set our tempers to a simmer and then to a boil. If we persist in still being nice, we get to cook ourselves an ulcer or develop high blood pressure. For an artist, being too virtuous is no virtue at all. It is destructive and counterproductive. Have I mentioned that it is no fun?

A sustained artistic career is made of two variables—talent and character. By "character" I do not mean the good or bad kind, I simply mean the character or tone of a personality, its exact nature. Great talent linked to an erratic character will yield an erratic career—bursts of promise subverted, flashes of glorious clarity and brilliance lost or muddled by the "flaw" in the stone of resolve. A sustained creative career requires discipline—the courage to evict what does not serve the goal of excellence. This is what it means to have character.

"What does not serve" varies person to person. For one it may be an overly dramatic friend. For another, too many high-octane dinner parties full of boast-and-toast talk. Whatever ungrounds an artist ungrounds his or her work. Whatever ungrounds an artist must be curtailed, avoided, or indulged in with care. As artists, we learn this from bitter experience. A virtuoso concert violinist learns that even a single scotch the night before playing certain works costs in terms of the necessary manual dexterity to safely undertake musical flight. Indulgence has a price. Airline pilots know the same thing as does the FAA. Pilots are checked for abuse of alcohol and other substances. If they overindulge, lives are endangered. For an artist, the life of his work is endangered. Self-indulgence spells self-endangerment. Our large self falls prey to our petty vices. It is enlightened self-interest to be selfish enough to be self-protective. Being self-protective may not seem "nice." We may say no to invitations that do not serve us.

As an artist, being nice is not nearly as important as being authentic. When we are what we truly are and say what we truly mean, we stop shouldering the responsibility for everyone else's shortfalls and become accountable to ourselves. When we do, astonishing shifts occur. We become aligned with our true higher power, and creative grace flows freely.

When we stop playing God, God can play through us. When I stopped rescuing my blocked writer-boyfriend, I moved from writing articles and short stories to writing books. That's how much energy he had consumed. When a composer dropped his high-maintenance girlfriend, he finally finished an album that had simmered a decade. An officially "burned-out" woman painter stopped volunteering her time to the all-consuming neighborhood environmental group and found she suddenly had time to both paint and teach, solidly increasing both her productivity and her income. Her volunteerism had long felt involuntary. Willing to seem less saintly, she felt herself far more free.

Teaching those around us what our priorities are—and remembering them ourselves—makes for harmonious relationships. Clarifying ourselves to others brings honest connections that are grounded in mutual respect. Honesty starts with us. Identifying those who habitually abuse our time and energies is pivotal, but identifying them is only step one. Avoiding them is step two, and this is where a lot of us stumble. It is as if we doubt we have a right to tranquility, respect, and good humor. Shouldn't we really suffer? Shouldn't we find it more spiritual not to upset the status quo? Artificial acceptance of people and

I love those who yearn for the impossible.

Johann Wolfgang
von Goethe

circumstances we resent makes us ill tempered. A little honest self-love does wonders for our personality, and for our art.

"But, Julia," I've heard people wail, "are you saying we should be selfish?"

Personally, I prefer selfish to simmering, cranky, hostile, and long-suffering. And is it really selfish to take time to have a self? You need a self for self-expression—and you need a self for a lot of other things as well. If the unexamined life is not worth living, the unlived life is not worth examining, or painting, or sculpting, or acting.

Too often, the rich world that feeds career-making work gives way to a hothouse world, and later works that feel recycled. For artists at every level, the necessity for nutritive inflow remains. Ironically, that inflow may be impeded by success itself, with the multiple demands made on our creative time.

A man at the very top of his art form professionally found himself so overbooked and so overburdened with advising others and lending his prestigious name to worthy causes that his life was no longer his own. The prestigious institutions with which he had aligned himself seemed to possess omnivorous appetites. Each request was "reasonable," each cause was "worthy." What he was was exhausted, burned-out, and baffled. "I'm at the top," he told me, "where I was always supposed to get, but I don't like it very much." Of course not. He had no time for his personal art, the beloved vehicle that had taken him to the top.

It is impossible to say yes to ourselves and our art until we learn to say no to others. People do not mean us harm, but they do harm us when they ask for more than we can give. When we go ahead and give it to them, we are harming ourselves as well.

"I knew I should have said no," we wail—until we start to actually do it. No, we cannot take on the one extra student. No, we cannot take on the one more committee. No, we cannot allow ourselves to be used—or we stop being useful.

Virtue—and the false virtue of being too virtuous—is very

Knowing what you can not do is more important than knowing what you can do. In fact, that's good taste.

LUCILLE BALL

tempting. The problem with worthy causes is that they are worthy.

"You cannot be healthy and popular all at the same time," an accomplished older actress once warned me. "People want what they want and if you don't give it to them, they will get angry."

True enough, but our artist also wants what it wants and if we don't give it to our artist, our very core gets angry. If we think of the part of our self that creates as being like a vibrant and gifted inner youngster, we begin to imagine how dispirited a series of "Not now, be nice, just be a good sport and wait until later" dismissiveness on our part can make it.

When we start saying "Can't, because I am working," our life starts to work again. We start to feel our artist begin to trust us again and to ante up more ideas. Again, think of the artist as being quite young. What does a child do if disciplined too rigidly? It sulks. It lapses into silence. It acts out—our artist can be fairly depended upon to do some or all of these behaviors when we insist on being "nice" instead of honest.

It is never too late to start over. It is never past the point of no return for our artist to recover. We can heap years, decades, a lifetime of insult upon our artist and it is so resilient, so powerful, and so stubborn that it will come back to life when we give it the smallest opportunity. Instead of being coaxed into one more overextension of our energies in the name of helping others, we can help ourselves by coaxing our artist out with the promise of some protected time to be listened to, talked with, and interacted with. If we actively love our artist, our artist will love us in return. Lovers tell secrets and share dreams. Lovers meet no matter how adverse the circumstances, sneaking off for a rendezvous. As we woo our artist with our focused attention and private time, it will reward us with art.

To live well is to work well, to show a good activity.

THOMAS AQUINAS

Be Nice to Yourself
(There's a Self in Self-Expression)

Did you know that secret? The awful thing is that beauty is mysterious.

FYODOR DOSTOYEVSKY

Many of us work too hard on being selfless. We forget that we actually need a self for self-expression. Take pen in hand and do a little archaeology—dig through your "shoulds" until you arrive at some "coulds." Complete the following sentences with 5 wishes. Write rapidly to evade your inner censor.

If it weren't so selfish, I'd love to try . . .
1.
2.
3.
4.
5.

If it weren't so expensive, I'd love to try . . .
1.
2.
3.
4.
5.

If it weren't so frivolous, I'd love to own . . .
1.
2.
3.
4.
5.

If it weren't so scary, I'd love to tell . . .
1.
2.
3.
4.
5.

If I had five other lives, I'd love to be . . .

1.

2.

3.

4.

5.

These lists are powerful dreams. They may manifest in your life rapidly and unexpectedly. For this reason, you may want to put these lists into your God Jar for safekeeping. Do not be surprised if "parts" of your "other" lives begin to show up in the life you've actually got.

Energy Debts

All actions require creative energy. We seldom acknowledge this. As artists, we must learn to think of our energy the way a person thinks about money—am I spending my energy wisely here, investing in this person, this situation, this use of my time? As a rule, artists are temperamentally generous, even spendthrift. This natural inclination must be consciously monitored. An artist must return enough to the inner well to feel a sense of well-being.

Whatever is worth doing at all is worth doing well.

Lord Chesterfield

A phone call with a tedious creative colleague is draining. What is getting drained is our creative bank account. A phone call or conversation in which our feedback is asked, used, and unacknowledged is like coaching someone on their stock market investments and not getting a thank-you for their big win. Conversely, a phone call that feels reciprocal is a win-win for both parties. You aren't just a site where someone is downloading information. You are a partner in a genuine dialogue that expands you both. I have a musician friend whose conversations are so rewarding, they send me racing to the page to write. Something in our give-and-take just plain gives.

As people and as artists, we crave to be seen for who and

what we really are. If we are in relationships where the dividends we need are never extended back to us, that is a bad investment. Too many of those, and we bankrupt our creative stores. We must ask not only "Do I love this person?" but "Is this relationship self-loving?" Any relationship that risks your artist's identity is not.

A creative person is intended to be fed and supported by both divine and human sources, but none of those needed nutrients can reach us if we have turned ourselves into a food source for others, allowing them to dine freely on our time, our talents and our reserves. If we give someone who is without scruples and needy full access to our time and attention, it is like giving them our creative checkbook. They will spend us willy-nilly, and when we turn to use our own reserves, we will find them missing.

The art of being wise is the art of knowing what to overlook.

WILLIAM JAMES

Creativity expands in an atmosphere encouraging to it, and constricts self-protectively in an atmosphere that is cynical or hostile. This is why artists can have a difficult time accessing their best work in academia. This is why our close friends must be safe and smart, but not so smart-aleck that our creative child is afraid to speak up. When we lose our voice or our energy creatively, it is not some mysterious malady. It can usually be traced directly to an encounter in which our energy was abused.

If someone squanders our time by refusing to be pinned down as to when rehearsals or writing sessions or deadlines can be accomplished, we are put on hold. We cannot invest in other directions because we are always aware that we might be "suddenly" called on to invest when the erratic person is available. If we put our life and our planning on hold to accommodate another, too often we will feel tapped out because we cannot really claim any time and energy as safely and positively as our own. We are "on call." It is like having the door to your creative house unlocked and not knowing when someone will enter.

Think of your energy as money. Does this person tie up too much of your time and energy for you to invest it elsewhere? Is he the human equivalent of an investment you cannot liquidate when you need to? If so, he is then not only expensive in himself, he is also costing you finding and making other more emotionally and creatively remunerative relationships.

Our creative energy is our divine inheritance. If people insist on squandering it and we cooperate, we will find ourselves creatively bankrupt, drained of goodwill and good feelings, short-tempered and short-fused. If our energy is squandered on their poor judgment, our continuing to invest in them robs us of the power to effectively invest elsewhere or in ourselves.

As artists, we must husband our energy as carefully as our money. We must spend it along lines that are personally and creatively rewarding. We must invest it wisely in people and projects that return our investment with measurable satisfaction, growth, and achievement.

Just as we expect and demand a fair return on our investments, we have a right to expect and receive a fair return on our investments of energy—both personally and professionally. Does this mean that we will never—or should never—extend ourselves in generosity toward our friends, family, and work? No. But it does mean that we must be alert to when and where our investment of energy is valued in return.

We must also be clear that "valued in return" may involve—and must involve—a return that is in some way compatible with what we extend. If a great apple pie is extended as a sign of love, "Could I have the recipe?" is not acknowledgment. It is ignoring the key ingredient—the love in the recipe. Similarly, if intellectual acuity is extended to a friend or a spouse or a colleague, that true ingredient must be acknowledged as well.

As an artist with thirty-five years of experience, I am the equivalent of the senior partner at a law firm. That is not ego, it is simply the level of my practice. While I may gladly undertake a "let's parse this out" political discussion on a close friend's creative career, I cannot undertake a regime of lunches involving creative counseling. I would come home both too fat and too thin, overnourished and undernurtured.

Every exit is an entry somewhere else.

Tom Stoppard

I am closer to the work than to anything on earth. That's the marriage.

LOUISE NEVELSON

As artists, all of us need to invest wisely in ourselves and in others. We deserve recognition and respect and acknowledgment for the actual worth of our investments of time, talent, and keen observation.

In our personal friendships, we require peers who see and acknowledge the skills we bring to the table. It is perfectly fine to talk with friends about our career situations and our fiscal dilemmas, but if those friends are giving us advice from their own considerable professional acuity and attainment, that should get some small nod from us, as ours hopefully does from them. This reciprocity of respect may be largely tacit, but it must be there or we may feel slighted or used.

Artists routinely apprentice and even adopt younger artists, but if you examine such arrangements closely, there is a reciprocal flow of energy from elder to younger, younger to elder. The apprentice helps, not merely helps himself. Such relationships can be controversial but mutually catalytic. Georgia O'Keeffe was both benefactor to—and benefitted by—her young protégé Juan Hamilton. Musical mentorships are commonplace. Aaron Copland helped Bernstein, who helped Copland. "Part of what I think we teach younger artists is professionalism," explains one master musician.

For the elder artists who teach and mentor, the rewards are real, but the demands can be unrealistic. In their desire to give, they may expend more than they can refund to themselves. A student who thoughtlessly misses lessons and expects and demands rescheduling can tip the balance from possible to impossible in a teacher's busy schedule.

If our teaching or mentoring feels thankless, we are either overextended or unthanked or both. As older, established artists, the company we keep may very well be underlings, and sometimes people help themselves to our help. When we are unhappy in a relationship, when we "blow things out of proportion," it is because the proportions within the relationship, and perhaps in our life as a whole, are somehow skewed. We are not crazy, but something is. We feel drained because we *are* drained. If the person who emptied the tank cannot help to fill it, well then, we must fill it elsewhere—and put a little red flag next to the person's name in our consciousness. When overtaxed by a friend, we must ask, Is this an understandable, rare situation—a death in the family, a job loss—that requires our marshaling extra help, or is this person habitually taxing, habitually dramatic and accident prone, a chronic abuser of our time and attention, a chronic undernurturer, or in between?

As artists, we have antennae sensitive to the thoughts and feelings of those around us. We can be chilled by indifference, hurt by lack of consideration, and we can be exhausted and diminished if we are in the company of those who talk down to us or treat us subtly like the identified patient: "Oh, you and your crazy ideas." As artists, we *need* our crazy ideas, and we need those who don't think they're too crazy. Symphonies and screenplays begin as crazy ideas. So do novels and nocturnes, bronzes and ballets.

Writers must write. Piano players must play pianos. Painters must paint and singers must sing. We can use our creative energy in the support of others, but if our artist gets lost in the transaction, if our aid and support is treated as generic cheerleading, if we are not acknowledged and nurtured in return in a way that fits our actual personal needs, then we are being inadvertently battered.

Alan sold a book and was required to do a substantial rewrite in order to bring the book fully into form. Rather than appreciating the pressure he was under, Alan's wife chose this "quiet time. You're just rewriting" to invite her extended family for a large and noisy visit. Wanting to be a good sport, wanting not to seem like a prima donna, Alan struggled with his growing anger as loud voices and interruptions cost him time and focus. Finally, exasperated and hurt, Alan rented a room in a nearby motel and retreated there with his computer and his unfinished book. It wasn't that he didn't love his wife and her family, it was that they

There are so many selves in everybody and to explore and exploit just one is wrong, dead wrong, for the creative person.

James Dickey

were unable to see that he was at the glass-mountain phase of a project—the heartbreakingly hard make-it-or-break-it period when an artist knows he just may not be quite good enough to bring to bear the excellence he knows he is required to.

One of the most difficult things that happens to an artist is the sorrow that occurs when misperceived in the public arena. This makes it doubly important that in our private arena our artist be acknowledged and respected. I am not saying that we should swoon around the house—or march around the house— wearing the air "I am a great artist." What I am saying is that if you are a writer and someone doesn't respect your writing time, she is not respecting you. If you are a pianist and someone doesn't respect your need to practice, he is not respecting your personal and professional priorities.

The world is made up of stories, not of atoms.

MURIEL RUKEYSER

Some people batter us often and for agendas of their own. Other people, excellent ones, may bruise us as they racket through a set of terrifying personal rapids. Learning to decipher which is which takes practice. As artists, we must practice generosity not only toward others but also toward ourselves.

Early in a creative career, sainthood isn't too common. But as we become revered and respected for our work, we can develop a weakness for being revered and respected. Our Achilles' heel can be the compliment that makes us feel that we alone can properly mentor a talented youngster. This seemingly harmless form of hubris actually undercuts our own usefulness to the young artists we tutor. Yes, yes, it's wonderful to be a wonderful teacher, a generous friend, but it's healthier to be ourselves, active artists acting on our own behalf. "You cannot transmit what you haven't got," 12-Step programs warn, and unless we make room for art, we resent making room for everything else. And some people—the gifted but needy student or colleague—always ask us to make too much room for them. And we cooperate!

Rather than speak our mind to someone else, we turn up the voice-over in our own head. This is that chiding voice that says

"Now, now. Be nice. Be reasonable. Be whatever is convenient for everyone else."

Ours is a culture that tells us "bigger is always better" and that "more" is better too. As artists, big is not always better and more is sometimes less. As artists, when we overdiversify, we also grow diffused. The name we have worked so hard to make means less as it is stretched too thin—along with our energies—in the name of being a "good sport," a "good guy," a "mensch." As artists, we know all too well how a helping hand at a timely intersection can move us up the ladder. Is it any wonder that as we first feel the rush of success, we often rush to help too many others? Directors may overcommit to "executive-producing" to help younger directors. They become a creative umbrella for less developed talents and often fail to see when that umbrella is so big that it puts their own work into the shade. Committing to help others, we may undercommit to ourselves. Instead of investing our energies wisely in husbanding what we have gained and making a modest expansion, we "go for broke"—a telling phrase—and in the end we break our own hearts by being overtired, overextended, and bankrupt of our own creative energies. When we "energy-debt" to others, the worst debt we incur is to ourselves.

Without sufficient containment for our own temperaments to thrive, without physical and psychic walls to shield us from the demands and dramas of others, we become overstressed. Our nerves short-circuit and our ideas lash like live wires—we are filled with energy, but it's not grounded and usable. Our art suffers and so do we. When we begin to set boundaries—no calls after eleven, no calls before eight, no work on Saturdays, and no on-demand makeup lessons for missed classes—we begin to experience a sense of faith. Why? Because we feel safe. It is hard to have faith in the future when we have no charity for ourselves in the present. When we ourselves feel like the food source, it is hard to find food for thought.

Creativity is really the structuring of magic.
Ann Kent Rush

Life is denied by lack of attention, whether it be to cleaning windows or trying to write a masterpiece.

NADIA BOULANGER

We cannot chronically and repeatedly make up the shortfalls of our colleagues without exhausting ourselves and our resources. We cannot chronically and repeatedly allow others to spend our time and our energy foolishly without discovering eventually that we have been robbed of our creative lives—and given the burglars the keys. We cannot take on "difficult" people and situations to prove our heroism and realistically expect to be either heroic or triumphant in the long run. Saving the day too often means that at the end of the day we have nothing left for ourselves, our own lives, loves, and passions. What we have is a life squandered and not cherished, misspent and not invested.

When we insist on playing God by trying to be all-powerful and all-understanding and all-giving and all things to all people, God can work no miracles in our own lives, because we never allow the time or space to let a divine hand enter our affairs. While it is true the divine source is an inexhaustible flow, as humans we are finite. We do tire, and we tire most easily from tiresome people.

TASK:
Invest in Yourself Energetically

Sometimes, it takes a little sleuthing to actually see our self-destructive patterns. We are so encultured to "not be selfish" that we may have difficulty setting aside the demands and expectations of others. Our own artist may be so concerned with helping to caretake other artists, we may find our stores of optimism depleted. When we reach for our inner resources, we find that our inner well has run dry, quite simply tapped too many times to help others.

Set aside a solid half hour's writing time. You are going to write—and receive—a letter from your artist's best friend suggesting that you make a few simple changes. The writer of your letter intends nothing but good and has been watching you and how you lead your life for a long time. There will be some simple suggestions—"Get more sleep"—and some complicated suggestions—"See less of Annie." Some of the ideas are going to be surprisingly do-able—"Take a life-drawing class"—and others will require some thought—"You need new friends." Allow your letter writer to say whatever is needed to bring you to reality in ways that you chronically sell yourself short. At the end of a half hour, read your letter carefully and place it in your God Jar. If you have carefully selected a "believing mirror," you may additionally wish to share the letter with that friend.

I am what is around me.

WALLACE STEVENS

CHECK-IN

1. **How many days this week did you do your Morning Pages?** If you skipped a day, why did you skip it? How was the experience of writing them for you? Are you experiencing more clarity? A wider range of emotions? A greater sense of detachment, purpose, and calm? Did anything surprise you? Is there a "repeating" issue asking to be dealt with?

2. **Did you do your Artist's Date this week?** Did you note an improved sense of well-being? What did you do and how did it feel? Remember, Artist's Dates can be difficult and you may need to coax yourself into taking them.

3. **Did you get out on your Weekly Walk?** How did that feel? What emotions or insights surfaced for you? Were you able to walk more than once? What did your walk do for your optimism and sense of perspective?

4. **Were there any other issues this week that felt significant to you in your self-discovery?** Describe them.

Discovering a Sense of Boundaries

Creativity requires vigilant self-nurturing.
The damaging impact of toxic inflow must
be countered and neutralized. This week's readings
and tasks focus on helping us to interact with the
world in ways that minimize negativity and
maximize productive stimulation.

Containment

My favorite Tarot card is the Magician. I think of it as the artist's card. He stands alone, holding one arm aloft, summoning the power of the heavens. He has no audience. His power—and our own—lies in our connection, personal and private, to the divine. As artists, we may perform in public, we may publish or show in public, but we must invoke and rehearse and practice and incubate and first execute within a circle of safety and privacy—or else.

Or else what?

Making a piece of art requires two very different forms of intelligence—the largeness of vision to conceptualize a project and the precision and specificity to bring that project fully and carefully to focused form. Often a project will reveal itself in large swaths very rapidly—like a series of lightning strikes. An artist will see clearly and quickly the large thing she is going to build. Then, years may follow as she labors to bring in what it is she saw. During those years, focus can be lost or diffused by distracting and destructive influences.

When you are conceptualizing something large, sketching in the lineaments of a book or play, a picky and inappropriate question can derail your process, sometimes catastrophically. If you say, "I have started to write a new novel" and the person across the table asks, "What's your closer?" that can be a very destructive question. You may not know that yet—nor should you. Material needs time to evolve and find its own feet. As you live with a piece, writing it and "finding" it, it will tell you the answers to those questions—however, if you overplot a piece of work first, trying to dictate its shape, you can run into the same problem a parent might have deciding at a child's birth that he should be a mathematician, doctor, lawyer, or opera singer—the child may not agree. Given a long enough creative childhood— and enough privacy—your project will reveal itself eventually to you as its parent. But a protective parent we must learn to be.

As artists, we must be very careful to protect ourselves and our work from premature questions and assumptions. It is not appropriate to describe our work in a few short sentences, watching the look of interest turn into one of "I'll pass" on the listener's face. Talk uses creative power. Talk dilutes our feelings and passions. Not always, but usually. It is only talk with the right person and at the right time that is useful.

As artists, we must learn to practice containment. Our ideas are valuable. Sharing them with someone who is not discerning is like being talked out of a precious stone—you knew it was a diamond until someone tossed it aside. Most of us do not have the self-worth to yell, "Hey, that's the Hope diamond you just discussed!" But it might have been.

In order for persons or projects to grow, they require a safe container. Both a person and a project need a roof over their head. Both a person and a project need walls for privacy. Just as it is uncomfortable to have people enter your home when it is

An essential portion of any artist's labor is not creation so much as invocation.

LEWIS HYDE

in chaotic disarray ("Oh, my Lord! What is my red lace bra doing on the piano?!"), it creates embarrassment and discomfort to show a project too early to too many people. What's worse, it's risky. Projects are brainchildren. They deserve our protection.

As the world of commerce has overrun the world of art, artists in all fields are routinely asked to "pitch" their work, or "write up a quick proposal." Any seasoned editor will tell you that a book proposal seldom bears much resemblance to the final book. An honest editor or studio executive will tell you that a great pitch does not often deliver a great book or a great film. This is no mystery. The energy that belonged in making the book or film was wasted and diffused by the "selling" of an idea that wasn't yet in solid form.

Art is not a pastime but a priesthood.

JEAN COCTEAU

Just as we wouldn't wake the baby so that the party guests could all coo and chortle and loom at her, we don't want to trot our projects out like performing seals. We all know the horror stories about toddlers who were told "Sing, darling!" Well, projects prematurely exposed to scrutiny tend also to develop a certain sullenness about growing up. We call our projects "brainchildren," and that word can be instructive. Just as it is traumatic to talented youngsters to trot them out and demand they perform for the dinner guests, with later psychotherapy and stage fright as a result, so, too, our projects can develop mysterious tics and phobias if they are prematurely auditioned and critiqued.

Writers' conferences are dark with the stories of books that miscarried by being read too soon and by the wrong eyes. "I showed an early draft to a friend who was a blocked writer. The comments were so negative, I never got the book back on track."

As a young writer, I, too, made the mistake of showing an early draft of a novel to a friend who wanted to write but wasn't writing. "Nothing happens in this novel," my friend complained, meaning no murder, no mayhem, no bloodcurdling drama of the kind she longed to write. The drama in my book was psychological—as I am sure was the writer's block that sent

Always the wish that you may find patience enough in yourself to endure, and simplicity enough to believe; that you may acquire more and more confidence in that which is difficult, and in your solitude among others.

RAINER MARIA RILKE

the novel straight to a bottom desk drawer, where it lived out the rest of its days despite an encouraging note from the one other reader I had sent it to, a New York editor who liked it.

Before we became so modern, many marriages began with meeting a friend of a friend. People vouched for the person they felt you might find interesting. And people vouched for you. In the arts, we need to be alert to the need for such checks and balances. If someone says to you, as to me, "So-and-so could help you with your musical," then you'd better find out if they have ever had any actual success helping anyone with a musical, or if they are an "expert" with nothing to share but their largely unworkable theories.

As artists, we are open-minded but we need not be gullible. Many of the people purporting to be able to help us shape our craft have very little experience with crafting something themselves. What we are looking for is people who have done what we want to do—not someone who has watched others do it. It feels different to be in the cockpit at Cape Canaveral than it does to watch from the ground. A great writer like Tom Wolfe may be able to accurately convey the experience, or damn nearly, but many "experts" in your art may not have enough knowledge of creative liftoff to safely teach you how to withstand its rigors.

It is experience that teaches what a tremor means and what it does not. As artists, we must find people who can share actual experience rather than a sanitized, dramatized, glorified, or press-filtered version. When "help" is volunteered, we must be certain it is timely and actually helpful. We must ask ourselves always, "Am I opening myself or my art to early and improper input, input that is ungrounded or inappropriate?" Another way to put it is: "Do they really know more about what I am doing than I do?"

The sacred circle of privacy is like the seal on a bell jar. It keeps the contents fresh. It keeps germs from getting in. It's unpleasant to say friends can be germs—but they certainly can be.

They can "spoil" a batch of paintings or a perfectly good play by their few ill-considered or even malicious remarks.

Cooking images are very apt and very clear: "Too many cooks spoil the broth" being a homelier way of saying "Practice containment." Keep your creative ingredients your own.

You do not want people prematurely tasting your project and making worried little murmurs. You do not want their ingredients added before you have done what you want with the ingredients you yourself chose.

You may not have added your spice yet when they say "Terribly flat." Instead of catching on, *Oops, this applesauce needs cinnamon,* you may think, *Oh, dear, bad applesauce,* and toss the whole batch out.

One of the most useful creative laws I know is this: "The first rule of magic is containment."

All in all, the creative act is not performed by the artist alone; the spectator brings the work in contact with the external world.

MARCEL DUCHAMP

TASK:
Practicing Containment

Most blocked creatives are blocked not by a lack of talent but by a lack of containment. Rather than practice discernment and discretion in whom we choose to show a project to, we throw open the doors and welcome comments from all corners. If we look closely at why we have abandoned certain projects and dreams, we can often find the offender—the ruthless commentator that caused us to lose heart.

TASK:
Rescue and Recall

Entire novels, movies, and musicals have been rescued, resuscitated, and restored through this simple reclamation tool. One best-selling nonfiction book owes its publication to this too. You might want to try it.

Take pen in hand and answer these questions as quickly as you can. That will give you the information with minimal pain; the information will give you back your power.

1. Have you ever spoiled a creative project by indiscriminate input too early?
2. What was the project?
3. What was the input?
4. What about that input especially confused or threw you?
5. How long did it take you to realize what had happened to you and your project?
6. Have you looked at the project again?
7. Can you commit to looking at the project again?
8. Choose a friend to whom you can commit that you will reexamine your project.
9. Reexamine your project. (Do this process as gently as you can.)
10. Call your friend and debrief your findings.

If you do not already own a God Jar, select or designate one now. A God Jar is a container for your sacred hopes and dreams. It might be a ginger jar, a cookie tin, a Chinese porcelain vase. My God Jar is Chinese porcelain and features two intertwining dragons, the symbols for creativity in Chinese lore. Into your God Jar should go the name and description of anything you are trying to incubate or protect. The play I am hatching goes into the God Jar—not into group discussion. The difficulty I am having in my rewrite also goes into the God Jar, as do my hopes for a successful resolution.

In addition to a physical God Jar, it also helps to select one person as a personal "believing mirror." A believing mirror is a carefully chosen individual who helps a project's growth by be-

A miracle is an event which creates faith. That is the purpose and nature of miracles.

GEORGE BERNARD SHAW

lieving in it even in embryonic stages. A believing mirror ideally practices a form of shared containment. The seed of an idea is protected and incubated by the warmth of their shared belief. Another way to think of a believing mirror is the old expression "secret sharer." It is a form of containment to select a trustworthy companion for our dreams and to confide their shape there only. Most of us need to talk to someone, sometime, about our creative aspirations. The right person to talk to is a believing mirror.

Inflow

Ours is a stimulating world—often an overstimulating one. We have cell phones, car phones, radios, televisions, and the constant barrage of media in all forms. Beyond this, we have our families, our friends, our jobs, and our other pursuits—all potential sources of stress and sensory overload. As our phones shrill, we, too, become shrill and rung out.

"I can't hear myself think," we sometimes say, and we are not lying about that. If "still waters run deep," the noisy rapids of our lives make it hard to be anything but shallow. Our deeper selves are muffled, overtaxed, and overextended. Our sensibilities are stripped of their fine tuning. We become numb to our own responses and reactions. Life is "too much" for many of us.

The act of making art requires sensitivity, and when we cultivate sufficient sensitivity for our art, we often find that the tumult of life takes a very high toll on our psyches. We become overwrought and overtired. Our energies are drained not by coping with our output of creative energy but from coping with the ceaseless inflow of distractions and distresses that bid for our time, attention, and emotional involvement. As artists, we are great listeners, and as the volume is pitched too high, our inner ear and our inner work suffers.

When a creative artist is fatigued, it is often from too much inflow, *not* too much outflow. When we are making something,

It always comes down to the same necessity; go deep enough and there is a bedrock of truth, however hard.

MAY SARTON

we are listening to an inner voice that has many things to tell us—if we will listen. It is hard to listen amid chatter. It is hard to listen amid chaos. It is hard to listen amid the static of ungrounded and demanding energy.

Contrary to mythology about us, artists are generous, often overly generous. We listen to others deeply, sometimes too deeply for our own good. We are susceptible to their hurt feelings and their pouting when we withdraw, and so sometimes we do listen to them even as our creative energy ebbs out of our own life and into theirs. This creates exhaustion, irritation, and, finally, rage.

It's not that we are unwilling to share our time and attention. It is that people must give us the courtesy of listening accurately to our needs about when and how we can do it. We may have huge energy stores, but they are *our* energy stores and we have the right to determine along what lines we want our energies to flow. For this reason, we may need to draw more boundaries than many people, and those who love us must be conscious that unless they can respect this, they are not a friend at all.

And when is there time to remember, to sift, to weigh, to estimate, to total?

TILLIE OLSEN

As artists, our inflow level must be kept manageable and we must "train" our friends and families and colleagues at work when and how we need our space, both physical and psychic. This may mean no calls in the morning before eleven. Or voicemail calls returned every day after three. It may mean "Patience. No contact on demand."

For many artists, expressing is almost a matter of emptying themselves to let inspiration move through them. We do not want to be in our human personalities and concerns when we are in the midst of creating. This is why busy executives have secretaries—to monitor their inflow and keep it from becoming overwhelming to their creative process. As artists, we may need this same protective shield and have to erect it ourselves.

Virginia Woolf said all artists need a room of their own—I think that room may be at Starbucks, or in the basement, or in the bathroom, sitting on the floor. It may be the words "Not now."

An artist requires solitude and quiet—which is different from solemnity and isolation. Artists require respect for their thoughts and their process, but that respect must start with us. An artist needs to be treated well—but often we are the ones who must begin that treatment, and one way we do it is by carefully setting our own valve on how much inflow is allowed to come into us. When we are embedded in family life, or in a sea of students, this can be difficult. If our phone rings constantly, we can't hear ourselves think. When something "gets to us," that is often quite literal because it *gets* to us. We want to "be reasonable." We want to not "fly off the handle." But it can be too much to handle the building up of something yearning to be expressed (inner pressure) and the nudging to conform (outer pressure) to what a "normal" person might act like. Creativity is a process of birth. Labor pain is not a time for manners.

Labor is intense and it is intimate. The whole psyche is turned inward to cooperate with what is being born. Similarly, when I write a book, I am listening to what I must write. When I am writing music, I am following a melody line that I must hear in my head. That takes attention. Attention requires focus. If we have friends and colleagues who, when we don't take their calls, do not get that we're busy, that is a form of abuse to us as artists. "Are you working?" must be asked and answered truthfully. Why? Because when we create, we are psychically very open. We can be flooded by energies. Creative energy—and psychic energy—can flow in many directions. When our friends interrupt our creative time to ask us to problem-solve for them, they are often inadvertently squandering our creative energies. They are deflecting our creative energy into flow lines that will illuminate their work and their lives and not our own. When people simply call and download in great detail, our creative energy gets depleted by trying to solve their problems. "So, don't do it," you might say. Easier said than done.

Creative work is often invisible to other people. If they see you typing, they may know you're writing. If they hear the pi-

Living in process is being open to insight and encounter. Creativity is becoming intensively absorbed in the process and giving it form.

Susan Smith

ano picking out a tune, they may realize music is afoot, but even the threat of interruption may strike them as bearable.

"This will take just a minute," they say without realizing that they are breaking the thread of your concentration and that finding the thread again may be very, very hard.

It is difficult enough to make a piece of art without the added burden of being available while you are doing it. For many very creative people it is hard to muster the self-worth to say "I will get back to you" or "I cannot talk now." As simple as such boundaries sound in the telling, you need only listen for a few minutes to the perceived "selfishness" of a creative parent to recognize that we have a culture where on-tap and on-demand attention are equated with love, and deferred gratification is equated with coldness.

"My father wrote first thing in the morning," the daughter of a famed creator recalls with scarcely banked fury. "Only afterward was he available to be a parent. . . ."

Perhaps, because much creative work is done in the home, the necessity of boundaries is more resented than, say, a banker father's work hours away from the house. Perhaps, too, there is a certain sibling rivalry as "brainchildren" are perceived as competition for parental or espousal attention.

A hardworking portrait artist whose commissioned work required long studio hours and great discipline to meet client deadlines like birthdays and Christmas ruefully recalled that "studio time was considered fair game. My friends would call from their office, unaware that they were, in effect, interrupting me at my office—and I had no secretary to deflect the calls."

For many of us, turning the phone off is an option we have never considered. TV and radio are also automatic—almost a form of civic duty. We "have to" be informed. Silence can be very threatening, but it is a threat worth trying in half-hour increments. Practice turning everything off—for one half hour—and tuning into yourself. A half hour is time enough for a bath,

Just a tender sense of my own inner process, that holds something of my connection with the divine.

PERCY BYSSHE SHELLEY

a letter, a bit of reading, a manicure, some meditation. It is just long enough to hear yourself think or catch a catnap. What you do with your half hour matters less than the fact that it is *yours*. Setting even such small boundaries is a huge step toward self-care—which leads to the self in self-expression.

TASK:

A Room of Your Own

For most of us, privacy takes a little planning. We love our friends, our family, and our art. In order to be alone together, "just the two of us," you and your art—you may need to sneak off like illicit lovers, or plan a weekend away like a married couple trying to keep the zing of romance in their relationship. Take pen in hand and list 10 ways and places you can have privacy with your art. For example:

Love the moment, and the energy of that moment will spread beyond all boundaries.

Corita Kent

1. I could get up an hour early.
2. I could stay up an hour late.
3. I could take my artist to Starbucks for a writing date.
4. I could borrow the key to a friend's apartment and go do my art there.
5. I could take a sketchbook or notebook and go sit in the back of a church.
6. I could take a train ride.
7. I could find a quiet reading room at a library.
8. I could arrange with friends to hide out and house-sit while they're out of town.
9. I could go home to my family; it could drive me to the page, the easel, the sketchbook.
10. I could plan and execute a tiny vacation. Even a day and a half of solitude could reorder my thoughts and priorities.

Day Jobs

If we do not limit our inflow, we become swamped by the life demands of others. If we practice too much solitude, we risk being flooded by stagnation and a moody narcissism as our life and our art become emptied of all but the big question "How am I doing?" What we are after is a balance, enough containment and autonomy to make our art, enough involvement and immersion in community to have someone and something to make art for.

Raymond Chandler sold insurance. T. S. Eliot worked in a bank. Virginia Woolf ran a printing press with her husband, Leonard. What gives us the idea that people with "day jobs" can't be real artists? Very often our day jobs feed our consciousness. They bring us people and ideas, stories and subjects, opportunities as much as obstacles. A day job is not something to "outgrow." It is something to consider, especially if your art feels stale. You may have cannibalized your own creative stores and need to restore them with contact from new sources. As artists, we need life, or our art is lifeless.

Art thrives on life. Life feeds it, enriches it, enlarges it. Cloistering ourselves away from life in the name of being artists causes us to run the risk of producing art that is arid, artless, and, yes, heartless.

For most artists, there is something risky about too much unstructured time, too much freedom to make nothing but art. We talk about self-expression, but we must develop a self to express. A self is developed not only alone, but in community. Community functions like resistance in weight-training—the contact with others makes us stronger and more defined. Day jobs help not only to pay the rent but also to build stamina and structure. Artists need both stamina and structure. Often, a day job provides both. A novel can be a vast savannah in which I wander alone—a musical may mean six years sailing across uncharted seas. Navigators needed the stars to structure their voyages. We artists, too, need other points of reference to stay on course.

Chekhov advised young actors: "If you want to work on your art, work on yourself." He did not mean "Contemplate yourself." He meant we ought to do those things that develop in us creative sinew. A day job can do that. So can some committed community service. So can taking the time to practice the art of listening to something other than our own concerns. A day job requires that skill.

Although we might like to think of ourselves as more rarified, artists are people, and people *do* need people. And things. And hobbies. And, yes, fun. If you strip your life down to get serious about your art, you will find that you get serious, period. If all you think about is your Art with a capital A, then it's always there, twitching and heaving like a space alien having its death throes in the middle of your stark, serene, and artsy loft. You begin to wonder how you will ever lift that thing or even get it out of the house for a walk. Your serious career begins to become your serious problem, which you can talk about, seriously, to other "serious" artists and, perhaps, to an endlessly empathetic therapist who understands how sensitive you are. None of this will get much art done.

The concept "I am a serious full-time artist" can get a little dreary—like one of those oversized New York artist lofts does in a chill winter light. What do you fill a space like that, a concept like that, with? Lofts are supposed to be empty to be chic. And if you start emptying your life of normal human pursuits so it looks like a "serious" artist's life "should," pretty soon you've got the same problem as that drafty acre of chic industrial space: groovy, but do you really want to live there? Doesn't all that empty hipness make you want to visit your aunt Rachel's homey, overstuffed three rooms, where there is a lot of bric-a-brac and comforting clutter and food in the refrigerator?

In our cash-conscious culture, we have a mythology that says you must be a full-time artist to be a real artist. We hear this to

A clay pot sitting in the sun will always be a clay pot. It has to go though the white heat of the furnace to become porcelain.

Mildred Witte Stouven

mean "no day jobs." The actual truth is we are all full-time artists. Art is a matter of consciousness.

A friend of mine gets cranky when he is separated too long from his piano. He also gets cranky when he is closeted too long with his piano. Our love affair with our art is like any other love affair—it needs separation as much as it needs togetherness.

Our life is supposed to be our life and our art is supposed to be something we do *in* it and with it. Our life must be larger than our art. It must be the container that holds it.

Life is not linear. Our Artist's Way is a long and winding road, and we travel it best in the company of others, engaged not in the inner movie of the ego but in the outer-directed attention that fills the well with images and stocks the imagination with stories. Rather than yearning to be "full-time artists," we might aspire to being full-time humans. When we do, art is the overflow of a heart filled with life.

That day job may not be a millstone after all. It might be a life-support system.

It is the soul's duty to be loyal to its own desires. It must abandon itself to its master passion.

REBECCA WEST

TASK:
Commune with Your Community

We have a great deal of "artist-as-loner mythology." It is as false as our mythology regarding the American West. Cowboys didn't settle the West. Families did. Communities did. Similarly, art is made by artists who know and love other artists and other people. When we think about who and what we love, we get ideas about who and what we would love to make. When we think about what my aunt Bernice would enjoy seeing, we begin to see in a new way, more focused and particular. Modern life is restless. We often move from city to city and in moving we lose touch with parts of ourselves and whole communities. We encompass a great many "chosen losses," and to make it up to ourselves, we must also learn to encompass "chosen gains." Ritual and regularity are a part of how we commit to community.

Take pen in hand and answer the following questions:

1. A daily ritual I could take in community is _____ _____.

2. A community paper I could read is _____.

3. A community store I could support is _____.

4. A community concern I could support is _____ _____.

5. A community service I could volunteer is _____ _____.

While you are upon earth, enjoy the good things that are here.

JOHN SELDEN

Sometimes our commitment is as small as a daily cup of coffee in the same coffee shop. Our community reading might be the local underground paper or a networking paper in our field, let us say *Back Stage* for actors or *The Village Voice Literary Supplement* for writers. We might buy our Christmas and birthday presents at the local independent children's bookstore. We might join a cleanup crew on "park day" or spend one hour a week reading to the elderly. None of these community commitments requires training, and they all offer us an anchor in the changing seas of life. All of us need a good dose of daily sweetness—the goodwill we put into life and the good cheer we draw from cherished familiar faces. Artists may need community and companionship more, not less, than other people. Our projects can take a long time to incubate, develop, and mature. In the meanwhile, we need a life and life needs us.

CHECK-IN

1. **How many days this week did you do your Morning Pages?** If you skipped a day, why did you skip it? How was

the experience of writing them for you? Are you experiencing more clarity? A wider range of emotions? A greater sense of detachment, purpose, and calm? Did anything surprise you? Is there a "repeating" issue asking to be dealt with?

2. **Did you do your Artist's Date this week?** Did you note an improved sense of well-being? What did you do and how did it feel? Remember, Artist's Dates can be difficult and you may need to coax yourself into taking them.

3. **Did you get out on your Weekly Walk?** How did that feel? What emotions or insights surfaced for you? Were you able to walk more than once? What did your walk do for your optimism and sense of perspective?

4. **Were there any other issues this week that felt significant to you in your self-discovery?** Describe them.

If we had to say what writing is, we would define it essentially as an act of courage.

CYNTHIA OZICK

Discovering a Sense of Momentum

Creativity thrives on small, do-able actions.
This week dismantles procrastination as a major
creative block. The readings and tasks aim at a sense of
personal accountability and accomplishment. The key
to a creative life is sustained, consistent, positive
action. This is possible for all of us.

Easy Does It, but Do It: Flow

Most artists get blocked not because they have too few ideas but because they have too many. Our competing ideas create a sort of logjam—and that is why we feel stuck. When we think about a project, we think, *I could try this and this and this and maybe I could try this and this and this and, oh, I could try that and then and what if and oh, dear!*

When we get to the *Oh, dear!* the mental gears either clutch up and freeze, leaving them stuck and immobilized, or they start to whir frantically, like a bike pedal when the chain has slipped. Is it any wonder we get confused and frightened? Sometimes, our friends unintentionally panic us, even our closest friends. I remember a testy, difficult lunch with my beloved friend and frequent director, John Newland. I had just started work on a new musical—songs and concepts felt like they were being dumped down a chimney into the top of my head—a little like Santa Claus gone berserk and just pouring the presents willy-nilly from the rooftop. John innocently asked, "What's your act one closer?" I didn't know. I had so many ideas, I couldn't even read the menu much less plot the show's proper build.

"Don't ask me that!" I wailed. "I don't know!" I snapped.

"It's just *me,*" John chided, "your old *friend*. Why are you so angry?"

I was angry because I was overwhelmed, I was overwhelmed because I had so many ideas about what I *could* do that I was panicked.

Whenever you feel stymied, stuck, or frantic, remind yourself, this is the result of having too many good ideas—even if it feels like you have no good ideas at all.

The trick is to establish a gentle flow, to keep that gentle flow trickling forward. This keeps the dammed-up ideas from bursting through and flooding you. It keeps the pressure from becoming so great, it clogs your mental system and shuts down your flow, leaving you even more tense, like an overfilled balloon.

Remember, creativity is not fickle, finite, or limited. There are always ideas. Good ideas. Workable ideas, brave and revolutionary ideas. Calm and serviceable ideas. The trick is to gently access them and allow them to flow. In other words, it's time for that 12-Step adage "Easy does it," because the truth is, easy *does* do it, and frantic, forced, and frenetic does not.

You must take some small step or the ideas will remain jammed up and the creative pressure behind the jam will continue to escalate. When it does, it will often manifest as attacks of self-doubt and self-loathing. "I am so stupid!" you might wail, when the actual problem is "I am so smart!"

What you are trying to do is move energy out of you. That is what starts the logjam gently moving. That is why you cannot achieve calm by listening to talk radio or watching TV—or listening to your friends' helpful suggestions for that matter. You want to quiet your mind by gently siphoning off its overflow, not adding to it.

The season is changeable, fitful, and maddening as I am myself these days that are cloaked with too many demands and engagements.

MAY SARTON

In our culture, we are trained to deal with anxiety by always putting more in. A drink, a shopping spree, a rendezvous with Häagen-Dazs—we tend to medicate our anxieties, not listen to them. The trick is to flow more out, not add more in.

This is where you can serve others and yourself. Instead of zoning out with the news, write your elderly uncle a letter. The operative word is "write." Do not call to talk. You do not want to tip the balance further by adding in more. You need to release thoughts. Think of a balloon that's too full. If you let air out, it zips ahead. If you blow more air in, things pop. When you feel tense and stuck, your life is like that too-taut, overfilled balloon. You are stretched too tight. This is why you cannot let in the well-meaning words of friends. This is why the chatter of a neighbor drives you suddenly so crazy. This is why you are a hair trigger. You are too full of creative energy and you need to gently siphon some off. Take a walk and remind yourself:

1. I do have good ideas.
2. I have many good ideas.
3. Slowly and gently, one at a time, I can execute them.

People become addicted to talk therapy because it does temporarily siphon energy off. People become addicted to over-medicating because it wins them momentary relief from their too-full state. So does overexercising. What is needed is to make forward motion creatively. The truer the dream, the more creative pressure it has, and the more important it is to begin with small actions to keep them from getting frozen up. Don't just talk. *Do.* You need to express yourself in some concrete, small way.

If your head is awhirl and you "cannot think straight," then start by straightening something up. Fold your laundry. Sort your drawers. Go through your closet and hang things more neatly. Straighten your bed. Go get the lemon Pledge and dust and shine your bookcase and your dresser—often, when we are

It is in the knowledge of the genuine conditions of our lives that we must draw our strength to live and our reasons for living.

SIMONE DE BEAUVOIR

engaged in such small, homely tasks, a sense of being "at home" will steal over us. When we take the time to husband the details of our lives, we may encounter a sense of grace. In 12-Step slang, "God" has often been said to stand for "Good Orderly Direction." Often, in making a sense of order, we encounter a direction we can valuably express ourselves in.

A letter, a memo, a stack of valentine's cards. This will prime the pump. In my creative practice, I write daily. Every day. Three pages in the morning. Almost always some more writing follows later in the day. When I began writing music, I at first binged on it and wore myself out. Then I was afraid to start again, and pressure built up. When I learned that it, too, yielded to the "a little daily keeps it flowing" technique, I slowed way down, and my productivity speeded way up.

No matter how stupid and overwhelmed you may feel in the face of the complexities and terrors of change, the problem is not—not *ever*—that you are stupid. It is simply that your excellent mind is working overtime and so you need to calm it down. Instead of discounting your anxiety or labeling your anxiety, use it as creative fuel.

You need to claim the events of your life to make yourself yours. When you truly possess all you have been and done, which may take some time, you are fierce with reality.

FLONDA SCOTT MAXWELL

TASK:
Easy Does It, but Do Do It

A close friend of mine accuses me of practicing the Martha Stewart school of creativity. A man who lives with his wife and servants, he has all but forgotten the sense of well-being that comes from doing one small something to sort our world and our own place in it. Most of us have many small areas where we could benefit from a little housekeeping. Take pen in hand and list five areas that you could neaten up. Choose one area and execute a little cleanliness-is-next-to-godliness energy—does this experiment put you in touch with a greater sense of benevolence?

A few examples of possible chores:

1. Polish my shoes.
2. Clear the surface of my desk.
3. Straighten out my bookshelves.
4. Sort my receipts into good order.
5. Throw out old magazines.

What we are after with this task is the experience of using stuck energy in a productive way, however small. Once we realize that our sense of being stymied by the outer world can actually be altered by simple and small actions on our own part, we begin to have more faith in the benevolence of the universe itself. In other words, if God is in the details, we had better be there ourselves!

Breakthroughs

One of the difficulties with the creative life is that when we have creative breakthroughs, they may look and even be experienced as breakdowns. Our normal, ordinary way of seeing ourselves and the world suddenly goes on tilt, and as it does, a new way of seeing and looking at things comes toward us. Sometimes this "new vision" can seem almost hallucinogenic in its persuasive shifting of perspective. What seemed certain now seems uncertain. What seemed out of the question now seems possible, even probable. It is as though we have had a strobe light sweep across our experience and freeze into bas relief a certain previously unquestioned assumption.

Creativity is grounded not in dreamy vagueness but in piercing clarity. We "see" a piece of work and then we work to shape it. We "envision" a new direction and then we move toward it. The creative journey is characterized not by a muzzy and hazy retreat from reality but by the continual sorting and reordering and structuring of reality into new forms and new relationships.

Life ought to be a struggle of desire toward adventures whose nobility will fertilize the soul.

REBECCA WEST

Courage—fear that has said its prayers.

DOROTHY BERNARD

As artists, we "see things differently." In part, this is because we are looking.

When we are willing to look—and willing to see what we see—we open ourselves to losing comfortable assumptions about the nature of "things." Those things may be creative—we paint a chair at skewed angles because that seems more "chair" to us suddenly—and this new viewing may apply to our human relationships as well. Suddenly and unexpectedly, we may apprehend them in a new and startling light. Sometimes such breakthroughs are frightening. When they are, we might call them "strobe-light clarity."

We might realize equally, "This relationship is going nowhere" or "My God, I am going to marry this man." Suddenly, our future has different casting than we imagined. We got a clear glimpse of ourselves solo or in an unexpected coupling. Such glimpses, a kind of "flash forward to your future," can be very disorienting. We "see" the shape of things to come, but that doesn't mean they are "there" yet. The bad relationship still needs to finish falling apart. The new relationship needs to finish coming together. We "know" what's going to happen, but we cannot force time to match our perceptions—and we ourselves actually need time to become grounded and able to handle the change we have foreseen.

When strobe-light clarity hits an area of our life or our work, we suddenly see the outlines of that arena with startling and heightened drama. "Why, I could paint this way!" we gasp, or "My God, she has no intention of ever standing on her own two feet. I am not helping her, I am enabling her!" When strobe-light clarity hits, it is harsh but distorted. We get a quick and terrifying glimpse of an unfamiliar truth that has the same disorienting effect as a strobe light flashed across the dance floor—everything jerks into new positions without our seeing the transitions. It can be tempting—in the flash of strobe-light clarity—to dismiss our former work or our former understanding as false. It is not false. It is simply outmoded. The way we used to paint was fine for then. And our friend may well have been authentically helped and is now only trying to create a wrong dependency. Strobe-light clarity is so sudden and so sharp that it is discontinuous. It is something we catch out of the corner of our eye: "What was that?!"

When we have such dramatic breakthroughs in our creative and personal reality, we must take care to integrate and absorb their meaning before acting on them. It is not that all of our prior understandings are inauthentic. It is more that they were incomplete. Our new insight offers a corrective to our prior understanding but it is a corrective that needs to be lived with a little before we act on it.

Strobe-light clarity is the creative equivalent of "This relationship is over." That may well be, but we do not need to move all of our belongings into the street. We can take a beat and assess our future options. When we decide, *I am bored with this art form as I have practiced it,* we are posing a question—"What next?"—that the universe is already in the process of answering. Creativity is always an interactive dance between our inner world and our outer world. Opportunity does not knock only as soon as we are willing to hear it. Arguably, it has been knocking for some time, and we have turned a deaf ear, a blind eye, to what our accepted consciousness had screened out and now is open to receiving.

Sudden breakthroughs *can* feel like breakdowns. It is helpful to think of them not as "breaking down" but as "breaking up." Think of your consciousness like a frozen river that breaks up in spring from a solid sheet to many floes. This is what is happening to your creative consciousness—what was solid is becoming fluid, new forms and new structures are becoming possible. New growth is afoot.

Instead of being unable "to see the forest for the trees," we suddenly see both the forest and the trees. *My God, I could include photographic snippets in my painting surfaces,* we think. We have shifted our mental furniture, repainted the old bureau a beau-

The great thing about getting older is that you don't lose all the other ages you've been.

MADELEINE L'ENGLE

tiful robin's-egg blue and given ourselves a whole new vista and venue.

The narrator should be first person and a male, we suddenly "know." And we "know," too, that it doesn't matter that we are female and writing this character. *Memoirs of a Geisha* is a brilliantly conceived and executed first-person narrative of an Oriental woman—written entirely by an Occidental man.

When we get a flash of strobe-light clarity, walls fall away. We see suddenly that we "can" do what we "couldn't" a moment before. We have a "flash" of invention and, like glimpsing the bright underfeathers of a bird, we suddenly realize our creative life is not colorless and lackluster, as we thought.

"I didn't realize what I was doing," we may gasp when we see that behind our own back and through our own hand, the Great Creator has orchestrated something new and original that we had no idea we were making. "Why, if I string all those heartbreak poems together, I have got the spine of a great performance piece. What a great idea!"

Strobe-light clarity is like a glimpse of yourself in a new and for-once-flattering mirror. It's like catching a glimpse of an attractive stranger and then going, "My God, I am that stylish woman." We look so different, so impossibly possible to ourselves that we are caught off guard. Our age falls away and we are abruptly young at heart, caught by the throat with the sudden emotion that says "This is real. . . ." We suddenly get just a glimmer of where we are heading and that new growth is possible, even impending at our advanced age—whatever it is.

Strobe-light clarity tells us this new growth will be terrifying. There is a "monster movie" drama to a sudden flash of insight. "Oh, dear God! What was that?!" we gasp. Seen so quickly and sharply, the most normal things can appear frightening. So it is with our new growth. The thought *I have got to go back to grad school* can be as scary as an ax murderer looming at us from the corner. As the light of reality grows around this sudden thought, the ax murderer begins to look more like a teacher and less like

Life was meant to be lived and curiosity must be kept alive. One must never, for whatever reason, turn his [sic] back on life.

ELEANOR ROOSEVELT

someone who is out to dismember our known reality. When you are in the grips of a sudden and startling flash of clarity, move slowly and gently with yourself so that you do not bolt in terror, tripping on the furniture of your consciousness.

Breakthroughs are not breakdowns. They just feel that way. Remember, you, too, are breakable. Be gentle with yourself while you grow accustomed to your new mental and emotional terrain.

We are not human beings trying to be spiritual. We are spiritual beings trying to be human.

JACQUELYN SMALL

TASK:
Geography

As a child, my favorite subject in school was geography. I loved the images of foreign cultures that startled my eyes—baskets and balls of rubber balanced atop heads; the plane dipping low over the head of the falls; hidden in the jungle highlands; the long, slender wands used by Egyptian healer priests to trace the body's energy meridians; the art and artifacts of other ages called across time and distance.

Begin by considering the following questions.

1. What culture other than your own speaks to you?
2. What age other than the one we're in resonates with your sensibilities?
3. What foreign cuisine feels like home to your palate?
4. What exotic smells give you a sense of expansion and well-being?
5. What spiritual tradition intrigues you beyond your own?
6. What music from another culture plucks your heartstrings?
7. In another age, what physical age do you see yourself being?
8. In another culture and time, what is your sex?
9. Do you enjoy period movies? Or movies, period?

10. If you were to write a film, what age and time, what place and predicament, would you choose to explore?

Now, collect a large and colorful stash of magazines and, if possible, catalogues. Find a good photo of yourself and place it in the center of a large sheet of posterboard. Working rapidly, select images from your magazines and catalogues and use them to establish your leading character—you—in an imaginary world filled with beloved objects and interests.

Finish Something

As artists, we often complain about our inability to begin. *If only I had the nerve to start X*—a novel, a short story, the rewrite on our play, the photo series we're "thinking" of. I would like to suggest that you start somewhere else—start with finishing something.

There must be some obscure law of physics that revs into action when artists finish something. And that something can be reorganizing the medicine cabinet, cleaning out the glove compartment, or taping your cherished road maps back into usable companions. The moment we finish something, we get a sort of celestial pat—sometimes even a shove—a small booster rocket of energy to be applied elsewhere.

How can you begin your thesis if you can't finish your mending? How can you fill out your grad school applications if your shower curtain is stained and torn, half on and half off its rings, while the new curtain waits expectantly folded on the toilet tank?

Most of us have households and studios filled with half-done projects: sorting the photos of our portfolio, a project half in albums, half in shoe boxes; realphabetizing the business Rolodex—another project half done; organizing the consecutive drafts of your last play, yet another "when I get back to it"

My favorite thing is to go where I've never been.

DIANE ARBUS

agenda—the list goes on. No wonder we drag our feet at the thought of starting something else. We've had too many false starts, too many half-finished, halfhearted projects.

Christian, a young composer, had great enthusiasm and a great many projects. He was always racing ahead on some new musical theme, going full steam until something else caught his eye and that something became the focus of a new burst of energy. Christian was the kind of young artist often called "promising," but he was too fragmented to deliver on that promise.

"Clean up your arranging room," an older composer advised him. "Make systems. Put everything in order and give every scrap of work its proper place."

Although he felt that he was wasting time and energy that he could be using on writing music, Christian grudgingly complied. As he began to assemble three-ring binders and put all of the work on each project carefully into place, a curious thing happened: self-respect began to rear its noble head.

I certainly have done a lot of work, Christian caught himself thinking. He saw that several projects were very near completion and that he had been denying himself the satisfaction of a job well done. Predictably, he almost did the same avoidant behavior on organizing the room itself. He worked on it until it was two-thirds done and then he stopped.

"How's that arranging room coming?" his friend, the savvy older composer, asked him. Christian confessed that he had stopped before finishing his clean-up.

"It's much better," he said defensively. "I know where almost everything is and you wouldn't believe how much work I have done, really. I had no idea how many projects I had come so far on."

"Finish that room. Get every last bit of it in order. You are close to the reward but not there yet. Finish it and see what happens."

Grudgingly, working under half steam, almost laughing at how he lollygagged and dawdled, Christian finally finished the clean-up of his little room. There was a place for everything.

It is good to have an end to journey towards; but it is the journey that matters in the end.

Ursula K. Le Guin

Every project stood squarely in place, sorted and simple to see. Christian felt a buzz of new energy. It felt like optimism but a bit more focused than optimism. It took him a while to name this new emotional component, but when he did he saw it was something different from inspiration, something more solid and firm than hope.

"I felt determination," Christian recalls. Many things that had seemed vague and illusory now seemed squarely within his grasp. A project at a time, moving folder to folder, Christian began completing work. Within a month of arranging his arranging room, Christian had multiple projects in final form, able to be moved to the next step, submitted for grants and competitions.

"I suddenly showed something more than 'promise,'" Christian relates. "I had actual finished projects. I wasn't just 'talented' anymore. I was something much better—productive."

There seems to be an unwritten spiritual law that if we want our good to increase, we must focus on appreciating and husbanding the good that we already experience. This can be done by writing gratitude lists enumerating the many things in our current life that are fruitful and rewarding. On a concrete level, it can be done by the careful husbanding of what we have. This means that buttons get sewn on, hems get tacked up, smudges get scrubbed off doorjambs. We make the very best of exactly what we have and we find that almost behind our back the Great Creator redoubles and reinforces our efforts and makes something even better. This is where the old adage "God helps those who help themselves" can be tested and found to be true.

A body in motion remains in motion, and nowhere is this law more true than in creative endeavors. When we want to grease the creative wheels, we do very well to muster a little elbow grease elsewhere. Mend the trousers. Hang the curtains. I do not know why hemming the droopy pant leg gives you the juice to get to the easel, but it does. I cannot tell you what it is about detoxing the mud closet that makes you see more clearly how to end a short story—or start one—but it does.

Finishing almost anything—sorting your CD collection, pumping up a bike tire, matching and mating your socks—creates both order and an inner order: "Now, start something," finishing something says.

TASK:
Learning to Navigate the Learning Curve

This is an exercise in encouragement. Faced with doing something new, we often forget we have successfully done many "somethings" old. Take pen in hand and list 10 things you have learned to do despite your doubt they could be mastered.

For example:

1. Spanikopita—I can actually make it and it's good.
2. Spanish—I can actually speak it well enough to communicate more than "How are you?"
3. The backstroke—I didn't drown, and now I like it.
4. How to change oil
5. How to operate my new computer
6. Calculus—another calculated risk I succeeded at
7. Ear training—yes, I *can* notate simple melodies more and more accurately.
8. Reading at open mic—I can speak into the microphone and hold my own most of the time.
9. I did learn how to work Photoshop on my computer.
10. I am able to give my dog heartworm pills without losing my hand.

Skills can be learned, and we can learn that the learning curve always involves excitement, discouragement, dismay, misery, and, eventually, mastery.

In order to carry out great enterprises, one must live as if one will never have to die.

MARQUIS DE VAUVENARGUES

No one needs to know that you've shut the world out and are meditating as you stroll down the street. Twenty minutes to a half-hour every day is a good amount of time to restore a sense of serenity.

SARAH BAN BREATHNACH

CHECK-IN

1. **How many days this week did you do your Morning Pages?** If you skipped a day, why did you skip it? How was the experience of writing them for you? Are you experiencing more clarity? A wider range of emotions? A greater sense of detachment, purpose, and calm? Did anything surprise you? Is there a "repeating" issue asking to be dealt with?

2. **Did you do your Artist's Date this week?** Did you note an improved sense of well-being? What did you do and how did you feel? Remember, Artist's Dates can be difficult and you may need to coax yourself into taking them.

3. **Did you get out on your Weekly Walk?** How did that feel? What emotions or insights surfaced for you? Were you able to walk more than once? What did your walk do for your optimism and sense of perspective?

4. **Were there any other issues this week that felt significant to you in your self-discovery?** Describe them.

Discovering a Sense of Discernment

This week poses a challenge: Are we actually able to go the distance? To answer in the affirmative, we must learn to keep certain demons at bay, most notably success, "the unseen enemy." The readings and tasks of this week aim at naming and declawing the creative monsters that lurk at higher altitudes. Anger is a frequent companion of this week's explorations. As we unmask our villains, we often feel a sense of betrayal and grief. This is replaced by a sense of safety as we name our true supporters more accurately.

Making Art, Not "Making It"

In the study of overeating, it has been discovered that certain foods are "trigger foods"—the first bite leads to the craving for more, more, and more. For many artists, fame is a trigger food, or can be. When fame is sought for itself, we always will want more, more, and more. When it occurs as the by-product of our work— which it does and often will—then it is more easily metabolized. But we must stay focused on *what* we are doing, not *how*.

When we are in the midst of making something, in the ac-tual creative act, we know we are who and what we are because we forget our public reception for a minute. We become the art itself instead of the artist who makes it. In the actual moment of making art, we are blessedly anonymous. Even when done in public, the act of making art is a private act. Creativity is always between us and our creative energy, us and the creative power working through us. When we are able to stay clearly and cleanly focused on that, then we are able to do very well.

We can always make art. What we cannot always do is make it in the venues we might choose or even in the field that we consider our rightful playing field. Actors who are not acting tend to forget that they can still learn a monologue, still try their hand at writing a one-person show, still try learning piano, watercolor, or clay. When we insist that we will express our creativity in only one field, or even in one corner of one field, we lose sight of two things: our versatility and our opportunity. We tend to isolate and to brood, resentful over not being appreciated, resentful over not being chosen when we can actually make choices of our own that put our creative power, if not our "career," squarely back in our own hands.

It is difficult to be depressed and in action at the same time. Actors forget that the key word is "act." Waiting to be chosen by an agent, waiting to be cast in a part, waiting to be well reviewed, they forget they can put on a show by reading at an open mic, recording monologues on a home video, throwing a benefit for their church group, going to old-age homes and performing. In a word, they can *act*.

Musicians can learn a new music, whether or not it can be seen as applicable to their particular métier. They can remember that the term is "play music," not "work at their career." Broadway melodies are enjoyable to play on the violin. The Beatles can be a welcome change from Bach. If we are really serious about our art, then we need to be serious about making it—not about being perceived as "a serious artist."

Self-respect lies in the writing and the playing, not in the reviews. Not even in the mental review of what has been done. Or how it was perceived in the public eye.

That phrase "the public eye" tells us the danger of focusing on "How am I doing?" instead of "What am I doing?" What exactly is the public eye? And why does it seem to always be closed or winking during our solos?

When making art becomes about making a career and making a profit—not that we don't enjoy those as benefits—then making our art is someone else's responsibility, not our own. We need a "lucky break," we say. We fall into talking about the way it is "in the business," and the odds against us, and the next thing that happens is that we feel powerless and depressed and mad— mad because we're not "making it" fast enough. And we don't mean art.

Clarence was a talented musician, so talented that "big things" had always been predicted for him. He played for "big names" on "big albums" and was always on the verge of his "big break." A chronic dissatisfaction that "it"—the really big break—hadn't happened yet kept Clarence from ever noticing and enjoying the many marvelous and exciting things that did happen. He had played with Bob Dylan and other idols of his. He had appeared on David Letterman's show and toured Europe with a red-hot band. His life looked glamorous from the outside but felt glamourless on the inside. He didn't play music for the joy of it. He played it to impress a producer or to rack up another Grammy nomination.

There has to be more to making art than this, Clarence caught himself thinking, and it was at this point that he saw the flyer calling for parents' help with the school music pageant. No one had contacted him directly. He was too big a fish for that. Looking at the little flyer, Clarence thought, *This might be fun. And the kids would be happy if I got involved.*

Clarence did get involved. Very involved. He had an extensive and expensive home studio where he could record tracks. The "little music pageant" began to have some very glossy and professional musical help. Next Clarence enlisted his wife—

We flood our minds with words! They mesmerize and manipulate us, masking the truth even when it's set down squarely in front of us. To discover the underlying reality, I've learned to listen only to the action.

JUDITH M. KNOWLTON

talented both as a costume designer and as a fine backup singer. Soon the entire house was filled with lively children's music and draped with brightly colored costumes.

"It's like Santa's workshop over here," Clarence told his friends, laughing. Laughter became a regular guest in the household as Clarence was relieved of his "serious focus" on his "serious career." Never before had the little school had such a sophisticated and happy production. There were even videotapes of the kids' star turns as they sang out to Clarence's professional music tracks.

Those who lose dreaming are lost.

AUSTRALIAN ABORIGINAL
PROVERB

"I think they got a lot out of it," Clarence said with satisfaction, "and I know I did."

Using his art artfully in the service of his family, community, and friends, Clarence reconnected to the joy that had made him an artist in the first place. He again came in contact with the generous part of himself that spilled out into music and self-expression. His art became about making something instead of about "making it." He now makes time every year for the children's music pageant. It gave him back the gift of giving by putting the "heart" back into his art.

Focused on success as a business goal, we often lose sight of success in terms of our personal spiritual well-being. We focus "out there" rather than on our own inner experience. Doing that, we can become lost.

"I always knew I was supposed to make good," says Joy. "Everyone was betting on me."

Joy had been a performer since childhood, when her parents first pushed her center stage. A talented actress with good comedic skills, she quickly got regularly cast in her small midwestern city, and when she made the "big move" out to Hollywood, she found regular casting there as well. She worked more than any of her friends and "really had very little to complain about" except for the fact that she just wasn't happy.

Entering a creativity recovery, she began writing Morning Pages and, as she did, began to wonder how much of her center-stage personality was really her own idea. "You're a born actress," her mother had always told her—but was she? Acting got her a lot of attention but brought little satisfaction.

As her self-exploration progressed, Joy noticed she really loved writing. Writing was what her serious "brilliant" sister did for a living, and it had always been off limits for her. She was the family cut-up and "star." Telling herself she was "just exploring," Joy began to let herself write. As she did, she found that she felt more comfortable in her own skin, more at home with herself creatively. She continued to work as an actor, but her writing held more and more of her attention. After a solid bout of urging from her best friend, she tried her hand at a monologue. It flew from her pen. She tried another. Then another. Then another. Before six months had passed, she had enough monologues for a one-woman show and the same best friend volunteered to direct it.

"I was terrified, stepping forward as a writer," Joy recalls, but her friend printed flyers, found a good venue, and was convinced that Joy's actor was just the midwife to her real talent as a writer.

"I didn't give up my actress, but I stopped acting as though acting were all of me," Joy remembers. Her one-woman show was a modest hit. Her friend next suggested she try a one-act play.

"With friends like you, who needs an agent?" Joy complained, but she set pen to page, and page to stage soon followed. It is several years later now, and Joy enjoys her success as a "hot" young playwright. She enjoys the process of making her art and finds "making it" a happy coincidence, not her goal.

"Once I let go of my idea that making art was about making it, meaning fame, I began to make the art I wanted to make and that gave me something that looks an awful lot like the life I always wanted to have."

When we surrender to becoming what we are meant to be instead of trying to convince the world of who we think we are, we find our proper creative shoes and can walk in them com-

One of the marks of an intelligent person is to be able to distinguish what is worth doing and what isn't and to be able to set priorities.

Anne Wilson Schaef

fortably. Not surprisingly, they sometimes take us far. Moving comfortably and at a less driven pace, we also enjoy the journey, finding pleasure in our companions and our "view" each step of the way.

TASK:
Make Something for Someone Else, Not to Be Somebody

They do not know that ideas come slowly, and that the more clear, tranquil and unstimulated you are, the slower the ideas come, but the better they are.

BRENDA UELAND

When we are focused on making a career in the arts, we often forget that our artful nature is a gift we can bring to the personal as well as the professional realm. We write for a living but do not take the time to write letters to our friends. We draw for a living but use our artistic skills only on paid commissions. Hobbies are out the window as "too frivolous," and as we focus seriously on our art, we become very serious indeed.

Take pen in hand, number from 1 to 5. List 5 people to whom you feel closely connected. Next to each name, devise one creative project you could undertake to show them your love and gratitude for their friendship. Select one project and execute it. For example:

1. My daughter—write out memories of raising her.
2. My sister—write out "artist" stories of her courage.
3. Carolina—draw her as a child and now as a friend.
4. Emma—make a photo album of our creative adventures.
5. Connie—make an "arts and crafts" recipe box for her.

We don't need to devote years, months, days, or even hours to a connection project, but it is often true that art made from the heart leads us to more and more art. As we free ourselves from our "get serious" mold, we often encounter new energies and new interests. When art becomes a part of our greater life, we often discover greater life in our art.

Velocity and Vulnerability

Any sudden change in velocity creates vulnerability for an artist. Two things come at us—opportunity and diversion or, more bluntly, useful things and opportunities to be used. When your life changes speed, it is often difficult to discern what is a genuine opportunity and what, on closer inspection, is an opportunity for someone else at your expense.

As our success and visibility as artists rise, so does the flow of two often difficult to distinguish things: opportunities and diversions. It is no coincidence that in Chinese the hexagram for "opportunity" and "crisis" are the same. As we become brighter and stronger as artists, others are attracted by that clarity and glow. Some of them will help us on our way, while others will try to help themselves, diverting our creative light to their own path. Those who actually offer us invitations and work in alignment with our true values and goals are opportunities to be cherished, and colleagues to bond with. Those who covertly present their own agendas in the disguise of a lucky break for us are opportunists, not opportunities. They represent a creative crisis in the making. They are what I call "piggybackers," and they must be identified and weeded out of our creative garden.

Piggybackers have a project they want to attach to your name, fame, reputation, and energy, and they seldom say "You could really help me," which would give you a chance to think about it on a clear level. Instead, they say, "I could really help you . . ." and they present their agenda cloaked in ways that make it look as though it could be compatible with your own. Maybe it is. Maybe it isn't.

When a piggybacker wants a share of your creative trough, he can be *very* persuasive. Flattery can flatten your will to resist. This is dangerous. Just as weeds and flowers can look a lot alike, a piggybacker can often successfully pose as something nicer.

Success can make you go one of two ways. It can make you a prima donna, or it can smooth the edges, take away the insecurities, let the nice things come out.

BARBARA WALTERS

Weeds are greedy, and choke out the garden by claiming too much territory. A piggybacker will do the same—and often, that is how you know them. Piggybackers often use flowery phrases: "I got this wonderful opportunity and I immediately thought of you, you're so wonderful, so gifted, so talented, so blah-blah-blah. . . ."

Piggybackers do not really care what your actual goal is. They care about harnessing your time, energy, and expertise to pursue goals of their own.

Piggybackers may have goals and agendas quite different from your own—although they are loath to reveal it. They may send you something fairly repellent to your values and yet insist you have huge swaths of common ground and that, therefore, you should endorse it. It is my experience that every time you are "generous" against your better judgment, you end up embarrassed.

Piggybackers like to offer you an opportunity and then, once you have signed on, try to run off with the project. Your "opportunity" gets trampled under their opportunism. In their race to win—and win big—artistic values get lost.

Arthur scored a substantial success with a best-selling book. For the first time in his adult life, he had money, recognition, and a seemingly assured future. Agents were eager to represent him, and publishing companies were eager to bid on his next project. Everyone was betting that Arthur would go on to bigger and better things—including Arthur himself. He had a winning personality and he was on a winning streak. It seemed nothing was beyond his reach—until he began to grab for all of it at once, telling himself that each opportunity was too good to pass up.

First, there was the infomercial. "It will sell who you already are and tell people who you are becoming." The filmmaker was persuasive and Arthur parted with 25,000 of his newly earned dollars, telling himself what the filmmaker told him, that it was "an investment in his future."

Next, there was the decision to join a prestigious think tank. All it took to "get in" was another $25,000. Most of the people involved had corporate sponsors, but since Arthur was really his own corporation . . . After listening to how much the prestigious credential would help him look more solid, Arthur was "in" again.

After a short while, it began to look like the line formed to the right. Everyone had a wonderful opportunity for Arthur to help himself and help them in the bargain. He really needed a high-powered and well-paid assistant. "They" really needed a better office than just a room in the house. "It"—the new big book—deserved a glossy, professionally designed proposal to "properly package" Arthur's good ideas. And, too, where was the Arthur Web site? Someone of his stature needed a "presence on the Web" to tell interested consumers who and what he was.

And what was that?

Arthur found himself overcommitted, overtired, overworked, and underpaid. His money and name underwrote a great many opportunities that simply didn't pan out in his real favor.

"I'd have done a lot better to buy nothing, bank my money, and wait for all of the furor around my 'fame' to die down." Instead, Arthur found himself struggling to meet his mortgage on his newly bought designer bachelor pad, meet the credit card payments on his newly acquired designer suits, and, as to getting any real writing done, he lacked the focus even to try. Ironically, his success had cost him everything that helped him make a success of himself in the first place—solitude, mulling time, the space and concentration necessary to forge some genuinely original thinking. Now Arthur fit the mold. He looked like many another Armani-clad huckster and he sounded the same— frantic and desperate to score.

As artistic visibility increases, so does artistic vulnerability. Velocity creates porosity—things and people whiz past our defenses and, if they breach our walls—"This will take only a minute"—they can create havoc. Their "minute" can take a

What I am actually saying is that we each need to let our intuition guide us, and then be willing to follow that guidance directly and fearlessly.

Shakti Gawain

*To have realized your dream
makes you feel lost.*

ORIANA FALLACI

great deal of time to detox from. It may cost us hours from our
writing or our practice time. Like any other human being, we
need time to metabolize our lives, our gains, and our losses.
Blinded by our celebrity—we look like a shiny nickel to a lot of
people—they can ignore our humanity. They attack our boundaries rather than understand them.

Three times in the last three decades I have unwisely involved myself with creative people and projects about whom I
had reservations. In each case, the human flaw I had suspected
resulted in a flawed project as well. Piggybackers are after the
glory of the "win" more than the good of the project. In their
rush for success they may rush a project and, like hothouse
tomatoes forced to grow too fast, such projects emerge card-
board and tasteless—attractive enough looking but not suc-
culent or nourishing—nowhere nearly as creatively tasty as the
real thing.

A creative name and reputation has weight and width. If we
lend our name and reputation to ventures of questionable merit,
we lose both our credibility and our chances of continuing to
gain ground ourselves.

No matter what level we make our art on—community theater to Broadway, small town open mic to major poetry venues—the question "Is this an opportunity or an opportunity to
be used?" must be asked.

We all want to be generous. We all want to find colleagues.
We all want to work. We must be alert to the caliber not only of
our own work but of those whom we align ourselves with.

As an artist, some risks are worth taking and some risks are
not. This is not snobbery. This is not exclusivity. This is discretion, discernment, and accountability to ourselves and our gifts.

The phrase "more trouble than it is worth" is something to
ask about any venture. Some difficult and daring things are
worth expenditure, worth the risk. Lesser projects and trouble-
some collaborators are creative quicksand—we get stuck and go

down with them. As artists, we must learn to stick to our art and not sticky situations.

As artists, we are open in a way that differs from many people's, so we are very vulnerable at being caught off guard. Inspiration can be caught out of the corner of the eye and on the fly, and so can opportunity, but this openness to creative possibility can also make us open to creative exploitation. Caught off center and off guard, we might agree to help someone do something that takes us far from our own work and priorities. Anytime your career shifts gears into something faster, think of what happens when you are driving a car: The shift from fifty-five to sixty-five is often the difference between seeing and enjoying the scenery and whizzing past things, saying, "Was that a gas station I just passed or a convenience store? Did I miss the exit?"

As artists, we easily miss the exit or get off at the wrong interchange. If you have someone else deflecting your attention, it is even easier. Think of trying to read the turnpike signs at a complicated interchange when someone is chatting in your ear about things not of bearing to the matter at hand: "How do we get there?" As artists, the "there" we are trying to get to is the work we can respect ourselves for and hopefully be respected for. The fame and hoopla are diversions, and after an expensive one, if someone—say, your agent or manager—is constantly calling you with opportunities that may serve them but not you, you will lose your focus, stop seeing clearly, and miss your opportunity to take a route through your own career that you like.

Opportunity knocks with a Christmas-morning feeling. There is often, for me, a hushed sense of awe as an opportunity slides into place: "Oh, this is so neat!" Sometimes we go just a little numb, as in "Pinch me. Can this be real?" Opportunists, by contrast, have more of a pressured feeling of last-minute shopping, the kind of impulse buy where you know you shouldn't but you do.

The simplest way to put it may be this: Facts are sober. Re-

I don't want to get to the end of my life and find that I just lived the length of it. I want to have lived the width of it as well.

DIANE ACKERMAN

assurances are not. Facts are what we are after in sorting the difference between an opportunist and an opportunity. Facts are "Well, let's see, I've worked on five Broadway shows and three national tours." Hype is "I have lots of experience working with singers." ("Lots," like what?)

When we are embarrassed by our own lack of credentials, when we feel lucky to be getting any help at all with our dreams, we may forget that we have a right to prices and accountability. As we begin to ask about both, either our sense of ease or our sense of unease will continue to grow. Discernment is a combination of gut instinct and a little careful reportorial work. We don't want to be told "There, there, don't you worry." We want to be told "I've done this six times and I've got three good friends I could call if I get in trouble."

As artists, we must be alert not only to our lucky breaks but also to our unlucky choices. We must learn when and how—pull the plug on people and ventures that do not serve our authentic goals and aspirations. All too often, the "big chance" offered us by another may be a big chance to be used.

Since you are like no other being ever created since the beginning of time, you are incomparable.

BRENDA UELAND

TASK:
Slow Down and Feel Strong

Speed creates an illusion of invincibility. We hurry through our days numbing ourselves to the deeper flow of our lives. We feel shallow and push ourselves to live harder when what we need is to live more deeply and quietly. A potent mantra for calming down is to repeat to yourself the phrase "There are no emergencies." If there are no emergencies in your life, what situation could you allow to unfold more gently?

Take pen in hand. Number from 1 to 5. List 5 areas in your life where you feel a sense of haste and pressure. Ask yourself if your sense of urgency is misplaced. Often we simply have anxiety about something unfolding naturally. We want to force our own growth like hothouse plants rather than allow situations—and ourselves—to ripen.

Turn again to your list of 5 haste-makes-waste areas. Can you reset your time line in each area so that you live more gracefully with ambiguity? One of the most common slogans in 12-Step work is "Easy does it." Too often, we hear this phrase to mean "Oh, calm down." The phrase means much more than that. It is the distillate of a vast network of spiritual wisdom that has learned that "Easy does it" actually means "Easy accomplishes it."

No person, place, or situation benefits from our harried pushing forward. Everything and everyone benefits from our slowing down—letting go and letting God—so that a natural pace and progression can be discovered.

A phrase from the drug culture, "Speed kills," warns us of the danger of too much velocity. We are vulnerable and exquisite creatures, complex mechanisms intended to move at a human and humane pace. We elect that pace every time we slow down to gather—and feel—our strength.

It is the creative potential itself in human beings that is the image of God.

MARY DALY

Creative Saboteurs

Most environments have some undesirable elements—mosquito season in the hot, wet South. Winter chills diving far below zero in the cold, ice-locked winter in Minnesota. Even idyllic environments have their hostile elements and, as artists, we need to know and name the elements in our environment that are clear and present dangers of the trail. In the Southwest, where I live half of every year, I have learned to walk with an eye peeled for rattlesnakes and even the stray tarantula. As an artist, I must pay equal heed to the psychologically dangerous denizens of my environment. I call these characters "creative saboteurs," and the appearance of any of them—just like the sighting of a baby rattler on an evening's stroll—can focus our attention on survival and off the beauty of whatever it was we were making. A creative saboteur doesn't always rattle before it strikes, so we do need a measure of self-protective alertness.

Because all environments have some negative elements, it is a fantasy to think we can completely escape creative saboteurs. I have found it more useful to take the same approach I take toward the more dangerous high-desert dwellers—know them, name them, and avoid them. A creative saboteur is not a friendly animal, and no matter how innocent it may try to appear, its very presence means you must be alert to impeding damage to you and your dreams.

Don't let them tame you!

Isadora Duncan

A playful name for a creative saboteur allows us to retain a sense of our own power. "Why, it's just a Wet Blanket Matador," we can say to ourselves when hit with the dampening impact of their uninvited and often ill-considered opinions and advice. The following is a typical exchange with a Wet Blanket Matador:

ARTIST: *I'm so excited. I think I've finally cracked the top of act two.*
WET BLANKET MATADOR: *Well, I'm sure it'll shift once you get it on its feet anyway. Structure really can't be determined solely by the playwright. It's also in the playing. Theater is a collaborative art, after all, blah-blah-blah. . . .*

This character will use an energetic wet blanket to deflect, dampen, and confuse your creative thrust.

As the artist/playwright, an exchange like this can dampen your enthusiasm. We are usually too well mannered to respond "Of course it's a collaborative art, but you have to have something to collaborate on, dim bulb."

Wet Blanket Matadors like to employ an air of sad superiority, as if they have seen you and your like come and go countless times before. Their tone is that of a worried camp counselor listening to an ill-advised twelve-year-old planning a picnic amid grizzlies. Wet Blanket Matadors will typically tell you, "Oh, no! South!" the minute that you say, "I've decided to go north." Their contrariness is comic once you catch on to their ability to *never* co-sign your perceptions. Successfully identified, a Wet Blanket Matador becomes less a saboteur than an occasion for comic relief.

Now let's look at a related character: the Amateur Expert. Like the Wet Blanket Matador, this citizen dwells in negativity but bolsters his opinions with the company of facts and figures that may have no relevance whatsoever to the actual success of your progress. Long on theory, short on experience, an Amateur Expert can give you a million reasons why something *won't* work but no functional advice to help something work. Amateur Experts are trivia freaks—they resemble fan club presidents in that they know what shampoo Rita Hayworth preferred but are unable to recognize a Hayworth in the making.

Both the Wet Blanket Matador and the Amateur Expert bludgeon creatives by their presumed superiority. They just "know" they "know better" than we do. . . . This persona is intended to deflect such pointed questions as "Exactly what have *you* ever done anyway?"

The next destructive character knows worse and cannot wait to tell us. Like a malaria-bearing mosquito, the Bad-News Fairy delivers a sting and a lingering malady. Rather than speak from her personal negativity, she carries—and delivers—the negativity of others. This is a typical exchange:

ARTIST: *I've just finished my new operetta and I'm pretty damn excited.*

BAD-NEWS FAIRY: *Of course, you know that operetta funding has just been cut by a million percent and, as my close friend Nigel Nix told me just yesterday, operettas as an art form are really of no interest to anyone anymore, especially him and Percy Pursestrings, who controls all funding you might be interested in.*

Grace does not pressure— but offers.

JOHN BOWEN COBURN

The thing that makes you exceptional, if you are at all, is inevitably that which must also make you lonely.

LORRAINE HANSBERRY

Notice that this saboteur always washes his hands. It's never *his* nasty little bacteria that are causing your creative cold. It's someone else's he just "happens" to pass on to you.

No roundup of creative saboteurs would be complete without mentioning that art snobs come in two primary colors: Very Important People and Very Serious People. VIPs like their clothes labeled and their art the same way. When they meet you, they want to check out your creative passport to make sure your skills have been stamped in all the right places. For them it's not that you can play the piano, but that you got into Juilliard. It's not that you can paint but that the Whitney owns one of your paintings. Forget that you're a writer, do you have an A-list agent or mere talent? These people are about who's who and not what's what. If you're Beethoven, you'd better be able to prove it. Contact with a VIP normally leaves an artist feeling very unimportant.

Now let's look at their close cousins, Very Serious People. The exchange here has to do with the notion that *you* are a mere artist, while *they* are a lover of *ART.* Your work, whatever it is, pales by comparison to the "great works" they ultimately know. To hear them tell it—and they will—art is a matter of life and death. And, of course, dead artists fare better than the living at "making the art" of *their* informed perceptions. Like oenophiles who horde vintage wines but won't drink it, the very serious art crowd can't be bothered with mere enjoyment and appreciation. What they "know" is "no."

As artists, we are often, far more often, more insecure than grandiose. We are stubborn as crabgrass, yes, but we are just as easily stepped on. Yes, we spring back—but sometimes only after years of discouragement. As we move our art into public venues, what we need is to find a few friends who encourage us by mirroring our competency—that, and the inner resolve to post a few signs that say "Keep off the grass."

Surviving a creative saboteur is like surviving a snakebite. It can be done and it makes a good story afterward. However, the first step—as with any snakebite—is to name and contain the poison. We cannot afford our own or anyone else's denial. We have been bitten. We have been poisoned. Damage has been done and the delicate and fine nerve endings of our art are badly hurt. Step one is to get away so that you are not bitten again. Do not stand stock-still in astonishment, poking the snake to see if it might want to bite again. Snakes bite. They bite once and they do bite again. If you think you have been bitten, assume you have been bitten and jump back. Don't listen to people who want you to "find the lesson" in your experience. There will be plenty of time for that afterward. For right now, put distance between you and the snake.

Do not engage with the people who want to talk with you about how rare this particular kind of poisonous snake is. Do not start to feel that the odds of your having been bitten make any difference in the fact that you have been bitten. Later on, after you have a few weeks' recuperation, you can enjoy lunch with someone who says, "Oh, he's always a viper and he bit me too," but such talk is for later, not right now.

First administer first aid. That means you acknowledge you have been bitten, don't pretend you have not, and reach for the antidote. The antidote is someone who supports you before, during, and after your creative injuries. This is a friend who doesn't say anything much besides "That's awful" and "What can I do to help?"

The answer to "What can I do to help?" is very straightforward: "Love me." That, and "Help me to forgive myself for having gotten fooled, hurt, bitten. Help me to let myself off the hook and not blame me for someone else's bad behavior. Help me to stop calling myself stupid. Tell me, accidents happen. There are snakes out here. Why, any one of us could have run into a nasty creature like you did."

It is spiritual law that if we cannot always avoid injury, we can always later turn it to good use. The silver lining of surviving snakebite is the compassion that it brings to bear both toward

Integrity is so perishable in the summer months of success.

VANESSA REDGRAVE

ourselves and later toward others. There will always be creative saboteurs. Their bite will always sting and, as we learn to identify them and avoid them, we can share our experience, strength, and hope with others: Creative saboteurs hurt us, but they can be survived.

TASK:
Perform an Exorcism

Creativity is a spiritual issue and that means we can invoke forces to cast out our demons. A spiritual-creativity injury is an excellent opportunity for a spiritual ritual of your own devising. Here are two of my favorites. They are both powerful and playful, a potent combination:

The beginning of compunction is the beginning of a new life.

GEORGE ELIOT

1. Exorcize a creative demon: Reflect on your injury and make a creativity monster embodying all the nasty elements of your tormentor. Making this monster is cathartic, but destroying it is more so. Burn it, bury it, abandon it in the wilderness twenty miles from your house, throw it over the gorge bridge, and send it downriver. Get rid of it. One student made a "word monster" using all the controlling rules of grammar and usage. She wrote more freely later.

2. Create a creativity totem: Make a being that embodies all the spiritual forces you would like to muster to your support. This can be a doll, a sculpture, a painted image, a piece of music, even a collage. Place it prominently and protectively in your environment. It is the act of making art that heals the broken creative heart.

CHECK-IN

1. **How many days this week did you do your Morning Pages?** If you skipped a day, why did you skip it? How was the experience of writing them for you? Are you experiencing more clarity? A wider range of emotions? A greater sense of detachment, purpose and calm? Did anything surprise you? Is there a "repeating" issue asking to be dealt with?

2. **Did you do your Artist's Date this week?** Did you note an improved sense of well-being? What did you do and how did you feel? Remember, Artist's Dates can be difficult and you may need to coax yourself into taking them.

3. **Did you get out on your Weekly Walk?** How did that feel? What emotions or insights surfaced for you? Were you able to walk more than once? What did your walk do for your optimism and sense of perspective?

4. **Were there any other issues this week that felt significant to you in your self-discovery?** Describe them.

In solitude we give passionate attention to our lives, to our memories, to the details around us.

VIRGINIA WOOLF

Discovering a Sense of Resiliency

This week dismantles the myth of
artist as superhero. No artist is immune
to negative emotions. The key to surviving such
emotions is accepting them as necessary, a known and
expectable part of the creative trail. The readings and
tasks of this week invite a sense of compassion for
the difficulties of our elected creative journey.
As the week focuses on the inner trials faced
by artists, it assures us that while the dark
night of the soul comes to all of us, by
accepting this we are able to
move through it.

Worry

It is valuable to think of creative artists as being like skittish race-horses, nervous until they are out the gate and actually running.

In my experience, no artist is ever immune to or beyond apprehension in many forms. Successful artists have learned to identify and deal successfully with these close-sibling emotions. It helps to make a few important distinctions, distill a few working definitions. Here they are:

Panic is an escalating sense of terror that can feel as if we are being flooded and immobilized by the glare of change. Panic is what you feel on the way to the altar or to the theater on opening night, or to the airport for a book tour. It is rooted in "I know where I want to go, but how am I going to get there?"

Worry has an anxious and unfocused quality. It skitters subject to subject, fixating first on one thing, then on another. Like a noisy vacuum cleaner, its chief function is to distract us from what we really are afraid of. Worry is a kind of emotional anteater poking into *all* corners for trouble.

Fear is not obsessive like worry and not escalating like panic. Fear is more reality based. It asks us to check something out. Unpleasant as it is, fear is our ally. Ignore it and the fear escalates. A sense of loneliness joins its clamor. At its root, fear is based in a sense of isolation. We feel like David facing Goliath with no help from his cronies and a concern that this time, his trusty slingshot might not work.

The more active—and even more negative—your imagination is, the more it is a sign of creative energy. Think of yourself as a racehorse—all that agitated animation as you prance from paddock to track bodes well for your ability to actually run.

In both my teaching and collaborative experience, I have often found that the most "fearful" and "neurotic" people are actually those with the best imaginations. They have simply channeled their imaginations down the routes of their cultural conditioning. The News at Five is never the good news, and so when they play the possible movie of their future they routinely screen the one with danger and dire outcomes. They do the same with creative projects.

Worry is the imagination's negative stepsister. Instead of making things, we make trouble. Culturally, we are trained to worry.

We are trained to prepare for any negative possibility. The news tutors us daily in the many possible catastrophes available to us all. Is it any wonder that our imaginations routinely turn to worry? We do not hear about the many old people who make it

I think these difficult times have helped me to understand better than before how infinitely rich and beautiful life is in every way and that so many things that one goes around worrying about are of no importance whatsoever.

ISAK DINESEN

safely home; we hear of the grandmother who did not. On the brink of opening a play, we therefore expect critical snipers, not raves. One reason Morning Pages work so well for artists is that they give a way to siphon off worry at the very beginning of our creative day. Similarly, the spot-check inventory of blasting through our blocks by the naming, claiming, and dumping of any worries, angers, and fears related to a project can also get an artist out the starting gate effectively.

Fears for our own safety and the safety of others, the sudden suspicion of brain tumors and neurological disorders, the "realization" that we are going blind or deaf, any and all of these worrisome symptoms indicate we are on the brink of a large creative *breakthrough,* not breakdown, although the resemblance between the two can feel striking.

Poised to shoot a feature film, I found myself abruptly plagued by the "conviction" that a sniper was about to shoot me in the eye. Where this phobia came from, I don't know, but it plagued me on the city streets. That it arrived on the brink of my shooting a film, I consider no coincidence. Also, noncoincidentally, once the camera was running, my sniper ran away.

Authors leave on book tours, huffing on their inhalers. Filmmakers populate the ER, suddenly beset by hives. Pianists know the terror of imminent arthritic crippling. Dancers develop club feet, stubbing their "en pointe" toes walking to the bathroom. We survive these maladies and the success that they presage more easily if we remember not to worry about worry.

After thirty-five years in the arts and twenty-five years of teaching creative unblocking, I sometimes think of myself as a creative dowsing rod. I will meet someone and my radar will start to twitch. Creative energy is clear and palpable energy, disguised perhaps as neurosis or fretfulness, but real and usable energy nonetheless. I feel a little like a tracker—the bent twig of someone's undue anxiety tells me that person has an active imagination that needs to be focused and channeled and that when it is we will have quite a flowering.

Any disaster you can survive is an improvement in your character, your stature, and your life. What a privilege!

JOSEPH CAMPBELL

One of my daughter's high school friends was a hyperactive teenager with bright, avid eyes and a restless energy that jogged him foot to foot as he exclaimed, "Look at that! Look at that!" his attention darting here, then there. Nothing escaped his worried attention. He literally looked for trouble.

That boy needs a camera, I thought, and gave him one for his high school graduation present. It's ten years later and he's a filmmaker. No surprise to me. His worrisome intensity lacked only the right channel.

When we focus our imaginations to inhabit the positive, the same creative energy that was worry can become something else. I have written poems, songs, entire plays with "anxiety." When worry strikes, remind yourself your gift for worry and negativity is merely a sure sign of your considerable creative powers. It is the proof of the creative potential you have for making your life better, not worse.

As performers, we *must* learn, and the rest of us *can* learn: We can learn to throw the switch that channels our energy out of worry and into invention. If we are to expand our lives, we must be open to positive possibilities and outcomes as well as negative ones. By learning to embrace our worried energy, we are able to translate it from fear into fuel. "Just use it, just use it," an accomplished actress chants to herself when the worried willies strike. This is a learned process.

In my experience, artists never completely outgrow worry. We simply become more adroit at recognizing it as misplaced creative energy.

I have sat in the back of movie theaters with accomplished directors who suffered attacks of asthma and nausea as their movies were screened for preview audiences. As a playwright, I have watched in horror as my leading lady stood heaving like a carthorse, hyperventilating in the wings before stepping onstage to perform brilliantly.

It is palpable nonsense to believe that "real artists" are somehow beyond fear, and yet that is the version of "real artists" so

Ideas have come from the strangest places.

JOYCE CAROL OATES

often sold to us by the press. We learn of an artist's nerviness—"Steven acquired his first camera at age seven"—but we seldom hear of an artist's nerves. It is for this reason that I like to tell the stories I was privy to in my twenties, when I was married to young Martin Scorsese, who was friends with young Steven Spielberg, George Lucas, Brian DePalma, and Francis Ford Coppola. From my privileged position as wife and insider, I witnessed fits of nerves and bouts of insecurity suffered through with the help of friends. Because all of the men in our intimate circle matured into very famous artists, these stories are quite valuable—not because they drop names but because they drop information. They tell us in no uncertain terms that great artists suffer great fears like the rest of us. They do not make art without fear but despite fear. They are not worry free but they are free to both worry and create. They are not superhuman and we need not expect ourselves to be so either. We need not disqualify ourselves from trying to make art by saying "Since it's so terrifying for me, I must not be supposed to do it."

Let me say it again: Some of the most terrified people I ever met are some of the greatest American artists. They have achieved their careers by walking through their fears, not by running away from them. The very active imaginations that led them into jittery terrors are the same imaginations that have allowed them to thrill us, enthrall us, and enchant us. Your own worries may similarly be the pilot fish that accompany your great talent. They are certainly no reason not to swim deeper into the waters of your own creative consciousness.

The really great writers are people like Emily Brontë who sit in a room and write out of their limited experience and unlimited imagination.

JAMES A. MICHENER

TASK:
Let the "Reel" Be an Ideal

Our imagination is skilled at inhabiting the negative. We must train it to inhabit the positive. On the brink of a creative breakthrough, we often rehearse our bad reviews—or, at least, our bad day. We imagine how foolish we will look ever to have hoped to have our dreams. We are adroit at picturing our creative downfalls.

Fortunately, success sometimes comes to us whether we can imagine it or not. Still, it comes to us more easily and stays more comfortably if it feels like a welcome guest, something looked forward to with anticipation, not apprehension. This tool is an exercise in optimism, and that word "exercise" is well chosen. Some of us may have to strain to constructively imagine our ideal day. But let's try it.

Take pen in hand. Set aside at least one half hour for writing freely. Imagine yourself at the beginning of your ideal day, a day in which all of your dreams have come true and you are living smack in the middle of your own glorious accomplishments. How does it feel? How good can you imagine feeling? Moment by moment, hour by hour, happening by happening, and person by person, give yourself the pleasure in your own mind's eye of the precise day you would like to have. For example:

"I wake up early, just as a beautiful morning light spills into the room and focuses on the wall where I have hung the covers of my best original cast albums for my Broadway shows. My bedroom has a fireplace and my row of Oscars and Tony awards balance happily on the mantel. I slip from bed so as not to wake my beloved, who is happily still asleep. It is a big day, day one of rehearsals for a new show. Casting has gone well. The director is superb. Everyone is eager and excited to be at work, and so am I. I have worked with many of these people before. We have a loyal, constructive, and brilliantly talented core group of talent that was working in what they call "Broadway reborn," as the melodic songs of our work echo the best of Rodgers and Hammerstein. . . ."

Let your imagination be a real "ham." Spare no expense and consider nothing too frivolous. Do you have telegrams of congratulations wreathing your makeup mirror? Did somebody send you two dozen roses, and a dozen fresh bagels for breakfast?

One word frees us of all the weight and pain of life: That word is love.

SOPHOCLES

When the phone rings with great news, who is calling to say "That's great!" Is it your favorite sister or the president? This is your day and you have it exactly as you want.

Allow yourself to inhabit your absolute ideal from morning until nightfall. Include your family and friends, your pets, time for a nap or high tea. Enjoy scones and excellent reviews. Accept a lucrative and prestigious film deal. Make arrangements to tithe a percentage of your megaprofits to charity. Stretch your mind and your emotional boundaries to encompass the very best day you can imagine and allow yourself a sense of peace, calm, and self-respect for a job well done.

There's only one corner of the universe you can be certain of improving and that's your own self.

ALDOUS HUXLEY

Fear

If you'll pardon the levity, most of us are afraid of fear. We think it's a bad thing. We *know* it's a scary thing. We're afraid of becoming afraid, scared of becoming scared. We know all too well how our fears can escalate into terror, and how our terror can either translate into frantic action or into paralyzing inertia. Because so many of our experiences with fear have been negative, we fail to see fear as positive or useful. It is both. Let me repeat: Fear is positive and useful. Fear says things like "I'm afraid that second movement is boring, and you might want to look at shifting a little of the harmony" or "I'm afraid my characters talk too much at the top of act two without the stakes being clear" or "I'm afraid there's something wrong with the bridge on my viola and I need to get it checked" or "I'm afraid I've overdosed on vermilion in this series and need my eye to fall in love with something else."

Fear is a blip on the radar screen of our consciousness. Fear tells us "Check this out." It is something we catch out of the corner of our eye. It enters our thoughts the way a dark shadow looms across a doorway. "Is someone there?" we may gasp. Yes, someone is there. Often it is a perception spoken by a part of

I did not wish to take a cabin passage, but rather to go before the mast and on the deck of the world, for there I could best see the moonlight amid the mountains. I do not wish to go below now.

HENRY DAVID THOREAU

ourselves that we have neglected and failed to attend. The punctilious part of ourselves may be correctly afraid that we *should* have written out the bass parts fully and not done the shorthand of "everything in treble clef, it's okay." It's *not* okay with the part of ourselves that believes, like the Boy Scouts, in being prepared. "I'm afraid I won't look professional enough," this fearful part insists. And it could be right. Fear asks that we check something for clarity. Fear requires action, not assurance.

As creative beings, we are intricate mechanisms. We have fine-tuned sensing mechanisms that extend beyond the ordinary realm of five senses. Sometimes we feel something large and good is about to happen. We wake up with a sense of anticipation and openness—spiritual attitudes we cultivate through Morning Pages and Artist's Dates. At other times, that very same openness brings to us a sense of foreboding. If we have bought into the currently popular spiritual position that fear is somehow "bad" or even "unspiritual," we will try to dismiss our fear without exploring its message.

"Don't feel that way," we will tell our fearful selves. "What's wrong with you?" By focusing on ourselves as the probable source of anything "wrong," we blind ourselves to the possibility that there might, in fact, be someone or something wrong in our environment.

Edward, a playwright, was committed to a large production of his newest and best play. The producer was all smiles and good vibes, all sunny promises and projections—yet Edward kept fighting a pit-of-the-stomach sense of apprehension in the man's presence.

"Stop it, Edward. What is this? Do you have some neurotic fear of success?" Edward's self-attacks were merciless as his fears continued to mount. "I am afraid this producer is too good to be true," Edward's instincts told him—in the form of bouts of insomnia and a few telling dreams about children's games in which the producer refused to play by the rules. As the dates for preproduction moved closer, Edward felt his fears rising further.

"It's all handled," the producer assured him, but Edward could not be assured. Beating himself up for "groundless fears," Edward finally picked up the phone and asked a few people a few questions. He learned that his producer wasn't producing anything. The venue was not locked down. Ads had not been placed. Deal memos for refreshments and concessions had not been finalized.

"I am so glad you called," a few people told Edward, "I need to be able to plan my schedule and, without a firm commitment on your side, I can't really do it."

Edward's producer was not productive. Edward's fears were not groundless, but well founded. The exploratory actions that Edward took—finally—on his own behalf taught him that he was traveling in company he could not afford. A few more phone calls and Edward learned that his producer's actions and attitudes had left a trail of burned bridges. Edward could not afford to have his name linked with a bad apple. He was involved with an opportunist, not an opportunity. Reluctantly but appropriately, Edward pulled the plug and disassociated himself from his troublemaking friend.

"I am so relieved you did that," a friend phoned to say.

"I didn't know how to tell you," another caller said.

"I hear you might be looking for a new producer and I would love to work with you," a third caller proposed.

Edward and his new producer worked rapidly and effectively. Edward experienced none of the mysterious fears and misgivings he had previously. His fear had truly been a messenger, and the message had been "Edward, you can do better and treat yourself better. You are right, here, to fear the worst."

When fear enters our lives, it is like a mouse scurrying across the floor of our creative consciousness. *Did I actually see something there, or was it a trick of the light?* we wonder. We get still and listen. Do we hear a faint rustling? Is that a tap of a twig on the window? A genuine problem of the arc of act two—or is it . . . there it is again. This time we turn on the overhead light. We

Every man feels instinctively that all the beautiful sentiments in the world weigh less than a single lovely action.

JAMES RUSSELL LOWELL

gently move the furniture away from the wall. Striving to still our hammering heart, we focus the flashlight of our consciousness into the dark and neglected corners, where we see, "Oh. I *do* have a mouse." Or "I have a dust ball the size of a healthy rat. I need to vacuum in here." In short, respected as a messenger, fear asks us to take a more accurate reading of our true perceptions to listen to *all* parts of our consciousness with care. As a rule of thumb, fear is *never* groundless. There is almost always some grounding action we can take in response to our fears.

Often we are so quick to label our fears neurotic or ill based or paranoid that we do not ask what signal our fear is really sending.

When you feel afraid, tell yourself, "This is good, not bad. This is heightened energy available for productive use. This is *not* something to medicate—or meditate—away. This is something to accept and explore." Ask yourself:

1. What signal is my fear sending me?
2. What affectionate name can I give to this messenger part of myself?
3. What grounded action can I take to respond to this fear?

Many fears are based on a simple lack of accurate information. Rather than take a small exploratory action in a needed direction—say, finding a new voice teacher or signing up for a computer class—we allow our fears to be the bogeyman who keep us from entering the gates to our dreams. "I'm afraid my voice may not be strong enough" translates into "Strengthen your voice." Each of us has fears that are particular to our own needs. When we listen to our fears with tenderness and care, when we accept them as messengers rather than as terrorists, we can begin to understand and respond to the unmet need that sends them forward. When we employ humor and tenderness to our fearful selves, they will often stop shaking long enough to deliver a needed message.

How many cares one loses when one decides not to be something but to be someone.

COCO CHANEL

TASK:
Admit Your Fears and Open the Door to Help

Very often the most damaging aspect of our fears is the sense of isolation and secrecy that they breed in us. We are afraid and we are afraid to admit we are afraid. Closeted alone with our fears, we forget that we are never alone, that we are accompanied at all times by a benevolent higher power who has sympathy and solutions for our problems.

Take pen in hand. The tool you are now asked to learn is extremely powerful and positive. It can be used in all times of emotional duress and it can be applied to any and all problems, personal or professional. This tool is affirmative prayer, and it works by singling out each negative situation and "claiming" divine attention and intervention upon our behalf. Let us say the problem is fear-born procrastination on entering a creative project. The prayer might go something like this:

Lord I disbelieve—help thou my unbelief.

E. M. FORSTER

"I am guided carefully and expertly exactly on how to begin work on my new project. I am shown carefully and clearly each step to take. I am supported fully and happily in taking each step into fruitful work on this new project. I intuitively and accurately know exactly how to begin and what to do to begin correctly."

In writing out affirmative prayers, it is important that we do not ask for help, we affirm that we are receiving it. Affirmative prayer is not a prayer of petition. It is a prayer of recognition and acceptance of the divine help that is at hand. Very often the action of writing an affirmative prayer clears away fear from our lens of perception. We suddenly see that we *are* guided, that divine mind is answering our request for help and support. We often intuitively know the right action to take and feel within ourselves the power to take that action. Fear becomes a cue for prayer and a deepened sense of our spiritual creative companionship.

Once you have written out your affirmative prayer, choose

the most personally powerful and resonant phrase in it to use as a mantra while you walk. Perhaps you wrote "My fearful self is clearly guided." You can distill that still further to "I am clearly guided," and you can walk with that reassuring thought until it begins to take on emotional weight.

Restlessness

Nothing is so perfectly amusing as a total change of ideas.

LAURENCE STERNE

For an artist, a bout with restlessness is best met with curiosity—not with the conclusion that your true cranky character is surging to the fore. Irritability is the flag waved by restlessness. Restlessness means you are on the march creatively. The problem is, you may not know where.

Restlessness is full of switchbacks, like a mountain trail. We feel one thing. Then another. We reverse ourselves. *I am full of energy and I have no energy,* we think. *I have no energy and I am full of energy,* we reverse the thought. We are a country of contradictions. North looks good and then south. Nothing feels right. Everything feels wrong. Nothing is right, but then, nothing is really wrong either. We are out of sorts. Under the weather—but the weather is fine except for our own emotional weather, which is stormy. We are volatile and changeable. Of course we are, we are restless. We cannot depend on ourselves to set a course—fortunately, we don't have to.

"Inspiration enters through the window of irrelevance," artist M. C. Richards has observed—many artists will tell you the same thing. It is as though the making of certain pieces of art on certain themes lie in our destiny, just below our conscious mind, where we feel that we are choosing. How our life and work will unfold. One clue at a time. A happenstance at a time, destiny and our destined work reveals itself to us. One day, often quite abruptly, clarity comes and we say, "Ah-hah! That's why . . ."

If you talk to enough artists, you will learn that lucky breaks and chance meetings are run-of-the-mill elements, stock characters that show up when our restlessness reaches unbearable levels. It is as though our restlessness calls to the very heavens for "something" to happen. And something—or many somethings—does. This is why, as uncomfortable as it is, as unpleasant, even unbearable—restlessness is a good omen. If you visit the reptile house at the zoo as a storm is coming on, you will see the creatures slithering in agitated anticipation. They know a change is on the way. Being alert to the possibility of change opens our ears and eyes to receive psychic signals more often and more quickly. Irritated, restless, ready for change, we snap, "Goddammit! What is it?" when destiny knocks. But destiny does knock, and it can be colorful and expansive if we will allow it to be. When we are restless and our lives feel colorless, it is a clue and a cue that they are about to become colorful—if we cooperate. Prayers, and especially creative prayers, are answered, but answered in ways we may not anticipate or appreciate. Again, this is why artists speak that spiritual-sounding word— inspiration. That is not some gauzy bromide, it is our actual experience. As artists, we *are* irrationally, intuitively, and insistently inspired. Sir Arthur Sullivan attended a traveling exhibition of Japanese art and returned home to write *The Mikado.*

About ten years ago I was living in Manhattan and I underwent an intense and nasty bout of cabin fever. I blamed it on the city. "This damn island," I groused, "it's like a giant cruise ship going through choppy seas with all of us shut up in our tiny cabins. I hate it. I want out. Out somewhere!" I started walking a lot.

Walking near the Morgan Library on Madison Avenue, I noticed a small corner bookshop with a neatly lettered sign, THE COMPLETE TRAVELLER. On "impulse," I opened the door. *This is stupid, Julia,* my rational side flicked on the voice-over. *Your commitments are going to keep you right here, so this is just an excursion in idiotic fantasy.* That's when I noticed the shelf full of old and battered books about explorers. I pulled one down. The thick,

Make friends with the angels, who though invisible are always with you. . . . Often invoke them, constantly praise them, and make good use of their help and assistance in all your temporal and spiritual affairs.

ST. FRANCIS DE SALES

creamy pages were dusty with age. They stuck together a little, even gave off a faint powder to the touch. Thinking, what the hell! I bought it—my father had loved boats and the sea.

Several months later, out on book tour, I was perched in Los Angeles on a cliff overlooking the Pacific, staring vaguely out the window toward—Australia? Hawaii? Somewhere. Suddenly, I remembered the book, tucked in my suitcase on another whim. Looking out the window at the vast flat sea, a few palm fronds dancing in and out of my sight line, I opened the book. That book opened an inner door. Suddenly, I heard music—a lot of music, wave on wave stepping ashore complete with lyrics. I grabbed a notebook and a pen, I grabbed my tiny toy keyboard, another traveling afterthought, and began notating what I heard.

The moment we indulge our affections, the earth is metamorphosed; there is no winter and no night; all tragedies, all ennuis, vanish,— all duties even.

RALPH WALDO EMERSON

My hotel, the old Art Deco "musicians" hotel, the Shangri-la, was a scant block or two from a mall where I found an electronics store and I bought a cheap tape recorder. The music was spilling through so fast, I needed to catch it on tape lest I miss some of it on the page. I heard soprano arias, booming bass parts, a large chorale—and I think I heard it all because in a fit of pique and irritability I went into a small travel store. That store was like Alice's doorway into Wonderland. An entire musical awaited my entry.

This story may not convince you that anything magic was afoot. You may not want to picture some invisible being giving me a quick shove—I don't blame you. And yet, it is my experience that when we are willing to be irrational and intuitive— even when we despise those words—we are rewarded by promptings, callings, that come to us from some mysterious and deft sources that guide and encourage us toward what might best be called destiny.

"I don't see why I should stick my head in this antiques store," we can catch ourselves grousing. And yet, opening an old photo album, some inner leaf turns within us and the notion for a novella rears its head.

When we insist on routine, when we insist on linearity, destiny will still knock, but it may have to work harder to get our attention. In my experience, destiny is willing to work very hard indeed—we are the ones who turn a blind eye, a deaf ear. We mire ourselves in a nasty mood and in our preconceptions about how change must come to us. We think, *It will have to be A or B or C.* In fact, when it does come, it is often, as my friend actress Julianna McCarthy ruefully notes, "H. Heliotrope."

Inner malcontent actually triggers outer change—if we are willing to listen to our malcontent with an open mind and listen to what will feel like a wave of irrational promptings. Those oddball, harebrained, nonlinear, and screwball itches, hunches, and urges are the path through the briar patch. Follow your strange creative cravings and you will be led into change a step at a time. I cannot prove this to you, nor would I. This is an experiment you must do for yourself and with yourself. You will never trust an unseen and benevolent partnering from higher realms unless you experience it for yourself and by yourself. As someone who is by nature exhaustingly skeptical—and equally exhaustingly open-minded and experimental—I am speaking from my idiosyncratic experience—and the experience of watching two decades of artists as they experimented and recorded the result.

"This is so stupid. What am I doing here?" we may ask ourselves when, on a whim, we have gone to an adult education class on the kooky subject of origami.

Yet, our lives are as intricately folded, as cleverly made, and as particular as that ancient pursuit. When we acknowledge the right of mystery to intercept and direct us, we acknowledge the larger issue that life is a spiritual dance and that our unseen partner has steps to teach us if we will allow ourselves to be led. The next time you are restless, remind yourself it is the universe asking "Shall we dance?"

We are never so ridiculous through what we are as through what we pretend to be.

FRANÇOIS, DUC DE LA ROCHEFOUCAULD

TASK:
Find the "Rest" in Restlessness

These are only hints and guesses,
Hints followed by guesses, and the rest
Is prayer, observance, discipline, thought and action.

T. S. ELIOT

In writing out a piece of music, a composer uses a "rest" to indicate a tiny, nearly imperceptible pause that is sometimes necessary before plunging ahead into the sea of notes.

Sometimes, and particularly when we are restless, it is a good idea to take a rest and allow our inner leadings to bubble up to the surface unimpeded. Certain atmospheres can create a sense of rest in us and, while we are all individual, here are a few restful places to try a five-minute breather:

1. **The back of a church or synagogue:** There is often a calm humility that comes from just a few minutes tucked in a pew, even for the nonreligious. We breathe in "faith."

2. **A large plant store or greenhouse:** There is a sense of "other realms" that is palpable in visiting a green space. Plants do have a secret life and they will share it.

3. **A forest:** Even if you live in the city and your forest is in a park, you will sense a different rhythm if you allow it.

4. **A carpet store for fine Oriental rugs:** There is a sense of the sacred in the intricate patterns and handmade excellence. The very amount of time required to make a beautiful rug reminds us of the beauty of our own life's tapestry.

5. **A travel store:** The reminder that ours is a rich and various world filled with adventures can often, oddly, calm a restless heart. An imaginary junket down a jungle river, a trek through the Scottish Highlands, a bicycle trip through France—all of these are options for us, and knowing that we have such spirited options can be strangely calming.

Insecurity

I am trying to learn to play the piano. I have a friend who plays the piano as one who can leap across peaks in the thinnest atmosphere with no fear of falling. He is nimble and daring and may not even feel a need for nerve, he is so nervy. I would love to play like that.

Today I made the mistake of looking up the mountain and seeing that the peak was still far above me and wrapped in mysterious clouds. I saw that the way up to it was a treacherous climb of switchbacks and crevasses. I knew I would fall. I knew I would fall. I knew it was all danger, all failure. In short, I compared myself to my gifted friend.

At the root of comparison is something a little nastier: insecurity. Instead of saying "I wish I were better than *I* am," we say, "I wish I were as good as *he* is." In one fell swoop we negate our work and our originality. No two players play alike, and there is that word, play. As artists, we do better focused on the play of learning than on the work of getting ahead. Centered on our own creative trajectory, each small gain is an encouragement. Each slight increment of mastery holds the sweet promise that the days of awkward repetition and frustrating blunders do lead somewhere after all. When we compete and compare instead of strive to emulate and empathize with other artists, we greet their skills with hostility and our own lesser skills with dismay. When we embrace the idea that all artists at all levels are still learning, still struggling, still evolving, growing, and grappling with their craft simply at a different altitude, we are encouraged by another's mastery to know: "It can be done." We need such encouragement. Our talent may be large, but our struggles may be large as well.

This morning, trying to play "When the Saints Go Marching In," I started crying in anger and frustration. Why didn't I learn this in fourth grade like everyone else? Where was I then?

Every autobiography is concerned with two characters, a Don Quixote, the Ego, and a Sancho Panza, the Self.

W. H. AUDEN

As artists, most of us contain a highly evolved and sharp-clawed inner perfectionist. This perfectionist has nothing to do with having standards and everything to do with self-punishing, self-flagellating, and self-defeating premature judgments regarding our potential. The root word of "potential" is "potency," or "power." Just as the eagle's fledgling is less formidable than the eventual eagle, so, too, our embryonic steps in a new art form fail to accurately convey our later creative flight.

My music room is a geranium red and my piano is a small Chickoring upright. Gold gilt letters declare "Established in 1823." The piano may know far more than I. It has one sticky key, D above middle C, but with my lame and halting progress, that hardly matters. I type better than I play and I type with two fingers. And yet, I have written seventeen books and numerous plays and screenplays. So, too, my primitive piano skills have allowed me to pick out beautiful melodies. The trick is, *allowed* me.

Grace is available to us always, at any stage of the creative journey. As beginners, we need the grace to begin. As apprentice artists, we need the grace to continue. As accomplished artists, we need the grace to again accomplish what it is we can. At all levels of creative endeavor, the Great Creator is present and partnering us.

"We are brought along like fighters," remarks the estimable actress Julianna McCarthy. She means that the Great Creator always gives us strength enough and support enough and guidance enough to meet the precise creative challenges at hand. We may be overwhelmed, but God is not. If we fail at Plan A, God has an endless supply of Plan Bs. There is always not only a fallback position, but also a net. That net is having the faith to try again.

When we say that making art is an act of faith and that as we make art we pursue a spiritual path, we are not talking loosely. There is grace in our every artistic encounter. Miracles do happen. We do not plan them. We hope for them and then we are open to the creator's mentoring hand in improving our suggestions. What looks difficult or impossible to us does not appear difficult or impossible to the Great Creator. As we set our egos aside and allow that creative power to work through us, miracles are routinely accomplished—seemingly by our own hand. Creative energy is like electricity. It will flow whether we allow it to or not. As we open our circuitry to conscious collaboration with higher forces, we are shaped by the energy that moves through us into the artists we dream we can become. The minute we relinquish the notion that our creative dreams are centered in the ego, the minute we begin to see them as spiritual adventures, we allow the Great Creator to shape us as only it can and will.

When I move a step at a time, I can edge up the mountain. If I go slowly and gently, playing "Twinkle, Twinkle, Little Star," I can even be proud to have edged up a ledge and I can say, "Wow, I am doing it." It takes vigilance to be gentle. It is easier to wail at myself, "Oh, my God, you will never learn."

We do not know how to ask ourselves for real growth. We do not know how to realistically dig in. We make our new art a mountain we cannot climb instead of trying our luck with a small incline and then a steeper one and then a slightly steeper one. Instead of being inspired by those creative climbers who hop crag to crag, we are discouraged.

I love the piano. How I play it can break my heart. That I play at all, at age fifty-four, when it is like going on a blind date and suffering through my insecurity, thrills me, and is a miracle.

There is certainly no absolute standard of beauty. That precisely is what makes its pursuit so interesting.

JOHN KENNETH GALBRAITH

TASK:
Exactly the Way I Am

At the root of most insecurity is the conviction that we must somehow be better—or other—than what we are in order to be acceptable. We want to play better than so-and-so—or at least as well as so-and-so. Lost in all of this improvement and striving for perfection is the idea that there is a great deal to like about ourselves exactly the way we already are.

Take pen in hand. Number from 1 to 50. List 50 specific and positive things that you like and approve about yourself exactly the way you are. These likable traits can be physical, mental, spiritual, personal, or even professional. For a glimpse at their possible diversity, consider these examples:

1. My handsome hands
2. The shape of my nose
3. The general use of grammar
4. The shape of my feet
5. My Spanish accent
6. My knowledge of American history
7. My knowledge of twentieth-century art
8. My pie-baking ability
9. My choice in walking shoes
10. My consistencies of letters to friends

There are as many kinds of beauty as there are habitual ways of seeking happiness.

CHARLES BAUDELAIRE

So often we are focused on what we would like to change—and change for the better—that we fail to celebrate what is wonderfully enjoyable exactly the way it is. We are often far closer to our own ideal—and ideals—than we dare recognize. Self-esteem is an active choice, not a sudden given. We can choose to actively esteem our many positive traits. By counting our blessings we can come to see that we are blessed and that we need not compare ourselves to anyone.

Self-Pity

Yesterday, wading through the rewrite of a play, I stepped into the black hole I call self-pity. I went down, sputtering, "But! This is silly! I have so much to be grateful for! Burble!"

The fact that I have been a writer for thirty years has done very little to armor me against a solid attack of self-pity. The fact that I have gotten through hard rewrites before, and will doubtless do so again, doesn't really matter. I am like any other artist—happy when I am working freely and unhappy when the work becomes too much like work. I write both because I love to write and because I have to write. I am called, and if I don't answer, the calling just gets louder until I do answer or I have a bout of self-pity because I "have" to answer.

At root, self-pity is a stalling device. It is a temper tantrum, a self-inflicted drama that has little to do, ever, with the facts. Self-pity isn't very interested in facts. What it likes is "stories." As Serah, the noted singer, likes to remark, "Facts are sober. Stories are emotion." Self-pity thrives on stories that go "Poor innocent me and terrible, mean them . . ." Self-pity likes to make us feel the world is an adversarial place and that the odds are stacked against us. Self-pity likes to point out the way we are never truly appreciated, valued, cherished. What self-pity really wants is a cheering section and a fan club. It wouldn't hurt, either, to have a few good designer suits to lounge around in, Camille-like, while our worried lovers hover and offer us sips of something cool. Self-pity is not interested in our getting over it. Self-pity is interested in our "getting over." Struck by a bout of self-pity, we want an appreciative audience for our suffering, not a bout of self-improvement.

Self-pity is not interested in our spiritual status. It turns a deaf ear to our peppy affirmations. For an artist, self-pity constitutes a chronic and formidable creative block. Self-pity has one job and one job only: It intends to stop us in our tracks. If self-pity can just keep us mired in what's-the-use, we will not have to do anything to find out. I am pretty sure that self-pity was a party guest in the Garden at Gethsemane. It was that satanic little voice that whispered "You can still wriggle out of this. They aren't going to appreciate you anyway."

"They aren't going to appreciate you" is often a trigger for self-pity. Please note that "they" (by which we often mean critics or even that more vague creature, "the public") has little or nothing to do with our own self-respect.

Any coward can fight a battle when he's sure of winning, but give me the man who has pluck to fight when he's sure of losing.

GEORGE ELIOT

Beauty is as relative as light and dark.

PAUL KLEE

Self-pity focuses our attention on how we are perceived rather than on what we are perceiving. It takes us out of our creative power and tells us that we are powerless, we will never "make it." Even if we already have, self-pity isn't interested in realistic self-assessment. It is interested in stalling us. For an artist, focusing on the odds "against making it" is like sipping a poisonous drink. It weakens us. When we focus on the impossibility of the outer world and its megalithic proportions, how small and weak and helpless and thwarted we all are, well then, we feel "what's the use," and the world doesn't get much better than that, does it?

Self-pity never asks "Well, what do you think of what you're doing, how you're living, what you are making?" That question might lead us to shake things up a little in some interesting directions. Self-pity doesn't want us to shake things up. It wants to shake us up, like one of those old-fashioned double-whammy martinis that puts you straight on the floor with its punch.

Self-pity wants you on the floor—and the floor feels like the floor even when it is the floor of a creative penthouse. All artists get attacks of self-pity, and we get them with our Oscars leering down from the mantel. We get them with our National Book Award glinting in the lovely golden light pouring through our study window. We get them—we get them—because if we don't watch out, we are about to do something big.

Self-pity is a scraggly red robin. It means that once we get over it, we are going to spring into action. Self-pity—as all of us know—is different from the vague gray numbness of garden-variety depression. Self-pity has an edge to it like a shard of glass. We can use that shard of glass to cut, not ourselves, but our sense of hopelessness, into ribbons. In other words, used properly, a good dose of self-pity is a jump start for creative action. "What's the use?" converts quickly into "What's next?"

If you don't medicate it with a walloping pitcher of martinis, an ill-considered love affair, a bout of overwork or overeating, a solid attack of self-pity is the signal that you are about to either make yourself sick or make yourself healthy. The healthy part of us cannot stomach self-pity and so it will be goaded into action. Oddly, that action may *not* be taken down the lash and laid across our creative back. The action may be something that starts with compassion: "Of course you are *hurt*. Your work was unfairly received. Cry a little."

Although self-pity *appears* to be grounded in the lack of appreciation from others, it is *actually* grounded in our *own* discounting of our self and our struggles. A few tears of sorrow over work ill used, a moment of surrender to our genuine fatigue and heartbreak—a little actual grief can very quickly take the claws out of self-pity's hold on us. When we say "Of course you feel bad," then we are on the brink of something a little interesting. We begin to raise the question "If this makes me feel so bad, what can I change?"

"I am tired of being talked down to by the academic poets," we wail, and then we start exploring master's programs. Someone points out publicly that we have a tendency toward something unforgivable in our painting—romantic blue washes, for example, and we think, *I'll show them romance! I'll show them shimmering light!* and we dig in, perfect our technique, and get even "more so" of the quality of question. We persist and persist and our fatal artistic "flaw" is often revealed to be our own strength. This was true of the hyperexpressivity of violinist Nadja Salerno-Sonnenberg. This was true of Hemingway's stripped and soldierly prose.

The answer to "What can I change?" often surprises us. We might get a stubborn "Nothing! I love that piece and I think I will play it more!" We might get "I am bored by this curriculum and I want to include a lot more." We might get "What I'd really like to get done is _____." In other words, the question "What can I change?" snaps us back onto our own creative spine. Now we are asking the questions that only we have the answers to: What do we respect? What do we like? What do we want to do more of? We spring into action on that.

Belief consists in accepting the affirmations of the soul; unbelief, in denying them.

RALPH WALDO EMERSON

Of course, most of this self-pity springing into action is often accomplished after a nap. Have I said that self-pity is often born of fatigue? It lays us flat because we may need to be there for a while. There is something about being horizontal—without the benefit of drink or drug—that allows the imagination to do a little lucid daydreaming. We get up from our bed of pain thinking, *I could try that.* And we do.

There are only two ways to live your life. One is as though nothing is a miracle. The other is as though everything is a miracle.

ALBERT EINSTEIN

TASK:
Take a Little Pity on Yourself

Most of the time when we are struck down by a bout of self-pity, it is because we feel underappreciated. The truth is, sometimes we *are* underappreciated. The efforts we make and the effort we expend seems to go unnoticed by everyone but us. It is as though we had a tiny, built-in resentment collector, an inner gauge that processes reality by tiny little clicks that say "You see? Not appreciated again."

We cannot make others appreciate us, but we can take the time, care, and attention to appreciate ourselves. "That was really nice of you," we can say. Or "How thoughtful!" One of the Toughlove spiritual laws advises, "Other people's opinions of me are none of my business." A more positive counterpoint might be phrased "My own opinion of me is all that matters."

Take pen in hand. Writing rapidly to avoid your inner censor, complete the following sentences valuing yourself:

1. It was generous of me to _____.
2. It was thoughtful of me to _____.
3. It was nice that I _____.
4. I was a good friend when I _____.
5. I was sensitive when I _____.
6. I did a good job when I _____.
7. I was very professional about _____.

8. I went beyond the call of duty when I _____.
9. I deserve a thank-you for _____.
10. I should get an Oscar for _____.

Self-appreciation takes practice, and it is the only reliable antidote to self-pity.

Doubt

Doubt is a signal of the creative process. It is a signal that you are doing something right—not that you are doing something wrong or crazy or stupid. The sickening chasm of fear that doubt triggers to yawn open beneath you is not a huge abyss into which you are going to tumble, spiraling downward like you are falling through the circles of hell. No, doubt is most often a signal you are doing something and doing it right.

Creativity is a spiritual issue, and although we seldom look at this squarely, the creative life features the same spiritual obstacles as any other spiritual path. The phrase "dark night of the soul" has gained common usage, and we think of it as it applies to the harrowing periods of doubt and drought that may come to someone on their spiritual quest.

Spiritual seekers of all stripe endure its painful ravages, whether they are Trappist monks like Thomas Merton or young Lord Buddha. What we don't talk about often is the fact that artists, too, are spiritual seekers, and we frequently suffer the dark night of the soul regarding our creative calling. Even worse, we often suffer it publicly.

To be an artist of depth, one cultivates a level of sensitivity that is acute. Performing artists, for example, listen with an ear cocked to the spiritual questions posed by a great piece of music or a great part onstage, and they open themselves to receive the energies required to manifest those questions creatively. Tackling these towering creative pinnacles, they are like tender

Beauty is one of the rare things that do not lead to doubt of God.

JEAN ANOUILH

birds who have learned to perch on skyscrapers as well as on trees. They still have all the acute sensitivity they have ever had, and they have also adapted enough to live in the fiercely competitive winds of high-altitude performance—but this does not mean it is easy. Artists facing an Olympian role *are* like athletes—highly trained, highly strung, and highly susceptible to injury, physical and psychic.

As I write, a gifted friend of mine is limping home after an extended tour. He is a musician of prodigious gifts, able to scale pieces whose heights and depths, whose creative cliffs, switchbacks, and drop-offs require the skills of a virtuoso. He has them. He uses them. And he doubts them. Doubt is a dangerous thing as you are leaping crag to crag above the artistic abyss. A well-placed doubt can send you tumbling—he recalls an entire Japanese tour bedeviled by troubling memory strain due to jet lag. He did not falter but feared he would, and carried that fear as a handicap, leaping ledge to ledge musically. This type of anxiety sends an artist to a place of darkness and terror that is difficult for most people to imagine.

In a sense, how we do as performers is none of our business. It is God's business how we do, and as we "suit up" and "show up," we are like monks doing matins—we fill a form and the form is larger than ourselves. Very often the beauty of a trained voice lifted in song can lift an untrained heart to a new altitude in connection to something or someone larger than our self. A great concert is an initiatory tribal experience. We touch the largeness of life through the largeness of the performer. Garland singing of yearning and love allows each of us to touch those feelings of yearning and love. The "somewhere over the rainbow" is a place located in the human heart, and art—and artists—allow us to access it.

Last night I had dinner with three young classical musicians, rising stars with phosphorescent talent. The dinner table should have floated like something from a hokey séance. There was that

It is not because angels are holier than men or devils that makes them angels, but because they do not expect holiness from one another, but from God only.

WILLIAM BLAKE

much creative power and light seated there, ordering pasta with pesto and arugula salad, fettuccine livornese and penne vodka.

"Do your teachers prepare you for doubt?" I asked them.

The young talents flickered like fireflies. The question alone created a certain shimmer of unease. One was headed to Japan on a tour with the Met, and was frightened by the prospect.

"Not really," one violinist said.

"We're told to just ignore it, I think," said a violist.

"Critics are often jealous," sniffed a second violinist defensively. She had not yet suffered a critical savaging, but she "had heard."

Under their cosmopolitan chic, these young artists were still novices hoping to get through on a wing and a prayer.

No, they were not prepared.

"Do not pick up the first doubt," creative elder Julianna Mc-Carthy warns me, the voice of six decades of experience on the stage, laying down the dictum.

For an artist, the first doubt is like the first drink for a sober alcoholic: We cannot afford to romance it. The first doubt leads to the second. The second leads to the third, and in no time you are staggering, hurting yourself on the sharp edges of the furniture.

One of the reasons artists need to talk to and hear from other artists is that the press is not a trustworthy mechanism for relaying information about the creative life. In the press, artists are either anguished or heroic, they are not what they must be—adroit, like spiritual samurai—to remain balanced amid turbulent doubts.

When a doubt moves at an artist, the artist must learn how to step aside and let the charge pass by. An artist cannot afford to be deeply pierced by doubt and finish the tour.

For an artist, doubt is both part of the territory and an ever-present danger. Doubt is the twister in Kansas. Doubt is the sickening temperature drop and unseasonable storm at twelve thousand feet. Doubt is the earthquake of the heart, the forest

Babies are necessary to grown-ups. A new baby is like the beginning of all things— wonder, hope, a dream of possibilities.

EDA J. LE SHAN

fire of self-criticism that threatens to take down everything in its blistering path. In other words, doubt is both normal and deadly, like coral snakes in Florida. Doubt is not to be toyed with.

There is a difference between doubt and self-appraisal. Doubt likes to come to the door disguised in the worthy suit of self-appraisal, "Maybe you should work on your . . ." Like a suitor, you should consider, but under that respectable overcoat is the dagger of despair: "Maybe you really are rotten at this." Doubt should not be allowed to enter—and it *will* try, at three A.M., in a strange city, with a polite knock, like a serial killer asking to share coffee while you phone the police.

The annals of art are dark with the destruction wrought by this satanic saboteur. Symphonies have been tossed into the fire; novels, too, have been burned at the stake. Stradivarius routinely smashed violins far better than those of his rival makers. "Feel the feelings but don't act on them. This, too, shall pass," artists need other artists to tell them.

As the cool light of day reveals, doubt and self-appraisal are not the same thing. It takes practice, but an artist can learn the difference. Self-appraisal has a certain steadiness of character. It knocks in daylight and poses a simple question, and if you don't listen, it goes away. Then it comes back, knocks again gently, and poses the same question. Gently. As something for you to consider. To think about. To look at changing. "Maybe it's time to get a new bow." Self-appraisal has an opinion, a thought for your consideration. It has an idea to hand you, not an indictment. It doesn't whisper at midnight when you are alone and exhausted. Doubt is what does that.

Doubt is the one who likes to separate its victim from the herd, get the lamb off always and then call in its cronies. Doubt strikes you when *you* are alone, but doubt itself travels in packs. Along with doubt come its nasty friends: despair, self-loathing, feelings of foolishness and humiliation. When doubt attacks, it's always with the same lot of lower companions like the bad boys in an Italian gangster movie. An artist needs to learn to spot

When it is not necessary to change, it is necessary not to change.

LUCIUS CARY,
LORD FALKLAND

these characters and see them as lowlife bullies and not as Boy Scouts bravely bearing the truth.

Doubt comes to the door in darkness, pretending to be alone and in need of your compassionate ear. But if you let him in, he'll bring his friends, and doubt can be very persuasive getting in.

Doubt is a great seducer. "I just want you to think about this," it whispers. Out come the artist's ears. Out comes the dagger. "Maybe you didn't and don't have enough talent after all. . . ." Feel the sharp piercing? It might be your creative lung collapsing around the blade.

No, as artists, we need lucid self-appraisal, not shadowy and sinister doubt. Self-appraisal is best practiced in broad daylight in the comfort of your own home and among very trusted friends.

All artists suffer doubts. Great directors watch from the back of screening rooms and have to breathe their hyperventilated doubt into brown paper bags. Brilliant actresses suffer stage fright as painful as rickets. Doubt is a part of the territory as an artist. Surviving doubt, learning to discern what is emotional terrorism and what is a proper, suggested course adjustment, is something an artist becomes more skilled at over time—and often only with the help of his creative elders who have suffered doubt themselves.

In a convent or monastery, a suffering novice can speak to a spiritual director. "Doubt is normal," they are softly told. "Why, without doubt, why would we need faith?" When, as artists, we suffer doubt, we do well to seek compassionate counseling. "Doubt? It comes with the territory, kid," director John Newland used to growl at me tenderly.

Art is a spiritual practice. Doubt is normal. We need faith to survive it and we also need charity. When doubt attacks, we must be vigilantly self-loving. We must not open the door to the stranger who hands us the bottle of scotch, the pills, and the gun. Keep the chain on the door, politely or not so politely defer taking the doubt that is offered. Sleep with the light on if you need to. Call a friend in the middle of the night. Find an old

The changes in our life must come from the impossibility to live otherwise than according to the demands of our conscience.

LEO TOLSTOY

comedy on television. Travel with a beloved children's book like a Harry Potter volume or *The Little Engine That Could.* Your artist does not need to be scared by things that go bump in the night. The dark night of the soul comes to all artists. When it comes to you, know that it is simply a tricky part of the trail and that you will see better in the morning.

TASK:
Doubt Your Doubts

Imagination is more important than knowledge.

ALBERT EINSTEIN

All artists experience doubt. Experienced artists learn to weather doubt without succumbing to self-sabotage. When doubt darkens the heart, it is wise to think of this gloom not as "reality" but as passing weather, like a badly overcast few days. During bouts of doubt, our judgments will not be accurate and should not be acted upon. Like a nasty cold snap, doubt is something to be survived, and so we should aim for actions that are warm, loving, nondramatic, and non-self-destructive. Rather than working on self-improvement, focus instead on self-care. Try to be actively selfish on your own behalf.

TASK:
The Self in Self-Expression

Take pen in hand and list 10 small ways in which you could be *selfish,* that might make it easier for you later to be *selfless.* For example:

1. I could let myself call my long-distance friend, Laura.
2. I could let myself subscribe to *Western Horseman.*
3. I could let myself buy a pair of parakeets for my studio.
4. I could let myself get a new easel.
5. I could let myself declare "me" off limits after seven, one night a week, and use that time and space to write.

6. I could let myself turn my phone off during my art hours.

7. I could let myself take a portrait seminar and get some expert tips.

8. I could let myself shoot a roll of black and white just because I'm crazy about it.

9. I could let myself make a weekly writing date to get me off the dime on my thesis.

10. I could let myself get that new recording I'm curious about.

Our personal journeys mark us.

David Halberstam

If you have difficulty thinking of 10 small ways to be creatively selfish, finish this sentence 10 times:

If I weren't so selfish, I'd _____.

CHECK-IN

1. **How many days this week did you do your Morning Pages?** If you skipped a day, why did you skip it? How was the experience of writing them for you? Are you experiencing more clarity? A wider range of emotions? A greater sense of detachment, purpose and calm? Did anything surprise you? Is there a "repeating" issue asking to be dealt with?

2. **Did you do your Artist's Date this week?** Did you note an improved sense of well-being? What did you do and how did you feel? Remember, Artist's Dates can be difficult and you may need to coax yourself into taking them.

3. **Did you get out on your Weekly Walk?** How did that feel? What emotions or insights surfaced for you? Were you able to walk more than once? What did your walk do for your optimism and sense of perspective?

4. **Were there any other issues this week that felt significant to you in your self-discovery?** Describe them.

Discovering a Sense of Camaraderie

Despite our Lone Ranger mythology,
the artist's life is not lived in isolation. This
week focuses your attention on the caliber of
your friendships and creative collaborations. Loyalty
and longevity, integrity and ingenuity, grace and
generosity—all of these attributes are necessary
traits for healthy creative exchange. The
readings and tasks of this week aim at
the difficult art of sorting our
personal relationships.

Keep the Drama on the Stage

Artists are dramatic.

Art is dramatic. When artists are not making artistic dramas, they tend to make personal ones. Feeling off center, they demand center stage. Feeling on tilt, they tilt at an imaginary windmill.

"This relationship is in trouble," they announce. "Why, it's got all sorts of problems."

Or "I'm sure it's nothing serious, but it's possible I'm going deaf. Did you hear what I said?"

All of us are creative, but those of us who are for a living had better learn to create with the same quotidian grace as our cousin who works at the bank, our father who administers his department at the university, or our neighbor who manages the hardware store. When we make our creative work and our creative lives too special and too dramatic, we uproot those lives from a sense of community and continuity—and that's exactly what we like to do whenever we get too nervous. Nervous, we create dramas to make ourselves more nervous.

We announce, "I've been thinking about *your* character, and I'm not so sure I should trust it. What do you think about that, wife?"

To the skilled ear, there is a predictively reactive tone to these sudden besetting dilemmas. Reality need not apply, the relationship is probably fine. Deafness would not drown out a compliment, and your character is less a question than the character you're dealing with: a nervous artist.

A friend of mine is a world-class musician who develops health problems on the cusp of every major concert tour. Health fears are his Achilles' heel. Mysterious maladies always arrive as his departure date nears. Another friend of mine, a fine writer, loses all humor and sense of personal perspective every time a writing deadline looms. His marriage is always "over" or, at least, on the rocks, until he settles down to write. People like these should furnish seat belts for those riding shotgun in their lives. You would think that *someone* would have the nerve to say "Oh, just stop it." As artists, we should say it ourselves, but drama gives us an excuse to not make art and so artistic anorexia is addictive. We get an adrenalized anxiety from not making art. We can binge on this chemical roller-coaster when work is due.

Artists love making art the way lovers love making love, and just as lovers become snappish when they need to go to bed and make love, artists become snappish when they need to make art. Artistic anorexia, the avoidance of the pleasure of the creative, is a pernicious addiction that strikes most artists sometimes and always takes us by surprise. Instead of making art, we make trouble—and we make it because we are bingeing emotionally on *not* making art. We need to get to the piano and practice. We need to do our vocal exercises. We need to show up at the easel or the page. We need to go full steam ahead, and when we don't,

Compassion is the antitoxin of the soul: where there is compassion even the most poisonous impulses remain relatively harmless.

ERIC HOFFER

we tend to blow off steam by venting inappropriately about any number of imaginary ills. Our aches and pains become the world's pain in the neck. Goddammit, art is a serious business, and you had better believe we will raise hell if anyone gets too festive in our vicinity.

"You just don't understand," we start snapping at people who do understand all too well. John Barrymore's performance as the imperious theatrical impresario in *Twentieth Century* should be required viewing for all artists prone to occasional bouts of self-importance. The *art* is what's important. We are intended to serve our art, not treat our friends and family as servants. The arrogant-artist archetype doubtless has its twisted roots somewhere in low self-esteem and posturing out of a need to disguise our vulnerabilities. If we have too much ego invested in our work and not enough ego strength coming from the rest of our lives, it's easy to act out the arrogant-artist archetype.

At root, we have lost our sense of humor and, as a result, our sense of scale. When we take ourselves too seriously and demand that others do the same, we inadvertently tighten our creative muscles and strain our own performance. Touring artists should probably carry a backpack of comedies. If we remember—or watch—*That's Entertainment,* we may loosen up, lighten up, and deliver the caliber of work we aspire to. There is a bumper sticker that reads "Angels fly because they take themselves lightly."

It is one of the paradoxes of a creative career that our careers take off once we loosen our fearful, ego-ridden grip. A sense of humor is attractive. It indicates a sense of scale. As an artist, a sense of scale is what gives our work proportion, perspective, and personality. As artists, we want to avoid being "over the top." The best way to do this is to avoid being top-heavy—that is, big-headed because we feel so small. As a rule of thumb, artists should repeat this mantra: Sudden problems in my life usually indicate a need to work on my art. Lest this sound like artist bashing, let me simply admit that I have bashed myself

Her great merit is finding out mine—there is nothing so amiable as discernment.

LORD BYRON

against the rocks of my creative imagination countless times before arriving at this conclusion.

A book deadline is not a NASA launch. A concert date is not a countdown for nuclear testing. As one cellist jokes, "I could be getting hit by a bus right now. Instead, I'm walking onstage to play a Brahms sextet." High profile and high pressure do not need to be synonymous. But the temptation to make them that way is enormous, particularly if we are feeling slightly off our game.

Our dogs should bite when they sense this senselessness drama coming on. My dog, Tiger Lily, a gold-and-white cocker spaniel, has learned to roll her eyes and pout eloquently whenever my humor evaporates. Tiger Lily's Westie sidekick, Charlotte, smells a rat whenever the household mood darkens unnecessarily. She has a small purple toy, Ratty, suitable for such occasions. When too much drama sets in, she presents Ratty at the offender's feet, with the strong, yipped suggestion that a game of catch might get us a lot further than whatever the hell game *this* is.

It is probably not an accident that the verbs *exorcise* and *exercise* are so similarly spelled. Most of the time when an artist is engaging in drama instead of art, he needs to move out of his head and into his body—if not into his body of work. A brisk walk up a steep hill, a few forced laps in the pool, and reality threatens to set in—the reality that the only drama in our very nice life is the one that we're creating ourselves. With our fine imaginations, artists can be drama addicts. We can also become physically addicted to our adrenalized anxiety in place of authentic creation. Too much drama is not fun, but it gives us something to do instead of making art. Until we break the code on this avoidance, we *believe* our dramatic scenarios.

"I know I should paint," we wail, "but does he love me?"

"All right, I should get to the piano, but I'm not certain I get enough respect from my peers."

"I'll get to the typewriter and work on the book as soon as I fire off a letter about my goddamn tennis shoes not holding up."

Man is an over-complicated organism. If he is doomed to extinction he will die out for want of simplicity.

EZRA POUND

"I'll pick up the viola and practice *after* I know where my musical career is going."

As artists, we can be con artists—not that we con others, we usually don't. But we do con ourselves. We con ourselves into thinking that our dramatic dilemmas mean more than our art, and that indulging in drama will ever-satisfy our creative impulses.

If we can just convince ourselves to indulge in a little terrifying doubt—about our talent, about our lovability, about our competencies, creative and otherwise, then we can usually manage to stall ourselves in our creative tracks and *really* give ourselves something to worry about. If we can stage a nice, nasty drama, we can often subvert or sabotage our genuine creative growth.

What a relief! How much easier to worry about boy/girl dilemmas than whether or not our book has the proper art, our rehearsal has been sufficient to move the music into our hands and hearts, our mastery of our new photographic equipment has actually sharpened the focus of our work.

Artists are dramatic. Channeled into our work, drama is fine, but artists risk being addicted to emotional drama. We can display an alarming predilection standing at the edge of the cliff, looking straight down, while asking gullible friends, "Will I fall?" or "Shall I jump?" "Why would anyone want to do that?" you may ask. The answer is that it gives us something to do instead of making art.

Art is the itch we have to scratch, but we're the only ones who can scratch it. And if we refuse to scratch the surface of our own dramatic resistance, if we refuse to allow ourselves the dignity of genuine creative risk, then you will know us by how close to the cliff we are standing.

What annoyances are more painful than those of which we cannot complain?

MARQUIS DE CUSTINE

TASK:
Keeping a "Ta-dah!" List

Facts are the opposite of drama. If you have been working with Morning Pages, you have probably become more and more accurate at generating grounded to-do lists that spell out the priorities of the day as revealed in the pages. In order to have a firm sense of self-respect as artists, we need to employ a second daily list. That list is the "ta-dah!" list, as in the bow well taken after a successful recital. "Ta-dah!"

In our era, the road to holiness necessarily passes through the world of action.

DAG HAMMARSKJÖLD

Rather than always focusing on what is left to do, we need to give ourselves a hand for what we've already done. Your ta-dah list is a nightly bow to personal applause for the many small creative actions taken in the course of a day. A ta-dah list might read:

1. Did my Morning Pages
2. Dropped Carolina a note
3. Put in 15 minutes at the piano
4. Repotted the geraniums
5. Read the essay in *The Atlantic* related to my thesis
6. Threw together a pot of soup
7. Inputted the bills to my computer home management program
8. Talked to Bruce—instant emotional restoration
9. Worked on actual writing of the thesis for one hour
10. Scheduled the dog at the groomer
11. Hemmed my droopy skirt
12. Ordered thesis-related book from amazon.com
13. Picked paint for kitchen windowsill
14. Tuned into the classical station for *Opera Hour*
15. Did the dark laundry

A ta-dah list can easily escalate to double this length. Often our days are far busier and more productive than we realize. Additionally, a ta-dah list may function as a subtle goad—"I'll love writing it down," we think as we tackle a creative something we've been avoiding. If to-do lists live out our priorities, ta-dah lists recognize our accomplishments. Ta-dah!—I did work on my art today. Creative lives are made of minutes—and minute amounts of work *do* add up.

The Good of Getting Better

As artists, we are not interested merely in expressing ourselves; that realm may belong to therapy. We are interested in expressing ourselves more and more accurately, more and more beautifully. This brings us squarely to the issue of craft, to our need for accurate assessment by others and ourselves.

Accurate and useful are most often found in the company of the grounded combination of personal experience and excellence. It is for this reason that artists have always apprenticed other artists. A great music teacher certainly shapes and colors the playing of her students—they become at once more fully themselves and somehow also recognizably "hers." It is, in part, a matter of shared technique, but it is also a matter of shared musical values. A great teacher both attracts and produces great students. It is a sort of spiritual lineage or, to cast it in the terms of the market, a "brand name." A great conservatory with great teachers puts a recognizable "stamp" onto its artists.

Sometimes, teachers and students seem to intersect by divine planning more than by set curriculum. This was the case for Emma and her teacher.

The great violin and viola teacher Joyce Robbins retired to southern California after a long teaching career in New York. A gifted viola player spending an unexpected year in California found Robbins and embarked on a course of study that changed her playing and perception of playing. She learned to hear.

"I just missed studying with this great teacher in the East. She had retired to California the year I enrolled. I never expected to

In the greatest confusion there is still an open channel to the soul. It may be difficult to find because by midlife it is overgrown, and some of the wildest thickets that surround it grow out of what we describe as our education. But the channel is always there, and it is our business to keep it open, to have access to the deepest part of ourselves.

SAUL BELLOW

go to California, but when I did I had to look her up. It was a three-and-a-half-hour round-trip commute to study with her, and I really got to know the California freeway system. On the other hand, I learned how actually to listen to myself as I played. I began to play more softly, with less stridency, and to listen to the actual sound I was making rather than just focusing on the technique of how I was making it. As a result, I began to sound much better. In the time since, whenever I hear a viola student with a particularly full and gentle sound, I wonder if he hasn't studied with my teacher and learned some of the same gift of hearing that she passed to me."

Yet, artists are everywhere and fine arts conservatories are not. A brilliant young painter in South Milwaukee may not have the familial or community support to study other than locally— and locally may offer some very fine teachers, or it may offer teachers whose own work is underschooled, underdeveloped, and unduly influenced by the supposed sophistication of a few powerful arts publications.

Try to discover your true, honest, untheoretical self.

BRENDA UELAND

Wanting to bloom where we are planted, we may seek out local teachers and either get lucky or experience an inner certainty that they are cramped in their creative calling and that they in turn can cramp us. Not wanting to be egotistical, many students stay too long at the fair, studying with teachers whom they have outgrown, often experiencing an uncomfortable creative constriction that manifests as teacher-student tension, even competition, that cannot often be directly addressed. How do we say "You see, I think I have outgrown you"? Often we say it best by simply thanking our mentor for time and talent given— then moving on.

Just as an excellent teacher can strengthen and clarify an artist, a bad teacher can damage, muffle, and muddy an artist. It is the impact of poor teachers that has blocked or battered many artists into at first healthy and later self-defeating hermeticism. Declaring themselves above, beyond, or outside the market, they court two possibilities, and usually encounter a mixture of both. Freed from outer influences, they may incubate and develop a strikingly original style. That's the good part. Freed from outer influences, they may also hit an artificially low ceiling, having taken their work as far as they can without further input.

Art, in some ways, is like any other skill—we enjoy doing it. Then we enjoy doing it well; then we enjoy doing it better. The refusal to allow ourselves the tools and techniques to move from "well" to "better," often calling it sort of faux purity, has nothing pure about it. We have allowed our pride and fear to taint our creative process. Yes, our inner creator may be childlike, but we have allowed ourselves to cross the line to *childish*. Defensive and defended, we have shied away from authentic growth.

A talented regional string player may struggle for years with self-perceived flaws, only to finally encounter an expert teacher who says, "You outgrew that instrument years ago, it's crippling you—get rid of it!" Not a perception likely to be jumped to by the artist alone.

Art, as remarked, is a form of the verb "to be" and, as artists, our spiritual and intellectual perceptions often lead and goad our need for increased technique. We can see it but we can't paint it. We can hear it but we can't play it. We need help. We can get help—or we can give up, discouraged by the gap between our inner standards and our own ability to meet them. Writer Tillie Olsen warns correctly of the danger of "the knife of perfectionism in art." If we keep its blade constantly at our creative throat, we fail to progress because we so stifle our learning process. A teacher is a guide through creative pitfalls such as these.

Each of us learns in our own way and at our own pace, and yet *someone's* excellent method will have something to offer us if we are willing to offer ourselves the opportunity to learn.

Authentic growth, however, is the goal, and that will not occur if we enroll ourselves in classes and curriculums that are themselves stagnant, stifling, or simply inadequate and ill advised. What we are after is excellence, and it can be found, but

I will tell you what I have learned myself. For me, a long five- or six-mile walk helps. And one must go alone and every day.

Brenda Ueland

we must look for it, not only in ourselves, as we have been, but also in others. We must be neither blinded nor dazzled by brand-name credentials—blinded to the possibility that they might mean something valid or too dazzled by what they *might* mean to see that in this particular practitioner they mean very little. In other words, we must be open to finding our teachers and open to being teachable—while simultaneously holding an awareness of our equally valid, genuine perceptions and skills that must be protected.

It is an often repeated spiritual axiom that "when the student is ready, the teacher appears." Over the years, I have heard many stories of miraculous intersections and meetings. The divine mind knows no distance, and so a student's prayer in Omaha is heard as loudly and clearly as a student's prayer in Manhattan. When we ask to be led, we are led. When we ask to be guided, we are guided. When we ask to be taught, we are taught. A young sculptor working in a small midwestern industrial city prays for guidance and is led to a renowned sculptor working ten miles away in the very same off-the-beaten-path locale. A talented actor in a tiny New Mexico town intersects with a retired Hollywood director, who helps secure him a scholarship at a famed acting conservatory. Guidance and generosity are always closer at hand than we may think. It always falls to us to be open to receiving guidance and to pray for the willingness and openness to know it when it arrives.

It is spiritual law that the good of our projects and our growth as artists must rest in divine hands and not merely human ones. While we are led to and drawn from teacher to teacher, opportunity to opportunity, the Great Creator remains the ultimate source of all of our creative good. It is easy to forget this and make our agent or our manager or our current teacher the source of our "good." When we place our reliance on an undergirding of divine assistance, we are able to hear our cues clearly, thank those who step forward to aid us, release

The best career advice to give the young is, find out what you like doing best and get someone to pay you for doing it.

KATHERINE WHILEHAEN

those who seem to impede us, and keep unfolding as artists with the faith that the Great Artist knows precisely what is best for us and can help us find our path, no matter how lost, distanced, or removed we may sometimes feel from our dream. In the heart of God, all things are close at hand, and this means our creative help, support, and success. As we ask, believe, and are open to receive, we are gently led.

TASK:
Becoming Teachable

Take pen in hand. List 5 personal situations that are, for you, lingering resentments, sore spots, and sources of self-pity regarding a lack of effective mentoring. For example:

1. My parents both got sick and I never got to Stanford for my poetry master's.
2. My viola was so difficult to play that I damaged my technique by compensating and am still undoing my bad habits.
3. My family had no idea what to do with a writer in their midst. They wanted me to be a lawyer. I had *no* literary support.
4. My hometown had never heard of modern dance. By the time I realized what it was, I was already in my twenties and on a career path as a physical therapist.
5. My very talented older sister got all the creative encouragement as a musician. I had to do the dishes while she serenaded on guitar.

These grievances are real, and you can't change them. You can, however, ask some pointed questions and take some nurturing actions. For example:

I happen to feel that the degree of a person's intelligence is directly reflected by the number of conflicting attitudes she can bring to bear on the same topic.

LISA ALTHER

1. Would I still like a poetry master's? There are many fine nonresidential programs for older students.

2. As to that viola technique, if you're not in a music program, there are still often excellent teachers who make themselves available for private lessons. The right teacher can undo the wrong learning quite quickly.

Address each of your historic grievances, looking for a present-tense action that creatively soothes your injured artist. Take those actions. Even the smallest can lessen self-pity's sting.

Before, During, and After Friends

We do not mind our not arriving anywhere nearly so much as our not having any company on the way.

FRANK MOORE COLBY

One of the trickiest issues in a creative life is the issue of private support and encouragement for our creative leaps—no matter how they are received. As artists, we do not need private adulation, but we do need before, during, and after friends, those people who love and accept us no matter what our current creative shape and size. We need friends who understand that a creative success may bring an onslaught of pressures nearly as devastating as a creative failure.

Friends must be found who understand how to cohabit with our varied creative needs. Sometimes, we are the lonely larva; sometimes, the beautiful butterfly. Our needs and necessities vary with where we are and how we are doing in our creative process.

It helps us to become conscious of our needs first of all for ourselves and then to share our insights with those we know we can trust. Too often, we try either to "go it alone" creatively or we do not ask for what it is we need in ways that can be acted on or understood. When our creative well is low from having worked a long time on a hard project, we need to be enough of a friend to ourselves to take a refreshing Artist's Date to fill the well back up with images and adventure. When a deadline looms and we are dead on our feet from overwork, it can be very hard to take such breaks. Instead, we tend to want to flog ourselves forward, and both the work and ourselves suffer. In such times, a call to a friend might say, "Pray that I can get out of the house to see *Harry Potter.*"

In 12-Step programs, participants learn the "sandwich" call. When they are about to do something difficult, they call a friend, do the difficult thing, and then call the friend back and report "Mission accomplished." There are stages of creative work when we can get so painfully stymied that a "sandwich" call is great first aid. We can call and say, "I can't get into my studio and I have work stacking up. I am going to go in for one half hour and just clean my brushes." We can call and say, "I am going to do the fixes on two pages and then call you to say I have." We can say, "I am going to read the first twenty-five pages of the manuscript to see what I think." Or "I'm going to rough out the choreography for the first movement."

Most of us have friends who are willing and ready to help us if we will just tell them how. In my early sobriety, I sold a script to Paramount and I was so terrified of rewriting it that my friend Jupiter used to come to my house, sit in my rocker, and read for an hour a day while I took my quaking self to the typewriter. An hour a day is a lot more work than no hours a day, and, as friends learn that small donations of time and support are more useful to us than grand gestures, they begin to know the cue lines: "Hook for half an hour and call me back." Or "Try to read the first twenty pages and call me back." Very often, we need help only to get a toe in the water. Once we are in, we can swim. Our help can be a phone call, a writing date where we both show up at Starbucks and scribble for an hour, a faxed check-in, an e-mail saying "I did it." The electronic age has allowed us to make our creative community far-flung. We can also "tame" a coffee-shop owner and faithfully eat a grilled cheese and work an hour in a back booth every day. For years, Dori's Bakery in Taos was like a zoo, full of writers, each of us with our table, nodding to each other and Dori as we sat down to

All who joy would win Must share it,—Happiness was born a twin.

LORD BYRON

*Transport of the mails,
transport of the human voice,
transport of flickering
pictures—in this century
as in others our highest
accomplishments still have
the single aim of bringing
men together.*

ANTOINE DE SAINT-EXUPÉRY

toil. Our friends will help us if we let them know how. Often, all we need is a little welcome company.

An artist in the midst of making a large creative jump—a concert tour, a book signing, a one-person show—is a vulnerable and sometimes volatile creature. And there are those who will attack and exploit that vulnerability and those who will protect and support it. An artist who is suddenly "hot" often gets burned. Without the solid anchoring of tried-and-true friends who stay the course, how is an artist to sort opportunity from opportunists, management from manipulation? Snipers are snipers, creatively as in life. They will hide and shoot. Some colleagues are snipers. Unfortunately, some friends are. Some families are. Often unconsciously jealous and resentful, they greet our good fortune with a chilly reception. A conversation with them can leave us feeling dismayed and dispirited.

Sometimes, it's sarcastic teasing: "So, how does it feel to be flavor of the week?" Sometimes, it's freelance spiritual advice: "Better watch out that you don't get too big for yourself." Sometimes, it's simple guilt: "I had a feeling this was coming, that you'd be too busy for me once you started on this project. It must be great to be so in demand." A friend of mine, a veteran actress, joked: "I don't know why we're so busy trying to get to the top; what's waiting at the top is envy and resentment." Yes, among other things, and it can be hard to find willing ears for some of our odd, success-driven adventures. I remember thinking, *Who can I call to say Sammy Davis, Jr., invited me to his house, and then told me I was a great dancer?* (I'm not sure my mother *was* the right choice.) The simple fact of your new life can sound like bragging and name dropping, even to yourself. We must find people who can see our vulnerability in such passages and neither encourage it to become terror nor discount it.

As artists, we need people who can see us for who we are— as big as we are and as small as we are, as competent and powerful as we are, and as terrified and as tiny as we sometimes feel. As artists, we need people who believe in us and are able to see our large selves, and people who are able to be gentle and compassionate with our smaller selves. I have a very small and cherished list of people whom I *could* call with a creative terror in the middle of the night. Ed, Jim, Bill, Bob, Julie, Emma, Bruce. I'm not saying I *do* call them to announce at two A.M., "I can't write. I've never been able to write. I've fooled the world and they're finding out at dawn," but if I had to call them, they would understand. Similarly, I hold a willing place on their midnight call sheet. None of us wants to be suicidally depressed at four A.M., but all of us sometimes are, and knowing that we *could* call often calls off the demons. Take a moment to make your midnight madness medical team. Sometimes, it is difficult to find people who can feel equally at home with both our largest and smallest selves.

For this reason, it is tremendously important to accurately distinguish who among our friends can accommodate each size. If you call a friend who loves "little" you with big news, you may meet an upsetting silence followed by a tepid "Gee, that's great!" that sounds like you've just said your exotic blood disease was now in remission. Call a friend who loves "big" you when you're feeling small, and you may feel as welcomed as a malaria-bearing mosquito. This is especially true if you are surrounded by people who are out of touch or shaky in their own creativity; they may never be able to see your need for validation and support as an artist. To them you're the lucky one, so what's the problem? This attitude may trigger you into your own caretaking, where you join them in neglecting your artist. A young novelist with a best seller gave all his earnings to his friends' worthy causes, "just to put everyone back in the same boat," struggling to keep their heads above water. A recording artist with a hit began frantically producing projects for needy newcomers. When people are judgmental or withholding around our success, we unconsciously try to buy them off—peace at any price, even if it's a piece of ourselves.

Consciously or not, the withholding of approval and appre-

Know that if you have a kind of cultured know-it-all in yourself who takes pleasure in pointing out what is not good, in discriminating, reasoning, and comparing, you are bound under a knave. I wish you could be delivered.

BRENDA UELAND

ciation is a powerful manipulation that moves us off our personal perspective and into pleasing others. This can be very expensive. When people are afraid of being artistically diminished themselves, they may never be able to do anything but diminish you. What we want to find are people who are able to be generous to us and to our artist.

We must learn to avoid those who blackmail us by pointing at our abandoning them when we are pulling our energies in and gathering them for a creative jump. We must find those who can both help ground us and help nurture us as we leap.

If the book is good, is about something that you know, and is truly written, and reading it over you see that this is so, you can let the boys yip and the noise will have that pleasant sound coyotes make on a very cold night when they are out in the snow and you are in your own cabin that you have built or paid for with your work.

ERNEST HEMINGWAY

A public appearance as an artist is best handled with a very clear understanding of the wallop the spotlight packs. Friends who see the glory but not its gory cost are the friends we may not be able to afford. Just as caffeine or an alcoholic drink can hit us hard on an empty stomach, so, too, the glare of the spotlight can throw us off center unless we are well fed spiritually, both before and after. Friends who see our success but do not see its stressors can tend to actually ask us to care for them just at those moments when we ourselves need care. This is why we need before, during, and after friends. We need those who can help us leap and help us land, help us celebrate and help us mourn. Some friends can do only one. Some friends can do only the other. We must find those generous enough in temperament and emotional range to do both.

It might be your aunt Bernice. It may be your little sister. It may be the doorman at your building or your best friend from grade school. All of us need a private cheering section when we undergo a public creative jump. We need those selected family members and friends who can provide us with the nutrients of love and creative support. If people see you only as the swan, that publicly graceful creature, and do not know about the feet churning beneath the water, then they are not the friends you truly need.

And yet, just as a swan is supported by water, which is see-through and ephemeral but "there," so, too, are we supported by higher forces that are unseen and ephemeral but "there." Our sincere prayers are answered. Furthermore, if we are lonely and beg for a little more in the way of human support, that support does show up.

Living lately in Manhattan, far from my nest in New Mexico, I have been craving before, during, and after friends, the day-in and day-out kind that I knew in New Mexico. To my shock and relief, I have been contacted by exactly that kind of person. An actor friend of mine from twenty-five years ago has turned up. A beloved teacher from thirty-five years ago. Another from fifteen years ago and a horseback riding girlfriend from further back than that. These friends knew me as young and wild as wistful and a lot of the ways that I still am when I get a chance to be. Today my mail contained notes from two of these recently re-met friends. My voice-mail had a message from my grammar school best girlfriend. All of these "miracle" reunions happened directly following a rather desperate prayer on my part, "Dear God, send me my real friends. I am too lonely with just you and me and good intentions."

Most of us are too lonely with just God and good intentions and no one knows this better than God. Instead of feeling so piercingly lonely, you might want to try, as I did, to pick up the phone and do some detective work. It took me three phone calls to find Sr. Julia Clare Greene, my high school writing teacher, but when I did and we talked on the phone, she did what a writer was bound to do: She wrote me. Now I have her picture and note tacked above my writing table, and it reminds me that I may have as many friends as I am willing to be friend to.

With thee conversing I forget all time.

JOHN MILTON

TASK:
There's a Somebody I'm Longing to Meet

Take heart and some heart steps. There are those who will tell you we should be "too mature" to need a cheering section.

That's stingy advice, and it's not founded in artistic reality. We both need a cheering section and need to *be* a cheering section.

Invent an imaginary supporter. Take a sheet of paper and write a want ad that expresses exactly what you would really like in a creative colleague. You may already know such a person. If not, your "ad" will help you recognize a possible candidate when he appears:

WANTED

A creative colleague with genuine enthusiasm and generosity for me and my work. Someone to share my hopes, dreams, and disappointments with, who will spoil me a little, cheer for me a lot, and believe in me when I can't believe in myself. Someone who can say—and mean—"That's beautiful, and so are you."

Catcher's Mitt

A compliment is something like a kiss through a veil.

VICTOR HUGO

As artists, we need to focus on process, not on product, and yet, we also need a catcher's mitt—somewhere or someplace where the ball we're pitching is aimed. In order to keep our art moving successfully on its true course, we need the right catcher's mitt. That is how we learn to throw the ball across the plate. Ideally, we want someone with enough range to catch a pitch that goes a little wild, someone with enough enthusiasm to yelp out, "Put it here!"

We make art to communicate not only to ourselves but also to the world. Someone or something must represent that world, and it must be the *right* someone or something. We must become smart about this.

The great writer Italo Calvino phrased it "The ears call forth the story." This is another way of saying that proper receptivity to our art helps to catalyze that art. "Oh, that's beautiful!" or "I love your phrasing" can be water to our creative garden. An eager "Tell me more about that" or "Show me that again" can bring our artist into blossom just as chill inattention or indifference can nip its growth or stunt it. So, too, skewed and premature criticism can cause it to compensate like a pine in a prevailing wind, and twist in an unnatural direction.

Early work is most often called forward by warmth. "That's going to be great!" You may remember the fairy tale about the bet between the wind and the sun as to who could make a traveler drop his cloak. The wind blew. The traveler, our artist, clutched his cloak. The sun shone gently, warmly, and pleasantly. Our artist took his coat off in the sun.

As a writer, your best catcher's mitt might not be an editor—it might be an avid, word-loving personal friend. Some of the best writing has been aimed to a specific someone—Rilke's *Letters to a Young Poet* was not generic. He didn't write them to "young people everywhere" but to one young mind and heart of interest to him. We can call such a person a muse, but we don't have to. You might like words like fuse lighter, spark, catalyst. It's someone whose particular intelligence lights your own. It is because of this alchemical attraction between souls that artists have always nurtured and encouraged other artists, and often championed their work. Haydn was nicknamed "Papa" because he was a catcher's mitt for Mozart.

At the end of his middle period, frustrated by his growing deafness—and the deafness of others to the music only he could seem to hear—Beethoven, in despair, made God his catcher's mitt and went on to write some of his most glorious music. Still, the story is a lonely one.

God can be the catcher's mitt for us as well, just as Christianity probably caught on because many people needed God in a human form in the same way many of us as artists need our catcher's mitt in a human form.

It is romantic nonsense to believe that we can, or do, make art in a vacuum. It is only a half-truth to say we make it to please ourselves. Even there we are pleasing a certain receptive aspect in ourselves, a sort of internal embodiment of our ideal viewer,

It is not what we learn in conversation that enriches us. It is the elation that comes of swift contact with tingling currents of thought.

Agnes Repplier

War talk by men who have been in a war is always interesting; whereas moon talk by a poet who has not been in the moon is likely to be dull.

MARK TWAIN

reader, or listener. I wrote *The Dark Room* to read to my friend Ellen Longo in installments. She was an avid reader and accountant. I wrote *Popcorn: Hollywood Stories* to make my first husband laugh at my version of the world we both survived.

Great art lies not in the generic but in the specific. It lies not in "More or less"—as we lamely conclude a thought to a bored listener—but in "Exactly like this!" as we excitedly show or tell someone perceptive. A tepid ear, a hurried glance, a lack of real focus—these can chill and even destroy an early work and a fragile worker. Yes, artists are resilient, but we are also like tender shoots. Our thoughts and our ideas must be welcomed or, like shy suitors, they get discouraged and go away.

Does this mean we want constant adulation and approval? Oh, probably. Does this mean we hate criticism and have no rigor, no discipline, no need for improvement? Emphatically, no. What it does mean is that our catcher's mitt must be receptive to our efforts, to our warm-up pitches and our looping fouls as well as to our sizzling fast balls and snaking curves that catch just the tiniest corner of the plate. Our catcher's mitt fields our creative energies, is open to all of them, and has faith in our artist's arm—wild, tired, serviceable, blistering. In other words, our catcher's mitt must be generous—which does not mean nondiscerning.

One of my best catcher's mitts is my friend Ed. When I tell him the writing is a little ragged, he says, "I'm sure it is, but it will tighten up later. It's great you're getting something down." When I tell him I am having a writing day that feels like I am suffering from rheumatism of the writing faculty, he says, "Everybody gets stiff once in a while. It can take a while to warm up. I am sure it's not as bad as you think it is, and you'll probably be limber again pretty soon." When I tell him, "I have so much work to do, I cannot believe it," he says, "True, but you've gotten through long rewrites before, and if you just keep chipping at it, you'll do fine."

Perhaps Ed's gentle coaching comes from the fact that he,

too, writes. Perhaps it comes from his years as a senior partner in a law firm, coaching hot young lawyers through pretrial jitters. Maybe it is his long years as a slow long-distance runner that have taught him the value of just logging the miles and not trying to sprint all the time. Maybe I am just lucky and Ed is very compassionate. Whatever the case, I need him. He is like the friend who turns up at the twenty-two-mile marker and gently runs me across the marathon finish line. I know Ed is a superb catcher's mitt because I have also had the other kind.

I have made the mistake of giving a rough draft of a book to one of my most fastidious and hypercritical friends. I have been told: "This book lacks your usual ease and poise. These essays are really heavy lifting and not very personable."

What do you say to that? "It's a rough draft, you idiot! There's a reason we call them 'rough'!"

I have also given rough drafts of my books to friends who are too nondiscerning. "I don't see how you could change a thing in this book. It's just perfect. Nothing seemed too long or too unfocused to me. I could always figure out what you meant and I just love the way you write anything. I could probably read the phone book if you wrote it. . . ."

Reviews like that from personal friends leave me pretty terrified that I *have* written the phone book. If the praise feels too syrupy, I get the terrible feeling that I will be like the wasp who gets her legs stuck in the sugary jam at a picnic—a good wallow until you want and need some liftoff. No, too much sugar from a catcher's mitt is not what we are really after.

What we want in a great catcher is what you see with a great catcher. Someone avidly crouched near home plate. Somebody slapping his mitt a little eagerly and saying, "Put it here."

How many are silenced, because in order to get to their art they would have to scream?

ANN CLARK

TASK:
Catch Yourself a Catcher's Mitt

The part of us that creates is youthful and vulnerable. It needs an atmosphere that is friendly and even playful, certainly compassionate, so that it can expand, experiment, and express itself. In many ways, a catcher's mitt is like a spiritual sidekick. Even the Lone Ranger wasn't really alone on all his great adventures. He had Tonto at his side.

Often, when we think about periods where we have been particularly happy, we will discover that we had an unacknowledged sidekick, a creative companion who cheered us on by taking a lively interest in our adventures.

Take pen in hand and do a little digging to discover some of your earlier companions and just what qualities they had that let you sparkle.

I believe . . . that every human mind feels pleasure in doing good to another.

THOMAS JEFFERSON

1. As a child, did you have a catcher's mitt for your creative efforts?
2. Who was your very best catcher's mitt? Mine was my friend Lynnie.
3. What did he bring to you that created joy and excitement in your artist?
4. Do you know such a person now?
5. Could that person be your catcher's mitt?
6. As a child, did you have a larger-than-life creative hero in your favored art? (Someone you just plain liked and identified with, not someone so intimidating, your artist would hide.)
7. What did your artist like in that artist?
8. What would that artist like in your artist?
9. Write a letter to your childhood catcher's mitt or your childhood creative hero.
10. Write a letter back to you.

CHECK-IN

1. **How many days this week did you do your Morning Pages?** If you skipped a day, why did you skip it? How was the experience of writing them for you? Are you experiencing more clarity? A wider range of emotions? A greater sense of detachment, purpose, and calm? Did anything surprise you? Is there a "repeating" issue asking to be dealt with?

2. **Did you do your Artist's Date this week?** Did you note an improved sense of well-being? What did you do and how did you feel? Remember, Artist's Dates can be difficult and you may need to coax yourself into taking them.

3. **Did you get out on your Weekly Walk?** How did that feel? What emotions or insights surfaced for you? Were you able to walk more than once? What did your walk do for your optimism and sense of perspective?

4. **Were there any other issues this week that felt significant to you in your self-discovery?** Describe them.

Action is character.

F. Scott Fitzgerald

Discovering a Sense of Authenticity

In the end, an artist's life is grounded
in integrity and the willingness to witness
our version of truth. There are no set markets
that assure us of safe passage. This week focuses
on personal responsibility for our creative caliber
and direction. Self-respect lies in the doing, not in
the done. For this reason, our personal resiliency is a
key to our creative longevity. Defeat is transformed
into experience by our willingness to start anew.
The readings and tasks of this week ask us to
practice a beginner's mind, opening ourselves
to renewed endeavors despite setbacks.

Encouragement

Artists are people whose "real" job, no matter what their paying
job, is the pursuit of excellence by listening carefully and well to
what is trying to be born through them.

Artists are not fragile, but we are delicate. We are subject to
the weather conditions in our life. Just as a long gray winter
spent indoors can cause depression, so, too, a period where our
creative life is led without the sunshine of encouragement can
cause a season of despair. We do not notice the darkening at
first. We just "don't feel much" like working. If we do work,
there will be forced and dreary drudgery to our time at the pi-

Why should we all use our creative power . . . ? Because there is nothing that makes people so generous, joyful, lively, bold and compassionate, so indifferent to fighting and the accumulation of objects and money.

BRENDA UELAND

ano, the easel, the page. We will feel like it's a long hill we are climbing and may even, mistakenly, glance up and say, "Oh, dear, so far to go. I'll never get there."

As artists, we routinely tap an inner well, and that well is fed by our spiritual condition. When we have kept our spirit carefully nurtured, the creative water seems to flow easily. When our spirit is dried out with unacknowledged discouragement, our inner well runs dry.

The antidote to depression is laughter, and this is where we are blessed if some of our friends have a good, bleak sense of humor. Sometimes, we can make a phone call that says "I am torn between suicide and doing my fingernails." Or "I am torn between making a gratitude list and leaping off my tenth-story window ledge."

The uncomfortable fact remains that there is always one positive thing we could do—and, damnably, there *is* always some positive something—even though we may still not have the heart to do it. We have to admit that our discouragement is, as one wag puts it, "a dirty job, but one that we have volunteered for, dammit."

There are some impeccably tried-and-true cheer-er-uppers that most of us are loath to try. It is, for example, very difficult to bake a pie and remain suicidal. It is very difficult to send out postcards without admiring ourselves, just a little, for our pluck and valor, even if our card says "Dear God, I am having a terrible time and wish you were here to do it with me." It is very hard to be depressed and watch a vintage comedy. It is hard to be depressed and make vegetable soup. Making almost anything can keep us from making trouble and, since most of us intuitively know this, we may take to our bed, giving our discouragement full rein to mug us. If we are in a 12-Step program, the dire complaints of a newcomer can lighten most despair. There is something very edifying about hearing someone share a truly catastrophic story when what we are worried about is something as elusive as "inspiration." Reading the hard knocks story of a literary great can cheer up most writers. Knowing that Rodgers and Hammerstein went penthouse to penthouse playing the piano and singing—to no good avail—to raise money for *Oklahoma!* can make the doldrums of "I don't feel like writing a song" seem laughably self-indulgent. Then, too, there is something wonderful to be said about just giving in to the full five-hanky storm of life that has a certain cheery effect. Finally, and this can work wonders, there is the possibility of calling someone truly boring. As they launch into breathtaking detail on something you could not care less about, the idea of going back to doing a little creative work can actually seem attractive. That and repeating the following:

All artists get discouraged. All artists have deep inner wells of self-pity into which we periodically dive. All artists are doing better than someone else and worse than someone else. All artists are doing better today than they have in the past and worse than they will in the future. All artists specialize in self-doubt. It is how we hone the creative imagination. . . .

We cannot control everything and everybody in our creative environment. We cannot leap across the dinner table and muzzle the fellow guest who casually observes, "At your age, you must be facing the fact that many of your dreams won't come true." We cannot—or, at least, we do not—hire hit men to take him out for murdering our hope, but that is what an offhand remark can do, especially if we are not alert to flag it as it passes. And we seldom are. "Let it go," we may say, only to have it go underground. When it does, it's poison.

As artists, we don't want to be petty, but the truth is, we *need* to be. If we try to "let go of" a creative slight, we very often simply bury it. There, tucked neatly into our subconscious, it can do its slow and poisonous work. Too embarrassed to repeat to a friend the "tiny" comment that hurt you on your way out the door from an audition, it becomes harder to audition next time. Why? Because we have been discouraged.

"Courage" comes from the root *coeur,* heart. It is easy to tell

We will discover the nature of our particular genius when we stop trying to conform to our own or to other people's models, learn to be ourselves, and allow our natural channel to open.

SHAKTI GAWAIN

if you have been discouraged if you check the emotional timbre of your heart. If you feel vaguely blue, a little cross, a bit grumpy, odds are you are "disheartened," meaning discouraged.

It is well worth it to sleuth a bit, to assume there is a cause for your discomfort instead of saying "I'm crazy. What's the matter with me?" Very often, "What's the matter?" is an ignored injury, however slight.

A friend asks to look at your video—and then doesn't. Weeks tick past and your filmmaker thinks, *Oh, what's the use?* You write an essay and send it to a colleague and no sound comes back to let you know that the penny dropped in the well has landed. You record a CD and out it goes to your family, where it falls, evidently, on deaf ears. You have "dragged home the invisible bone," the trophy of all your hard work lies on the floor unnoticed and unapplauded.

"No big deal," says your adult self. But your artist? Your artist has the character traits of a terrier puppy. It was proud to have made that bone and dragged it home, defending it against other dogs and managing to lay it at master's feet. So, how about a pat on the head? Like it or not, whether we hate the Disney description or not, artists *do* need pats on the head. We *do* need encouragement. We *do* need praise and we *do* need comfort. It does not matter how accomplished we are; it is a daunting and damaging thing to have our work ignored.

"I meant to" and "whoops" add up to discouragement. We "should be" more mature—but we really shouldn't. What we should be is alert to the damage of discouragement and clever about addressing it directly. If no one else is cheering us on, we must cheer ourselves on with tokens of our esteem for work well done. We must care for our manuscripts well, not leave them in shabby stacks where we spill coffee over them. We must set Artist's Dates and celebrate our finishing a new story or finally laying to rest the portrait for the grumpy client from hell who could not be pleased, although the portrait was pleasing to

Discontent and disorder [are] signs of energy and hope, not of despair.

DAME CICELY VERONICA
WEDGWOOD

everyone else who saw it. We must actively seek out friends who do not shame us around our discouragement and friends who can celebrate with us any small victory. In short, discouragement comes from an experience of stinginess—on the part of a critic, a colleague, a friend, our family. Encouragement just as clearly comes from an experience of generosity. Ideally, from others and ourselves.

At its root, discouragement is a decision in favor of stinginess. We are voting that the universe has done its last nice thing for us and that we have come to the bottom of Santa's bag of toys. No one will ever be spontaneously nice to us again—and we certainly aren't going to point the way by mustering any authentic and healing compassion for ourselves either.

We know how to stay discouraged when we are discouraged. We know how to choose our best negative friend to call. Most of us have a secret number emblazoned in our consciousness under the heading "Dial this number for pain and rejection." Most of us know how, if we are really feeling bad, we can feel just a little worse by calling it.

Jennifer has an excellent candidate for the worst person you could possibly call. He is a romantic ex. Someone who still owes her a great deal of money and who manages to ask for one whopping favor every time they speak. Superb at reporting the health and longevity of his stellar romantic involvements, where he is truly appreciated, this ex is skilled at remarks like "I heard you were in a terrible relationship—is that true?" Jennifer experiences the temptation to call this ex as a sign that the devil is alive and well and knows exactly where she lives. And yet, and still, Jennifer can fight calling this man the way a newly sober alcoholic can fight taking the first drink. It just doesn't seem possible to stay away from the pain and rejection that such a call can inevitably bring. Not when it's a clear-cut choice between encouraging herself and reaching for Mr. Poison.

All of us have some version of Jennifer's dilemma. We face

My business is not to remake myself,
But make the absolute best of what God made.

ROBERT BROWNING

the choice of thinking, *Actually, I'm doing pretty well and should really respect myself for my progress,* or, as we so often choose to think, *I am a spineless wonder, incapable of mustering the integrity, resolve, and inspiration necessary to address a postcard.* We all have people who think we are rather nice and doing pretty well and we all have other people who think—as we do often—that we could do better and be better if we would just listen to them. . . .

For most of us, the idea that we can listen to ourselves, trust ourselves, and value ourselves is a radical leap of faith. The idea that we can tell ourselves "Hey, you are doing pretty well and so much better than you did last year" amounts to a revolution. The possibility that we can trust ourselves, our decisions, and our painstaking progress, that this trust might be enough, even admirable, requires that we muster a soupçon of optimism. Optimism about ourselves and our chances is an elected attitude. We can choose to believe the best and not the worst, but to do that we must become conscious of our own negative voice-over and decide to change our mental sound track.

Optimism is critical to our spiritual health. Is our creative glass half full or half empty? Have we wasted a decade or two not getting where we would like, or are we strong and seasoned and facing another couple of decades where our age and maturity and sheer experience may allow us to actualize areas beyond our grasp when we were younger? It's a matter of perception—and faith.

The good news and the bad news is that artists are like plants that can thrive or wither with only a few simple variables. It is hard to kill an artist, but it is very easy to discourage one. All that it requires is a certain withholding quality, and that can cast a spell over a very fine piece of work.

We all know people who tell us our dreams are foolish, pie in the sky, whimsy, and that we should be grateful for what recognition we have won and settle for a lower creative ceiling than

Just trust yourself, then you will know how to live.

JOHANN WOLFGANG
VON GOETHE

our high-flying dreams require. (Those people have settled themselves and are uncomfortable with anyone willing to continue with substantial risks.) Fortunately, we also know people who do not bother to think about the odds or age or anything but the work at hand. Those people are the ones we must consciously choose to listen to. It is to those people that we must take our creative cuts and bruises for poulticing.

If we are to "take heart" and go on with our work, then we must take our heart seriously. We must listen to its pains and we must bring to it its joys. A heart does not need to be told "Oh, toughen up." It needs you to plan a tiny cheering ceremony and execute it. That done, you will find "the heart"—the courage—to work again and well.

Perhaps loving something is the only starting place there is for making your life your own.

ALICE KOLLER

TASK:
Taking Heart

If we are to "take heart" and encourage ourselves, we must first find our heart. Our truth lies in what we love, and as we remind ourselves that we have loved and do love, we find our way unerringly back to the place from which accomplishment is possible.

In horseback riding circles, fine riders will talk of "throwing my heart over a fence" and then "jumping after it." What they are talking about is the courage to commit, to be full-hearted. When we are discouraged, we are literally divorced from our hearts. We forget how large our hearts are and how daring. When we trust our hearts, we trust ourselves. The following exercise, taught so beautifully by Oscar Hammerstein as *My Favorite Things,* is a lesson that all of us can teach ourselves whenever the going gets tough.

Take pen in hand, number from 1 to 50, and list 50 specific and particular things your heart loves. For example:

1. Red-winged blackbirds
2. Raspberry pie
3. Lemon curd
4. Beatrix Potter drawings
5. My daughter Domenica's bangs and sooty eyelashes
6. West Highland terriers
7. Plaid ribbons
8. Homemade rice pudding
9. Lily oil
10. The tassels on field corn
11. William Hamilton cartoons
12. Making this list

It's almost impossible to make a list of heart loves without concluding we live in a rich, savory, and enjoyable world where—if we will just "take heart"—things are bound to work out well.

Sometimes, we meet with creative encouragement that we savor, cherish, and act upon. Sometimes, however, we meet with creative encouragement that we discount and disown. Take pen in hand. Number from 1 to 10. List 10 examples of creative encouragement that you acted on *or* ignored. Next to those you acted on, note the action taken. Next to those you discounted, note an action that *could* be taken.

"I have no name:
"I am but two days old."
What shall I call thee?
"I happy am,
"Joy is my name."
Sweet joy befall thee!

WILLIAM BLAKE

Integrity

What if we experiment with the idea that creativity is a spiritual and not an intellectual transaction? Not so long ago, cathedrals were built for the honor and glory of God. Art and artistry were routinely put to the service of higher realms. Higher realms were routinely credited for the worldly successes of creators.

Brahms exclaimed, "Straightaway the ideas flow in upon me, directly from God!"

"The music of this opera *(Madame Butterfly)* was dictated to me by God; I was merely instrumental in putting it on paper and communicating it to the public," Puccini confided.

If these men, masters at their art, could bow to mystery rather than their own mastery, might there be something medicinal for us in what they say? What if creativity itself is, as our creative ancestors teach us, actually a *spiritual experience,* a way to touch the divine and allow it to touch us? What if we reclaim the making of art as our birthright? Not some frippery on the edge of our serious business of making money. What if we remember and insist that art is central and dignified and important to the human experience?

We are an expression of the Great Creator, and we in turn are intended to create. It is not mere ego but our divine birthright to create. We carry creativity within us as surely as we carry our blood, and, in expressing it, we express our full humanity, which is far more than material. When we fail to answer this calling, when we turn it aside and listen to voices that deflect us, we are not in alignment with our own nature, nor with what might be called our destiny.

When we are headed in the right direction creatively, we feel a sense of satisfaction in each day's journey. We might not be moving as fast as we wish, but we are moving in the right direction and we do know it. At day's end, we can tote up our ta-dah list and say, "I placed three important phone calls. I reached out to check information that I needed. I jotted notes and got a few good paragraphs down."

Conversely, when we are not moving in the right direction, we experience a sense of unease. We have a growing sense of being off the beam. Something isn't sitting right with us. We feel stagnant or else stalemated. Sometimes, when we are moving in a wrong direction and events pick up velocity, we experience an alarming sense of being out of control. Something is "off," we know it and it is getting more and more "off." This is the time to step on the brakes. When we skid to a halt and the

Where there is great love there are always miracles.

WILLA CATHER

spinning stops, we can say, "I was headed straight for the cliff and I didn't have to go over."

Most of us experience the presence of what I often call "my beeper." I will get a "flash" that something is not quite right. If I ignore it, I will get another flash. My beeper will beep until I pay attention to it, checking in on the ominous feeling I am trying to ignore. Recently, my beeper went off that something I had written was not quite right. "Oh, it's bound to be fine," I tried to reassure myself. "How bad can it be? I wrote it. Everybody—three editors—read it. What's my problem?" When my beeper persisted and no amount of "It's fine" felt fine, I finally called back the questionable text right as the presses were ready to roll. Was it fine? Absolutely not. An immediate, thorough, page one, start-it-all-over rewrite was what was called for. I gladly rewrote the offending piece and felt I had had a very close call indeed.

And so, a sense of rightness will most usually mean all's well. A sense of wrongness will also usually mean something is wrong. Listening to such gut feelings is always worth the time and trouble it takes. When we let God be God and work through us, we experience both a sense of serenity and excitement. We experience integrity—which comes from the root word "integer," meaning "whole," unfragmented by doubt or discomfort. When we experience a sense of oneness with God, ourselves, and our fellows, we can safely know we are in our integrity.

If this language sounds "serious" and "spiritual," so is the matter at hand. "Know thyself," the Greeks inscribed above their temple door. As artists, we must take this to heart, working to express our inner imperatives and not just filling the form provided by the marketplace. Settling for convention over authentic self-expression, we are falling, in the biblical phrase, for false gods. In the long run, this works out no better for us as artists than it did for those worshiping the golden calf. The

Two things make a story. The net and the air that falls through the net.

PABLO NERUDA

"market" is the golden calf. When we worship it, we deaden our souls, risking, over time, our attunement to the work that would move through us. Commerce has its place, but that place is not first.

You will often hear an artist say, "Ah, they had only a shoe-string, so I didn't get my going rate, but it was really enjoyable to work on that film." Or "I *love* helping a new composer get something properly recorded, so I brought in a few of my friends and we really did a nice job." Or "They needed some publicity shots for their dance company, and I just loved helping them out. I mean, what's much more fun than shooting a batch of little ballerinas? And that troupe is first rate."

As artists, we have a different kind of accountability than many people. What pays us and pays off in the long run is really the caliber of our work.

As artists, we have an inner Geiger counter and it ticks loud and clear when we are near pay dirt—first-rate, high-caliber ore that means we are working at the top of our form. Because this device is an inner one, it isn't easily fooled by the prestige of a certain venue or the lack of prestige of another. What it detects is quality. It knows the real thing when it is near it. This is what "accountability" is for an artist, the blunt assessment: Is it any good? Fame, money, prestige—none of them can fool this inner meter of excellence. It boils down to the simple fact that artists respect good art—and we respect ourselves when we make it.

The great musician Stephane Grappelli remarked: "A great improviser is like a priest, talking only to his God." In a sense, all artists are like priests as they listen for the voice of inspiration, aspire to excellence, and hold themselves accountable to that high ideal more than to any boss or paycheck. When we violate our creative ideals, we violate our artistic conscience—and we become very uncomfortable.

Whenever we indulge in what might be called "paint by numbers" art, we are engaging in cynicism and skepticism. We

If you don't tell the truth about yourself, you cannot tell it about other people.

Virginia Woolf

I honestly think in order to be a writer, you have to learn to be reverent.

ANNE LAMOTT

are on a subtle level out to "fool" people. We are looking down at our audience and saying "If I just feed them what they are used to getting, I can fool them." Does this mean that we must always and willfully break the mold? No, a first act that is twice the normal length is too long for an audience to sit through comfortably—or perhaps at all. On the other hand, a first act that breaks arbitrarily because "it has to" is not an act that is listening to "where it wants to break" and finding the shape that is authentic for it as a piece of art.

As artists, we are always engaged in a delicate balancing act. We both know how things "are done" and we must strive to listen accurately to see if that's how our particular piece of art wants to be done. If we ignore all convention, then our rebellion is probably just as destructive and willful as if we blindly follow all rules, cynically calculating that if we "do it right," we can get away with something less than good because it's "done the way they always do it."

This is how skeptics are born. It also promotes a nasty hybrid of blade-runner artist—adapted to such a poisonous environment and promoting an ill-considered, self-aggrandizing myth that *their* adaptation is "normal," and that any "real" artist should be able to survive anything. Nonsense. Artists such as these like to appear on late-night talk shows, telling war stories and focusing as much on their corporate derring-do, the *Star Wars* of the studios and super-agents, than their art. Promoted in the press, and self-promoting, these artificially inflated *artistes* may intimidate genuine artists of a quieter stripe.

In cultures where creativity is embedded in the warp and woof of daily life, shyer souls may practice their creativity with more impunity. In this country, the artist is an endangered species. Grants are diminishing. Public appreciation is also more difficult to find. Too much power has gone into the hands of too few—reviewers stand in for viewers.

Fearing this process, fearing their capacity to survive it, many gifted artists allow discouragement to darken their creative land-scape. Of course they do. They may lurk too long in the shad-ows because they lack support—the before, during, and after friends—to help them tolerate their turns center stage. Many public art situations are toxic to artists themselves. We learn to deal with them, but we do not do it easily. Just as the body must develop antibodies, so in our current culture must the artist's soul. Not everyone can do this. Many excellent artists cannot.

In my twenty-five years of teaching, working to unblock damaged artists, it is my experience that it is not that artists lack quality but that, as a culture, we lack sufficient quality of *charac-ter* to nurture and appreciate the artists among us. Until we fiercely advocate and nurture ourselves, we feel stifled. Until more of our reticent artists make more art, we risk continuing to believe the assessments of those who critique but do not create. The quality of our artists is not the true issue. The qual-ity of our critical climate is. We do not have genuine receptiv-ity to the arts.

In light of these facts, many superb artists are not stamped with sufficient critical approval and so they may doubt the very caliber of their art. Making art takes courage—and, although our Lone Ranger, artist-as-loner mythology would tell us oth-erwise, it requires support.

The people who snort about there being a lack of quality in amateur art have not seen enough diamonds in the rough. They like to buy their art at Tiffany's stamped with a brand name and someone else's approval. They haven't had the courage to walk through church and hear a beautiful, if untutored, soprano, and commit cash on the barrel for her education. They have not been in a school hallway or on a sidewalk and seen a student sketch that caught them by the throat with its unexpected vir-tuosity—and inquired enough to know how they could help and support that young artist. It takes courage and heart to make art, and it takes courage and heart to support art makers. A cel-

If you don't risk anything, you risk even more.

ERICA JONG

ebrated pianist who hails from a small midwestern town always cites the generosity of an older couple from his home city who staked him a no-strings-attached year's rent in New York when he was trying to make his way. This couple had the wisdom to serve the art in the artist, to see the unpolished stone and help it find its setting. In our culture, their discernment and commitment are unusual.

Our culture diminishes both art and artists. Art is secular now, mere ornament, where once it was central to civilized life. Artists are seen as dispensable or, at best, marginal types, gifted perhaps, but mere filigree.

Good art is a form of prayer. It's a way to say what is not sayable.

FREDERICH BUSCH

Artists are everywhere, and if we do not see them—or see ourselves as perhaps being them—it is because as a culture we have bunkered our artistic soul in the safe citadel of cynicism. We co-sign the assessment of critics who are chic and "critical" but creatively impotent. Quality is not the issue, care is. When I teach that we are all creative and I say that we should all use that creativity to express ourselves, I am sometimes greeted by derisive skeptics who snort, "Don't you think you might be unblocking an awful lot of bad art?"

Let's be real: There is already a lot of art in the world that isn't exhilarating in its excellence. In fact, those who hang back from "inflicting their art" on the world seem to often be those who create more beautifully.

As an artist who teaches, I have far more often been humbled by the superior quality of someone's unblocked work than shamed by the quality of newly unblocked work. It is often ego strength and not the strength of the art itself that determines how far forward an artist is willing to put himself. We have made such a spotlight-riddled, harrowing public spectacle of the arts in this country that many people with enormous talent quite sensibly choose to live outside the limelight.

In our current cultural climate, we have too much acid in the soil of our creative garden. The limelight is acting like lime itself—poisoning the communal root system and support so necessary for arts and artists to flourish. Our critics are likely overly aggressive gardeners, busily weeding and heaping on the acid chemicals, unskilled in encouraging the tender green shoots that hold promise to bloom.

In our culture, we must consciously build safe hatcheries for our art. We must find people and establish places that allow us to flourish. We must become creative about being creative.

As creatives, we must learn to carefully and consciously put our money where our mouth is. We must learn to take the authentic risk of bettering ourselves. Setting aside a genuine hour a day to work on the play will get us further in the long run than telling ourselves we will write the play after we redecorate the apartment—which is why we are taking one more time-consuming freelance job so we can have the right computer table so then we can "really" write. Dreams become reality when we start to treat them as if they are real. When we stop postponing and evading them, and when we can answer "Today, I worked on my dream" with a grounded specific.

Creativity isn't something vague that we are going to do. It is something real that we actually *do* do. It is the refusal to sell ourselves short by shortchanging our artists with empty talk—or empty paychecks. We may have to work at a day job and that day job may give us structure and support, but it is a dangerous lie to tell ourselves that our paycheck from our advertising agency will ever give us the same satisfaction as writing the play we have dreamed about since grammar school.

Often, when we are afraid to try to make what we really want to make, we will say, "I can't make that." The truth is, we could, but we are frightened to try: Not trying, we do not really know whether we could or couldn't make our heart's desire. Very often when we say "I couldn't do that," we are again embracing an ideal of false independence, eschewing spiritual help. We are embracing an idea of God as a withholding God whose intentions for us are counter to our own dreams. Believing, even unconsciously, in such a toxic God, we do not see the Great

The imagination has resources and intimations we don't even know about.

Cynthia Ozick

Creator as a cocreator, a partner, in our dreams. Rather, we see God as a barrier, a withholding parent who denies our dreams. Most often, we are who denies them.

It is at this point that we must muster our integrity and be honest about what it is we really want. We must take the leap—or even the small hop—of faith that moves us slightly toward our true dream. This honest motion on our part is what triggers support for our authenticity—instead of support for a false self we can no longer comfortably inhabit.

"But what about the odds?" You may catch yourself grasping at straws. Odds are a favored guise of false gods. Odds are the denial of miracles. Odds are faith in being faithless, faith in being hopeless, faith in being stuck where we are, isolated from any power that might overcome the odds.

As we commit to our real dreams, we commit to ourselves. As we commit to ourselves, we also commit to trusting the power that created us. We are then aligning ourselves not with false gods but with the true power of the universe, the Great Creator through whose power all dreams are possible.

Surprise is where creativity comes in.

RAY BRADBURY

TASK:
Pat Yourself on the Back

You have already accomplished many worthy things. It is a good idea to have ready at hand a list of 25 things you are proud of. This list is where you value your own character and put down in black and white some of the things you have done right. It is important in writing this list to place on it what you are actually proud of, not what you "should" be proud of. There should be at least one entry that makes you grin at the memory, perhaps an episode where you stood up to a bully or managed to think of the exact right comeback at the actual moment of attack.

Take pen in hand and list 25 specific things you are proud of.

Do not be surprised by a positive leading to more positives, for example:

1. I am proud I taught Domenica how to ride a horse.
2. I am proud I took her to Sunday pony rides when she was a toddler.
3. I am proud I let her ride double with me to get her balance.
4. I am proud I signed her up for lessons and stood on the sidelines, watching.
5. I am proud I stuck up for Carolina in religion class.
6. I am proud I told the nun that Christian Scientists were as good as Catholics.
7. I am proud I brought my mother wagon loads of wild violets for her garden.
8. I am proud I tried to save the tomato worm by taping it back together.
9. I am proud I picked Tiger Lily from all the puppies at the pound.
10. I am proud I still write Morning Pages even when I am not teaching.

A list such as this one goes a long way toward establishing a beachhead of integrity.

Style begins when you seek and discover your strengths, then bank on them for all they're worth.

SARAH BAN BREATHNACH

Getting Back on the Horse

We are intended to make something of ourselves. When we feel supported by others, this is a festive feeling. There is a sense of community and a sense of shared purpose and humor—like we're the creative equivalent of a quilting bee or a barn raising. The collective group energy feels firm and exhilarating and fine. We don't wobble because there are helping hands to steady our ladder as we try to climb. Surrounded by support, making something—and something of ourselves—is easy. This is why the great summer music camps like Tanglewood and Aspen and Marlboro matter. This is why painting institutes and writing retreats are so valued. All of us need such support. We don't always have this luxury.

Sometimes, support fails us. Instead of help, we meet hindrance.

Sometimes, we suffer a horrifying creative injury. Our bones may not be broken, but our confidence is. An actress is emotionally disemboweled by a director who makes Hannibal Lecter look like an amateur. A pianist is reviewed by a critic who thinks "beat" is a musical term meaning "to club."

Creative cataclysms like these are common. They are the dangers of the trail. Artists are sensitive animals, and we do get spooked. Certainly, the sensitive horse of our talent gets spooked, and we may get pitched right off it. "I am never trying *that* again!" we vow—meaning the novel; the finger-twisting, heart-shredding concerto; that torture rack, the stage. And the longer we don't try "it" again, the more we convince ourselves we could *never* try "it" again. We say, "It hurt me once, and . . ."

There is one and only one cure for a creative injury, and that cure is to make something. If we do not make some small something, our injured yet active imagination will make an even bigger deal out of what happened to us. Sometimes, the only comfort we can find is naming ourselves. If no one else will pronounce us "artist," then we must say our name to ourselves—and the only way to say it is through art. The bandage must fit the wound. If your musical has been trounced, write some music. If your painting has been pounced on, paint something, even a kitchen chair. If your poetry has had its feet broken, walk to an open mic and read something. A famous director I know well, always conscious that critical reception might curtail his chances to do large-budget works, would remind himself on sleepless nights, "If I can't shoot 35, I can shoot 16, if I can't

Try again. Fail again.
Fail better.

SAMUEL BECKETT

shoot 16, I can shoot Super 8. If I can't shoot Super 8, I can draw, I can sketch. . . ." In other words, he knew his medicine for his creative losses, however huge and catastrophic, lay in the phrase "I can—and will—create."

We *are* intended to make something of ourselves, and sometimes that "making" has to be done without palpable support. We feel defeated and deflated by our interpersonal relationships. We feel like people have let us down, and often they truly have. Even more discouraging, we feel we have let ourselves down— we feel we "haven't been smart enough." And sometimes, we've done that too. As artists, we have off nights and off years. It is part of the territory. It is arguably a *necessary* part of the territory.

During my twenties, it seemed that everything I touched turned to gold. I was an award-winning journalist first—scooping *The Washington Post* and getting written up in *Time*. Next, I married a great love, Martin Scorsese, and worked side by side with him, contributing writing to his films. I became a popular newspaper columnist and had a winning streak as a screenwriter, selling a trio of films to Paramount and writing a successful television movie starring Don Johnson as Elvis. These were heady times.

Enter my thirties. First, a terrible divorce. Then I made a feature film but had my sound track stolen. I dubbed the film and released it in Europe to good reviews, but there was no American release, no "payoff" for three years of work. I wrote novels but didn't get them published. I wrote plays that won prizes but not productions.

Enter my forties. *The Artist's Way* was published. A dozen more books followed throughout the decade. The novels I had written finally saw print. My plays were produced. Instead of the pangs of failure and anonymity, I now learned the dangers of success. The best word for my forties might be "rigorous."

Throughout all of this time, I steadily, on a daily basis, kept writing. I kept working with the tools of creative recovery and even survival for myself and others. I knew from experience that

The way to find your true self is by recklessness and freedom.

BRENDA UELAND

a creative career took faith. In short, no loss of "time" when I was out of favor, no up or down when I was in vogue, ever went without later providing its usefulness. Everything—and I do mean everything—is fuel for the creative fire.

As a teacher and as an artist, I experience creative growth as characterized by periods where creative syntax and confidence shatters. We write "badly" because we are no longer writing as we were and not yet writing as we will. In our culture, there is little understanding of the growth process of an artist—which is often conducted in a very public arena. For the very public artists, for filmmakers and novelists in particular, there is little room for the work made during necessary periods of creative flux. Concert musicians report the same dilemma—a style matures idiosyncratically and spasmodically, moving not from beauty straight to beauty but from beauty through something different to more beauty. Few reviewers value the "something different" stage.

Art is made from talent and character. Adversity strengthens our character and can strengthen our art as well. It creates empathy and compassion for the adversity of others. This deepens our heart and our art. Adversity is educational, and like many educations, it is terribly hard to recover from without help. That help, in human or nonhuman form, as coincidence, as timely call, as "impulse" to do something off your beaten path, is a guidance and support we can rely on—but act on it we must. We are not so much rescued as joined.

When I first met veteran director John Newland, we were both living in a tiny mountain town. He was there in official retirement from a long and illustrious career—a retirement that lasted about four minutes before he was directing high school plays, community theater, college acting classes, anything that let his skills and experience have some play, however restricted. For myself, I was in what might best be called a "battered" period. I had taken a few creative tumbles—most notably around

You aim for what you want and if you don't get it, you don't get it, but if you don't aim, you don't get anything.

FRANCINE PROSE

discouragement on my musical work—and I was reluctant to get back on the horse. After all, falls hurt, and wasn't I getting a little old for them?

Feeling more than a little sorry for myself, I met up with Newland. I had gone to see an evening of high school monologues he had directed—my daughter was in his cast. I watched from a rickety seat in the tiny auditorium as student after student presented tough and edgy work, daring for our little town, daring for anywhere. I was used to community theater being more tame.

Who the hell did this? I wondered. Someone was putting up some great work. At evening's end, I was pointed to a tall, handsome man with a face like a ravaged cathedral and a shock of snow-white hair to top his alpine height.

"John Newland," he said, shaking my hand. "You've got a talented kid. I hear you're talented yourself, so let's eat some lunch and talk about things."

I met Newland for lunch and found his optimism to be the best thing on the menu. My age? "You're just a kid. I've got forty years on you and I'm still working." My discouragement? "Let me read that musical of yours. I'll bet it's good. We'll put it on." My worry about my career? "You've got another forty years to go, so buck up and let's do something."

We did do something. We put up my musical *Avalon,* and into that small auditorium three thousand miles from New York walked the woman who would become my musical collaborator. She "happened" to be playing chamber music in the same auditorium. A classical violist, she brought a small herd of her classical friends to hear *Avalon* on Newland's and my opening night.

What a good composer, she was thinking even as I sat curled up in the back row, wondering if I would live through the experience of hearing my music performed for the first time. She introduced herself that evening and she reintroduced herself when I moved in next door to her in New York, by "chance," four months later. Within months we were happily collaborat-

Art is our chief means of breaking bread with the dead.

W. H. AUDEN

Creative minds have always been known to survive any kind of bad training.

ANNA FREUD

ing—not, I believe, because I was smart enough to figure out my career but because I was willing to get back on the horse and know it when John Newland rescued me and then she did. It is my observation, after many years of teaching, that such "timely" rescues are par for the course. When an artist sends up a despairing prayer, the Great Creator does hear and answer it.

As artists, when human powers fail us, we must turn to the Great Creator for help. We must "surrender" our sense of isolation and despair and open ourselves to the spiritual help we frequently experience as an unexpected inner strength. Let me be clear about one thing: Artists at all levels experience adversity—some of us quite publicly, some of us in painful privacy. One way or another—bad colleagues, bad reviews—we fall off the horse.

It is a spiritual law that no loss is without meaning in all of creation. And so, the bitter defection of our creative colleagues who say "Thanks" and then try to shove us off the ladder (failing to mention our contributions at press conferences, claiming credit for our ideas in staff meetings) is actually, somehow, a boon to us. Yes, the shove hurts—and the treachery and the disillusionment. But we more often than not land in a pile of straw. We find our fall mysteriously cushioned. "Angels" appear. Sometimes, we sense them internally, as inspiration, the minute we ask "What's next?" and not "Why me?"

Because creativity is a spiritual issue, injuries to that creativity are spiritual wounds. In my experience, an artist's anguished prayers are *always* answered by the Great Creator. Even as we sob to the fates, and rightly, "I cannot go on," we are going on, and we are going on with spiritual assistance. Something is stirring that means we are already going on. We are gaining ground, first as awareness, and next as action. Creativity is a spiritual practice, and like all spiritual practices, it contains the tool of self-inventory.

We want colleagues of both talent and character. To find them, we must forge brighter our own talent and character. Very often, the people who do betray us and our values are those whom we have felt a vague stirring of unease about and then dismissed that as paranoia. Our gift is that in the future we will hear our forebodings as spiritual telegrams and not as neurosis.

Sometimes, remarkably often, creative angels show up externally. (In the theater world, the term "angel" is actually used.) As our villains slink from the scene of the crime, our heroes and stagehands step forward to try to put up a new and better show. "What if you try this?" a friend asks. Instantly, we see a path—or, at least, a next right step—if only we will take it.

As artists, when we are sold down the river, we must look to see in what ways we are selling ourselves short. Yes, the others have been bastards—that is real and irrefutable and painful. What is often more painful is seeing our participation; usually the spot where we shrank back from trusting ourselves is the very point that turned the tide against us. This does not make other people's foul play our fault. It does not mean they shouldn't have acted differently and better—what it does mean is that we will act differently and better in the future. That is the part we can change.

But the way to change this is not through berating ourselves for our stupidity. It is not by trying to make their flaws our fault. It is not by claiming we "drove them to it" somehow. It is by treating ourselves kindly, listening to ourselves gently. It is by telling compassionate people and forces exactly how hurt we are and admitting we need help that we heal. Call your aunt Bernice and tell her that a critic broke your heart. Write a letter to Oscar Hammerstein II, who endured a decade of failures after the success of *Showboat,* and tell him you're on a losing streak, does he have any thoughts. Call the college teacher who thinks you're a huge success no matter how you feel right now. Call yourself home to that part of you that *is* strong enough to continue. That is when the help comes—it bubbles up within us and it enters as lightly as wind stirring a curtain. There will always be help.

I have a sense of these buried lives striving to come out through me to express themselves.

MARGE PIERCY

What we are charged with in "making something of ourselves" is making ourselves willing to listen for that help and to accept it in forms we don't expect. Then act we must.

As artists, we are engaged *always* in a collaborative process with the Great Creator. Stakes that seem impossibly high to us, casting that feels all wrong—these, when we ask for spiritual guidance, may be revealed to be necessary to the plot, important to the growth and maturation of our own creative process. As artists, it is important to remember that all breaks are lucky because bones are often strongest at the broken places. Art is healing, and artists heal.

As artists, the Great Creator *will* help us if we help ourselves. How do we find this creative help? We find the creator by creating.

As artists, we do not control our creative world, but we control a lot more of it than we care to admit. We evade knowing how much we do control because it is more comfortable and comforting to coast on the spit of our career resentments than to experience the terrifying vulnerability of trying yet again to bring our work into the world.

Most artists feel and respond like spurned lovers to the thought of really committing to their work. Like a broken-hearted bachelor or shy spinster whose tender dreams were abused, we refuse to be vulnerable again. We "know" how it's worked out before. We "fear" how it may work out again, and so we do not even make a coffee date with our creative dreams to see if this time might be different.

Turned down by a callow agent, we say, "Oh, they're all like that." But are they? Blasted by a cynical gallery owner or a bitter dramaturge, we conclude, "I'll never get into a gallery" or "My work will never be accepted." All too often we don't try again—fearing more damage to our broken creative hearts. We know too well that in our heart of hearts, our creative dreams do not die any more than our romantic ones, and we are frightened by the whispers of these dreams—the undead plays, novels, and paintings that we have shoved into our creative closets, where they live with the muttering ghosts of our broken dreams.

As artists, we are dreamers, and what we fear is the nightmare of our work being shunned, mishandled, or ill perceived. Fearing this, we allow our discouragement to globalize from one person to "they," from a single tough review to "always," from a stinging rejection to "they'll never." We elect a defensive cerebral cynicism.

We begin talking about how "they" will never appreciate our work. We feel alone and abandoned, and we are—not because "they" have abandoned us but because we have. We have given up not only on ourselves but also on God. We have said, "What's the use?" instead of "What's next?" Rather than risk the vulnerability of moving out again on faith, we have hidden our dreams and our hopes under what we call "realism about the market." We have said, "Oh, they're all like that" rather than allow ourselves the terror of discovering they might not be.

Artists, like gifted horses injured at the fence, may shy away from trying the fence again. And yet, a gifted horse can and must be rehabilitated. As artists, we are both the horse and rider of our talent. When we are thrown, we cannot let that throw us. It's part of the territory.

Get back on the horse.

"Healing,"
Papa would tell me,
"is not a science,
but the intuitive art
of wooing Nature."

W. H. AUDEN

TASK:
Ouch! Let Me Make It Better

Creative injuries tend to be secret injuries. "It shouldn't bother me so much," we say. Or "I just seemed to lose interest after that." We deny to others and to ourselves the devastating impact a creative upset can have on us. We fall down from the horse, and rather than get back on, we tell ourselves we have lost interest in riding.

Unmourned creative injuries create scar tissue. We "toughen

up," but the wound festers underneath. "I'm just not interested," we say, when we are *very* interested indeed—just injured.

The following exercise is one in compassion and forgiveness. We deserve compassion for the pain we suffered due to our creative injury. We deserve forgiveness because we have allowed ourselves to be stopped, stalled, or stymied and we usually judge ourselves harshly for that.

Take pen in hand and again number from 1 to 10. List 10 creative injuries or disappointments you have not allowed yourself to grieve, get through, or get over. Be very careful to be gentle with yourself. This is an extremely vulnerable and volatile process.

As you review your injury list, look for a very small and very gentle step you can take to move your artist back toward the arena where the injury occurred. But the steps must be very small and very gentle. Let us say, for example, that you wrote a novel and received some encouraging and some discouraging agents' letters in response to your manuscript. A first step might be rereading the positive letters and the first twenty-five pages of your manuscript. Allow yourself to go slowly and carefully. If you put up a play and received some savage reviews, you might be avoiding theater entirely. Get yourself a set of theater tickets. In other words, coax your artist out to play, then put your artist straight back to work.

Rationality squeezes out much that is rich and juicy and fascinating.

ANNE LAMOTT

CHECK-IN

1. **How many days this week did you do your Morning Pages?** If you skipped a day, why did you skip it? How was the experience of writing them for you? Are you experiencing more clarity? A wider range of emotions? A greater sense of detachment, purpose, and calm? Did anything surprise you? Is there a "repeating" issue asking to be dealt with?

2. **Did you do your Artist's Date this week?** Did you note an improved sense of well-being? What did you do and how did you feel? Remember, Artist's Dates can be difficult and you may need to coax yourself into taking them.

3. **Did you get out on your Weekly Walk?** How did that feel? What emotions or insights surfaced for you? Were you able to walk more than once? What did your walk do for your optimism and sense of perspective?

4. **Were there any other issues this week that felt significant to you in your self-discovery?** Describe them.

Always be a first-rate version of yourself, instead of a second-rate version of somebody else.

JUDY GARLAND

Discovering a Sense of Dignity

The key to a successful creative life is the
commitment to make things and in so doing
make something better of ourselves and our world.
Creativity is an act of faith. As artists, we are sourced in
the Great Creator, meaning that our funding of strength
and power is limitless. This week focuses on the survival
of those difficulties encountered at the highest creative
peaks. Our graceful ability to encompass difficulty
rests in our ability to be faithful. The reading and
tasks of this week aim at acquainting the
creative practitioner with the survival
tools necessary for the successful
accomplishment of a sustained
creative life.

The Glass Mountain

Today, with charming Currier and Ives snowmen lurching to
life under tiny hands in Riverside Park below, I grapple with the
icy slopes of depression. *My* mood is the glass mountain of fairy
tale lore: I slither down every time I try to clamber up.

"It's the holidays," a friend of mine called to advise gravely—
secure that her depression, her heightened sense of nasty odds,
held common ground with mine.

I don't think so.

Today's depression and doubt is par for the course at the stage

There is only one journey.
Going inside yourself.

RAINER MARIA RILKE

I am in on a new project, this one a musical. I've got the jigsaw puzzle laid out on the floor and I can see a corner here, a corner there, but the big hole in the middle is exactly replicated by my own anxiety: Will I ever find the real substance of this piece? Trying to land a project—a book, a play, a song cycle—is like trying to land a big fish; as in Hemingway's *Old Man and the Sea,* the world boils down to that fish and me, and I am worried it will get away. As artists, we are often laboring to land big fish against big odds. What's worse, our fish are often invisible fish to the eyes of others, who see us as Daddy, as Mommy, as professor, as girlfriend or boyfriend, and not as someone engaged in a heroic struggle to drag something huge from the archetypal creative sea.

We want to pass for regular citizens. We do not want to turn our phones off or hide in the darkest corners of libraries, writing longhand. And yet, painting, writing, sculpting, and composing does take yards of quiet, uninterrupted time. How to manage this without seeming arrogant or standoffish? People come up with different solutions. My phone is off, but my voice-mail explains my writing hours and when a caller can expect a call back. Novelist John Nichols writes midnight to dawn, an eccentric practice, but it keeps him from snapping people's heads off—"I'm writing!"—when they call him during the day.

So reluctant are we to make a big deal of our work that we may make too small a deal of it. We do not communicate clearly the swaths of silence and solitude we sometimes crave. We fit our work into the crannies of life, and that's good a lot of the time. It lets us have a life, and that life enriches our art. But we do not talk often about sneaking out of our marital bed and stealing down the hall to write, to paint two to four in the night. We do not talk about running away to write our crime novel, holing up in a fleabag motel, on a stolen weekend from our marriage and law practice.

A pianist preparing for a concert tour may be teaching—and

teaching well—but he's preparing for a concert tour, wrestling down huge reams of music with his bare hands, even if he continues to teach his conservatory class load. A novelist listening to a book tell its tale may be listening to his children as well, but that book is always talking too, sometimes in whispers, and he *must* keep an inner ear cocked. A playwright cantilevering a new play from page to stage is worried about that brainchild finding its legs, and so listens like a new mother with ears in the night while "real" children, miffed and pouting, complain to their friends, "Mommy's writing."

Sometimes, mommies and daddies—no matter how we love our children—do need to write. Unexpressed art rises inside an artist until it reaches a level of restlessness and longing that must be addressed by making art—nothing else will scratch the itch. Nothing else is "wrong," although it may seem to be.

"What's wrong, Mommy?" our children wonder, sensing our distance and distraction. We have to fight not to snap their heads off if we are mulling a plot line.

"Nothing, Mommy needs to write."

"What's wrong, darling?" asks our significant other.

"Nothing, I just need to paint."

The year I taught film at Northwestern University and at Chicago Filmmakers while also teaching the Artist's Way privately and some classes of the Right to Write, I really needed to write. Teaching was taking too much of my time and focus and my family was taking the rest. I arranged for a brief getaway to Taos, and as I was waiting to board the plane a man's voice began speaking in my head. I grabbed for pen and notebook and began taking dictation. The writing was so welled up in me that it was the fast-paced flood, imperious and imperative: I must get it down. I wrote on the plane ride from Chicago to Albuquerque. I wrote on the bus ride from Albuquerque to Taos. I settled into my motel, still writing, and woke up to days of writing breakfast until dinner, ensconced at the outdoor table at

Your hand concentrates for you. I don't know why it should be so.

DAME REBECCA WEST

*Freedom means choosing
your burden.*

HEPHZIBAH MENUHIN

Dori's Café, where they were used to writers. Every night I would get a plaintive call from my family, "When are you coming home?"

"Not yet," I would answer. "I have to ride this out." I stayed in Taos for most of the month and most of a first draft of the novel. I reluctantly went home and began retreating to a corner coffee shop, where I hid in a back booth and wrote the rest. It was several months before I was back to my family in the role they preferred me in: "Mommy" and "wife." I had simply built up too large a debt to my writer not to give it absolute first place for a while. This experience taught me to be careful, to always honor my writer a little more fully. It is easier for a family to adjust to a daily writing schedule than it is for them to adjust to a season of abandonment. It is also easier for them to learn to batten down the hatches and make do during the glass-mountain phase of finishing a book than it is for them to live through that phase being conducted a thousand miles away with only phone calls of reassurance. Every project has a glass-mountain phase, a period when nothing is going well enough because the work is simply so hard. Families and friends learn to know and weather this. They do if we give them an explanation and a chance.

We work so hard at "normal" because we've heard so much about artists being crazy. We have heard too many stories of Jackson or Anne Sexton, too many of Sylvia, and Zelda, and fragile Scott. Our reluctance to be *that* kind of person has made us practiced liars—some lies are necessary and self-protective. Women know this. As an experienced artist, I carry my work like a secret pregnancy. I am *always* aware of inner life and the need to protect it. My apology if this metaphor seems gender linked. The creative men I have known and lived with often cast their creative projects as secret military campaigns, an equally gender-linked phrase, calling for secrecy, strategy, and protection.

Trained as we are to be mommies and daddies, and teachers and bankers, lawyers and judges, and so many responsible things, sickened as we are by the woeful tales of artists as irresponsible monsters, we may have difficulty mustering sufficient responsibility to our art and our artists, to protect them during the occasional, necessary times of hard climbing as a large project finally lurches into form—or does not. This delicate and treacherous stage, the glass mountain of creative doubt, is a slippery slope we face alone. It is on its icy flank that we must find small footholds, edging our way upward from concept to actual conception—a difficult birth, as pivotal as conquering our creative Everest—or nearly. "I hear it! I hear it! But I can't get it into my hands," a pianist friend once wailed to me. "I hear it, I hear it! But I haven't got it all on the pages," I have wailed back when a large wave of music knocked me sideways and I struggled to write notes fast enough as I went under.

As artists, we don't talk a lot about the quotidian anxiety of creation, at its worst during the glass-mountain phase, but difficult enough all the time. By and large, for most of us, the need to make art, the cost of making that art, and the higher cost of not making it is not something we lightly air. Our glass mountain is *our* glass mountain, and, like most fairy tales, it is invisible to others but very real to us. Art is a vocation, a calling, and if no one hears the call as loudly as we do, that doesn't mean it isn't there, that doesn't mean we don't hear it, and that doesn't mean we don't need to answer when it calls.

Over time, family and friends become more and more adroit at recognizing the symptoms of our creative calling. "Do you need to write?" or "Do you need to get to the piano?" they may begin to ask us. Most of us have drawn to ourselves partners who do love our artist—especially once they are assured that our artist has no desire to leave them. A novelist's wife knows that no meal will ever be as satisfying as a good round at the page. Sandwiches and slices of pie have a way of appearing at the edge of our writing table, where they are gratefully devoured. There is doubtless a special niche in heaven for those who have helped us to birth our creative children. Mere book dedications seem inadequate thanks compared to the gratitude we feel when we are

It's only when we truly know and understand that we have a limited time on earth—and that we have no way of knowing when our time is up—that we will begin to live each day to the fullest, as if it was the only one we had.

Elisabeth Kübler-Ross

well understood, a gratitude matched only by the terror we may feel when we are misunderstood, as artists sometimes are by those who mistake our need to make things for a need to make something special—and elite—out of ourselves.

We are the hero of our own story.

MARY McCARTHY

When I was young, I had a very good friend, Nick Cariello, who was very political. He invited me to visit his other good friends, who were even more political than he was. I remember a long, winey evening of talk, angry talk, about how artists were just like everyone else. They should not be considered special. They should take out the trash just like the rest of society.

"Yes, we can do our turn at that," I said. "But if you make an artist carry trash eighteen hours a day, an artist will still have to make art. It's our calling." And it is our calling. And so, we do carry the trash. But we carry, also, our stories, our symphonies, our dance, and our dreams. We carry them in daily life, and, every so often, up the glass mountain that is our Everest.

TASK:
Scaling the Glass Mountain

Take pen in hand and answer the following questions as rapidly as possible:

1. Do you have a project edging into the glass-mountain phase?
2. Can you protect your work schedule a little more rigorously than usual?
3. How can you steal extra solitude, even a half hour a day?
4. Can you manage an escape from family, friends, and telephones?
5. Have you made friends with Starbucks, the back room at the library, a back booth at Wendy's, writing in your car?

You may have in your vicinity a spiritual center where you can take a personal creative retreat and share communal meals. Many nuns, priests, and monks are great support during periods of creative doubt. Many convents and monasteries offer hermitage space to gather steam so that projects can be finalized. The sisters at Wisdom House in Litchfield, Connecticut, artists themselves, have long taught Artist's Way courses, and when staying on their grounds I have often walked my way into the quiet necessary to find renewed faith to finish projects.

Perhaps too much of everything is as bad as too little.

EDNA FERBER

Landing

In order to make our art, we expand and contract. Expand and contract: big ideas and the minute, painstaking work of getting them down in finer and finer detail. As we concentrate like this, we are first big and then single-pointed. In the heat of the creative moment, our thought—or flow—is hot, thick, dense, fast, and light, like good ink. We are skywriting for a path.

Our creative size has a tidal aspect—we ebb and we flow. Or, if you would, we expand and contract, altering sizes and shapes like one of those luminous mysteries of the sea, the jellyfish, which closely resembles a parachute. When we are at the height of a creative flight and trying to land, we, too, resemble a beautiful, full-bellied parachute trying to touch earth. Lovely? Yes. But safe? Not necessarily. Completing a draft of a novel may spark thoughts of suicide rather than celebration. Creative post partum can be unexpected and *deep.*

Parachutes often land with a lurch. Our creative flights may land the same way. Our chute collapses around us and we stumble around blindly. Or the chute stays somewhat open and we tumble across the field, dragged along by our leftover velocity. In other words, a creative landing may leave us a little bruised, battered, and suddenly claustrophobic as our creative chute collapses and our normal life threatens to smother us.

When we are making things, we sometimes get very, very big. Or simply very, very free. In the height of the creative moment, we are not constricted and downsized by our daily rigamarole—our age, our family tensions, our feelings of being a cog in the wheel. It is hard to come back to our normal size after such a heady expansion—and often, we don't, at first.

Creative flight is exactly that—flight. We get a higher than bird's-eye view of our life and our dreams and often many other things as well. We "see" the big picture, and such a vision can leave our ordinary perception shattered. We are staggered by the magnitude of what we have seen, and our own size feels foreign.

As we try to land back in our own life, we may shoot past our real size and feel like someone very small. This is why astronauts undergo debriefing, and why veteran artists, over time, learn specific skills to help themselves reacclimate to their lives and families. Finishing a long project is also a little like driving cross-country—when you get home, you may need to hide out and sleep for a couple of days before seeing your friends—otherwise, reentry can be bumpy. This is normal, just scary. It is hallucinogenic, like *Alice's Adventures in Wonderland:* I was so big and now I am so small. Or our life may feel like Mother Hubbard's—we feel pinched and can't quite wedge ourselves back into the shoe we normally walk in. It's not so much that our head is too big but that it's still full of very big ideas.

The creative world is full of cherished and hoary stories of what artists act like and look like when they visit the ethers in creative flight. In the pitch of taking down the music for my first musical, I put a silk smock dress on and wore it backward—perhaps for days—without noticing. Seized by an idea that we fight to land, who has time to think about clothes, to worry about looking normal? A famous novelist I know often forgets to put in his teeth.

Comfort is the key during creative flight. Everything else

O world invisible,
* we view thee,*
O world intangible,
* we touch thee,*
O world unknowable,
* we know thee.*

FRANCIS THOMPSON

goes by the board. And then the flight ends, and you think, *Oh, I should wash my hair, call my brother, sweep the kitchen, or clean and pitch from drawers.* Intuitively, we try to ground ourselves by a sudden binge of cleaning, scrubbing, cooking, calling friends. Reentry is a volatile process. We become seasoned only after time, learning to send up flares to show our progress: I am still in the chute and hope to emerge next week.

As a sober alcoholic, I am wary of anything too high and too fast. Euphoric is more of a memory than a sought-after state. And yet, when I do get a sudden rush of voltage, I find it a little thrilling as well as daunting. I know it is dangerous and I must remember that I will need to land carefully.

We do not land with grace, perhaps, but we can learn to land more and more safely. We can learn to let the intense energy of our fever-pitched work ebb from us more gently as we practice. Does a bath work? Cleaning? Calling a certain very old friend— that can be truly grounding.

Learn the craft of knowing how to open your heart and to turn on your creativity. There's a light inside of you.

Judith Jamison

Above all, we can remind ourselves: The ground does exist, and we find our feet again.

"I try not to talk with anybody for a couple of days," a seasoned novelist explains. "I know that when I have finished a big piece of work I am a little weird and so I try to give myself enough space to be weird in private." I might make a pot of soup. I might read a bad detective novel. I might take my dog out for some really long walks. Eventually, I start to feel normal again. I notice I need to scrub the floor or vacuum the car. I realize my running shoes are getting worn out and I think maybe I can handle going to town and getting a new pair. I might even put that off a day until I can't stand not going. The point is that a big piece of writing is a little like a big storm. It leaves you shaken and disoriented and things need time to settle down. You don't want to talk with your friends and sound like you just went through an alien abduction. You want to wait until you can ask how their kids are and if the movie at the art house is worth getting over to see. In other words, you don't want to reenter the world until the world has more in it than you and your capital-A Art. For me, that's a few days' transition, and when I try to skip it, I act pretty strange and people do notice. I like to let the dust settle now.

TASK:
What Makes You Feel Grounded?

Take pen in hand and list 10 activities that always make you feel more grounded, for example:

1. Making soup
2. Vacuuming
3. Changing my sheets
4. Doing the laundry
5. Baking a pie
6. Watching those horse-training videos
7. Waxing the car
8. Cleaning the refrigerator
9. Calling my best friend from grade school
10. Cleaning my office and paying bills

The regular use of this tool is one of the most confirming rituals possible in a creative life. Like the daily ta-dah list, this tool helps to put a sense of grounded celebration into our creative life. It does this because it emphasizes life itself. While we may "live for our work," our life is, and must be, larger than our work. By allowing the dailiness of life to step forward again, we become, in a sense, our own parents, saying "Welcome home" after each of our creative flights. A student-turned-colleague adds the writing of congratulatory postcards to herself as a regular part of this routine. "Good work!" the postcard exclaims. She has postcards on successfully completing arranging assignments, recording assignments, and musical workshops. As her jumps get larger and more public, her private practice of self-congratulations grows even more important. Our work feels not only good, but better, when we place it within the comforting confines of our ongoing routines and relationships.

What you are after is a grounded sense of connection to your life and relationships before, during, and after creative flight.

Age and Time

And the day came when the risk [it took] to remain tight in the bud was more painful than the risk it took to blossom.

ANAÏS NIN

There is a remarkable book of flower photographs by Irving Penn, who made his initial mark as the signature photographer of *Vogue,* photographing models at the height of their youthful bloom. His lens captured Suzy Parker, as glorious as a hothouse orchid, a woman as trained to a forced and topiary beauty as a single perfect bloom forced to perfection. Perhaps, as a reaction to this hybrid, highly bred haute couture, Penn turned his camera to the world of flowers in bud, in bloom, and past prime in ripening and glorious decay.

Penn's shots are remarkable. We admire the buds in all their nascent glory. We admire the vibrancy and potency of blooms at their perfect prime. But the revelation of the book is the beauty of the flowers as they pass from ripeness to gentle decay, falling from perfection to what Penn reveals as a different perfection. There is a poignancy and power to beauty nearly spent. It holds the remnant of what it was, and its fading grandeur reminds us that we die to bloom again. We are "gone to seed, according to plan."

Oh, if only we took our sense of aging from the natural world. If only we watched the mentoring and grave care and leadership and wit of older animals mentoring the young.

I worked with director John Newland during his seventies and eighties. A tall, snowy-haired man with a gloriously ravaged face and a hawk eye for cant and shenanigans, he was far more daring than the younger directors who have supplanted him in his field. Like Miles Davis, he had learned "Do not fear mistakes. There are none." He cut shabby scenes with a merciless glee. He allowed a full range of rage and daring—in fact, he demanded it. He knew the full range of the human keyboard. He expected all octaves to be accounted for and wasn't satisfied when they were not.

Yes, youth passes behind us, but we are blind so often to what we are gaining and to the beauty of what we become as artists. There is not a note of silvery sound or a hair turned silver that isn't perfect and beautiful. It is difficult not to rage at the passing of physical beauty and strength, the exquisite daring and dexterity we once possessed, the turn of a phrase or a haunch as perfect as a ripe peach, as gleaming and golden as the hard-won golden apple—of course we miss these things.

But we gain in beauty. We gain in tenderness. We gain in longing and desire and in satiation if we get the chance—not merely or only exquisitely in our sexual and our physical selves but our creative selves as well.

At fifty-four, I am still willing to learn. I am willing to entertain the idea that everyone who is learning something they care about—whether it is the piano, as with me, or the emotional weather of someone they are newly involved with—anyone who is learning will feel this treacherous mix of vulnerability and frustration, of hope and discouragement. There is an exciting element of self-respect: You are trying.

I think that one of the benefits of doing something "at my age" is that I have lived long enough not to think that "hard" means wrong or even un-do-able. It may just mean hard. And, too, I no longer think my hard is worse than someone else's hard. I think all beginners have high hopes and dash themselves against their own expectations and dreams like waves against a cliff until they get it: over and over, like a wave, yes, but perhaps, a gentler one. Water *does* wear away rock. Practice *will* make if not "perfect," then "better." Take me and the piano.

Clearly, it is mind and muscle and heart that must be trained.

I wish that life should not be cheap, but sacred,
I wish the days to be as centuries, loaded, fragrant.

RALPH WALDO EMERSON

All of them must learn patience, the virtue I hate, and repetition, the idea God had the sense to use daily. Ah, yes, the sun rises and the piano waits. I simply need to tell myself, make a routine, not a special occasion, out of this. Appreciate the players leaping up on the craggy heights, but don't be discouraged by them. They show you what players can do and what a piano can do. And even that word "piano" means "softly."

I also worked, during his seventies and eighties, with veteran actor Max Showalter. At eighty-two, he traveled to Taos to teach at a creativity camp that I was leading. He commandeered the piano and held a hundred of us spellbound for several hours as he replayed his seven decades in show business and his eight decades of life. "You have to be positive. They have to know life is good—every scrap of it," Max told me. He lived every scrap of his life fully—he husbanded a great and glorious half-acre of garden when I first knew him in Hollywood in the 1970s and thirty years later he had another glorious half-acre transplanted to Connecticut. In both gardens, we took pictures of each other and of our visions of life. Max caught a photo of me as a budding young woman and, in our last photo together, my hair has glints of silver in the gold. We talked on that visit of the garden of talent he was also husbanding, working with his good friends at the Goodspeed Theatre and in community projects to shepherd young talent into his old trooper's version of the theater: "A place of promise where we all can get bigger than life. *NO!* As big as life allows us and that's plenty."

It is the soul's duty to be loyal to its own desires. It must abandon itself to its master passion.

REBECCA WEST

TASK:
The Communion of All Saints

Have you considered asking your creative saints, those artists you admire who have passed over, for help? This personal practice, far from being heretical, honors the fact that art making is a spiritual lineage. Our artistic ancestors *are* sources of inspiration, not only in the survival of their work but in the survival of their creative spirit. By involving them directly, we correctly honor their contributions to our lives, and this practice often yields great creative fruit. Do you have any resistance to this process?

As a culture, we are quite primitive and arrogant in our refusal to honor and acknowledge the inflow and imprint of our ancestors.

Experiment: Select one creative elder who has passed on. Ask for help and input on a problem you are facing. Writing very rapidly, transcribe what you hear. Haydn may tell you to use proper files for your musical compositions and organize your workroom.

A young composer became accustomed to an extra sense of guidance in daily affairs—"Stop in this music shop," "Call your old professor," etc. As these leadings palpably paid off in creative terms, the notion of asking for inspiration from creative ancestors seemed, if not reasonable, interesting. Schooled rigorously in the classics, with at least a rudimentary notion of each composer's supposed temperament and life situation, our young composer began asking for specific help. Doing so, she reported that she found Haydn strict and very smart, she found Mozart goofy but inspirational, she found Beethoven kind, focused, and passionate, and that her own compositions were improving enormously. By asking to be inspired, she felt she was.

One day in her Morning Pages, she wondered if such inspiration was just her "imagination." Immediately, she heard, "There are a lot of souls over here who are very interested in what we did, and very interested in what you're doing. We like to help when we can."

Consider this: what if "original sin" is denying instead of celebrating your originality? Each of us possesses an exquisite, extraordinary gift: the opportunity to give expression to Divinity on earth through our everyday lives. When we choose to honor this priceless gift, we participate in the re-creation of the world.

SARAH BAN BREATHNACH

Service

In centuries past, art was made for the honor and glory of God. Viewed in this light, a career in the arts was a career of service, not egotism. There is a cue there for us.

The dedication of our work to a higher cause than our own self-promotion frees the work from preciousness. It becomes not about how good we are but about how good we can be in self-less service to something larger than ourselves. Sometimes we can dedicate a book to a person whom we wish to reach. Rilke's classic letters to a young poet tapped his own inner reservoirs of wisdom and generosity.

As artists, we are the bearers of gifts, spiritual endowments that come to us gratis and ask only to be used. A gift for music asks that we give voice to it. A fine photographer's eye asks that we focus it. We are responsible to our gifts for the use of our gifts, and this is a form of accountability too.

But if you have nothing at all to create, then perhaps you create yourself.

CARL JUNG

Some of the best playwriting—Shakespeare's included—was done with an eye to making wonderful roles to serve the talents of friends. Anytime we elect to serve, we open the doors for higher inspiration. We may target a piece of work to someone or something that we feel is worthy; this elected humility re-moves the tightening that occurs when our work is all about us and our brilliant careers. We may be brilliant in passing but we will no longer be straining for brilliance. Asking to be of serv-ice, and to be open to the proper inspiration to serve through our work, we then become teachable, and when we are teach-able, our work always improves.

When our work is made only in the service of our hope for fame or recognition, it is hampered by our self-consciousness as we wonder, *How am I doing?* When we are able to work with-out such self-consciousness, we are able to work more freely and more fully. Our ego steps aside and is no longer a constrictive valve narrowing our creative flows and focus. We think less about "us" and more about "it," the work itself.

I remember sitting under whispering trees at a music park, listening as a brilliant pianist lashed through a blistering per-formance as dramatic as the incoming storm. I was seated be-tween two grown men who listened to the cascading notes as enraptured as small children, their faces lit with Christmas radiance. Magic was afoot, or, perhaps better, at hand. Later I learned that the musical magician we had so admired had played all evening uphill, against an inner critic that cited that missed chord, this muffled mordent. With a monk's devotion, he had played anyway—such nights are an artist's Gethsemane, a night to be endured only on faith.

"I have to remind myself there is something larger than me and my skill, something more important than my ego's perception," the pianist confided to me. That something is in art itself, the creative power that moves through us, healing and transforming those who encounter it.

"It was like watching Magic Johnson play," one of the men whispered to me on that bench. It was an accurate remark. That word "magic" again, and consummate skill. On Magic Johnson's off nights, he still "hits" more than others. His sailing long ball swooshes still have spooky ease. This is often true for artists. Our "best" nights to others may internally feel our worst. Our perceptions must not be allowed to capsize our professionalism. Novelists with long literary careers report ruefully the great reviews on the books they like least, and the tepid receptions to the works they most cherish. In a sense, the reception of our work by ourselves as well as others is none of our business. Our job is to do it. We work, and the work works through us.

Actors talk ruefully of having terrible nights with rapturous reception, and tepid response to the nights they felt themselves most connected. In a sense, a singer is merely the vehicle for a song, and the song is merely a vehicle for music itself. No matter how accomplished and acclaimed we may become as artists, there is always, at core, this essential anonymity: We are in service of something larger than ourselves.

We have very strange notions about art in our culture. We have made it a cult of the individual rather than what it has always been, a human aspiration aimed at communicating and community. We "commune" through art, both with the forces of inspiration when we work and with other humans who en-

We can't take any credit for our talents. It's how we use them that counts.

MADELEINE L'ENGLE

counter us and those forces through our work. To commune is to attune with an open heart, something impossible if we are thinking only of ourselves.

Manhattan abounds in musicians and music schools. Some of the very best of each are to be found in the vertical canyons of this tiny and overcrowded island. One of the finest music teachers in Manhattan teaches with the greatest amount of innovation—and out of a spirit of service.

"Beginning piano books are just terrible," he says. "Some of the very best students hate to use them. They just don't respond to the music in them and so they become bored." Boredom, of course, is the enemy of learning, and so this music teacher has composed a whole series of beginning music lessons with music he wrote himself and fairy tales to match. Who wouldn't want to learn the waltz that was danced when Sleeping Beauty was awakened with a kiss? Who wouldn't want to play the song a mighty organ played when it fell in love with a gifted young student? Piece by piece, lesson by lesson, seeking only to serve his gifted and disenchanted students, this master teacher has built a curriculum that is lively, innovative, and eminently playable.

"Here, let me write something out for you," he will say, and draw the lines of a staff and make handwritten music paper. "Wouldn't it be fun to learn this?" And the big black notes march across the page, crooked and enticing.

Setting aside all ego and snobbery, setting aside how music "should" be taught, this great teacher teaches from a spirit of love and service. Is it any wonder that his students develop a love of music that serves them very well?

As artists, we are intended to be conduits for inspiration. There are high thoughts and high intentions and higher realms that can speak to us and through us if we allow it. When our ego and our ego-driven fears are given a central place as regards our art, we have rolled a large boulder into our own way, and our career cannot unfold unimpeded because it must divide to make

Love is the spirit that motivates the artist's journey . . . it's a powerful motive in the artist's life.

ERIC MAISEL

its way with unnatural intensity and velocity around the boulder settled in the stream of our good. On rivers and in the rivers of creative flow, such rapids are treacherous. We are far better served by being of service.

Contemplating a piece of work, we do better to think *Whom is this work for? Whom will it serve?* rather than *How will it serve me?* Once we find a path for our work to be of service—even if that path is merely to create a wonderful role for a friend—then our work goes smoothly forward. It is not about "us" anymore. We have retired as self-conscious creator and aligned ourselves again with all of creation, a worker among workers, a friend among friends. When we do so, our work is less buffered by our own harsh fears. Our fears are set aside every time we simply ask again, "How can I make this work more serviceable?"

Director Steven Spielberg once remarked to an interviewer that he hoped at heaven's gate, God might say to him, "Steven, thanks for listening." This listening for inspiration, this willingness to align our creative will with a sense of higher guidance, is not contrary to a career but a better and more grounded way to establish one. A career solely grounded in the idea of self-advancement is not grounded enough in the advancement of ideas. For all their estimable craft, artists who fail to deepen their goals and their ideas find that their careers run into a certain shallow sameness over time.

Chekhov advised actors, "If you want to work on your career, work on yourself." It might equally be advised, if you want to work on yourself, work to make your career of service to something larger than yourself. Dedicate yourself to something or someone other than yourself. This expansion will make you larger both as a person and as an artist.

We used to routinely call God "the creator." We had a consciousness that our own creativity was a divine gift, an opening for God to work through us. When we enshrined ourselves and our individuality rather than our shared humanity at the center of our consciousness—a shift for which therapy may be thanked

To believe your own thought, to believe that what is true for you in your private heart is true for all men—that is genius.

RALPH WALDO EMERSON

for a great deal of useless narcissism and also an unpleasant conviction that art was about compensating—we lost our proper
understanding of art as service. We disenfranchised ourselves
from our birthright as creators and we lost the understanding
that art was an act of the soul and not of the ego. Whenever we
take art back to the realm of the sacred, whenever we make it an
act of service in any form, if only to such an idea as beauty or
truth or humanity, but perhaps better when it is more person-
ably serviceable, we again experience the ease of creative flow
and the lessening of our creative doubts. When we ask to "listen," we create works worthy of being heard and we ourselves
hear the heartbeat of our common humanity, which is grounded
in divinity.

*Whatever you can do or dream
you can, begin it;
Boldness has genius, power and
magic in it.*

JOHANN WOLFGANG
VON GOETHE

We may make a piece of art to promote planetary understanding. We may make beautiful music for the glory and service
of music itself. We may write a play for alcoholic women to take
heart. We might paint to express gratitude to our creator for the
beauty of Queen Anne's lace. When we make our art in a spirit
of service, it lightens the burden of our ego. It makes for clarity
of focus, purity of intent, and follows a spiritual law that might
be simply stated as "Form follows function." When the "form"
of our work is open to higher consciousness, its function is
raised as well.

Art moves through us. It is colored by our individuality, but
we are not precisely its origin. Or, to put it differently, a piece of
art may originate with us, but we originate somewhere larger
ourselves. We are, each of us, more than we seem, more than
the sum of our merely human components. There is a divine
spark animating each of us, and that divine spark also animates
our art. When we ask to be of service in our art, we fling open
a window in our creative studio. Through that opening, the
greater world of inspiration can enter us. A painter friend of
mine talks about art needing a "hole for the imagination." I
think I might phrase it as "When we dedicate a piece of art to
something larger than our ego, that something larger becomes a

*The gift turned inward, unable
to be given, becomes a heavy
burden, even sometimes a kind
of poison. It is as though the
flow of life were backed up.*

MAY SARTON

felt presence." A great painting, poem, or piece of music carries that indefinable something more. We sense it and, although we try to name it and define it, it eludes definition and containment. There is a breath of the divine that blows through us as artists and blows through our art as well. Walk into a cathedral and you will sense something larger than the artisans. Our hired hands, as artists, also hold a hand with a higher hand. Take Bach, hired to write music so that his church would have something to play once a week at service—that word again. What Bach wrote was more than merely serviceable. Inspired by a spirit of service, he wrote the cantatas, the "little songs," that we love and cherish centuries later.

Arguably, we are all in service to an artist greater than our own. Life itself works through us. We are the carriers of dreams and desires that may have originated generations earlier. Music runs in families. So does a gift for drama and for words. When we elect to make art from a spirit of service to a larger whole, we are really simply becoming truthful. We are all part of a larger whole and, in acknowledging that truthfully, we move a notch closer to humility, to a simple and sheer plainness that allows the beauty of the grand design to be seen through us. If beauty is truth and truth beauty—and I believe that this is so—then our acknowledgment of our place in a larger scheme of things strikes a first true note from which more beauty follows.

TASK:
Beauty Is Truth and Truth, Beauty

Each of us carries an inner capacity for awe. One of us will be wonderstruck by a musical sequence. Another of us is rendered humble and serene by the sight of a butterfly's wing. Each one of these gateways to the divine is there waiting for us to use it to make contact. There are some things that simply make us happy, some things that we plainly and for no apparent reason love. For this reason, we say, "God is in the details." Each of us experiences the touch of the Great Creator when we allow ourselves to touch upon something that we love.

Because the part of us that creates is youthful and innocent, an ideal place to collect "artist toys" is a good children's bookstore. Go to one now. If dinosaurs are your love, get a dinosaur book. If dogs make you happy, find a book of the dog. Make it a point that your bedside table contains at least one book on a topic that simply delights you. Delight opens the door for the Great Creator to touch us with a sense of well-being. You may love zebra finches or just plain zebras. Let yourself celebrate what you love and that you are the person who loves it. As you connect to the childlike part of you that loves and enjoys the material world, you are connecting to the sense Aristotle had when he remarked, "In all things of nature there is something of the marvelous."

Allow yourself to marvel.

Only the heart knows how to find what is precious.

FYODOR DOSTOYEVSKY

EPILOGUE

I WOULD LIKE TO END this book on a grace note: that is to say, I would like to acknowledge the place of grace in the making of art and artists. It is a great grace that we are born creative beings. It is a great grace that we access that creativity. Although you may language it differently, all creators feel the hand of the Great Creator touching them through their work. Art is a spiritual practice. We may not, and need not, do it perfectly. But we do need to do it. It is my belief that the making of art makes us more fully human. In becoming more fully human, we become more fully divine, touching in our finite way the infinite spark within each of us. Focused on our art, we connect to the artful heart of all life. The creative pulse that moves through us moves through all of creation. It could be argued that creativity is a form of prayer, a form of thankfulness and recognition of all we have to be thankful for, walking in this world.

SUGGESTED READING

My experience as a teacher tells me that those who read this book are better off doing something, rather than reading another book, but I have included many of my favorites just in case you feel compelled to research further. These books represent some of the very best in their fields. To keep it simple, try to finish Artist's Way work before adding this input.

Aftel, Mandy. *The Story of Your Live—Becoming the Author of Your Experience.* New York: Simon & Schuster, 1996. Persuasive and useful.

Ban Breathnach, Sarah. *Simple Abundance.* New York: Warner Books, 1995. Grounded in my own work and expanding on it, this is a profoundly touching book.

Berendt, Joachim-Ernst. *The World Is Sound: Nada Brahma.* Rochester, Vt.: Destiny Books, 1991. Eloquent and persuasive book on sound theory.

Bolles, Richard Nelson. *What Color Is Your Parachute?* Berkeley: Ten Speed Press, 1970. Whimsical and pragmatic guide to goal setting.

Bonny, Helen. *Music and Your Mind.* Barrytown, N.Y.: Helen A. Bonny and Louis M. Savary, 1973, 1970. An explicit guide to using music as an antidote for mental and emotional pain.

Bradley, Marion Zimmer. *The Mists of Avalon.* New York: Ballantine Books, 1982. A powerfully evocative novel of female spirituality in pre-Christian England. A mesmerizing novel of goddess worship in Arthurian times.

Brande, Dorothea. *Becoming a Writer.* 1934. Reprint. Los Angeles: Jeremy P. Tarcher, 1981. The best book on writing I've ever found.

Burnham, Sophy. *A Book of Angels.* New York: Ballantine Books, 1991. An elegant, deeply felt exploration of the spiritual powers and forces at play in our lives.

Bush, Carol A. *Healing Imagery and Music.* Portland, Oreg.: Rudra Press, 1995. A profoundly useful guide to listening for healing.

Came to Believe. New York: Alcoholics Anonymous World Services, 1973. Useful and touching book about embryonic faith.

Campbell, Don G. *The Roar of Silence.* Wheaton, Ill.: The Theosophical Publishing House, 1994. Seminal book on sound healing—clear, passionate and useful. All of Campbell's many books are important and persuasive, but this one remains a primer.

Cassou, Michelle, and Steward Cubley. *Life, Paint, and Passion: Reclaiming the Magic of Spontaneous Expression.* New York: Jeremy P. Tarcher/Putnam, 1996. Passionate and experienced into-the-water book for visual artists.

Chatwin, Bruce. *Songlines.* New York: Penguin Books, 1987. An exquisite, mysterious and powerful book.

Choquette, Sonia. *The Psychic Pathway.* New York: Random House. Crown Trade Paperbacks, 1994, 1995. Safe, grounded, practical guide to opening to spiritual gifts.

Choquette, Sonia. *Your Heart's Desire.* New York: Random House, Crown Trade Paperbacks, 1997. An extremely clear, step-by-step guide for manifesting dreams as working reality.

Eisler, Raine. *The Chalice and the Blade.* San Francisco: Harper & Row Publishers, 1987. Seminal book on the differences in masculine and feminine life approaches.

Fassel, Diane. *Working Ourselves to Death.* San Francisco: HarperCollins, 1990. A strong-minded intervention for workaholic personalities.

Fox, Matthew. *Original Blessing.* Santa Fe, N.M.: Bear & Company, 1983. An important corrective book on Christian tradition; brilliant, impassioned, compassionate.

Franck, Frederick. *Zen Seeing, Zen Drawing.* New York: Bantam Books, 1993. A fine treatise on the value of "attention" in the creative life.

Gawain, Shakti. *Creative Visualization.* Mill Valley, Cal.: Whatever Publishing, 1986. Helpful in learning to create and hold a vision.

Goldberg, Bonni. *Room to Write: Daily Invitations to a Writer's Life.* New York: Jeremy P. Tarcher/Putnam, 1996. A masterfully provocative and wise writer's tool.

Goldberg, Natalie. *Writing Down the Bones.* Boston, Mass.: Shambhala Publications, 1986. The best pen-to-paper writing book ever written.

Goldman, Jonathan. *Healing Sounds: The Power of Harmonics.* Rockport, Mass.: Element Books, Inc., 1992. Powerful and gentle teaching book on sound healing techniques.

Grof, Christina, and Stanislav Grof, *The Stormy Search for the Self.* Los Angeles: Jeremy P. Tarcher, 1990. A provocative book about the misunderstanding of spiritual experience in our culture.

Harmon, Willis, and Howard Rheingold. *Higher Creativity.* Los Angeles: Jeremy P. Tarcher, 1984. A valuable and often instructive book on creativity in front-line famous authors and others.

Hart, Mickey. *Drumming at the Edge of Magic.* San Francisco: HarperCollins, 1990. A great book on music as a spiritual experience.

Heywood, Rosalind. *ESP: A Personal Memoir.* New York: E. P. Dutton & Co., Inc., 1964. A delightful book of personal encounters with higher forces.

Holmes, Ernest. *Creative Ideas.* Los Angeles: Science of Mind Communications, 1973. A tiny, powerful and important book of spiritual law as applied to creative manifestation.

James, William. *The Varieties of Religious Experience.* Boston: Mentor Books, 1902. Seminal fountainhead describing different forms of spiritual awakening, much insight into creativity as a spiritual matter.

Jeffers, Susan. *Feel the Fear and Do It Anyway*. New York: Fawcett Columbine, 1987. An into-the-water book for getting past fear.

Leonard, Jim. *Your Fondest Dream*. Cincinnati: Vivation, 1989. Another into-the-water book; many brainstorming techniques.

Lewis, C. S. *Miracles*. New York: Macmillan, 1947. Inspirational, prickly, and provocative. A challenge in open-mindedness.

Lingerman, Hal A. *The Healing Energies of Music*. Wheaton, Ill.: The Theosophical Publishing House, 1983. Excellent book on music as medicine, learned yet friendly.

London, Peter. *No More Secondhand Art: Awakening the Artist Within*. Boston: Shambhala Publications, Inc., 1989. A manifesto for personal art as process, not product.

McClellan, Randall, Ph.D. *The Healing Sources of Music*. Rockport, Mass.: Element Books, Inc., 1994. A kindly yet wide-ranging source.

Maclean, Dorothy. *To Hear the Angels Sing*. Hudson, N.Y.: Lindisfarne Press, 1990. A lovely book, a fascinating spiritual autobiography by one of the founders of Findhorn.

Mathieu, W. A. *The Listening Book: Discovering Your Own Music*. Boston: Shambhala Publications, Inc., 1991. A companionable book that demystifies music as a life path.

Matthews, Caitlin. *Singing the Soul Back Home: Shamanism in Daily Life*. Rockport, Mass.: Element Books, Inc., 1995. A wonderfully rich book for grounded spiritual practice.

Miller, Alice. *The Drama of the Gifted Child*. New York: Basic Books, 1981. Seminal book on how toxic family dynamics dampen creativity.

Nachmanovitch, Stephen. *Free Play*. Los Angeles: Jeremy P. Tarcher, 1991. A wonderful book on creative freedom.

Noble, Vicki. *Motherpeace—A Way to the Goddess Through Myth, Art, and Tarot*. San Francisco: Harper & Row Publishers, 1983. Creativity through the lens of the goddess religion.

Norwood, Robin. *Women Who Love Too Much*. Los Angeles: Jeremy P. Tarcher, 1985. Seminal work on codependency.

Peck, M. Scott. *The Road Less Traveled*. New York: Simon & Schuster, 1978. A book for early spiritual skeptics.

Shaughnessy, Susan. *Walking on Alligators*. New York: HarperCollins, 1993. A companionable, savvy guide for anyone working to appreciate the worth of process as well as product.

Sher, Barbara, with Annie Gottlieb. *Wishcraft: How to Get What You Really Want*. New York: Ballantine Books, 1979. A potent, catalytic book for creative living, similar to my own work and my current thinking.

Starhawk. *The Fifth Sacred Thing*. New York: Bantam Books, 1994. Mesmerizing novel of spiritual ecology.

Starhawk. *The Spiritual Dance*. New York: Harper and Row, 1979. Brilliant on creativity and god/goddess within.

Tame, David. *The Secret Power of Music*. New York: Destiny Books, 1984. A lucid introductory overview of the healing powers of music.

Ueland, Brenda. *If You Want to Write.* 1938. St. Paul, Minn.: Schubert, 1983. The care and maintenance of the writer as a creative artist. Shrewd, personal and pragmatic.

W., Bill. *Alcoholics Anonymous: The Story of How More Than One Hundred Men Have Recovered from Alcoholism.* Akron, Ohio: Carry the Message, 1985.

Wegscheider-Cruse, Sharon. *Choicemaking: For Co-dependents, Adult Children and Spirituality Seekers.* Pompano Beach, Fla.: Health Communications, 1985. Recommended for dismantling co-dependent workaholism.

Woititz, Janet. *Home Away from Home: The Art of Self-Sabotage.* Pompano Beach, Fla.: Health Communications, 1987. Important for arresting the mechanism of aborting success.

Wright, Machaelle Small. *Behaving As If the God in All Life Mattered.* Jeffersonton, Va.: Perelandra. Ltd., 1987. A spiritual autobiography about work with "earth" and other energy forms.

SPECIAL INTEREST

These books are intended as special help on issues that frequently block creativity.

Alcoholics Anonymous. *The Big Book.* New York: Alcoholics Anonymous World Services. Care and maintenance of a sane and sober lifestyle for alcoholic and nonalcoholic alike. Inspirational guide.

Alcoholics Anonymous. *Came to Believe.* New York: Alcoholics Anonymous World Services, 1973. Useful and touching book about embryonic faith.

The Augustine Fellowship. *Sex and Love Addicts Anonymous.* Boston: The Augustine Fellowship, Sex and Love Addicts Anonymous Fellowship-Wide Services, 1986. One of the best books on addiction. The chapters on withdrawal and building partnership should be required reading.

Beattie, Melody. *Codependent No More.* San Francisco: Harper & Row, 1987. Excellent for breaking the virtue trap.

Cameron, Julia, and Mark Bryan. *Money Drunk, Money Sober.* New York: Ballantine Books, 1992. A hands-on toolkit for financial freedom. This book creates new language and a new lens for money management. It grew out of *The Artist's Way* because money is the most often cited block.

Hallowell, Edward M., M.D., and John J. Ratey, M.D. *Driven to Distraction.* New York: Touchstone Books/Simon & Schuster, 1994; first Touchstone edition, 1995. Invaluable book on attention deficit disorder.

Louden, Jennifer. *The Women's Comfort Book (A Self-Nurturing Guide for Restoring Balance in Your Life).* San Francisco: HarperSanFrancisco, 1992. Applicable to either sex as a practical guide to self-nurturing.

Orsborn, Carol. *Enough Is Enough: Exploding the Myth of Having It All.* New York: G. P. Putnam's Sons, 1986. Excellent for helping dismantle the heroic workaholic personality.

RESOURCES

Sounds True
413 South Arthur Avenue
Louisville, CO 80027
1-800-333-9135
A wellspring of spiritual sound and wisdom from all world traditions.

Transitions Bookplace
1000 West North Avenue
Chicago, IL 60622
1-312-951-7323
Largest American clearinghouse for titles like these.

Also, of course, www.barnesandnoble.com and www.amazon.com

INDEX

ABOUT THE AUTHOR

JULIA CAMERON has been an active artist for more than thirty years. She is the author of seventeen books, fiction and nonfiction, including *The Artist's Way, The Vein of Gold,* and *The Right to Write,* her bestselling works on the creative process. A novelist, playwright, songwriter, and poet, she has multiple credits in theater, film, and television. She divides her time between Manhattan and the high desert of New Mexico.

© Aloma

To order call 1-800-788-6262 or send your order to:

Penguin Putnam Inc.
P.O. Box 12289 Dept. B
Newark, NJ 07101-5289